POWER AND ITS DISGUISES

D0462450

Anthropology, Culture and Society

Series Editors:
Dr Richard A. Wilson, University of Sussex
Professor Thomas Hylland Eriksen, University of Oslo

POWER AND ITS DISGUISES
Anthropological Perspectives on Politics

Second Edition

JOHN GLEDHILL

Pluto Press
LONDON • STERLING, VIRGINIA

First published 1994
Second Edition 2000
by PLUTO PRESS
345 Archway Road, London N6 5AA
and 22883 Quicksilver Drive,
Sterling, VA 20166–2012, USA

www.plutobooks.com

British Library Cataloguing in Publication Data
A catalogue record for this book is available from
the British Library

ISBN 0 7453 1686 7 hbk
ISBN 0 7453 1685 9 pbk

Library of Congress Cataloging in Publication Data
Gledhill, John.
Power and its disguises : anthropological perspectives on politics /
John Gledhill.—2nd ed.
p. cm.—(Anthropology, culture and society)
Includes bibliographical references and index.
ISBN 0–7453–1686–7
1. Political anthropology. 2. Power (Social sciences) I. Title. II. Series.

GN492.G55 2000
306.2—dc21
00–026069

09 08 07 06 05 04 03 02 01 00
10 9 8 7 6 5 4 3 2 1

Designed and produced for Pluto Press by
Chase Production Services
Typeset from disk by Stanford DTP Services, Northampton
Printed in the European Union by TJ International, Padstow

CONTENTS

PREFACE TO THE SECOND EDITION

This second edition has been prepared at the end of my third year at the University of Manchester. Occupying the chair once occupied by Max Gluckman, I have approached the task with considerable fear of failing to measure up to the tradition that I have inherited. Much has, of course, changed since Gluckman's day. My predecessors as heads of the department, Marilyn Strathern and Tim Ingold, set their own distinctive stamps on its development. But political anthropology remains central to Manchester's work. I have already learned a lot from my new colleagues and from three generations of outstanding undergraduate and postgraduate students. Special thanks are due to John Hutnyk and Karen Sykes. I shamelessly took over some of John's ideas for a stimulating second-year Political and Economic Anthropology course when he left Manchester in 1997, and he remains a good friend and fellow advocate of a more politicized approach to what we do. Karen patiently answered my dumb questions about Melanesia and steered me towards readings that rapidly pointed a scholar drowning in administrative tasks in the right direction. But I have benefited greatly from working with every one of my new colleagues at Manchester, even if the fruits are only partly visible here and I must absolve all of them from responsibility for my mistakes or misunderstandings. A special acknowledgement is, however, also due to Katrin Lund, whose work as tutorial assistant on the second year course contributed immeasurably to its success. I would also like to thank Matthew Gutmann, Ananth Aiyer and other friends in the United States for their useful suggestions for the second edition, although I will certainly have fallen short of satisfying their demands for a tougher line on certain theoretical tendencies.

Since I have been teaching with new ethnographic material and addressing new issues, the temptation to rewrite the book radically was hard to resist. It had, however, proved valuable to teachers in its original form, and the positive feedback that I have received from colleagues in Europe and the United States suggested that the main priority was to ensure that it remained up to date. I have introduced some new material and ideas, and developed and nuanced some of the existing lines of argument. A considerable amount of what is new is, however, simply to keep up with what has happened in some of the places I discussed since the original edition was completed in 1993. This exercise also proved valuable from the point of view of looking at explanations of the changes that have occurred and considering their broader theoretical implications. There are many contributions to which I have still failed to give the place they are due. I must excuse myself to their authors on the pragmatic grounds of lack of space, but I hope that the book's principal message is that there is always much more to be explored and rethought.

Since much of the book remains as it was, I remain deeply indebted to my old colleagues at University College London and must reiterate my gratitude to them all, again with the absolution that none should be held responsible for either my views or my mistakes. Particular thanks are due to Rob Aitken, who shared the class teaching with me when I tried the original book out as a lecture course, and now figures as a published authority in its bibliography. I continue to owe a special debt to Bruce Kapferer, who has not only forced me to think about a lot of things over the years, but was generous enough to give me access to an unpublished manuscript which I plundered freely of its rich ideas. Our dialogue continued for a year in Manchester while he was with us as Hallsworth Senior Research Fellow in 1997. To Richard Wilson, the editor of this series, and another scholar from whom I continue to learn much on a regular basis, I owe even more than when he first invited me to write the book and steered it through to publication. What I know about political anthropology has been influenced by a large number of other scholars, in Britain, Mexico and the United States, many of whom are cited extensively in the text. Even so, I continue to omit much work that I value greatly because it is not accessible to English-speaking readers, as those who consult some of my more specialized publications will readily see.

Although most of the case studies used to illustrate the arguments of this text are drawn from the work of other anthropologists, I have used a little more of my own ethnography in this edition. Thanks are due to the Economic and Social Research Council of the United Kingdom, the Wenner-Gren Foundation for Anthropological Research and to the London University Central Research Fund for financing this work.

Last but certainly not least, I remain indebted to Kathy Powell for her friendship and continuing contributions to my thinking about politics and anthropology.

POWER AND ITS DISGUISES

1   LOCATING THE POLITICAL: A POLITICAL ANTHROPOLOGY FOR TODAY

We actually know a great deal about power, but have been timid in building upon what we know.

(Wolf 1990: 586)

Half a century ago, the subject matter and relevance of political anthropology still seemed relatively easy to define. Under Western colonial regimes, one of the most valuable kinds of knowledge which anthropologists could offer to produce was that relating to indigenous systems of law and government. Most colonial governments had opted for systems of indirect rule. Colonial authority was to be mediated through indigenous leaders and the rule of Western law was to legitimate itself through a degree of accommodation to local 'customs'.

In the last analysis, however, the laws and authority of the colonizers were pre-eminent. Anthropologists in the twentieth century found themselves in the same position as clerics in the Spanish-American Empire at the dawn of European global expansion. The authorities were interested in witchcraft accusations and blood feuds with a view to stamping out what was not acceptable to European 'civilization'. Yet there were some areas of indigenous practice, such as customary law on property rights, which colonial regimes sought to manipulate for their own ends, and might even codify as law recognized by the colonial state. This bureaucratic restructuring of indigenous 'traditions' and social organization was generally carried out within a framework of European preconceptions, giving anthropologists an opportunity to offer their services in the cause of making colonial administration work.

A particularly intractable problem for the colonial regimes was that of finding persons who could play the role of authority figures in areas where state-less or 'acephalous' societies predominated. Much of the classical writing of British political anthropology was devoted to showing that the chiefs the colonial authorities recognized in the 'segmentary' societies of Africa did not possess real authority over their people. The classic case is the Nuer, a pastoral people in the southern Sudan, studied by E.E. Evans-Pritchard (1940, 1987). Evans-Pritchard argued that the Nuer political system was an 'ordered anarchy' based on the principle of 'segmentary opposition'. The population was organized into clans and lineages based on male lines of descent from founding ancestors. Local groups formed 'segments' of larger, more inclusive, kin-groups defined in terms of descent. Nuer social and political structure could thus be represented as a hierarchy of nested lineage segments of differing scale: the 'clan', the biggest group, segments into 'maximal lineages' founded by brothers, each maximal lineage segments in turn into different 'major' lineages, and the segmentation process continues through levels of 'minor' and 'minimal' lineages. Evans-Pritchard saw this structure of lineage segmentation as a consequence of the political principles that operated in Nuerland. Obligations to aid others in fighting were expressed in terms of kinship. Groups which were opposed at one level of segmentation, that of minor lineages, for example, would join together in a conflict which opposed the higher segmentary unit to which they all belonged to another unit of the same structural level, such as a major lineage. This principle of 'fission and fusion' also provided the Nuer with a principle of unity in conflicts with other 'tribes'.

Evans-Pritchard described Nuer politics as 'ordered anarchy', since even villages had no single recognized authority figures. There was an indigenous figure called the 'leopard-skin chief', but he was merely a ritual mediator in disputes, lacking any power to summon the parties to jurisdiction or impose settlements, let alone a wider political role. People seldom achieved redress without threatening force. Nuer society did not, therefore, possess the kind of leaders who could act as agents of 'indirect rule'. If the colonial authorities mistook ritual mediators for genuine political authority figures, such agents might provoke resentment when they tried to act, as representatives of an imposed alien power whose ideas of justice conflicted sharply with indigenous ideas.[1]

The classical British texts on political anthropology of the 1940s and 1950s thus offered a commentary on the tensions that colonial rule produced and on the reasons why it might be resented, but tended to take colonial domination itself for granted. Nevertheless, in a magisterial survey of anthropological perspectives on politics, Joan Vincent has argued that it is 'historically inaccurate to regard the discipline simply as a form of colonial ideology' (Vincent 1990: 2). She bases her case on several different arguments.

---

1 Evans-Pritchard's classic work on the Nuer has been subject to many critical re-evaluations: see, for example, Beidelman (1971), Gough (1971) and the modern study of Hutchinson (1996), discussed in Chapter 2. For overviews of this tradition of Africanist work, see Middleton and Tait (eds) (1958), and Mair (1962). Mair's contribution is particularly interesting because she began her career at the London School of Economics teaching colonial administration, going on to pioneer the anthropological study of the politics of the 'new nations' of Africa. She vociferously defended the British structural-functionalist school against the charge that it had turned the discipline into a servant of colonialism (Vincent 1990: 257).

Firstly, Vincent contends that early anthropological voices often offered trenchant critiques of the consequences of European domination. In the 1880s, before anthropology departments became established in American universities, fieldworkers of the Bureau of Ethnology of the Smithsonian Institution were not merely documenting the sufferings of Native Americans and producing the first academic monographs on the 'resistance movements of the oppressed', but entering into political confrontations with the federal bureaucracy (ibid.: 52–5).

Secondly, in Britain, the first ethnographic surveys funded by the British Association in the 1890s were not conducted on 'exotic' societies but on English and Irish rural communities, and were motivated by concern about the potential social and political consequences of industrialization and mass urbanization. The Edwardian pioneers of fieldwork-based anthropology in the British colonies, notably W.H.R. Rivers, failed to convince the Colonial Office of the value of funding a professional anthropology which might improve the government of subject peoples (ibid.: 119–21). Between 1900 and 1920, the Royal Anthropological Institute approached the government formally on several occasions, but the official response towards anthropology remained one of suspicion, compounded by the class prejudices of Colonial Office. The first professional anthropologists generally came from non-establishment social backgrounds (ibid.: 117). It was private foundations associated with the global expansion of American capitalism that showed the greatest interest in funding anthropology. Rockefeller money not only supported the development of American anthropology within the USA's growing international sphere of interest, but much of the classic fieldwork of British anthropologists in the 1920s and 1930s (ibid.: 154).

Nevertheless, as Vincent herself shows, the critical strands of an anthropological approach to politics were not those that became hegemonic in the discipline in the period after 1940. This was the date when the British structural-functionalists established 'political anthropology' as a formalized sub-field. Their anti-historical functionalist theory created a breach between the American and British traditions which was not fully closed until the 1960s, when new approaches to political anthropology associated with the Manchester School, discussed in Chapter 6, became the mainstream on both sides of the Atlantic (ibid.: 283). Anthropologists working in colonial countries were seldom 'agents of colonialism' in a direct sense. Wendy James summed up their dilemma as that of 'reluctant imperialists' (James 1973). Yet most of the profession did display 'willingness to serve'. More significantly, the analyses of mainstream academic anthropology, in both Britain and the United States, proved incapable of confronting the fact that its object of study was a world structured by Western colonial expansion and capitalist imperialism in a systematic way. As I stress throughout this book, it remains necessary to strive for the decolonization of anthropology today. The problem is not simply the relationship between the development of anthropology and formal colonial rule, but the historical legacies of Western domination, the continuing global hegemony of the Northern powers, and contemporary manifestations of racial and neo-colonial domination in the social and political life of metropolitan countries.

Anthropologists whose own politics were generally rather conservative (Worsley 1992) could make a valuable contribution to showing how indigenous notions of authority and justice might conflict with Western notions during the era of formal colonial rule. Their approach was, however, clouded by the assumption that the West and its way of doing things represented the future for all humanity. Political anthropology became an analysis of the tensions of transition. For a while it remained that, as the old colonies became new and independent nations, supposedly embarking on their own roads to a 'modernity' which was seldom subject to any profound scholarly reflection.

The political experience of these 'new nations' was, however, soon to cause Western anthropologists considerable anguish, and the kinds of theoretical paradigms and research agendas that seemed appropriate in the 1940s and 1950s gave way through the 1960s and 1970s to more critical perspectives. A new generation of Western-born anthropologists that had played no role in the colonial regimes felt free to denounce its predecessors. The professional advancement of anthropologists within the ex-colonial countries themselves turned on the heat. The main pressure for rethinking came, however, from a changing world.

In Africa, both the economic and political visions of the modernization theorists of the optimistic post-war era seemed illusory by the late 1960s. The negative consequences of failure to achieve sustained economic development were reinforced by civil wars and the appearance of some particularly vicious regimes in a continent where even the best of governments seemed distant from liberal democratic ideals. On the economic front, some parts of Asia presented a brighter picture to Western liberal eyes, but those countries that advanced economically were not conspicuous for their progressive stances on human rights. The Indian sub-continent remained economically weak, and combined destructive patterns of inter-state violence with intra-state political conflict. The Indonesians followed up violent internal political repression with brutal colonial expansion. Latin America, which had already experienced more than a century of violence and political instability since independence, not only failed to translate impressive per capita economic growth rates into greater social justice for its impoverished masses, but experienced a wave of military regimes.

The combination of a generally unsatisfactory outlook on 'development' and a dismal report on 'democratization' favoured the rise of radical paradigms. At first, explanations couched in economic terms tended to win out, since inequalities within the global economy were manifest impediments to the universalization of prosperity. A substantial number of repressive regimes around the world owed their survival, and in some cases their very existence, to the intervention of imperialist powers. The dependency paradigm, initially associated with André Gunder Frank and a series of Latin American writers,[2] but subsequently diffused to other parts of the world, explained the politics of the periphery by arguing that the bourgeoisies of 'underdeveloped' countries were subservient to metropolitan interests, siphoning off their countries' wealth in alliance with foreign capital. Given that analysis, the national state of the peripheral country is charged with maintaining the kind of social order needed to perpetuate dependent development.

Yet dependency theory proved as popular with democracy's enemies as with its supposed friends. If a nation's miseries depend solely on the unequal distribution of economic power on a world scale, and Third World bourgeoisies are in hock to foreign interests, then the colonels can leave the barracks to take over government in the name of a defence of national and popular interests against the imperialist enemy and its local bourgeois clients. Strong government and state-directed economic development becomes the anti-imperialist alternative to the treacherous machinations of civilian politicians tied to private vested interests. If things go badly, this is because the North is determined to continue exploiting the South. Dependency theory thus not merely proved weak at explaining variety in political responses to underdevelopment in scientific terms: it was sometimes coopted by the torturers.

Dependency theory and its more 'academic' successor, the world-systems theory pioneered by Immanuel Wallerstein (1979), did, however, force 'international relations' onto the anthropological agenda. World-systems analysis stimulated lively debate about ways in which global processes were modified by 'local' historical variables to produce variety in the way particular regions of the periphery developed (Smith 1984). Marxist theories of imperialism also enjoyed a revival in the 1960s and 1970s, particularly among indigenous anthropologists whose intellectual formation was based on reading Lenin and Rosa Luxemburg. It now became commonplace to argue that the end of formal colonial rule did not spell the end of 'colonial' relationships between North and South, the old politico-administrative form of colonialism simply having been replaced by new, and more insidious, neo-colonial relationships.

At the same time, however, an awakened anthropological interest in history provoked further exploration of the consequences of the colonial process itself and non-economic dimensions of Western domination. The 'new nations' of the period after the Second World War were formed by the

---

2 For critical surveys of this and other 'radical' perspectives on development and under-development, see Goodman and Redclift (1981), Kay (1989), Escobar (1995), Kearney (1996) and Gardner and Lewis (1996). The alternative development strategy advocated by the dependency theorists could be seen as simply another variant of the developmentalist ideologies that became globally hegemonic after the Second World War, in contrast to the kinds of 'grassroots' models advocated as 'alternative development'.

colonial powers out of a frequently incongruous series of pre-colonial 'societies'. Pre-colonial states and 'statelets' were amalgamated together into colonial territorial units along with sundry stateless agricultural and pastoral-nomadic groups on principles that made less sense once colonial rule ended, since it was the presence of the colonial power which had provided the territorial unit with political and social unity. Furthermore, the colonial powers had not been content simply to cast the mantle of their rule over peoples already living in the territories they colonized. Colonial capitalism also transplanted people from continent to continent, some as labourers and some to develop services that the locals were deemed incapable of providing. Thus, some of the new nations of Africa and the Pacific were left by their European colonizers with substantial Asian populations occupying advantageous social and economic positions, laying a basis for future conflict. Surveying Caribbean history, Sidney Mintz has observed that our current heightened awareness of mass migrations in an era of so-called 'globalization' is partly explicable by the fact that so much earlier population movement in the capitalist world economy involved non-White people moving within circuits that segregated them from the populations of North Atlantic countries, whereas today former colonial 'others' are an increasingly important presence in Northern countries themselves (Mintz 1998: 124).

Eager to divest themselves of a colonial empire that no longer seemed economically beneficial after the Second World War, and unable to find politically feasible ways of resolving the contradictions they had created, the British must bear a heavy responsibility for the course of events in various parts of Africa and in the Indian sub-continent since independence. There is, however, a more general principle at issue here than the particular messes created by the extended process of decolonization, to which all the colonial powers made a contribution – including the United States. The contemporary configuration of the world into political units, nations, peoples and religious communities results from a global process of carving out empires and spheres of influence through direct military interventions and indirect political meddling in the 'internal' conflicts of states that achieved or conserved political independence from the great powers in the nineteenth century.

Developments in regions which retained political independence, such as the Russian Empire, the Ottoman world and China, were also reshaped by the carving up of the world into colonial territories and the global commercial expansion of the industrial powers of north-west Europe and the United States. The 'non-bourgeois' elites of Japan and Russia sought to promote economic modernization to underpin their geopolitical position in a world of rifles, heavy artillery and battleships. Western expansion did not produce cultural homogenization, much less a universal tendency towards bourgeois society and liberal democracy as envisaged by the optimistic social theorists of nineteenth-century Europe. It did, however, transform the nature of social and political life in ways which are as recognizable in the case of 'Islamic fundamentalist' Iran as they are in countries on the immediate frontiers of Western Europe.

Anthropology's distinctive contribution to the social sciences is often defined in terms of its favoured *methodology*, the direct study of human life 'on the ground' through ethnographic fieldwork. Anthropologists live for an extended period with the people they study, observing the details of their behaviour as it happens and conducting an extended dialogue with them about their beliefs and practices. The fieldwork method is not, however, peculiar to anthropology, and I would prefer to stress the importance of anthropology's *theoretical* contribution as a social science that attempts to examine social realities in a cross-cultural frame of reference. In striving to transcend a view of the world based solely on the premises of European culture and history, anthropologists are also encouraged to look beneath the world of taken-for-granted assumptions in social life in general. This should help us pursue critical analyses of ideologies and power relations in all societies, including those of the West.

In my view, a political anthropology adequate to the world of the late twentieth century must seek to relate the local to the global, but in a more radical way than has been attempted in the past. A crucial question is anthropology's relationship to history (Wolf 1990). One problem is that the sub-field of political anthropology has failed to reflect adequately on what is peculiar to the political life and systems of Western societies in world-historical terms. Progress has been made in strengthening historical perspectives that explore how the present state of the world is the product of social processes of global scale, impacting differentially on regions with specific local social characteristics, through different agents of global change, such as particular types of capitalist enterprise or colonial regimes. Yet anthropology has continued to talk about local 'societies' and 'cultures' in a world where the politics of the former Yugoslavia are influenced by the politics of Serbs living in North America, and the politics of the Indian sub-continent or the Middle East erupt onto European streets.

Furthermore, what we often take as the 'core' of political life in 'democratic' regimes, going out and voting, seems to be an increasingly unpopular activity in the country which now claims to guarantee all our freedoms, the United States. The whole of the Western world seems to be experiencing a notable public disillusion with institutional political life and the role of professional politicians. The world to the east of Western Europe seems to manifest a greater enthusiasm for nationalism than democracy. How are we to understand such processes without asking more profound questions about what states, nations and democracy mean in Western terms and how these Western forms emerged historically?

Ethnographic research methods remain essential for investigating the dynamics of political processes at the local level, particularly where we are dealing with the way institutional politicians interact with popular social movements, or with informal aspects of power relations in which the way people understand the situations they face and the options open to them must be central to the analysis. Such studies enable anthropologists to challenge analyses and explanations offered by other disciplines in ways that are *politically* as well as intellectually significant. I explore ethnographic examples in considerable detail throughout this book to underscore these points. Yet taking their cues from the insights afforded by ethnography, anthropological perspectives on larger-scale phenomena may *also* differ from those of other disciplines. As we will see in Chapters 5 and 7, anthropological studies have shown that understanding the behaviour of apparently 'Westernized' post-colonial political elites demands an understanding of the distinct cultural frameworks which orientate their actions and make them meaningful. Even within Western Europe, differences in political cultures are significant enough to make cultural analysis of political life essential. Addressing these issues takes us beyond the local level and the immediate field situation towards formulating broader kinds of models and looking at historical processes seriously.

Anthropological writing about political life therefore has much to offer, but there is still a need for sustained rethinking if we are to maximize the potential of anthropology to illuminate this facet of human experience. In order to clear some of the ground, I will begin by examining some of the premises of 'political anthropology' as it was defined in the classical writings of the British school. I will show how its premises can be subjected to a double critique: as both a form of ethnocentrism and as an inadequately critical analysis of the historical specificity of the Western reality which served as its point of departure.

HOW NOT TO USE THE WEST AS A POINT OF DEPARTURE

Anthropology occupies an uncomfortable place in the social sciences and humanities. From the discipline's earliest days, anthropologists assumed that their work had a universal significance. Anthropology was to be the study of the whole of humankind, in all its cultural diversity. Yet in practice this pretension to universality was inhibited by the fact that anthropology crystallized as a discipline within an institutional framework in which sociology, law, economics, history and political philosophy were already established fields. In the eyes of practitioners of these other specialisms, anthropologists should deal with the exotic peripheries of European colonial expansion, the 'peoples without history' whose distinctive lifeways were shortly to be expunged by the relentless march of a truly universal Western modernity (Wolf 1982).

Anthropologists began to elaborate accounts of the special scientific contribution their field would make as soon they achieved an institutional place in academia, through the creation of departments and chairs in the subject, both at home and in the research institutions set up by European powers in the colonial world. Although some, like Malinowski, expressed apprehension that the disappearance of the world of the 'savages' might mean the disappearance of their own jobs, the same circumstances that marginalized anthropology actually provided excellent grounds for justifying its continuing importance. The mainstream social sciences were created to analyse Western societies and Western modernity. Anthropologists could challenge their claims to universality on two fronts: first, by arguing that they embodied eurocentric premises that limited their usefulness for analysing non-Western societies, and second, by arguing that conventional social science accounts of Western modernity itself were limited by the absence of a relativizing perspective. Anthropology had something distinctive to say about all human societies, including the industrial societies of the West, because it alone possessed an adequate comparative perspective on human institutions and experience. A radical anthropological critique of conventional social science would assert that the latter was hopelessly entangled in ideological conceptions reflecting the world-views of the dominant groups in Western societies. Although no social scientist could entirely escape the cultural preconceptions of his or her native milieu, the anthropological project offered the best means of promoting open and critical minds because it forced the analyst to pay attention to cultural difference. On this view, understanding of 'the other' is the precondition for greater understanding of 'ourselves'.

This maximalist account of the anthropological project remains one that can be advocated in principle, but more modest claims for the discipline's role have tended to prevail in practice. Funding agencies, non-governmental organizations (NGOs) and governments are told that the world needs anthropologists to add 'cultural' dimensions to research projects designed by specialists in other fields. Thus anthropologists help reinforce the conviction of others that they are exclusively specialists on non-European peoples, as illustrated, for example, by perceptions of anthropology's relevance in AIDS research. Anthropologists also sell themselves as researchers who do fieldwork and thereby come up with details of local situations other methodologies would fail to capture. Both these selling points of the discipline are valid, but they also invite continuing marginalization. It is a rare research proposal which contends that anthropology offers a root-and-branch alternative perspective on some fundamental contemporary human issue.

Professional anthropologists are not, of course, free to pursue their intellectual convictions in an unrestrained way. Part of our contemporary problem of self-definition arises from the way more powerful agencies and interest groups shape our horizons. Such constraints are not, however, entirely new, since the founding schools of anthropology had to react to the definitions of anthropology's role produced by the colonial order. Then, as now, anthropologists responded to the pressures placed upon them in diverse ways, and frequently conflicted amongst themselves in doing so. In order to understand what anthropologists of different generations have said (or not said) about politics it is necessary to explore the politics of anthropology itself, a theme which will be discussed in depth in Chapter 9. Since the development of anthropology is related to Western domination, it is clear that political anthropology is a sub-field in which the need for critical self-awareness of the way historical contexts have shaped research agendas and interpretations is particularly important.

Because anthropology was originally assigned the task of investigating societies defined by their 'otherness' and 'non-Western-ness', it has taken a long time for anthropology to get to grips with the West itself. Too much of what classical sociology had to say about Western societies was taken for granted as a valid baseline from which to work out what was different about the non-European world, including the way sociology defined a society in general terms and identified 'societies' with bounded territorial units. Hidden behind this apparently universal definition of what 'society' is were two specifically European preoccupations. Firstly, nineteenth-century European social theorists were preoccupied with problems of 'social order' arising from elite anxieties about the impact of mass proletarianization and urbanization – the fear of the 'dangerous classes' produced by industrial capitalist development (Wolf 1982: 7–9). Secondly, Europeans developed a very specific conception of the 'modern state', which also shaped their ideas about society and culture (Gledhill 1999: 11–14). When British structural-functionalist anthropologists asked the question: 'What is political organization in African societies?', they brought too much of this ethnocentric baggage with them.

In his Preface to *African Political Systems*, edited by Fortes and Evans-Pritchard and first published in 1940, Radcliffe-Brown concludes on the following note: 'The political organization of a society is that aspect of the total organization which is concerned with the control and regulation of the use of physical force' (Fortes and Evans-Pritchard 1987: xxiii). This definition (and the rest of the discussion which precedes it) derives its inspiration from Max Weber's definition of a 'political community' as: 'a community whose social action is aimed at subordinating to orderly domination by the participants a "territory" and the conduct of persons within it, through readiness to resort to physical force, including normally force of arms' (Weber 1978: 901).

Weber's original discussion was concerned with identifying the *distinctive features* of the *modern state*, which he defined as a type of political community possessing a monopoly of the *legitimate* use of force in addition to the association with a 'territory' highlighted in the quotation. Radcliffe-Brown, however, had to extend his discussion to include 'stateless' segmentary societies. Fortes and Evans-Pritchard proceeded to explain that authors in the volume charged with studying such societies – as distinct from what they defined as 'primitive states' like the Zulu or the Bemba – were unable to base

their analysis on a description of governmental organization but were 'forced
to consider what, in the absence of explicit forms of government, could be
held to constitute the political structure of a people' (Fortes and Evans-
Pritchard 1987: 6).

This looks suspiciously like a familiar anthropological procedure in dealing
with the 'exotic': we begin by defining the phenomenon that does not fit into
existing Western conceptual frameworks in *negative* terms as an absence of
something we understand (or think we understand) and proceed from there.
After asserting (ibid.: xiv) that 'in dealing with political systems ... we are
dealing with law, on the one hand, and warfare, on the other', Radcliffe-
Brown observes that:

In many African societies a person who is accused or suspected of witchcraft or some
other offence may be compelled to take an oath or submit to an ordeal, the belief
being that if he is guilty he will fall sick and die. Thus, the *rudiments of what in more
complex societies is the organized institution of criminal justice* are to be found in these
recognized procedures by which action is taken by or on behalf of the body of
members of the community, either directly or by appeal to ritual or supernatural
means, to inflict punishment on an offender or to exclude him from the community.
In African societies the decision to apply a penal sanction may rest with the people
in general, with the elders, as in a gerontocracy, with a limited number of judges or
leaders, or with a single chief or king. (ibid.: xvii, emphasis added)

This line of analysis is utterly ethnocentric, despite Radcliffe-Brown's claim
that his definition of political organization lays the basis for 'an objective
study of human societies by the methods of natural science' (ibid.: xxiii). It
begins from a model of how power and political organization are supposedly
constituted in modern Western societies, and proceeds to classify other
societies in accordance with their *distance* from this baseline. Thus
'recognized procedures' for sanctioning persons accused of witchcraft
become 'rudiments' [of] organized institutions of criminal justice' in more
complex societies.

Pierre Clastres has criticized traditional political anthropology for universalizing the Weber-derived identification of political power with coercion,
subordination and violence. Radcliffe-Brown certainly sees the political as
invariably centred on coercive power, even if coercion takes a 'moral' rather
than physical form (ibid.: xvi). What, Clastres asks, do we do with
Amerindian societies in which: 'if there is something completely alien to an
Indian, it is the idea of giving an order or having to obey, except under very
special circumstances such as prevail during a martial expedition' (Clastres
1977: 5–6)? Are these societies in which political power *does not exist* at all
and which therefore lack any political organization, or is there something
wrong with the assumption that all power is coercive, and that the forms
of power found in modern Western state societies (and other civilizations)
are universal?

One problem with looking for institutions in 'stateless' societies that perform the same sorts of functions as state institutions elsewhere is that it becomes difficult to separate out 'political' organization from other aspects of social organization, in just the same way as it is difficult to identify an autonomous 'economic domain' where production, consumption and exchange are organized by kinship or other types of social relations that have multiple functions. Fortes and Evans-Pritchard remark, for example, that in very small-scale societies 'political structure and kinship relations are completely fused' (1987: 7). Ted Lewellen (1992) has argued – against the critique of the sub-field offered by the political scientist David Easton (1959) – that anthropology's failure (or refusal) to mark off the political as a distinct 'sub-system' of societal organization is a virtue rather than a vice. As Lewellen shows, there are grounds for refusing to separate the 'political' and the 'social' even in analysing 'modern' large-scale societies, but there are also dangers in taking theoretical short-cuts here. We need to think about how the political *has come to be seen* as something separate.

In his analysis of the rise of 'historical bureaucratic societies' (the imperial states of the pre-modern period), the sociologist S.N. Eisenstadt argued that it was in such societies that a political domain first became 'disembedded' and achieved relative 'autonomy': rulers' goals began to conflict with those of traditional aristocratic groups enjoying hereditary status by virtue of their birth and specialized organs of political struggle, such as court cliques, emerged (Eisenstadt 1963). Yet it is also possible to argue that the perceived autonomy of the 'political' in Western societies is one of the key *ideological* dimensions of Western 'modernity' – not something we should take as an objective fact, but a way of *representing* power relations that obscures their social foundations and the way they work in practice. The problem with taking a model of Western systems as a baseline is that we are in danger of de-emphasizing fundamental differences between forms of social life. In this case the basic issue is whether the way 'stateless' societies organize themselves actually checks the development of the forms of power associated with state societies. An investigation of how particular societies resolve universal problems may prove less interesting than a study of how and why they come to have different problems to resolve.

The point of Clastres's critique of traditional political anthropology is precisely that it obscures one of the major lessons to be learned from the study of the so-called 'primitive societies': that it is possible for societies to exist and flourish without any division between oppressors and oppressed, coercers and coerced. 'Stateless societies' are not societies that have yet to 'develop' politically but societies that have *resisted* the emergence of the form of political power which generates the state (and social inequalities). Clastres sees the birth of the state as the first crucial 'rupture' (*coupure*) in human history, one that is far more important in world historical terms than the transition to agriculture.

Fortes and Evans-Pritchard might have responded that Clastres's analysis smacks of the intervention of political-philosophical interests into the 'scientific' field. Clastres clearly wishes to make a critique of 'civilization' as an alienating form of existence by reconstructing the 'savage' as a negation of all forms of inequality and oppression. He is offering a 'political' version of Marshall Sahlins's analysis of hunter-gatherers as the 'original affluent society', in which the rest of human history moves downhill all the way (Sahlins 1974). Does the world of 'stateless societies' really know no coercion, oppression or inequality, between, say, men and women? The answer, I will argue in the next chapter, is negative. Yet this is not really what Clastres's argument is about. What is being challenged here is the *ethnocentrism* of universalizing a particular model of social and political power, ultimately derived from a model of the modern Western state. This procedure leaves us with little option but to rank societies on an evolutionary scale in terms of the amount of this sort of power present within them, which leaves the 'primitive' world close to zero on the scale. It obscures qualitative differences in the nature and deployment of power in different types of societies, including those of the Western industrialized nations themselves.

It also obscures another important issue for understanding the variety in 'traditional' African political systems: how far did the historical coexistence of 'states' and 'stateless' peoples in a single region reflect the way groups of indigenous people sought to resist the kinds of inequalities associated with political centralization? Traditional models presented 'stateless' societies as having a deficit in terms of institutions possessed by more 'complex' societies, due to technological, ecological or demographic conditions. There is another possibility: that state and 'stateless' societies formed interrelated and interdependent parts of a single, dynamic social process on a regional scale. State-builders sought to extend their dominion, whilst 'tribal' groups sought to preserve their autonomy and resisted the development of centralized power within their communities – being transformed, as we shall see in Chapter 2, from the 'pristine' organizations that existed in a world without states in the process.

To sum up the argument thus far: the problem with traditional political anthropology was that it started with the political organization of 'modern' societies as its baseline and set up typologies of 'other cultures' according to the categories thus defined. This reduced 'stateless' societies to a negative category, but it also produced a categorization of societies that did have states as 'primitive' versions of Western-derived archetypes. This would be particularly undesirable if the 'modern' state of Western civilization used to generate universal concepts of 'the political' turned out to represent another major break in history.

A number of comparative sociological studies of the 1980s, discussed in more detail in Chapter 3, argued that the Western relationship between 'state' and 'civil society' represents a radical discontinuity in world history, which plays as important a role in the constitution of the modern global social order as the birth of capitalism. There are really two issues to examine here. The first is concerned with understanding the differences between agrarian civilization in Europe and other parts of the world, and the reasons for Europe's dramatic global expansion. That can lay the ground for investigation of the second issue: the impact of Western forms of social and political organization on the rest of the world.

At first sight, contemporary global political organization appears extremely diverse, much more diverse, in fact, than economic organization. Yet there are general tendencies. One example would be conflicts between national governments and elites and regional separatist and 'ethnic' movements. It could, and should, be argued that each case of conflict of this kind needs to be *contextualized*, to be placed in its particular historical and cultural setting. The apparent similarity between phenomena may evaporate as we begin to understand that the conflicts not only have different historical causes, but also have different meanings to the groups that organize them. Nevertheless, the way 'ethnicity', for example, becomes politicized in the contemporary world may reflect a subtle universalization of some of the features of the politics of Northern societies to the South, despite the differences which continue to exist between forms of political organization and political cultures.

The importance of this issue becomes obvious if we reflect on the way Northern politicians and media tend to explain modern political and social conflicts in terms of an absence of 'modernity'. 'Ethnic' identifications are often presented as primordial and atavistic, aspects of a 'traditional' social order surviving under the veneer of modernity and reasserting themselves because a given region has not succeeded in achieving the kind of modernity the North has attained. 'Tribalism' is often the term used to mark the 'primitive' characteristics of this form of conflict. The objections to such an explanatory framework are manifold. Firstly, the leadership of 'ethnic' and 'regionalist' movements are generally thoroughly 'modern' politicians vying for power with another elite faction commanding the central state machine, and the symbols which rally popular support to the cause are generally invented or reinvented rather than primordial (Hobsbawm and Ranger 1983). Secondly, both the means and the ends of the conflict centre on 'modern' conceptions of political and economic organization, the achievement of states within states, or political units which possess partial or total autonomy from the existing centre and recognition by other political units as sovereign bodies. The implication of rejecting a view of certain kinds of conflict as indices of imperfect transitions to 'modernity' is that there is a deeper sense in which Western colonial expansion and more recent tendencies towards 'cultural globalization' shape the diverse forms of modern political and social conflict and are, indeed, what underlies the proliferation of 'difference' that seems so integral to modern political processes.

As a prelude to further discussion of this point, we should review what social theorists now argue is peculiar to the modern Western state.

THE DISTINCTIVENESS OF THE MODERN STATE

A number of comparative historical sociologists have emphasized the way in which the 'modern state' differs from its predecessors in terms of its 'penetration' of everyday social life (Giddens 1985, Hall 1985, Mann 1986). The governmental apparatus of the kind of state which began to develop in north-west Europe from the sixteenth century onwards affected the day-to-day lives of those it claimed to rule to a far greater degree than even the most centralized non-Western states. Thus Giddens argues that the 'class-divided' societies of the pre-modern era remained essentially *segmental*. As a Chinese proverb puts it: 'the country is great and the emperor is far away'. Imperial China had an elaborate administrative system, but in Giddens's view this type of pre-modern bureaucracy gave the central government far less power over society than that enjoyed by the national states of early modern Europe. Furthermore, Giddens suggests, pre-modern states were not really *territorial*. Imperial governments always claimed to be masters of all they surveyed, but lacked the administrative, communicative and military infrastructures necessary to make that claim a reality. 'Traditional' states had *frontiers* rather than *borders*. The administrative reach of the political centre was relatively low and its control was patchy on the periphery of its domains. The Weberian definition of the state as an institution that possesses a monopoly of the legitimate use of force within a territorial domain is therefore appropriate only to the modern European state.

Giddens traces the break away from traditional state forms to the emergence of 'Absolutist' states in Europe. Post-medieval European states were based on centralization of administration and the formation of standing armies, accompanied by a transition from feudal to private property relations. Monarchs consolidated their own power at the expense of feudal aristocracies, which had previously been able to exercise some of the powers of government themselves at the local level, including the ability to tax. Giddens argues that this political transformation created a climate peculiarly favourable to the separation of the 'economic' and 'political' and 'private' and 'public' domains. The apparent 'autonomy' of the political domain and the separation of 'public' and 'private' are central to Western ideas, but products of history, not universals. As I suggested earlier, they constitute ideological representations that need thinking about more critically when it comes to attempting an anthropological analysis of how power relations actually work in the European context.

Giddens argues that a combination of constant warfare between rival states and internal pacification linked to centralization of power produced a kind of 'selective pressure' towards the development of states that had efficient centralized tax systems. This also promoted the development of money economy and credit systems that gave an important impetus towards capitalist development, bolstered by the state's guaranteeing the absolute rights of private property. On this model, the development of a 'capitalist world economy' centred on Europe which is seen as the motor of Western global expansion by Wallerstein (1974) is only one facet of a European world system developing on the basis of transformations of political and military power. Capitalism, in the sense of merchant capitalism, flows across borders and is 'transnational', but the consolidation of Wallerstein's capitalist world economy is universally accompanied by military force and the state system develops according to its own logic.[3]

This is initially the product of military competition *between* different states which in turn strengthens tendencies towards administrative reorganization and greater fiscal efficiency *within* states. Giddens suggests, however, that the final transition to the modern nation-state depended on the way the internal social pacification process became linked to what he calls 'the consolidation of internal administrative resources'. The military arm of the state, a professionalized army, was now mainly pointed outward, towards other nation-states, whilst internal control was increasingly based on other kinds of 'surveillance' techniques and institutions – a point on which Giddens derives his inspiration from Michel Foucault, whose wider theoretical contribution is discussed in Chapter 6.

In Giddens's view, this development was the result of the emergence of industrialism and a new type of urbanism and relationship between town and country associated with industrialism in the 'core' areas of the European world-system. He argues that the changing nature of internal control in European states was based on processes Foucault (1979) calls 'sequestration'. Foucault is referring to the creation of carceral organizations – prisons, asylums and workhouses. A new social category of 'deviants' is removed from society and *disciplined through training of the body and surveillance* – a

---

3 Wallerstein contends that capitalism can only develop where a number of politically independent states organize the 'world-system' division of labour between manufacturing centres and the peripheries which supply them with raw materials. Following Weber (1951), he argues that politically decentralized 'world economies' avoid the overheads of imperial bureaucratic superstructures, permitting reinvestment of profits to sustain continuous growth of production and trade. Wallerstein does, however, argue that the way European societies were structured politically before the sixteenth century is relevant to understanding why their 'world system' escaped subjection to the control of a single, imperial, political centre. This emphasis on the novelty of 'the modern world system' has, however, been contested by Jonathan Friedman (1994). Friedman not only argues that there are fundamental similarities between contemporary economic globalization and cycles of decentralization in the wealth accumulation processes of earlier civilizations (which he also sees as 'capitalist' in a broad sense, derived from Weber rather than Marx), but that the developments that Giddens associates with Western modernity, such as the public–private distinction, individualism and 'control of the subject' through new forms of institutional power, are related to such cycles and have appeared several times before in history in, for example, the Hellenistic, Roman and Chinese worlds. Like Aihwa Ong (1999: 241), Friedman takes Giddens to task for treating nation-state formation processes as autonomous phenomena relative to the economic dynamics of global systems, in an approach that is generally 'atomistic' and contingent when it should be holistic and systemic (Friedman 1994: 224).

transformation of modes of exercising power from the public torture and destruction of the body that had characterized earlier forms of punishment. Giddens, however, regards Foucault's emphasis on prisons and asylums as excessively narrow, emphasizing a more general shift in the sanctioning capacities of the state from the *manifest use of violence* to the *pervasive use of administrative power.*

Firstly, police forces replace the use of troops in everyday social regulation, in conjunction with an elaboration of sanctioning mechanisms of codified law and imprisonment. There is a general extension of surveillance mechanisms into everyday life. Secondly, everyday life is now based on industrialism, so the workplace itself becomes a site of surveillance. Violent sanctions on the part of employers and workers do not disappear overnight, but, in the industrializing nation-states of the core, capitalist employers were not allowed any direct legal access to the means of violence for use against their workers. 'Dull economic compulsion' became their main power resource. In the long run workers had no practical alternative but to accept the disciplines of capitalist wage labour and became habituated to its rules, which came to seem 'normal' and 'natural'. At first, however, they seemed to be quite the opposite, so that capitalism was born in a world of vagrancy laws and workhouses, institutions in which the 'disciplines' of capitalist wage labour were imposed on a recalcitrant dispossessed rural population.

Giddens therefore identifies certain links between industrialism and industrial urbanization on the one hand, and the forms of internal pacification which become characteristic of the nation-state on the other. Of course, the methods used to discipline the vast mass of human beings whose dispossession was the basis for industrialism were a kind of (class and state) violence. The classification of the uprooted poor as 'vagrants and criminals' and their incarceration in workhouses was hardly humane, and physical coercion played an important role in getting people into these institutions in the first place. Nevertheless, in the longer term, the new *mass societies* associated with industrialization were forged on the basis of new technologies of social control that differed in important ways from preceding forms of state power. These new technologies were far more pervasive in people's lives than their predecessors and thus the nation-state overcame the segmentalism of older state forms.

Giddens then proceeds to explain the form of nationalism found in Western industrial societies as a concomitant of the nation-state and industrialism. Once the state achieved an administrative and territorial unity, nationalism, based on a symbolic sense of shared history, culture and language, became a way of lending the administratively integrated unit a conceptual unity. Much of this symbolic unity was fabricated out of 'invented traditions', and Western nationalism for Giddens therefore has a political character. It is also an ideology which lends itself to oppositional movements, particularly where uneven development creates social dislocation in regions within the 'national unit' and claims to administrative sovereignty or autonomy are pressed by disadvantaged groups. Nevertheless, even these oppositional movements are now channelled through the administrative and political apparatus of the modern nation-state regime, through struggles for amendment of national constitutions and legal recognition of the rights of particular national or ethnic groups. As Wilson and Donnan argue in criticizing what they see as an unhealthy tendency for political anthropology to focus on a 'new' politics of identity, privileging the self and its representation, gender, sexuality, ethnicity and race, much of this new politics 'would be nowhere without the state as its principal contextual opponent' (Wilson and Donnan 1998: 2). This suggests something about the deeper changes brought about by a 'modern' type of state organization.

WIDER IMPLICATIONS OF HISTORICAL DISCONTINUITY

Talal Asad has argued that the contemporary production of social, cultural and political difference on a global scale ultimately rests on the universal 'formation of modern states on European patterns throughout the world' (Asad 1992: 334). Given the variety of contemporary political regimes, it may seem implausible to talk about a diffusion of the modern state form throughout the world, but Asad is pointing to something deeper than forms of government.

He suggests that the crucial transformation in European society came with the notion that there existed a separate legal and constitutional order that the ruler had a duty to maintain, a notion which emerged in north-western Europe in the period from the late thirteenth to sixteenth centuries. This is the historical moment when the word 'state' first comes into general usage. It becomes possible to see the state rather than the person of the ruler as the sole source of law and legitimate force within its territory. With that change emerged the 'citizen' who owes allegiance to the state, of which both he and the politically dominant class were members, together with the distinction between the 'public' sphere and the 'private' sphere, also emphasized by Giddens, which corresponds to the distinction between state and 'civil society'.[4] What is distinctive about this new type of political organization is

---

4 The notion of 'civil society' plays a crucial role in European theories of politics and is central to the way European thought constructed a negative 'Orientalist' discourse emphasizing the West's superiority to rival civilizations (Said 1978, Turner 1994: 34). Seventeenth-century models of 'bourgeois individualism' defended the political freedom of the propertied individual against the monarchical state, arguing that freedom depended on the existence of a 'civil society' standing between the autonomous individual and the state. The institutions of civil society – churches, guilds, voluntary associations, families and communities – protected the interests of individuals and enabled them to assert their interests against those of the state. Models of 'Oriental despotism' defined non-Western political regimes as ones in which the institutions of civil society do not exist, and a similar argument is often advanced today to explain the absence of democratic governance in countries that allegedly have 'weak civil societies'.

that all groups in society become compelled to pursue their interests 'within the domain organized by the state', through political struggles focused on legal categories. Working-class politics, for example, becomes struggle about labour laws, whilst struggles in colonial contexts often revolve around getting colonial administrations to recognize 'custom' as a legal category.

Within a modern political system, Asad argues, all social issues become *politicized* in this way. Indigenous groups demand the legal recognition of their special status, whilst gender and sexual politics become possible once the law makes it possible for sub-groups of free and equal citizens to acquire certain distinctive rights. Such struggles cannot always be pursued successfully, but it is important that people now attempt to secure rights in this way even in profoundly authoritarian circumstances. Repressive regimes increasingly find themselves forced to justify practices which violate human rights as universally understood. Asad in fact suggests that 'repressive regimes' are states which share the *pretensions* of all 'modern states' to intervene profoundly in the social practices of everyday life but have not succeeded in developing the power infrastructures needed to effect the kind of 'penetration' of social life achieved in the North. They are essentially *weak* states, resorting to physical coercion because they cannot secure their ends through the more subtle and manipulative practices of power associated with Northern 'surveillance' societies.

The modern state does not necessarily function in a way that guarantees 'the greatest happiness to the greatest number'. The deep regulation of social (and personal) life through law can be deeply disadvantageous to particular groups even in a democratic society. In the context of the world colonized by the West, however, what Asad stresses is how the spread of modern forms of power underpins the homogenization of certain understandings of 'modernization' and 'progress', despite the continuing cultural and social differentiation of the global social order:

> The West has become a vast moral project, an intimidating claim to write and speak for the world, and an unending politicization of power. Becoming Western has meant becoming transformed according to these things, albeit in a variety of historical circumstances and with varying degrees of thoroughness. For conscripts of Western civilization this transformation implies that some desires have been forcibly eliminated – even violently – and others put in their place. The modern state, invented in Europe, is the universal condition of that transformation – and of its higher truth. (Asad 1992: 345)

Asad's argument remains salient even if the model of state 'modernization' and its relationship to nation-building offered by Giddens turns out to be an inadequate or incomplete account of Western European development, and may be even less applicable to the development of national states outside Western Europe. Considering the processes that led Catalans living on the borders between France and Spain to identify with one country or the other, Peter Sahlins (1998) argued that national identity is not always imposed on 'peripheral' or borderland regions from the top down and the centre outward, as envisaged by a model of the state as creator of national culture and consciousness. Looking at the provincial backwater of Chachapoyas in Peru, David Nugent (1997) demonstrated that, under Latin American social conditions, people who live in 'peripheral' regions could embrace ideologies of 'modernity' independently of the national state. Indeed, the Chachapoyanos demanded that the state intervene in their lives to fulfil its obligation to deliver modern systems of government and 'economic progress', in order to displace aristocratic oligarchies whose arbitrary and rapacious rule remained founded on colonial models of racial hierarchy. 'Western modernity' is not always a process of enforced conscription, although the Chachapoyanos were to come to appreciate the more negative implications of social and economic 'modernization' and state power, and to rebel against them, at a later stage in their history. There may also be 'alternative modernities' that are not purely Western in their configuration even though they are forged in response to Western expansion, as Aihwa Ong has argued for the case of China (Ong 1996). Nevertheless, Ong (1999) also argues that contemporary East Asian states deploy 'modern' forms of disciplinary power in a way that enables them to play by the rules of liberal market society and embrace a global culture of consumerism whilst appearing to 'say no to the West'. This reinforces Asad's analysis of the deeper transformative impact of Western forms of power.

POLITICAL ANTHROPOLOGY RECONSTITUTED

From an anthropological perspective, it can, however, also be argued that the Western tradition of political analysis places excessive emphasis on the state and on formal political institutions of government. That understanding power relations in society involves more than an understanding of the formal institutions of the state is a point some theorists outside the anthropological tradition, notably Antonio Gramsci, argued long ago. It is also necessary to recognize that power remains incompletely centralized even in Western societies. The anthropological study of 'local-level' politics, the main theme of Chapter 6, can play as important a role in helping us to understand the North as it does in the case of the societies of the South. As Marc Abélès has argued, given the crisis of legitimacy now afflicting the political life of the North, it seems more necessary than ever to move beyond a focus on the state to an analysis of how power is acquired and transmitted in society as a whole. We need to appreciate the 'multilayered complexity of political reality'. This includes political action in everyday life and the symbols and rituals associated with these everyday political actions, the concretization of 'political culture' at the point where power is affirmed and contested in social practice (Abélès 1992: 17).

Here Abélès is again suggesting that the 'autonomy' of the political in modern societies is an illusion. Power actually rests on the everyday social practices that are the concrete form taken by relations between the governing and the governed. These relations are not simply expressed in forms of social action we could explicitly label 'political'. I will take up this issue in Chapter 4, in considering the problems of analysing 'resistance' to colonial exploitation and oppression and look at it again in Chapters 6 and 8. It is central to the life of modern 'metropolitan' societies, not only for the reasons Abélès gives, but because these societies now contain large numbers of people who do not feel incorporated into the political life of the nation in which they reside, the migrants and refugees drawn into the centre by economic and political forces but then subjected to practices of social discrimination and exclusion. We might already suspect that these systematic practices of discrimination are not simply reflections of the nature of modern capitalism, but another side of the coin to modern 'political' nationalism as Giddens defines it. Discrimination in the metropolis may encourage migrants to re-identify with their countries of origin, strengthening what Basch *et al.* (1994) have termed the 'deterritorialized nation state' (see also Glick Schiller 1999). Yet other scenarios of a more 'post-national' kind are possible, as illustrated by Mixtec Indians moving in transnational space between Oaxaca State, in the south of Mexico, to agribusiness farms and urban slums in the borderlands of northern Mexico and California (Kearney 1996).

Action that contests existing power relations may take many forms, including, for example, the parodying of the institutions and symbols of the regime which has characterized certain colonized groups' responses to situations of domination and struggles for autonomy and recognition (Keesing 1992). Much of it is in constant danger of slipping from view simply because of its everyday and inchoate quality. Anthropology has an important role to play in bringing these dimensions of modern political life back into view – and recognizing them brings a political, ethical and moral dimension to *doing* anthropology.

This suggests, however, that emphasis on the historical discontinuity constituted by the rise of Western state forms can potentially have negative as well as positive consequences. It is important not to replace the Weberian ideal-type model with another theoretical straitjacket on the understanding of difference. Anthropological perspectives can enrich the account of Western political life provided by sociology and political science. Yet it remains important to recognize that contemporary political processes everywhere reflect the impact of Western global expansion in both its direct, colonial, forms and in other, more indirect ways.

Even struggles for cultural autonomy and against Western domination take place under conditions that have been shaped by that domination. The West has not merely played a crucial role in drawing up the political map of the modern world, but it has also transformed the ways in which social conflicts are politicized and in which states and groups seeking power pursue their objectives on a global scale. Though particular situations always reflect the interaction of the local and the global, local social and cultural histories now find expression in action in ways that are part of a common experience of modernity, as I stress in Chapter 7. Only concrete, contextualized analysis of particular situations will enable us to understand what is happening and why it is happening (in Europe and the United States as well as other parts of the world). But little that is happening anywhere can be understood without reference to the historical discontinuities produced by the rise of the modern state and modern forms of power.

2 THE ORIGINS AND LIMITS OF COERCIVE POWER: THE ANTHROPOLOGY OF STATELESS SOCIETIES

Although Clastres's polemic against traditional political anthropology would be an appropriate starting-point for a discussion of 'stateless' societies, the late Stanley Diamond advanced a critique of the state which is broader than Clastres's observations about indigenous South American societies. Diamond's 1951 PhD dissertation was an ethnohistorical study of state formation in the West African kingdom of Dahomey, but his wider paradigm for a 'dialectical anthropology' reflected his New York Jewish background and experience as a volunteer with the British Army during the Second World War in North Africa. There he met Black African 'volunteers' from South Africa. Pressed into service by the South African government through the good offices of chiefly clients of the regime, these men were sent to die in an unknown land in an unknown cause in place of Whites (Gailey 1992: 4).[1] A humanistic rather than 'scientific' Marxist, Diamond focused on the repressive consequences of state formation – bureaucratic oppression, racism, marginalization, ethnocide and genocide – and the cultural resistances which state and colonial-imperialist domination provoked.

Diamond's analysis juxtaposes 'the kin community' and 'civil society' (Diamond 1974). He defined 'civil society' as the culture of civilization, the ideologies, apparatuses and agencies associated with political organization based on the state. A particular civil society may oppose a particular state regime. Aristocrats may use peasant unrest to displace a ruling dynasty. Persons from a different social class may wrest control of the state from an established elite, bringing about change in the ideologies associated with state power. Yet, in Diamond's view, even the most radical action of civil society against a regime does not undermine the existence of states as such. Radical resistance to the alienation provoked by the culture of civilization is mounted within the sphere of 'kinship': the world of intimate personal relations, material reciprocity and mutual aid networks, community as the enactment of shared culture in the everyday life of the lower classes. Even in

---

1 I have drawn on Christine Gailey's account throughout this discussion of Diamond's life and work.

the modern world, this deep level of social life remained the basis for grassroots re-creation of identities and a popular cultural creativity resistant to the increasingly powerful attempts by civil structures to repress, control and define appropriate social behaviour. Diamond's notion of 'kin–civil conflict' has wide ramifications for political anthropology.

Kin-communities provide a model for pre-state societies based on consensual authority embodied in custom rather than power relations embodied in law, but Diamond's deeper purpose was to highlight the continuing existence of a contested domain even in the most 'totalitarian' of societies, such as Nazi Germany. No system of civil domination, however technically perfect, could suppress all forms of resistance. There is much more to be said about cultural resistance to domination in modern societies, and also about its possible limits. Nevertheless, Diamond deployed his dynamic concept of the state as an apparatus seeking to impose its writ on a resistant kin-community in path-breaking analyses of the development processes of early states.

In his analysis of pre-colonial Dahomey, Diamond showed how this West African 'proto-state' strengthened its domination over the local kin-community by intervening to control the reproductive and social roles of women. Irene Silverblatt (1987) has explored similar processes in the Inca Empire of Peru. The Inca state forced the local kin-communities of the empire to surrender women to it, known as *acllas*. Since giving women to higher status people, hypergamy, was a basic Andean way of expressing hierarchic relations, this practice had profound symbolic significance in political terms. 'Conquerors' were conceptualized as male in the Andes and the ranking of different local kin-communities (*ayllus*) was expressed in terms of contrasts between female original inhabitants and male conquerors. Conquered groups provided women for secondary marriages to the conquerors. Thus, according to this ideology, only males could found conqueror lineages and intermediate lineages formed by intermarriage between conquered and conquerors.

This is an ideological discourse on status, but it had practical significance in terms of the organization of the Inca Empire. The pre-hispanic Andean power system had a different cultural logic to the European system that replaced it. The Inca demanded that their subjects provide them with women for secondary marriages, and the children of these unions became Inca. As Zuidema (1964) has shown, the structure of the empire was represented in indigenous thought as a tripartite division overlaid on a quadripartite division of the empire into four quarters (*suyu*) and a division of Cuzco itself into two moieties. This corresponded to a division between priestly and kingly power. The tripartite division was between a category called Collana, a second called Cayao and a third called Payan. It had various meanings: it could refer to a division between Inca conquerors, the original lords of the land, and offspring of union between the two, or it could mean aristocratic rulers, the non-aristocratic population and the Incas' assistants or servants.

The root meaning, however, was that Collana were the primary kin of an Inca ego, and Cayao the rest of humanity unrelated to an Inca ego, from whom Collana men could choose secondary wives, thus producing the third category, Payan.

This tripartite division was full of ideological possibilities. It could be used to talk about class and the relationship between the Inca and those they conquered. It could be used to honour male leaders of subordinate groups or it could be used in a way that emphasized Inca superiority. Lastly, the category Payan, the children of Inca and non-Inca, could be used to emphasize the *hierarchic unity* of the Inca state – the way Inca power *encompassed* other groups and made their future reproduction depend on their relationship with the superior kin category, Collana.

This brings us back to the role of the *acllas*. The *acllas* were given to the Inca as a kind of tribute, to become brides of the Sun who remained virgins unless the Inca himself decided otherwise. The political hierarchy established by conquest was thus represented symbolically by the Inca in kinship and gender terms: the category Cayao could stand for 'conquered women' *and* for the non-Inca population as a whole. Furthermore, the Inca himself contracted his primary marriage with a sister, thereby symbolizing his ability to marry any woman in the empire. In addition to this symbolic function, however, the *aclla* performed a number of distinct practical functions within the Inca power system.

Firstly, they were political pawns. The Inca king gave *acllas* to members of the Incaic nobility as a reward for loyalty, but he also manipulated the status significance of the alienation of women to bind non-Incaic provincial elites to the empire. Local headmen felt honoured by being asked to provide a daughter to the Inca and were seen by their communities as gaining prestige by doing so. Silverblatt gives an example of a father who hands over his only daughter to be sacrificed to the Sun. The significance of the act is that the father is now recognized by the state as the headman (*kuraka*) of his *ayllu* and governorship of the area will now pass to his male descendants. The woman was finally buried alive in the lands bordering her community appropriated by the Inca state, and so this example demonstrates the second significant function of the handing over of *acllas*, the symbolization of Inca domination and the relationship between conquest and hierarchy. The system thus had a subtle edge to it: its logic made ambitious local chieftains into accomplices of Inca domination.

The Inca demand for women provoked resentment in the conquered communities, however, and was quite often used as a punishment against those that rebelled against the empire. To reinforce control, representatives of the Inca state claimed the right to distribute women within conquered communities: peasant marriage became a yearly mass event presided over by state officials. But the removal of *acllas* from their communities was a much stronger expression of domination: women made 'Wives of the Sun' were turned directly into dependents of the state. Virginity is the key symbol here.

Andean women's sexual conduct before marriage was not rigidly controlled in the kin-communities, but the *acllas'* sexuality was policed by the empire and only the Inca and persons given his permission were permitted access to them. So the second significant point about the *aclla* was that the state now exerted power over the demographic reproduction of the Andean community in a way which also reinforced Incaic domination.

The third important function of the *acllas* was as priestesses of a state cult, and even those who were sacrificed at least had the compensation of being honoured and revered. Besides officiating in state rituals in Cuzco, the *acllas* performed an important role as ritual mediators between their home communities and the capital, distributing holy bread to provincial shrines and *kurakas*. All the different dimensions of the removal of women from *ayllu* communities into the *aclla* category demonstrate the principle that whilst the logic of the institution begins with the gender and marriage symbolism of conqueror–conquered relations which was already part of Andean ideology before the Incas, the Incas used this symbolism to elaborate new modes of practical political domination.

This intertwining of class and state formation with gender transformations of this kind is probably typical of early state formation, although European colonialism produced a further deterioration in the position of women in these societies and gender relations are further transformed by modern capitalist commodity relationships (Gailey 1987). The superiority of Diamond's framework for exploring political life as a dynamic process over formal descriptions of governmental and legal institutions is apparent. Yet there is more to be said about those societies which remain 'kin-organized'.

The world of 'non-state peoples' can be an extremely violent one, a world of incessant warfare, killings and torture. The absence of the civil institutions of the state and authoritative community leaders does not guarantee equality or even balanced complementarity of social roles as far as gender and inter-generational relationships are concerned. Inequalities based on age might be transitory, since most individuals will eventually become adults and elders, but those between the sexes are a different matter (Molyneux 1977). Stateless societies may be structured in a way which inhibits the emergence of permanent centralized authority and social stratification, but how far can it be argued that they rest on consensual rather than coercive relations?

Some anthropologists working on Australian aboriginal society, such as John Bern (1979) and Peter Worsley (1992), have argued that kinship and marriage in 'stateless societies' should themselves be seen as *political* phenomena, concerned with gerontocratic forms of power and male domination of women.[2] 'Gerontocracy' may be not be an innocent

---

2 Tonkinson (1991) has, however, argued that these patterns were not universal in Australia.

phenomenon, a difference between men reversed over time, since 'big men' may secure more women than others in the tribe. It may also entail a permanent coercive oppression of women in addition to the transitory measures which elders adopt to frustrate the desires of younger men to possess the women they seek to monopolize. Worsley argues that the fact that younger men generally contest the monopoly of women claimed by elders turns struggle over possession of women into the main form of political conflict in 'stateless' societies (1992: 44). It is a primary source of the fighting and feuding which 'primitive law' has to mediate, and the problem to which gerontocratic strategies of social control are addressed.

Before I pursue the implications of this argument, it is necessary to introduce a note of caution. Feminist scholarship in anthropology has alerted us to the pitfalls of looking at gender relations solely from a male point of view, taking indigenous male representations of women at face value. To speak of 'sex roles' is to assume that there are distinct 'male' and 'female' points of view and patterns of behaviour that characterize all persons of the same physical sex in a given culture, and that these enjoy an autonomous existence, independent of the interactions between men and women and ongoing negotiation of relations between them (Strathern 1988, Guttman 1997). 'Maleness' and 'femaleness' can only be understood in relation to each other. The assumption that persons (or gods) can be unambiguously assigned to one of two genders may be problematic even in cultures that stress the distinction between male and female and expect men and women to play different roles in everyday life. From the point of view of relationships between the sexes in 'stateless' societies, we need to be alert to the possibility that ideologies and practices of male domination may be 'complicated, if not counteracted, by women's influence in socio-economic, domestic and religious matters' (Knauft 1997: 237). It is just as androcentric to look at power relations between men and women from an exclusively male vantage-point as it is to ignore the ways in which the notion that stateless societies are 'egalitarian' might need qualification from a perspective that considered gender.

The issue of power relations based on age and gender does, however, suggest a need to scrutinize more closely the vision that Pierre Clastres offers of the political life of 'societies without states'. In the next section, I argue that Clastres himself does not fully transcend the baggage of the classical sociological tradition and its models of 'social order', even if his critique of the thinking of classical political anthropology remains valid.

THE EXTERNALIZATION OF THE POLITICAL AS THE NEGATION OF POWER

Clastres begins with the paradox posed by the aboriginal institution of chief-tainship. Most South American indigenous groups possessed recognized leaders, but these were of the kind Robert Lowie termed 'titular chiefs' – chiefs who possessed no ability to issue commands which would automatically be obeyed. In Western terms they seem practically powerless, at least in peacetime. Chiefly authority was stronger in wartime, approaching a capacity to demand absolute obedience from other members of the war band. Yet once fighting stopped, any power an individual acquired as a war leader evaporated, and it was common for leadership in war and peacetime to be assumed by a different individual. History records war chiefs who sought to perpetuate their power by trying to extend hostilities beyond the point which their communities regarded as legitimate: the South American Yanomami warrior Fousiwe, and the North American Apache chief Geronimo, both found that no one bar a few equally egocentric young warriors would follow them (Clastres 1977: 178–9). This, Clastres contends, demonstrates that chiefs were incapable of imposing their personal desires on a recalcitrant society and translating prestige acquired in warfare into permanent authoritative power. After all, 'no society *always* wants to wage war' (ibid.).

Even the most warlike of societies suspends hostilities periodically in order to replenish food stocks and to undertake ceremonial activities which demand a cessation of aggression against other groups. Yet Clastres's suggestion that war-weariness ultimately sets limits on the development of coercive authority ignores arguments from both Amazonia and Melanesia that the reproduction of war is integral to the reproduction of a maleness engaged in a struggle to assert its domination over femaleness which I consider in more depth later in this chapter. According to Clastres, power is regulated by 'society' blocking the egotism of (male) 'individuals'. This framework obscures the possible structuring of 'stateless' societies by coercive relations other than those associated with political centralization.

To explain how the separate power associated with the emergence of the state might break out of the regulatory mechanisms of the 'primitive social order', Clastres appeals to increasing demographic density as the factor which cannot be completely regulated by social practices. He is not, however, a simple demographic determinist. He argues that the transition to statehood is socially contested as demographic density increases, using the example of the Tupi-Guarani in the fifteenth century. This group surpassed the norm for the South American lowlands in terms of demographic density and local group size. It also displayed tendencies towards a strengthening of chiefly power, which were, however, being challenged at the time of European conquest by prophetic shamans, who went from community to community urging the people to abandon their forest homes and migrate to the East in search of a promised 'Land without Evil'. Clastres argues that the millenarian vision of the Guarani prophets thwarted the dynamic of state formation by mobilizing society at large and unifying different tribes more effectively than the chiefs had done, although it resulted in terrible suffering for those who responded to the call. The Guarani case is ultimate proof of the resistance of 'stateless societies' to political centralization.

The Indian chief as presented by Clastres is a 'peacemaker'. His main resource as a mediator is the spoken word. Yet not only may people decide not to heed the word of the chief, but his ritualized oratorical discourse is not really spoken in order to be listened to (ibid.: 130). The chief stands up to deliver his speech in a loud voice when the group is gathered together at daybreak or dusk, but no one gathers round and no hush falls. In a sense, the people are feigning a lack of attention, because they may indeed settle the dispute afterwards, but the content of the speech is a prolix repetition of the norms of traditional life. These empty words are not the words of a man of power, but the duty of the individual selected to speak for the community, to embody its normative principles. Thus, Clastres argues, 'normal civil power' is based on the 'consent of all'. It is orientated towards maintaining peace and harmony and is itself 'profoundly peaceful' (ibid.: 22).

Not only does society deny chiefs coercive power, it also denies them scope for accumulating material wealth, by insisting they display generosity at all times: in some South American groups, finding the chief is a matter of searching for the poorest and shabbiest-looking member of the community. Lowland South American chiefs did possess one privilege generally denied to others: polygyny. At first sight, the 'gift' of women to the chief might be construed as reciprocation for the chief's services to society, the flow of speech and presentations that it is his duty to provide. Yet even with the support of his wives' labour, the chief could not amass much wealth, and much of what was demanded of him consisted of things like bows, arrows and masculine ornaments that the chief himself would have to make. Clastres suggests that the notion of a quantitative exchange of equivalent values between the chief and the group is inconceivable in this case. The absence of an obvious exchange principle is reinforced by the fact that the office of chief tended to be inherited patrilineally (ibid.: 30). The same family line retained its disproportionate share of the group's women. Furthermore, the things the chief gives to the group – goods and speech – are not reciprocated in kind, since people do not give to chiefs and only chiefs can speak.

Clastres therefore suggests that it is the very denial of reciprocity in the relationship between chiefs and community that is crucial. The circulation of gifts, linguistic signs and women is constitutive of society, but chiefs are people who fall outside the web of reciprocity:

Power enjoys a privileged relationship toward those elements whose reciprocal movement founds the very structure of society. But this relationship, by denying these elements an exchange value at the group level, institutes the political sphere not only as *external to the structure of the group*, but further still, as *negating that structure*: power is contrary to the group, and the rejection of reciprocity, as the ontological dimension of society, is the rejection of society itself. (ibid.: 32, emphasis added)

This, Clastres argues, is how lowland South American indigenous peoples provided themselves with a defence mechanism against appropriation of coercive power by chiefs. As a speaker and displayer of generosity, the chief was totally dependent on the group of whose values he was custodian. If he failed to keep the peace or provide relief in times of famine, he was removed. Polygyny appears to be a privilege, but the chief acquires women as a pure gift. This places him outside the normal framework of reciprocities and expresses his dependence on the group.

Despite the impressive evidence provided by the millenarian revolt of the Guarani prophets, Clastres's own material suggests that the defences of 'primitive societies' against state formation could come under pressure. Some pre-colonial lowland societies may have been in the process of succumbing to new modalities of political power (Roosevelt 1989), and Clastres does not take us very far towards understanding how and why states did form in the highland zone of South America. Michael Mann (1986) has argued that state formation is an exceptional process in early human history, dependent on unusual circumstances. Archaeologists are also increasingly drawn to the view that state formation should be seen as an historically contingent process rather than something inherent in the political-economic and social structures of kin-based communities, a 'latent potential waiting to unfold as soon as the right conditions appear' (Patterson 1993: 103). Once this unusual event has occurred in a given region, however, the expansion of states transforms peripheral societies, which might not otherwise have developed as they did (Friedman 1994: 18–22). It is still possible to conceive of local populations actively resisting the imposition of the new forms of domination associated with the state. Given that there were contacts between highland and lowland societies in South America, Clastres may not really be analysing populations that existed in some 'pristine' world of 'society before the state'. The main problem with his analysis is, however, its exclusive focus on the power or lack of power of 'chiefs'. It does not attend to the potential existence of other modalities of domination in 'stateless societies'.

This seems a strange omission in Amazonia, given the number of anthropologists who have sought to make links between warfare, male bonding and antagonism directed against women among the indigenous peoples of this region (Murphy 1959, Chagnon 1988). Joan Bamberger (1974) used lowland South American examples to argue that myths that speak of a time of matriarchy that provokes male rebellion are ideological charters for practices of male domination. Gregor (1985) has developed this argument by arguing that Amazonian patriarchy was sustained not merely by symbolic terrorism but by ritualized gang rape.

This line of argument has, however, been challenged by Cecilia McCallum (1994). McCallum argues that a vision of a violent male quest for domination over women is discrepant with the strong moral emphasis on respect for others, self-control and pacificity that she found among the peoples of the Alto Xingu (the area of Gregor's study of the Mehinaku), and contrasts strongly with the tenor of male–female relationships in everyday life. She suggests that Bamberger and Gregor treat ritual as a kind of 'political theatre' which recreates 'ideal type social relations' in a way that imposes 'debased forms of symbolism and representation' drawn from Western cultures onto complex ritual cycles that are about making, unmaking and remaking persons and the social relations between them (McCallum 1994: 91, 109–10).[3] For McCallum, constructing females as objects to be consumed and controlled by males universalizes Western models of sexuality that have no place in the Xingu, where the complementary roles of male and female sexuality are integral to the construction of all personhood and sociality.

The Xingu Park is a special kind of environment, a show-case for the Brazilian state's claims to protect indigenous people, and McCallum is working with 'pacified' groups that have sought refuge within it. Nevertheless, she offers a powerful argument against imposing Western ideas about power, gender and sexuality onto other cultures that might also be supported by considering what happens to indigenous peoples who have been strongly drawn into 'modernity'. Knauft argues that the growing association of masculinity and male agency with trade goods and money in both Amazonia and Melanesia has increased individuation and the autonomy of the nuclear family, with a consequent commodification of female sexuality (Knauft 1997: 244–5). He suggests that increasing emphasis on male sexual control and increased tensions in domestic relations reflect growing insecurity provoked by the transformation of a traditional sexual licence practised with discretion into an exchange of sexual favours for goods or even prostitution, and by the fact that men are forced to leave home to acquire the commodities needed to fulfil their status aspirations (ibid.: 246). This analysis is consistent with Strathern's argument that Western models of the person, exploitation and domination derive from the logic of commodity economy and 'possessive individualism',[4] contrasting with Melanesian notions of personhood as objectifications of relationships which include cross-sex as well as same-sex relationships (Strathern 1988: 338). Yet Knauft is less eager than McCallum

---

3 Ritual processes often have the quality of 'unmaking' normal social relations or even enacting community destruction in order to rebuild and reassert the integrity of those relationships. McCallum argues that the Xinguano view of social life is 'person-centred' and not concerned with building corporate groups or 'society' (ibid.: 105). A good example of a ritual process that focuses on building 'community' is the Festival of Games of San Juan Chamula in Chiapas, Mexico. This complex cycle enacts the cosmic destruction of the community before reconstituting it as a collectivity able to defend its autonomy against non-Indian oppressors (Gossen 1999).

4 'Possessive individualism' reflects the idea that 'society consists of a series of market relations' (Macpherson 1962: 263–4). The crucial idea is not, however, possession of property in land or moveable goods, but property in *one's own person*. Those who entered a wage contract or became dependent on poor relief partially alienated property in their persons, and this is how, in the seventeenth century, political rights were linked to property in things. Such people should be 'included in their masters' as far as having a voice in government was concerned, but not be denied the civil and religious liberties that all men had a 'natural' right to defend against arbitrary monarchical rulers (ibid.: 142–8). See also Gledhill (1997).

to eliminate discussion of antagonism between men and women entirely from analysis of indigenous societies before the impact of 'modernity'.

SEXUAL POLITICS IN STATELESS SOCIETIES

The people of the Western Highlands of New Guinea have also acquired notoriety in the anthropological literature both for the warlike nature of their men and an apparent antagonism between the sexes. Again, we should not assume that these communities represent fossilized 'stone-age societies' which have always lived in the manner which has been observed ethnographically, not only because regional conditions of life were influenced by the expansion of colonial power long before it penetrated the area directly (Worsley 1970: 333), but because they have their own, pre-colonial, history. Gilbert Herdt (1987) writes that war was the ultimate reality for the group he studied in the 1970s, the Sambia, because it was a pervasive fact of daily life. We can accept that circumstance and explore its contemporary significance without further analysis of historical causes. We know, however, that the Sambia established themselves as a fringe-area group in a larger regional society dominated by more numerous tribes speaking a different language. Their fears of ancient enemies formed in a matrix of concrete historical experience (Herdt 1987: 21–3).

The Sambia lived in small hamlets based on a core of patrilineal kinsmen. Clansmen of a given hamlet were allied in ritual and military matters with those of other hamlets nearby who saw themselves as descended from a common (fictitious) ancestor. Members of clans united in these 'phratries' saw themselves as brothers or age-mates: they could call on each other for assistance at times of war, and in some cases hamlets belonging to different phratries jointly sponsored collective initiation rituals, forming an 'interphratry' confederacy. Yet fighting with bows and arrows could break out between hamlets of the same phratry and confederacy, even if it was less likely than fighting between hamlets of different phratries that were not linked together by marriage alliances. Although intermarriage between hamlets cross-cut phratry boundaries, and, like the interphratry initiation rituals, helped moderate violence when it flared up, it was a weak political bond, since 'bonds of blood were stronger than marital bonds' (ibid.: 50). The confederacies themselves were accordingly fragile.

Local fighting was subject to institutionalized constraint. Feuds between hamlets, premised on sorcery accusations, adultery or retaliation for an insult, would be settled by 'ritualized' exchanges of arrows on designated fight-grounds. The principle that the fighting should not be lethal could not be observed in practice on every occasion, prompting warriors to rationalize a death by saying: 'He stood in front of my arrow' (ibid.: 49). Bow-fighting was practised as a military game which was part of the process of training boys to be warriors and was also a means by which adults could compete for martial prestige, but ritualized bow-fights between hamlets could escalate into 'big-fights'. In these, killings were more likely, war leaders prepared plans for ambushes and raids, and shamans turned lethal sorcery on the hamlet's enemies. Initial escalation usually followed an 'accidental' killing. The original parties would mobilize allies for support, and this process tended to lead to further escalation as 'stranger' groups were drawn into the conflict through alliance networks. They arrived wielding clubs and axes, the most lethal weapons at the Sambia's disposal.

This level of escalation and the accompanying bloodshed did, however, prejudice inter-hamlet relations to a point where the continuation of basic social life was threatened. Truce ceremonies, enacted between warriors on the fight-grounds, might lead eventually to a restoration of peace through blood compensation payments, but compensation was not as significant an institution in the Sambia case as in other parts of the Western Highlands. Extended periods of fighting only tended to die down after blood revenge had been exacted and food supplies had been disrupted by women's inability to tend the gardens. Although truces tended to be short-lived, peace did permit elders to negotiate new marriage alliances and conduct collective initiation rituals, allowing social life to continue in as 'normal' a manner as the Sambia could hope to achieve given their commitment to violence. Although it was inter-tribal warfare against groups defined as eternal 'enemies' to be slain in which the Sambia warrior ethos reached its destructive height, assassinations and sorcery accusations abounded in the competition between warrior big-men even at the local level.

Sambia men spent much of their time preparing for war and guarding against surprise attack, including sorcery attacks ascribed to women acting in league with their enemies. Sambia society was not entirely devoid of peace-making institutions. Patterns of conflict were regulated by a degree of ritualization and the structure of alliances which linked patrilineages in one hamlet with those of another, though these cross-cutting ties could equally well pit men of the *same* hamlet against each other in inter-hamlet fights in which their hamlet as a whole was not directly involved. The Sambia recognized different forms of warfare. They tried to limit the intensity of fights by specifying the weapons to be used and level of combat, but violence could escalate even from 'controlled' and apparently harmless beginnings. Faced with constant warfare and fragile political alliances, Sambia villages put up the stockades and trained their boys to be aggressive warriors. As Herdt points out, warfare is a complex phenomenon that can have many causes, including the ambition of leaders and competition for resources. His own analysis focuses, however, on the way that violence was driven by a Sambia 'warrior ethos', founded on a need to compete that destroyed resources and devalued humans, and ultimately rested on the desires of Sambia men to dominate women.

There is a danger here of ascribing Sambia aggression to male psychological drives. This, and the alternative argument that 'male solidarity' and 'gender antagonism' are 'functional' responses to conditions of endemic warfare, has been addressed in an innovative analysis of the political dynamics of Melanesian warfare in the Sepik area by Simon Harrison (1993). Most analyses of 'primitive warfare' accept the Hobbesian argument that the state imposes peaceful relations on individuals who are 'naturally' inclined to violence outside the immediate moral universe of kin communities (Sahlins 1974). Yet Harrison notes that what the state accomplishes is not the abolition of internal violence but its classification as 'illegitimate' (Harrison 1993: 149). Melanesia refutes the assumption that peaceful sociality is a condition that 'stateless societies' are only able to maintain within the narrow circle of village social ties, since Melanesians are perfectly capable of maintaining peaceful relations with distant trading partners. Harrison suggests that we focus instead on the way male ritual cults are organizations for *producing* war, for *negating* conditions of peaceful sociality that are assumed to be 'normal' (ibid.) He sees such male ritual as an 'imposition' that embodies male symbolic idealizations of 'power' which are *political* in two senses: they construct a 'community' that is an enduring entity 'externally bounded against "enemies" and internally structured by inequalities of age and gender' (ibid.: 148).

[Thus] what men are demonstrating in ritual, and in warfare itself, is a kind of power and freedom from accountability that open up two interdependent spheres of action: both to kill and make war, and to act politically in their dealings with women and juniors. (ibid.: 144–5)

This account can readily be applied to the Sambia. Men assert that their dominance is necessary to defend 'society'. It rests on a peculiarly male essence, *jerungdu*, which is a life-force substance embodying uniquely masculine qualities of bodily and spiritual strength. Semen supplies *jerungdu*, and men must possess it in abundance if they are to be true men, something they must demonstrate by sexual and military prowess. This amounts to an injunction to dominate both women and other men. But *jerungdu* is not innate: neither women nor boys possess it, and it must be acquired from 'real men'. In Sambia cosmogony, the original couple from whom they spring are hermaphroditic age-mates, but one is bigger and older. Since both have penises, the stronger of the pair copulates through the mouth of the partner. This process transforms them into male and female, though the primal male has to cut open a vagina on the female to allow the first child to emerge into the world (Herdt 1987: 167). The first-born son is forbidden sex with his mother by his father, and told to have fellatio with his younger brother, who thereby in turn becomes masculinized. The founding myth of the Sambia thus explains what is at the core of their initiation rituals: what Herdt originally termed a 'ritualized homosexuality' that allows transmission of manhood through semen to boys from bachelors, youths who have themselves acquired maleness and become strong enough to take their place in the male society of warriors and give maleness to younger boys.

In a new preface to his first book on the Sambia, originally published in 1981, Herdt abandons the term 'homosexuality' for these same-sex practices, renaming them 'boy-inseminating practices' to eliminate the connotations of Western concepts of sexuality (Herdt 1994: xiv). They belong to a family of practices found in association with 'stratification by age, with emphasis upon the intergenerational qualities of power, knowledge, manliness, prowess in war, honor and virtue being transmitted from older to younger male' (ibid.). The Sambia did not respect same-sex relations in men who were fully socially adult. Those who continued to prefer oral sex with boys rather than vaginal sex with women which could produce children were 'rubbish men' who had failed to make the full transition to manhood. Herdt argued that the logic of Sambia notions of sexuality was determined by male models of power and what was ultimately a *fear* of women. *Jerungdu* is a form of power restricted to men that can only be acquired from men, and how much of it one has determines how much of a man one is. The role of bachelor as sperm-giver and boy as sperm-taker cannot be reversed, and the transition to sex with women is made possible only by the growing strength of one's manliness: vaginal sex with a woman threatens pollution and even depletion of *jerungdu*. Sambia men were often loath to start having vaginal sex with their wives, favoured the missionary position and orgasmed quickly. Newly-wed men often continued to take semen from male partners for a while after they began to have sexual relations with women, something they kept secret from the former.

The lengthy Sambia initiation cycle subjects boys to an arduous process of physical ordeals designed both to foster warrior virtues and to end the grip of mothers over their male children. One of the most dramatic episodes in Herdt's ethnography is a moment when young men physically attack the mothers of initiated boys after the nose-bleeding ceremony, in which cane stalks are forced down the nostrils of the screaming children and the blood is collected on fern leaves. Two men try to ram the bloodied leaves down a woman's throat, and another charges into the group of mothers, with bow and arrows in hand, and curses them, provoking anger and demands for revenge on the women's part. Herdt suggests that: 'It seems that the blood and the sight of women here can create violent reactions in [young men]. Something in their gender identity is so touchy, like an unhealed wound' (ibid.: 152). The symbolism of the initiation rites in fact reveals a frequent association of key male symbols with femaleness. The phallic ritual flutes used in the initiation rituals to teach the mechanics of fellatio are supposedly hostile to women and children. Yet they also have female associations: they are called 'frog female' because they sound like a frog croaking in the forest, only women hunt frogs, the initiates' mothers fed them frog two days before and the forest edge-land is where dangerous female spirits live. Not only is the spirit of the flutes female, but the myths say they were made by women. But these are dangerous women, not the submissive, obedient women of Sambia male ideology.

The rites separate boys from the world and power of women, but Sambia seem unable to deny the necessity of the female contribution to social reproduction even as they engineer this separation: semen is likened to mother's milk (ibid.: 150). Women, it is conceded in the heart of these male rites, are naturally fertile and reproductive, and men are not (ibid.: 190). The ritual process aims to remove female residues from the body of the initiate and all 'femine feelings' and behaviour. Yet its repetitiveness and the aggression towards women manifest throughout the cycle suggest that men never truly believe that their cultural mimicking of women's natural fertility is sufficient to establish the superiority of male power over 'natural' female power. If the women knew that men acquire their power only by *playing the woman* to an older man, the basis for male gender domination would be threatened. The secret fear of Sambia men is that women are really more powerful than they are.[5]

The secret society organization of Sambia men is therefore a *political* organization in Harrison's sense. It involves a transfer of control over young men from their mothers to the elders. The latter need to control the products of women's labour and of their bodies, including the female children who will be needed to obtain wives for the bachelors. They also need to control the bachelors themselves, who cannot yet be allowed sexual access to the women around them. To accomplish the last objective, elders resort to repetition of the nose-bleeding ordeals. Herdt suggests this is a kind of 'symbolic castration', steering bachelors' sexual impulses away from women towards younger initiates (ibid.: 185). Ritual beliefs about the polluting nature of women's bodies reinforce bachelors' avoidance of women, and warfare redirects any anger youths might feel towards the elders towards external enemies.

Yet the power claims of Sambia masculinity remain fragile. Sambia recognize the power of female and hermaphrodite shamans, and women who are shamans can participate in the healing of men. Once again, notions of motherhood and the natural fertility of women surface, and this time not simply in myth but in social practice. That coercion and violence enter into relations between the sexes among the Sambia reflects the cracks in the power structure over which male elders preside. Here power is negated in Clastres's sense because the male part of society is dedicated to the negation of the power of the female part, which it is nevertheless forced to acknowledge, in its myths and in its dreams.

---

5 Some New Guinea peoples went further in exorcizing the spectre of female power. The Iqwaye cosmogonic myth denies the necessity of the female role in sexual reproduction by having man and the cosmos created from a primal self-creating being with his own penis in his mouth: as the creator and first man vomits his own semen and blood, thus were created all things in this world. The creator Omalyce was at once his own father, mother and son. The Iqwaye therefore close their ideological system more successfully than the Sambia (Mimica 1988: 74–87).

· Herdt concedes that he did little work with women in his first fieldwork. His analyses were written from his own male point of view as well as from that of his male informants. As Gutmann points out, following Young (1983), the assumption that women are 'muted' or inarticulate in 'traditional societies' is in danger of becoming a self-fulfilling prophecy (Gutmann 1997: 848). Herdt's ethnography shows women as present throughout the ritual sequence which lies at the core of his analysis. They actually confront men at various points. He argued, however, that the assumption by women of a complementary role to men in performing the ritual indirectly reinforced the male position, despite the fact that women and men ended up confronting each other, verbally and physically, as a group (Herdt 1987: 134). Yet though the Sambia men said that they regarded the women merely as spectators, their role as an audience was neither trivial nor passive: women acted in a way which sanctioned the necessity of initiation, because their antagonism to men as husbands in the rites reinforced the separation of the male world into which the initiate was moving.

There is a point in the initiation rite, during the moonlight rituals of the dance-ground, at which the women perform their own ceremony, the Firewood Ritual. Herdt describes the rhetorical chastising of initiates and adult men by women in these nocturnal events as 'rituals of rebellion' (ibid.: 132), following Gluckman's analyses of ritualized confrontations that allow the tensions provoked by domination to be expressed and *released* in a way which allows the system to continue functioning (Gluckman 1954, 1955). The ultimate effect of the ritual dramas enacted is to realize the separation of the initiate from the female power domain of motherhood.

Yet men worry about hiding the 'secret' of the flawed nature of their power from women. How can we be sure that the women do not know the secret, and are Sambia men themselves convinced of their ignorance? Female contestation of male dominance claims in Sambia society might run deeper than the opposition visible in the ritual process. Even that ritualized opposition seems less than trivial given that it provokes violence that is not entirely ritualized. Ritual is, however, not 'everyday life', and as McCallum suggested, we should also take everyday relations between men and women into account in framing our interpretations. Her own analysis suggests that the dangerous states of being created in the making and unmaking of an order of things in ritual contexts can produce 'unscripted' reactions from the participants. Yet although the Sambia case is consistent with the kinds of generalizations Strathern has made about the role of both male and female in creating 'personhood' in Melanesia, these same generalizations are integral to Harrison's model of the political role of male cults as an effort to establish the kind of freedom of accountability that is evident in a different form in the behaviour of war chiefs (Harrison 1993: 144). The elimination of all notions of 'domination' from 'stateless societies' therefore seems unwarranted. The tensions that result from the attempt by older men to privilege their own status through ritual cults seem, however, of a quite different order to the effects of contemporary forms of male domination, expressed in the commodification of women's bodies, the divide that Knauft suggests separates the Melanesian past from the present.

CIVILIZATION, MOTHER OF BARBARISM

The issues raised by an exploration of ways in which the workings of 'stateless societies' inhibit centralization of political power make it more difficult to explain how the *first* states in human history formed. We cannot, however, assume that the 'stateless societies' we know about from ethnography represent the kinds of societies which existed before there were any states or civilizations at all (Fabian 1980). No anthropologist has been able to study a human community unaffected by Western civilization by ethnographic methods, let alone the societies which *actually* preceded the formation of the earliest civilizations of the Old and New Worlds.

The problem of 'the Origins of the State' is therefore one to which political anthropology can make a contribution only in collaboration with archaeologists. The nature of that contribution, in my view, lies primarily in using ethnographic data to problematize theorizing about the social mechanisms that might have led to the centralization of power and to pose questions about the nature of power and inequality in early state societies (Gledhill 1988a). There are areas of the world, such as Polynesia, where close cooperation between archaeologists and anthropologists has already shown its potential (Sahlins and Kirch 1992). In most cases, however, the interface is indirect and theoretical. It is seldom possible to combine even ethnohistorical and archaeological data in an investigation of state *origins* in most regions of the world for the simple reason that indigenous or early colonial written sources usually relate to later episodes in cyclical processes of state formation and collapse, the beginnings of which lie in a remote past.

Much of the vast literature on early state formation is not, however, about state 'origins' in the literal sense, but later episodes in such long cycles. Seen in terms of the 'ecological paradigm' that stresses the role of demographic pressure as the underlying motor of social evolution, all processes of social and political change result from essentially similar causes. If, however, we stress the importance of cultural strategies of power and the actions of social agents in forming alliances and negotiating relations of domination as central *variables* in these processes, explanations are likely to be much more complex (Brumfiel 1992, Patterson 1993). Each successive episode will reflect the impacts of previous historical experience and transformations in social practices and world-views associated with the civilizational process.[6]

---

6 As Diamond stressed, 'civilization' is a cultural system in which the hierarchic principle becomes a presupposition of social life. It is, however, also important to note, as Edmund Leach showed in his classic *Political Systems of Highland Burma*, that hierarchical and non-hierarchical models of local politics can continue to coexist in an unstable and oscillating state on the margins of more stably hierarchized polities (Leach 1954).

All societies in a region may be changed by state formation, including those on the periphery of expanding centres. This area of research is important to political anthropology in another sense. It encourages anthropologists to think about societies studied ethnographically as components in larger regional systems, and to reflect on how their organization might have been affected by these wider relationships *before* the era of Western colonialism. If we fail to do that, then we not only treat the West's 'others' as 'peoples without history', but miss opportunities to understand why particular human communities organized themselves politically in particular ways.

In his path-breaking studies of the nomads of Inner Asia, Owen Lattimore (1962) suggested that the social and political structures of these pastoral societies should be understood in the context of their long historical interaction with the agrarian heartlands of China. The nomad chiefdoms were organized into a structure of clans whose segments were ranked. Although the power of the chiefs was limited in peacetime, the hierarchic order of a chain of command was present in embryo in this political organization. At one level, this seems merely another case of the distinctive powers accorded to leaders in war and peacetime mediators, but Lattimore suggested that there was a deeper logic to nomad organization. Imperial China liked to think of the barbarians as its inferiors and subjects, but practised a complex diplomacy on the borders of its domain, accepting the nomads' gifts as tribute paid by those who acknowledged Chinese hegemony, while carefully distributing resources of far greater value in return. These buffer mechanisms were indices of Chinese weakness: periodically the nomads erupted across the border as the imperial state grew weaker and exhausted its energies putting down peasant rebellions and unruly provincial lords. Lattimore suggested that these moments revealed the underlying rationale of the nomadic clan organization: it enabled the nomads to achieve rapid consolidation of administrative control over the territories they conquered, including re-establishment of tribute payments by the local peasantry.

In a general overview of the relationships between 'centres' and 'peripheries' in the processes of state formation, Gailey and Patterson (1988) suggest that: 'the emergence of state societies has immediate effects on the stratification and production relations of surrounding societies' (ibid.: 86). Not all states are the same, however, and these writers draw a distinction between 'strong' and 'weak' tribute-based states. An example of the former is the Inca state after the 1430s, and the latter category would include African kingdoms like Dahomey, which relied on external slave-raiding to supplement the tribute the centre extracted from the subject population within its borders. Gailey and Patterson focus on how the development of each kind of state influenced the development of peripheral societies. They classify peripheral societies whose nature has been changed by articulation with states into two broad groupings.

Heavily militarized strong tribute-based states promote the development of societies based on what Marx described as the 'Germanic mode of production'. The organization of production is atomized at the household level, although households' access to common lands and other resources depends on their participation in larger communally organized activities, such as age-grade ceremonies and military raiding. The relationship between the peripheral society and the neighbouring state has several dimensions. The periphery supplies the state with exotic prestige goods and with slaves captured from neighbouring groups. Any members of the community who achieve privileged positions in this trading system may not only become wealthier, but be drawn into the state system itself, as retainers, military officers or functionaries. They are, in fact, peculiarly suited for such roles: as 'strangers' they can be used in place of members of the state elite who may harbour political ambitions of their own, particularly the collateral kin of the existing ruler. Over time, differences in wealth emerge between households in the peripheral society, but this alone does not necessarily lead to their transformation.

That comes where slave-ownership becomes the basis for the emergence of an internal elite or when militarism is turned inward on the peripheral society itself, and poorer households are forced to turn to their more powerful neighbours for protection and come to accept the dependent status of feudal retainers. Should the tribute-based state itself collapse, the peripheral society may remain household-based without continuing its raiding or attempting to subjugate neighbouring peoples, revert to a less militarized and economically atomized 'communal mode of production', or undergo a transformation into a weak tribute-based state on the lines of the Mongol state that emerged on the periphery of China after the collapse of the Sung dynasty in the thirteenth century.

The second type of peripheral social formation Gailey and Patterson discuss is that associated with the 'lineage mode of production'. This concept owes its origin not to Marx but to the French Marxist anthropologists Claude Meillassoux and Pierre-Philipe Rey (Rey 1975). These societies are defensively organized in *non-military* ways to resist the encroachment of weak tribute-based states on their lands and people (through slave raiding). Use-rights to land, labour and products are restricted to members of corporate kin groups (which are not necessarily unilineal descent groups). Control of resources and people remains communal, but higher-status persons within the corporate kinship group exercise a differential control. This has implications not merely for inter-generational relations but for gender: tighter kin control over resources not only weakens cognatic claims to labour and produce, but, in patrilineal-patrilocal settings, the role of sister is diminished in importance relative to wife-mother roles by the diminished contact with natal kin. Male control over marriage is strengthened, and with it, gerontocratic authority. Gailey and Patterson suggest that lineage societies may themselves transform into weak tribute-based states, when the state neighbouring them itself collapses. Alternatively, they may revert to less restrictive communal relations, and can also transform into 'Germanic' systems and militarize themselves where they compete with neighbouring Germanic societies (or communal control over resources at the corporate group level weakens). If that proves impossible, the population may simply migrate out to more remote 'regions of refuge'.

Gailey and Patterson present 'Germanic' and 'lineage' societies as examples of how state formation and expansion transform kin communities on their periphery. They are both transformations of a 'communal mode of production' where 'property needed for subsistence is held by the group as a whole and rights to use it are available to all on the basis of gender, age/life status, and kin connections' (1988: 80). Differences in status and wealth may exist within the political community. It may be one in which there is a permanent institution of 'chieftainship' even if chiefly power is unstable, chiefs are removed from office by assassination and usurpation, and different kin groups rise and fall in status as individual chiefdoms develop, expand and collapse. Societies that belong to the communal mode of production do not, however, display the atomization of control of resources by households found in the 'Germanic' mode, nor the restrictions on access to resources to members of kin corporations found in the 'lineage mode'. Claims to usufruct of resources can be made bilaterally, so that the boundaries of kinship groups remain flexible. People can choose to affiliate to mother's or father's natal group, as was the case with the Andean *ayllus* (Spalding 1984).

For some, this attempt to rework Marxist concepts for new purposes may seem an unappealing reduction of ethnography's rich variety into a tight classificatory scheme. Nevertheless, it is hard to deny the importance of the principle that motivates it. The forms of human social and political organization cannot be seen simply as the unconstrained exploration by 'people' of a series of logical possibilities, as if every human community sat isolated on an island in the midst of a limitless ocean. It has also proved difficult to explain social structures simply as 'adaptations' to local techno-environmental conditions. Other societies are part of any human group's environment. The political communities we term 'states' are expansionary organizations that draw in human and material resources from beyond their borders. In some cases, drawing in resources and people from the 'external' periphery is essential for the reproduction of the state itself, since its elite cannot extend their exactions from the population they rule beyond a certain point without provoking revolt (Carneiro 1981). Thus centres both create and (unintentionally) transform peripheral societies. State and stateless societies develop in ways that are fundamentally interdependent.

'STATELESS SOCIETIES' UNDER THE MODERN STATE

It would be inappropriate to end a discussion of ethnographic 'stateless' societies without underscoring the need to understand their transformation by colonial and post-colonial states. To do so, I will return to the classic

African case of the Nuer and Sharon Hutchinson's updating of Evans-Pritchard's work (Hutchinson 1996).

Today the Nuer experience national state power with a vengeance in the form of the Arab-dominated, Islamic regime in Khartoum, which renewed a brutal civil war against the peoples of the south of the country after a decade's hiatus in 1983. Civil war brought Nuer more violence than they had ever known and their sufferings drove many of them into a life of poverty as migrant workers and refugees in urban slums. Adjustment to the new order of things proved traumatic. Many migrants from the south were forced to seek a livelihood doing the most degrading kind of work, such as emptying latrines. Nuer initially considered that a cow purchased with 'the money of shit' could not live, and extended this idea of the polluting consequences of degrading work to other types of labour (Hutchinson 1996: 84). In a delicious example of how women selling beer tried to keep money polluted by association with degrading work separate from the rest of their income, Hutchinson records how one woman remarked, with a smile, that 'It's going straight to the government' (ibid.). 'The government' was hardly a novelty for Nuer by the 1980s. The state was already part of their lives at the time when Evans-Pritchard presented them as a paradigmatic case of an 'acephalous' political organization, since it was the colonial state that made the world safe for anthropologists to construct such models.

Hutchinson traces Nuer experience of national state power through the colonial period to the 1990s. Nuer themselves talk about this experience as 'the age of government' – and also as 'the age of the gun'. Nuer themselves made efforts to get guns from early colonial times (ibid.: 111), and their history is one of both resistance and accommodation to the state. Although Nuer hate and despise the Arab government in Khartoum even more than they hated the British, they do not entirely reject another kind of state-like authority today, that of the Sudanese People's Liberation Army (SPLA). Hutchinson shows that the SPLA has in fact been extending administrative policies begun by the Anglo-Egyptian colonial administration (ibid.: 146–9).

Hutchinson argues that Evans-Pritchard's model of Nuer 'ordered anarchy' was undermined by developments in the colonial period. In part, this was because the British did actually manage to create new kinds of leaders, although the result of these efforts was to fragment the Nuer political system even more. Far from fostering social peace, colonial policies actually accentuated the centrality of feuding in Nuer life, and the old systems of ritual mediation became less effective (ibid.: 131–2). When a man died in traditional inter-community disputes, the kin of the killer had offered a woman in marriage to the dead man's kin, so that he could live on in the children born to her. The British thought it would be a better idea to ramp up the rates for blood compensation, removing the old incentives to restore peaceful relations through marriage. But the most fundamental change Hutchinson charts through the colonial and post-colonial is that in Nuer ideas about the polluting effects of homicide.

Traditionally, a killing among Nuer could kill the slayer through a mysterious transmission of blood between them, the form of pollution called *nueer*. The role of the 'leopard-skin chiefs' centred on the removal of this pollution, and one of Hutchinson's informants told her that *nueer* pollution itself should be seen as 'one of our chiefs' in the past (ibid.: 124). The danger of pollution underpinned the rules of violence in Nuer society, an ethical code that prevented use of the most lethal weapons in fights between kinsmen and neighbours. The use of guns and the role of colonial courts began to undermine these ethical codes. Government-appointed chiefs began to pervert the blood compensation rituals by taking most of the sacrificed animals for themselves and the police who supported them. The major change lay, however, in the differences between guns and spears as killing instruments, and the fact that so many people were killed in Sudan's first civil war (1955–72). Gun killings were at first compared to death by lightning (ibid.: 108). People who died in this way were initially seen as killed by God, and became *col wic*, potentially dangerous lineage guardians who had to be propitiated and whose kin had to give priority to getting them a 'ghost wife' (ibid.: 138–40). But the number of people dying from guns increased whilst the number of cattle available for bridewealth payments fell radically because of the devastation caused by war. The SPLA commanders therefore decided to promote the idea that people killed in the war were not *col wic*, and that killing in a war with the government did not involve pollution dangers (ibid.: 140). There were precedents for this in past history, since Nuer who had acted as government chiefs and policemen had been involved in judicial executions, but did not hold themselves personally responsible for the deaths.

In saying that killing for the SPLA was morally different from feuding, the SPLA was effectively making its own claim to be recognized as a legitimate government. But the implications were radical. Before, Nuer had located the meaning of gun-related violence in a concept of a divinely ordered world: now they were losing confidence in supplicating God as a way of dealing with violence, and seeing violence itself as increasingly inevitable as the Sudanese post-colonial state disintegrated. The gun became a symbol of masculine power in an increasingly individualized Nuer society, a way of winning back self-esteem (ibid.: 153). Gun symbolism became a fetish, replacing the cattle and spears of Evans-Pritchard's day. The problem is, however, that each successive state regime commands more fire-power than Nuer do, and men have great difficulty seeing themselves as successful in fulfilling traditional roles as defenders of women, children and herds. Because guns are too expensive for individuals, the gun has ironically become a means of promoting a continuing collective solidarity at a time when the older binding force of shared claims on cattle acquired from marriages is declining (ibid.: 150–1). Yet, on balance, the overall picture Hutchinson paints is bleak. Although there is still some continuity of old Nuer cultural concepts which were central to the construction of sociality and regulation of violence, the experience of successive state regimes has undermined those systems without replacing them with alternatives that work.

This is, of course, the opposite of what classical anthropology, with its faith in the civilizing mission of the Pax Britannica and the ultimate superiority of the modern liberal state and its institutions, assumed would be the future of colonized peoples. It is also not a particularly good advertisement for the supposed benefits of 'government' in general.

3 FROM HIERARCHY TO SURVEILLANCE: THE POLITICS OF AGRARIAN CIVILIZATIONS AND THE RISE OF THE WESTERN NATIONAL STATE

Debates about the 'origins of the state' may seem more relevant to political philosophy than to contemporary political anthropology. Yet it is less obvious that the same can be said about the analysis of the great 'agrarian civilizations', the combination of a stratified, agrarian-based society with one of the world 'religions of the book', such as Buddhism or Islam. The agrarian civilizations of the Near and Far East were world-historical rivals of the Latin Christian civilization of the West, and the multi-ethnic religious communities they established continue to be a force in modern global politics, as Europeans were so sharply reminded by the tragic events in Bosnia in 1993. The European response to the Bosnian problem suggests that the shifting frontier between Christendom and Islam remains salient to the very identity of 'Europe' and 'the West'. The later Kosovo crisis reminds us that that Western Europe's identity is also entangled in the division between Catholic and Eastern Orthodox Christianity, a consequence of the collapse of the Roman Empire in the West and its partial survival in the East in the form of the Byzantine Empire. Although Islamic governments ultimately failed to make a decisive collective intervention in the Bosnian conflict, individuals from Islamic countries volunteered for service with the Muslim forces. The presence of nationalist Russian volunteers in the Bosnian Serb forces was followed by the celebrated dash by a Russian column to take control of Pristina airport before the advancing NATO ground forces. Although the motivations of the actors involved in the break-up of Yugoslavia should be sought in the present, and ethno-nationalism is clearly a more general global phenomenon, history, and not simply twentieth-century history, remains important for understanding the deeper meanings with which contemporary actions may be invested (van de Port 1999).

This underscores the point I stressed in Chapter 1, the usefulness of trying to understand 'modernity' at a global, cross-cultural, level. Such a perspective not only sheds light on the contemporary politics of religion but illuminates other aspects of the division of the world into geo-political blocs which are based on essentially similar forms of political and economic organization but articulate their cleavages through a reassertion of cultural-historical differences. It is true that local conflicts are often ignited by political leaderships pursuing self-serving quests for power and that the past to which their rhetoric appeals may be almost entirely a contemporary fabrication. Yet the generalized social mobilization such promptings can invoke – including the obscene violence which neighbour may come to perpetrate upon neighbour – suggests that the demagogues are unleashing deeper, societal processes. These processes may reflect distinctive popular understandings of society, culture, identity and the meaning of history itself, shaped by the way Western domination has transformed but not erased variations in forms of social life.

This is an area where the analyses of comparative sociology tend to be deficient, although the comparative analysis of agrarian civilizations (including the West) is a field to which the anthropological contribution itself has been limited. Historical sociologists have largely been interested in explaining the 'rise of the West' and accounting for the global hegemony the Western powers achieved. Traditionally, these analyses focused on supposed structural 'blockages' which prevented non-Western civilizations achieving the economic and military 'dynamism' which enabled the north-west European powers to achieve capitalist industrialization and thus create colonial empires founded on military superiority. They are not centrally concerned with non-European agrarian civilizations in their own right, and are prone to emphasize the way such civilizations ultimately 'stagnated' socially and economically in comparison with Europe. Historical sociology remains in danger of perpetuating the intellectual vice known as 'Orientalism' (Said 1978, Turner 1994), in which the West understands 'the East' as an inverse image of its own preoccupations and understanding of itself, reducing the variety and complexity of alien cultural forms to a homogenized 'exotic other': Europeans contrasted oriental 'despotism' with European love of liberty, or juxtaposed the supposed character traits of a standardized Western 'individual' with what were generally, though not invariably, negatively characterized 'oriental' proclivities. For Edward Said, 'Orientalism' was the means by which the imperial gaze created a system of knowledge appropriate to world domination, but as Bryan Turner has noted, there is an equally important sense in which the 'problem' of Orientalism was not the Orient but the Occident. We should not take the assumptions it makes about Western civilization as unquestionable truths (Turner 1994: 34, see also Carrier 1995).

Modern historical sociology is aware of these pitfalls. Nevertheless, a focus on explaining the 'rise of the West' distracts attention from cultural features of non-Western civilizations which do not seem germane to explaining differences in historical development. Comparison of this kind may also involve the use of sociological categories derived from Western experience which embody ethnocentric premises about the way 'societies' in general are structured. Analysis of non-Western agrarian civilizations as 'whole systems' in their own right is essential because there *are* radical differences between cultural systems at this level.

Louis Dumont (1970, 1986) has argued that the Indian caste system and, with it, the political organization of Indian civilization, cannot be properly understood without recognizing that 'hierarchy' in India is founded on a totally different cultural logic to 'social stratification' in Western societies. Both types of society have social 'inequalities' in our terms, but these 'inequalities' do not have the same meanings to social actors in hierarchic societies as they have for social actors born in societies premised on Western notions of individualism and egalitarianism. The crux of Dumont's argument is that, in India, political power is encompassed by and subordinated to religious status. As we will see later, Dumont's position has been criticized on the grounds that, despite its radical relativism, it actually belongs to a sociological tradition dating back to Marx and Weber – and represents another variant of 'Orientalism' – because it depicts political power in India before colonialism as having less significance for social life than it actually had. Dumont's emphasis on the cultural logic of hierarchy as an eternal principle always present in Indian constructions of power has also been criticized as ahistorical, structuralist idealism. Nevertheless, as we will see in Chapter 7, powerful arguments can be made for its continuing relevance to contemporary politics, once we possess a theory of how historically rooted cultural models can be *reactivated* in a way which influence the behaviour of contemporary actors.

Culture *is* important. Although it is difficult to see how comparative analysis could be possible at all without assuming we can discuss, say, the relationships between 'classes' and the 'state' in different agrarian civilizations, we need to define what these general terms denote within particular cultural and historical settings: is Japanese feudalism, for example, the same as European feudalism, even if both are at some level of abstraction examples of something similar?[1] The national states which succeeded non-European agrarian civilizations subjected to colonial domination may today *appear* to have Westernized elites and modern forms of political life. At one level *they do*, since Western colonial domination has transformed them profoundly. Yet it may not be possible to explain their contemporary politics without understanding that distinct cultural models of the nature of society, government and the state continue to shape events today and make their

---

[1] This question has been seen as important because Japan was the only Asian power to make a rapid transition to capitalism. It is tempting to explain this by saying Japan's 'feudal' political organization provided 'structural preconditions' for capitalism otherwise found only in Europe. This argument is demolished by Moulder (1977), who argues that Japan's 'development' can only be explained by her unique place in the evolving world system. Lacking the resources that Western industrial powers were interested in controlling, Japan was coopted as a 'junior partner' in their project of securing military domination of Asia rather than 'peripheralized'.

'modernity' no less modern but still *different* from that of the West. We should also bear in mind that neither modern nor ancient societies have just one culture: we can also identify class and regional cultures of various kinds which may be central to political processes.

POLITICAL SYSTEMS IN THEORIES OF EUROPEAN DEVELOPMENT

Although the limitations of comparative historical sociology should be noted, I do not wish to disparage its considerable achievements. The new insights modern research has produced into European development offer us a better appreciation of what is distinctive about Western historical experience and redress deficiencies in anthropological thinking. I will focus here on issues germane to problems discussed later in this book, beginning with the relationship between political and socio-economic change in Europe.

Different theorists date the origins of a distinctive European trajectory of development to different historical periods. Some, like Perry Anderson (1974a, 1974b), argue that the role of Roman civilization was crucial to later European development. Others start with European feudalism or emphasize a variety of later historical turning points, such as the geographical expansion of the European world in the sixteenth century, the rise of Absolutist states, or the development of industrial capitalism. Some analyses argue strongly *against* drawing a polarizing opposition between the history of Europe and Asia (Turner 1979). Theda Skocpol's comparative analysis of the French, Russian and Chinese revolutions suggests that the political and agrarian structures of the three 'proto-bureaucratic' *anciens régimes* overthrown by these classical social revolutions were more similar to *each other* than France was similar to England (Skocpol 1979). Skocpol argues, however, that the fate of these regimes was determined by the development of an international state system within which they could not compete successfully with more 'modern' powers, echoing the emphasis of others on the European multiple-state system as a driving force in modern history.

Many analyses suggest that it is not adequate to see 'modernity' – defined in terms of individualism, mass society, the modern state and its disciplinary technologies, a notion of historicity as 'progress' and a dominant culture of scientific rationalism – as the product of socio-economic change alone.[2] Giddens (1985) argues that not all features of modern societies

---

2 Few modern theorists see it as the consequence of unique social changes in Britain, although arguments based on the cultural peculiarities of the English have been advanced by an anthropologist (Macfarlane 1987). Macfarlane's writings on 'English individualism' display at least an elective affinity with neo-conservatism, and form part of a movement in 'revisionist' historiography which argues that nothing truly 'revolutionary' happened in the course of Western development. They remain largely silent on the coercive nature of what I will persist in seeing as fundamental transformations.

derive from the capitalist organization of the production process and capitalist property relations, and that military and political transformation proceeds according to its own, autonomous, logic, although this view has been criticized by anthropologists such as Friedman (1994) and Ong (1999), as I noted in Chapter 1.

Giddens's position is clearly at odds with Marxist emphasis on the 'transition to capitalism' as the key to understanding Western development. 'Orthodox Marxist' theory has its own political dimension, but this is tied to a particular class-based theory of social change. The assumption is that capitalism is the product of class struggle, and that this struggle has two sides to it. In the first place, modern capitalism rests on 'free wage labour' and the mass proletarianization of 'peasants', who are driven off the land and forced to sell their labour power to capitalists. Proletarianization is a precondition for capitalist production as Marx defined it, and the 'pre-history' of capitalism therefore entails a coercive transformation of the 'traditional' agrarian system on the part of the ruling class and the state, since peasants resist being driven from the land and into wage labour. 'Free wage' labour also entails major transformations of the legal system, to guarantee the rights of private property and sanctity of contracts on the one hand, and to dissolve the bonds of personal dependence associated with feudalism on the other. Thus, capitalism implies a second type of political transformation according to orthodox Marxism: until the bourgeoisie have captured control of the state from the landowning aristocracy, they cannot enact the laws required for the full development of modern capitalism. The consolidation of the capitalist mode of production therefore depends on political revolution. Britain's 'bourgeois revolution' is the civil war of the seventeenth century, and France's achievement of modern capitalism was delayed because her 'bourgeois revolution' was not consummated for another hundred years.

This orthodox account is not, however, accepted by all modern Marxist writers. Against the prevailing emphasis on 'rising urban bourgeoisies', Brenner (1982) argued that agrarian capitalism was an essential precondition for industrial capitalism and the product of agrarian class conflict within English feudal society, differing political structures being important mainly as factors influencing the different outcomes of such conflicts in France and Eastern Europe. In almost complete opposition to this approach, another major debate developed about whether Britain ever achieved a full transition to capitalism.

Perry Anderson (1987) and Tom Nairn (1988) argue that Britain's economic decline, and the peculiarities of British class structure, political institutions and nationalism, should be explained in terms of the limitations of the country's capitalist development. The pioneer shift towards capitalism did not produce the large-scale capitalist industry which developed later in France, Germany and the United States. Small-scale industrial capitalism did not achieve full domination over merchant capital. Accordingly, the British 'bourgeoisie' never succeeded in producing a 'bourgeois' state and political system. The Nairn-Anderson thesis has been robustly criticized by Ellen Meiksins Wood (1991). Wood offers the intriguing counter-argument that the fact that our paradigmatic conceptions of 'bourgeois' society, the modern state and political culture come from Continental Europe, in particular France, simply reveals the top-down, statist, nature of capitalist development in those countries, and the fact that pre-capitalist social property relations persisted in them long after they had disappeared in England, where capitalism took over society much more comprehensively at an early stage. Thus, the absence of a 'modern' state and political culture of the Continental kind in Britain reflects the fact that it was the bourgeoisie that established capitalism there, from below, rather than the state, from above. British culture is therefore the *most* capitalist in Europe.

Wood's argument still leaves Britain as an exceptional case within the overall pattern of European development, however, and it reinforces non-Marxist arguments that analysis of political change in eighteenth-century France in terms of a notion of 'bourgeois revolution' is misconceived, as Skocpol shows in her analysis of the breakdown of the *ancien régime*.

In pre-revolutionary France, wealthy merchants could buy public offices and convert themselves into noblemen. France had a unified upper class, which included both hereditary aristocrats *and* (pre-industrial) bourgeois, and it was a political revolt against Absolutism by this elite that precipitated the revolutionary crisis. What prompted upper-class calls for 'representative government' – which the elite viewed as government which would conserve their privileges – was the Crown's removal of its exemption from taxes. This policy was dictated by the fiscal crisis caused by the costs of competing militarily with other states which had more dynamic economic systems. France's peasant farmers, burdened by state taxation and feudal exactions from landowners, were not distinguished by their productivity.

At first the conflict pitted wealthy, cosmopolitan aristocrats against poor members of the nobility, who sided with the king because they feared that political 'modernization' would lead to the abolition of the seigneurial dues which provided their comparatively meagre incomes. Yet what started as a political conflict between those at the top of French society was transformed into a social revolution based on class war between landlord and peasant. All French peasants resented the seigneurial regime, but it was especially resented by small-holders, who owned their land, but were still subject to petty aristocratic exactions dating back to the medieval period. Once the peasants saw the state apparatus was too disorganized to repress them effectively, resentment turned to rebellion.

A more 'radical', Jacobin, political leadership did emerge to lead the mass conflicts which developed in both countryside and city, but it was a leadership of 'petty bourgeois' urban intellectuals and professionals, not a rising capitalist bourgeoisie of either the mercantile or industrial variety. The outcome of the French Revolution was broadly favourable to capitalist development: feudal institutions were abolished in favour of a full private property regime and peasant solidarity collapsed as soon as the small-holders were freed from the seigneurial impositions that had given them common cause with fellow villagers dependent on landlords. Yet it seems necessary to recognize the Absolutist state as an autonomous actor in this historical drama. The immediate problem to be resolved after the revolution was the reconstruction of the state,[3] a process which did not bring France political stability through the whole of the next century.

The case of *ancien régime* France has wider implications. The state in agrarian civilizations cannot be reduced to a simple instrument of ruling-class dominance, because such systems generally involve conflicts between imperial governments and landowning ruling classes. In the case of China, the imperial dynasty ruled through the *literati*, a corps of bureaucrats which was theoretically openly recruited on the basis of ability to pass an examination in Confucian philosophy. In practice the *literati* were generally younger sons or adopted wards of landowning 'gentry' families (Barrington Moore 1969). This made it difficult for the state to achieve its goal of ruling through administrative personnel who lacked autonomous social power and would not fall under the control of regional landlord cliques that might put private interests before those of the empire. Nevertheless, incoming Chinese imperial dynasties frequently took actions designed to reduce the power of the landed upper classes: the Manchus actually abolished serfdom in the eighteenth century, so that emancipated peasants could again become free members of peasant communties paying taxes only to the state itself.

Mann (1986) and Hall (1985) describe the long-term effect of these processes as a 'power stand-off' between ruling class and imperial state. Skocpol's argument that pre-revolutionary France and Manchu China were variations on a theme has much to recommend it at first sight, but Mann has argued that even Europe's 'imperial' states reflected important differences in European conditions in terms of the balance of power between decentralized social (class) power and the power wielded by monarchical states. These differences are central to what he identifies as the special historical dynamic of European societies.

A SPECIFICALLY EUROPEAN DYNAMIC?

Mann takes the view that capitalism was a product of the larger European system of civilization, and that England achieved early supremacy simply

---

3 Marx himself explained post-revolutionary developments in France, in particular the rise of the populist regime of Louis Bonaparte, in terms of the continuing *weakness* of the capitalist class and continuing resistance of the peasantry to social and economic modernization. This analysis is most trenchantly expressed in Marx (1968), the text which contains his (in)famous analogy between the French small-holding peasantry and 'potatoes in a sack'. Marx himself therefore did not adopt the simple 'bourgois revolution' model.

because she had 'a certain edge' over her rivals. He differs, however, from many other theorists who share that premise, in arguing that Europe was set on a distinctive course of development from 800 AD onwards, though he shares some common ground with Perry Anderson (1974a). Like Anderson, Mann emphasizes the puny nature of the early medieval state, and stresses the importance of the extreme political decentralization which followed the fall of the Roman Empire: the 'parcellization of sovereignty' and autonomy of the medieval *city* from political control by the feudal landed aristocracy.[4] Both agree that this shaped the subsequent economic development of European societies. What Mann adds to Anderson is the idea that what he calls the 'multiple acephalous federated state system' of Europe created an expansionist economic dynamic in two spheres, the agrarian economy itself, and international trade and commerce, within the special framework provided by the Christian Church (Mann 1986: 395–6).

Christianity is central to Mann's model of this early 'European dynamic', as it is to John Hall's answer to the question of why European civilization was not reunified politically under an imperial state but achieved a dynamic economy under highly conflictive conditions of political decentralization. The Catholic Church, as a transnational organization, provided the framework of pacification required for the development of European trading systems and commerce, and, as a holder of lands and producer of commodities, also played a direct role in reviving and developing economic activity after the Dark Ages. Hall notes that Christianity sought to 'penetrate' lower-class society (Hall 1985: 126), and Mann develops this point in another direction by linking Christianity to the issue at the forefront of Marxist analyses – 'class struggle'.

Mann argues that the extreme decentralization of European feudalism heightened class stratification between lord and peasant, while Christianity intensified the degree of conflict in agrarian class relationships. Here he emphasizes the *contradictory* nature of Christianity. After the early Church reached an accommodation with secular state power, its hierarchy dedicated

---

4 In the European context, we associate feudalism with the existence of a landlord class, but Weber defined feudalism in political terms, as a system of domination in which rights to exercise authority are delegated from higher to lower-ranking power holders in return for services of a military or administrative character through a contractual relationship of personal loyalty between lord and vassal. What is granted, the fief, does not have to be rights over land, but could simply be rights to tax free peasant communities or juridical or military authority (Weber 1951: 255–7). European feudalism was particularly decentralized because local elites enjoyed power in the economic, juridical, political and military spheres simultaneously. Sovereignty was not simply decentralized, however, but *parcellized*: different lords held jurisdictions over single peasant villages, so that the peasants could play one master off against another, and some peasants retained 'allodial' tenure of the land, free of overriding claims by landlords. Parcellization of sovereignty left some sectors of feudal society comparatively free of control, and Anderson argues that this gave forces favourable to capitalism a chance to consolidate themselves absent in non-European state systems.

itself to producing an 'immanent ideology of ruling class morale'.[5] Yet Christian doctrine continued to offer an alternative view of the world – a *classless* ideology which provided a sense of social identity for its socially and culturally heterogeneous congregation. According to Christianity, rich and poor, lord and peasant, stood equal on the Day of Judgement. However much the Church tried to preach obedience to authority, it could never suppress this dangerous popular 'message' – that Christians should seek social improvement in this world, if necessary in opposition to this-worldly authority.

Christianity and a weak state promoted class struggle. Mann argues, however, that lords retained the capacity to outflank peasants organizationally. Peasant rebellions mostly remained localized. So he does not regard Brenner's key process, 'class struggle' between lord and peasant, as the *decisive* source of social change in Europe, but as something sustaining an impetus towards transformation.

The second major aspect of Mann's 'European dynamic' is agrarian. He argues that European expansionism was underpinned by the intensive exploitation of nature, and that peasant farmers made an important contribution to agricultural innovation. Mann suggests that the intensive exploitation of the land was a response to the localism and political fragmentation of Europe – the more extensive agriculture of the Romans would be a reflection of the different political organization of their territorial empire. The problem, however, with arguing that agrarian dynamism characterizes Europe *in general* is that in much of pre-industrial Europe, as in other agrarian civilizations, bursts of agricultural growth were followed by stagnation (Brenner 1982, Wolf 1982).

Nevertheless, Mann's emphasis on the relationship between Christianity and class conflict and the impacts of politico-economic decentralization does seem relevant for understanding why agrarian capitalism emerged for the first time in Europe and not somewhere else in the world. It also leads him towards a theory of how property relations influenced the development of state forms. European civilization saw an unprecedented extension of 'private' property rights. This is not a question of 'private property' in its modern sense – ownership vested exclusively in a single judicial person – but a matter of how far the state could interfere in dominant class appropriation of resources (Mann 1986: 399). The European state had less control in this respect than historical contemporaries like the Chinese and Ottoman

---

5 Most empires in history have been cemented together by such elite ideologies, society below the elite level remaining segmentary and often basing itself on a quite distinct value system, including religious practices. In the Chinese case, Confucianism was the ideology of the mandarins, and only interested itself in questions of personal salvation in the later stages of Chinese history, after Buddhism and Taoist mysticism had already largely filled the void it left in popular religiosity.

empires. European monarchies which tried to increase their power over society had to adapt to the unassailable strength of class power. As Hall puts it: 'the European state evolved slowly and doggedly in the midst of a pre-existent civil society' (Hall 1985: 137).

Mann divides the process of state consolidation in Europe into two phases. From the mid-twelfth to later fifteenth centuries, 'feudal' federations are replaced by more centralized territorial states, though these 'national' units were still cemented together by 'particularistic, often dynastic, relations between monarchs and semi-autonomous lords' (Mann 1986: 416). Like Moulder (1977), Mann argues that the primary impetus towards centralization came from international war. Feudal levies were supplemented by professional soldiers, costs escalated and competition forced states to emulate their neighbours. Mercantile activity came increasingly to depend on the protection of states, but the states themselves depended on loans from merchant capitalists to fund their wars, because their powers to tax were still limited. There was thus a symbiosis between the monarchies and merchant capital, and mercantile interests saw state warfare as economically advantageous, adding their weight to demands for territorial expansion coming from younger sons of the nobility denied land under European systems of primogeniture inheritance. Since military expansion was about capturing markets as well as land, state economic policy evolved on the lines known as 'mercantilism', orientating itself towards building up the 'national' economy at the expense of rivals, although European societies were not yet 'nations' in the modern sense of the term as defined by Giddens.

The second phase of state consolidation based on national states began in the late fifteenth century: the lord–vassal chain gave way either to the Absolutist system of bureaucratic administration centred on the Royal Household, or to the 'Constitutionalist' form of government based on representative assemblies. As inter-state military competition intensified, all European monarchies switched to professional armies and permanent tax-collecting machines staffed by bureaucracies. Yet the wealth of the ruling class as a whole remained vastly greater than that of the state.

Mann defines 'Absolutism' as a system in which the monarch rules through a permanent bureaucracy and army, excluding the dominant classes from an institutionalized voice in government, and argues that it was only possible where the state did not need to tax the dominant class. Spain had the bullion of the New World, but still faced a more or less permanent fiscal crisis which forced the Crown to sell public offices to the highest bidder. Whereas the French had a relatively secure agrarian tax base among peasant small-holders, the Spanish imperial state suffered a constant erosion of its tribute-base among the indigenous communities of the New World. By securing the consent of the nobility by refraining from taxing them, and imposing their exactions on lower classes, Absolutist regimes promoted divisions in society, and were ultimately less effective as tax-collecting organizations than 'Constitutionalist' states like England and Holland. This made them less effective military competitors on the international scene in the longer term. 'Constitutionalist' states fostered the unity of the propertied classes, and Mann describes them as 'organic class-nations', mobilizing the entire fiscal energy of their populations, since the ruling class contributed to state revenues (Mann 1986: 480). This laid the basis for the development of the modern technologies of power discussed in Chapter 1. Hall makes a similar point in contrasting the 'organic' European state with the 'capstone state' of China, though he also notes the underlying similarity between *ancien régime* France and China in this respect (Hall 1985: 138–9).

Mann, however, regards 'Absolutist' and 'Constitutionalist' states as two sub-types of a single, historically distinctive European state form. His argument is based, among other things, on an argument about how French and Spanish Absolutism behaved in their colonial worlds: the fact that Spanish Absolutism could not overthrow private property rights or interfere in the economy as much as an ancient imperial state was demonstrated by its performance in the Americas, where even its own officials would go in for contraband trading in defiance of imperial economic policy. I would accept that the history of the Spanish and French imperial states does reflect the strength of decentralized class power in the European world, but it is worth noting that even eighteenth-century observers were beginning to see the Absolutist regimes as anachronisms which could not survive the challenge posed by more dynamic societies developing in Britain, Holland and North America. In themselves, they were not harbingers of a new world-historical era.

In my view, the 'dynamic' of European development lay, in part at least, in the long-term stimulus to cumulative transformation engendered by the decentralized international system of competing state units. Mann's analysis shows how the extreme political-economic decentralization of medieval European society and the particular nature of Latin Christian civilization underpinned the emergence of a 'multiple acephalous states system' which was both resistant to empire formation and conducive to further transformations of society and polity. Yet 'Europe' has always been characterized by a diversity of state–society relations and political cultures, which is what makes its contemporary unification and even its identity so problematic. Although the European *arena* of civilization made it possible for the first 'modern' national states and capitalist economies to emerge, the structures of many European social formations would, in a different context, have remained inimical to the genesis of 'modern' society. In this sense, Mann's argument for a common European social dynamic leading towards capitalism and beginning in 800 AD has an unacceptably teleological quality.

Mann's entire emphasis on the long-term is rejected by Giddens. Giddens argues that 'progressivist' interpretations of history 'in which the dynamism of the modern West is traced to a sequence linking the Classical world, feudalism and modern societies' underplay the distinctive qualities of 'truly modern' states in comparison with all forms of 'traditional states', including

European ones (Giddens 1985: 83). He focuses his own analysis on transformations ensuing from sixteenth and seventeenth-century Absolutism,
and emphasizes the emergence of industrialism, rather than capitalist social
property relations, as the key to the development of modern technologies of
power. It was industrialized war which produced not merely nineteenth-
century colonialism but the global spread of the nation-state form. The
experience of industrialized war, and the mass mobilization associated with
it, shaped the pattern of *economic* development of Soviet Russia, Nazi
Germany and Japan in the period between the two world wars. The organization of the economy during the Second World War provided a paradigm for
the 'Fordist-Keynesian' restructuring of capitalist economic regulation
through state intervention which characterized the post-war years up to the
late 1970s (Harvey 1989). War also set the political parameters of the world
order which developed after 1945 – not merely the politics of the 'Cold War'
but the kinds of political regimes which emerged among the defeated.

Giddens therefore argues that industrialized militarism is another key
dimension of 'modernity'. Yet from the perspective of the late 1990s,
abandonment of a focus on capitalist social-property relations as a shaper of
historical change seems unwise, and there are costs in abandoning the long-
term analysis of the distinctiveness of post-Roman European civilization in
favour of Giddens's 'discontinuist' model. Mann and Anderson offer
important insights into the historical roots of relations between civil society
and the state, religion and politics, and individual and society in the
European arena.

There are, however, strong objections to any framework which sees
'modernity' as the product of endogenous change taking place within the
historical-geographical space that defines 'the West' as 'Europe'. In fact,
rather than talk about the 'rise of the West' it might be preferable to talk
about the development of 'North Atlantic civilization' in a way that relates
developments within Western Europe to the existence of the colonial empires
founded by European powers. We can make a distinction between an 'old'
colonial world, constructed between the sixteenth and eighteenth centuries,
and the 'new' capitalist imperialism represented by the nineteenth-century
colonial process, in which industrial capitalist centres carved up the world
politically in order to create new markets, control areas supplying food for
their urban populations and raw materials for industrial processes located
in the metropolis, and invested capital in 'modernizing' colonial production
to serve the needs of industrialism. One anthropological account of the role
of the 'old' colonialism in the 'rise of the West' is provided by the global perspectives offered by Eric Wolf (1982) and Sidney Mintz (1985).

Rather than seeing change on a global scale as resulting from the interventions of an active metropolitan 'core' on a passive colonial 'periphery',
Wolf and Mintz both emphasize ways in which developments in colonized
regions influenced developments in metropolitan societies, and more
complex ways in which changes in different parts of the evolving global

system were interrelated as changes in one area influenced, facilitated or impeded developments in another. As Mintz observes, the colonial world served as a 'laboratory' for subsequent developments in Europe. Though sugar cane originated in Melanesia, and Europeans borrowed the technology for growing and processing it from the Islamic world, Caribbean sugar plantations prefigured the factory system of the Industrial Revolution in the way they organized time and the division of labour (Mintz 1985). This idea of the old colonial world as a 'laboratory of modernity' can, however, be taken much further.

Ann Stoler (1995) has argued that the experience of Europeans in their 'old' colonial territories shaped nineteenth-century ideas about race and sexuality in Europe. Furthermore, she suggests that all the key symbols of modern Western societies, including liberal notions of citizenship and nationalism, were shaped in an historical context of which colonial relations were constitutive, and that this underlies the very concept of 'culture' and the idea of 'Europeanness' itself. There is an obvious relationship between the historical 'invention of the white race' and the Atlantic slave trade, even if racism was reinforced in the United States by the transition to an industrial capitalist economy, as David Roediger argues (Roediger 1994: 64). But Stoler suggests that racial divisions were important for defending general 'European' superiority, given that there were lower-class Europeans in the colonies who needed to be separated in status from 'the natives' and inhibited, as far as possible, from the kind of wholesale miscegenation that would break down racial hierarchy. Within the colonies, racial and class discriminations became blurred: the 'children of the Indies', as the offspring of Europeans and non-Europeans were dubbed in colonial Indonesia, were said to lack the internal controls and 'suitability' for disciplined work required of a citizen claiming a right to participate in a liberal democratic nation (Stoler 1995: 130).

Stoler therefore argues that the evolving colonial social order shaped the way that emerging European bourgeoisies distinguished themselves from the old aristocracies, defined the notion of the rights-bearing free and equal citizen, and subsequently set about disciplining the 'dangerous' new industrial working classes at home. As the case of the Irish demonstrates, the new working classes could themselves be racialized and 'othered' within North Atlantic societies, but Stoler's suggestion is that the 'disciplines of the body' emphasized as the quintessence of modernity in the work of Michel Foucault (1979, 1985) has a colonial dimension linked to 'race' and sexuality that Foucault's own eurocentric argument ignores.

Her argument thus suggests a major criticism of the basic assumptions of the 'rise of the West' discourse. Western European thought came to depict Europe as a 'modernity' bringing civilization and progress to the 'backward and underdeveloped': yet European societies' first colonial territories, in the Americas, Caribbean and Asia, could be seen as the historical laboratories in which the ideas and practices that came to define 'modernity' were first worked out (Stoler 1995: 15–16). As an ironic and important further twist to this perspective, she cites Timothy Mitchell's observation that Foucault's paradigmatic example of modern disciplinary power, Jeremy Bentham's panopticon, first appeared in the Ottoman Empire rather than Northern Europe (Mitchell 1991: 35).

AGRARIAN CIVILIZATION OUTSIDE EUROPE

Taking the silenced contributions of the Islamic world to European development as a cue, I will focus here in particular on the relation between religion and politics, since this is a theme of such contemporary interest as well as a central element in the theories of European distinctiveness we have considered. It will also lead us into areas where anthropologists have contributed centrally to important debates.

I begin by revisiting the case of China, where the endless repetition of the imperial form of government reflected a 'power stand-off' between the state and landlord class. China appears to be amongst the most 'bureaucratized' of pre-industrial states, but the imperial bureaucracy was tiny in comparison with the scale of the empire (Hall 1985: 41). As Weber (1951) observed, the amount of tax revenue siphoned off into the private pockets of that bureaucracy was substantial. The imperial government sought to prevent its administrators from being coopted by the landlord class by rotating them in posts regularly and preventing them from serving in provinces where their families held land. These measures were not conducive to administrative efficiency. Mandarins were often unable to speak the local dialect and became dependent on assistants 'recommended' by the local gentry. The fact that the Chinese *literati* were generally recruited from the gentry class was not, however, a total disaster from the state's point of view. Gentry lineages were large and had problems maintaining their economic and social position. Sending a member into the bureaucracy offered a means of adding to the collective wealth of the kin corporation. The gentry thus benefited from empire, even if they clashed with it over control of the peasant surplus.

Confucianism gave the mandarin class a specific identity which was centred on and ultimately supportive of state institutions, although it could not be relied on to sustain mandarin allegiance to any particular dynasty (Hall 1985: 40). This helped damp down periodic tendencies towards 'feudalization'. Landlords sought to escape state taxation and increase their estates, and sheltered peasants who preferred dependence on a local lord to a rising burden of state taxation, but the dominant class never withdrew their support from the imperial state in the decisive way that brought about the fall of the Roman Empire in the West. Hall lays great stress on the monolithic nature of Chinese elite culture in explaining the persistent re-establishment of an imperial government after bouts of feudalization (ibid.: 52). Confucianism did not 'penetrate' Chinese society, but this civilization knew no struggles between church and state once the mandarins succeeded in suppressing the threat posed by Buddhism. No neighbouring powers threatened Chinese integrity. Nomadic invaders simply took their place within the imperial institutions, and north and south China achieved economic, social and political integration.

This, Wallerstein (1974) observes, converted the imperial state unit into a self-sufficient 'world system', although it is important not to see China as a *closed* system. Despite periodic interventions by the Chinese imperial centre, the coastal cities of south China have two millennia of cosmopolitan history behind them. Access to them by strangers from the sea was considerably easier than overland through the mountains. Guangzhou (Canton), at the head of the Pearl River delta, today at the forefront of China's new capitalism, possesses a mosque that is thirteen centuries old and still serves a small Hui Chinese Muslim community of 6,000 (Ikels 1996: 13). Even when the Ming Dynasty (1368–1644) attempted to prohibit sea trade, Chinese merchants continued to build networks throughout East and South-East Asia. When European traders finally arrived in numbers, they had to break into markets encapsulated by a Chinese-dominated trade and tributary system that ramified throughout the region (Ong 1996: 78).

As a 'world system', Islamic civilization appears similar to Christian civilization: no empire ever succeeded in encapsulating the Islamic cultural world within its political boundaries. Yet as an encompassing religious order, Islam appears more totalizing than Christianity. It establishes a framework for the whole of religious and secular life, including the political domain, and is both this-worldly and other-worldly. The last of the world religions to emerge onto the historical stage, Islam, like Christianity, bases itself on a concept of the individual before God. Its social cosmology is therefore distinct from the Hindu-Buddhist hierarchic model of society in which the individual has no meaningful social existence outside collectivities and the part is always encompassed by the whole. Yet it is also distinct from Christianity. The Muslim requires no priestly mediation to approach God and acquire grace and salvation. Islamic stress on the individual's duty to obey the teachings of the Koran, the source of *all* law, gave the scholar-lawyers, the *ulama*, a pivotal political role. The Chinese *literati* and Catholic Church hierarchy both offered ideologies serving the interests of the state, but under Islam, political and religious power could become deeply antagonistic.

The pastoral tribes of Arabia were united by the Prophet Mohammad after pressure from two neighbouring agrarian civilizations, Byzantium and Persia, had awakened a sense of common ethnic identity which the Prophet's vision transformed into the expansionist model of the Islamic community pursuing its holy mission through war (Hall 1985: 86–7). Given the rigorous monotheism and totalizing perspective of that vision, Islamic conquerors did not readily adapt themselves to the existing structures of power in the agrarian civilizations they invaded. Matters were complicated by the charismatic nature of the Prophet's original leadership and the nature of his social message, which stressed the obligations of the rich towards the poor. Firstly, after Mohammad's death, factional struggles for control of the Islamic community produced the opposition between Shi'ites and Sunnis. Sunnism accommodated itself to the structures of social and political power beyond the Arabian heartland, whereas Shi'ism remained in tension with temporal power by insisting that legitimate successors must be descendants of the prophet, establishing the Shi'ite Islamic community as a community of suffering founded on the martyrdom of the Prophet's grandson at the hands of worldly usurpers (Gilsenan 1982: 55–6). Secondly, in Hall's view, the codification of Islamic law, the *Shari'a*, reinforced the potential for conflict between political power and the religious community led by the *ulama*.

The *ulama*, it must be stressed, are not priests. Islam tolerates no mediators between God and the individual: they acquire their authority in society as interpreters of 'the Word as text' (Gilsenan 1982: 31). Hall, following Crone (1980), suggests that it was of vital significance that the codification of Islamic law took place outside imperial Iran and in opposition to the Umayadd caliphate in Syria, in the demilitarized commercial cities of Iraq. The *ulama* were alienated from the political regime produced by the Sunni military ruling class of the caliphate. They defined mainstream Islam in a way which idealized the law of an egalitarian tribal Arab past, endorsed by Allah himself. The accumulation of both secular and religious power was condemned. God's community was to lead a simple life: the caliph should provide only necessary governance and there was no space in this political theory for a wealthy priesthood or parasitic ruling class. Islam was stronger on theories of collective morality than coherent theories of the state (Ayubi 1991).

Urbanized Islamic politico-military elites tried to overcome this menace to the legitimacy of their rule by attempting to incorporate the *ulama* into the state apparatus as a scholar-bureaucrat stratum, but the *ulama* preserved their distance from state institutions, with the exception of the Ottoman case discussed below. They did so, Hall suggests, in part because codification of the *Shari'a* meant 'their doctrinal code had set' and was not susceptible to further modification by revelation (Hall 1985: 90–1). But Hall also offers a second explanation, focusing on how the practice of politics in the classical Islamic world was structured by the continued interaction of urban communities and segmentary nomadic pastoralist tribes which remained the bearers of Islamic culture and the key military force in the Islamic world. In contrast to Europe, where cities raising their own troops or hiring mercenaries were able to defend themselves within what was a 'relatively pacified' environment, the cities of the Middle East faced a tribal hinterland 'capable of great military surges' (ibid.: 93).

The defence of urban civilization depended on the protection that might be secured from one of the Islamic tribal groups of the exterior, but once the protector turned into a ruler, a rising tax burden proved bad for commercial life, and government remained alien to the civil society it governed. As internal discontent mounted, the *ulama* would withdraw their support from the ruling house, declare it impious, and invite in another tribe to restore Islamic purity. Thus the actual existence of a tribal hinterland around the areas of sedentary life provided the material base for the continuing antagonism of religion and politics, and the cultural unity of the Islamic world beyond the boundaries of any individual state. The classical Islamic world was not simply a world of multiple political centres – like Europe – but one of unstable centres: few regimes lasted even a century.

This theory of Islamic politics is ultimately derived from a 'native' source, the fourteenth-century scholar Ibn Khaldun (Gellner 1981). Gilsenan, however, offers another explanation of the political role of the *ulama* which overcomes an objection to Hall's argument, namely that since the Koran always required interpretation, its potential challenge to despotism and social inequality could be defused. The *ulama* could and did provide dissimulated ideological and moral underpinnings to oppressive political and social relations simply by passing over certain kinds of acts and relationships in silence, as well as by defining acts and relationships as 'Islamic' by specifying how they were to be regulated by the 'eternal law' of God (Gilsenan 1982: 35). What they could *not* do, however, was establish a social *monopoly* on interpretation of the Word of God, because believers did not depend on the *ulama* to perform their religious duties, and holy men did not have to be *ulama*. It was this, Gilsenan argues, which prevented any state taking over the sacred tradition simply by coopting the *ulama* as a corps of *literati*. Cooption seldom suited the *ulama* themselves, and even in modern times, there is always a tension between the universalism of the Islamic religious community and particularistic attempts by states to appropriate Islam for its own ends, such as the construction of nationalism. The *ulama* never became a social class nor even a corporate group, not simply because they were recruited from a broad social base, but because they occupied different structural and social positions in different Islamic states.

Despite the instability of classic Islamic polities, later history did produce three substantial empires, the Safavids in Persia, the Mughal Empire of India, and the Ottomans. One factor which undermined the basis for decentralized, contractualist, Islamic society was military: the adoption of gunpowder. All three empires also formed in areas with a long historical tradition of strong tribute-based states exploiting an agrarian peasantry. Yet the Persian Empire of the Safavids began to collapse in the mid-seventeenth century after the *ulama* withdrew their support from the empire's Iranian-born rulers, when the latter reneged on their undertaking to convert all their subjects to Shi'ite Islam. The Mughal Empire, aligned with Sunnism, adopted the quite different strategy of using *Hindus* as its bureaucracy and indigenous *Rajputs* as its elite soldiers. It began to collapse after late seventeenth-century emperors attempted to create a purely Islamic state (Hall 1985: 106).

The longer-lasting Ottoman Empire is the one case in which the *ulama* were successfully integrated into the state. They were not simply exempted from taxation, but acquired wealth from land and buildings made over to them as religious endowments which was largely independent of the state. Since these estates were not subject to the Ottoman norm of confiscation by the state on the death of the holder, but could be passed on to heirs, sons of the Ottoman politico-military aristocracy often entered the corps of *ulama* to acquire hereditary property rights (Gilsenan 1982: 38). The alignment between the *ulama* and other sections of the elite was reinforced by their role as tax-farmers, linked to the merchants who sold the peasant grain they collected in kind, and the fact that the highest-ranking *ulama* were members of the military ruling estate. Ottoman *ulama* were loyal to the state and deeply conservative.

Nevertheless, once the empire stopped expanding, at the start of the seventeenth century, a protracted process of decay set in. This was reinforced by European commercial penetration, which induced feudalization in the Anatolian provinces as local notables became estate-owners producing export crops for the world market, property rights in land were transformed, and peasants turned into proletarians (Islamoglu and Keyder 1977). Hall suggests that the *ulama* did not turn against the state, but continued to participate in its politics as an organized faction, along with the military and the court officials. Sultanic power declined and lost its autonomy relative to these factional power blocs, but the empire continued, paralysed by the inability of any single faction to impose its will.

Matters were not so clear-cut, however. As the Ottoman state reacted to Western pressure in the mid-nineteenth century by 'reforming' land law and other legislation on Western lines and embracing 'secularization', the *ulama* found themselves able to play a more popular role as providers of subsistence and support for impoverished peasants and rural–urban migrants. Religion was displaced from its close relationship with the state into new areas in which the poor articulated their experiences of capitalist development in terms of the assertion of their own claims to be the true believers and the distorted ideological grid of a demonology of foreigners (Gilsenan 1982: 41–6). Even within the late Ottoman Empire, then, we can discern the development of the populist, fundamentalist, forms of Islam which became an integral part of Middle Eastern life in the twentieth century as these societies have responded to what Ayubi (1991) terms 'distorted capitalist development' and bureaucratic authoritarianism. Kemalism's attempts to create a secular state in Turkey founded explicitly on the principles of Western modernity failed to exorcize Islam – or even the ghost of the Ottoman world as an alternative vision of national identity and dignity – despite continuing commitment to the Kemalist project on the part of the military (Mardin 1993).

If political and religious power were in tension in the Islamic world, there was no question of the *ulama* withdrawing entirely from the political domain. It is often argued that Indian civilization is distinctive because the religious elite, the Brahmans, did withdraw from involvement in politics to concentrate on organizing society through the caste system, leaving the political domain not merely unstable, but ephemeral. Kingship in India is secularized, and political power is defined as hierarchically inferior to religious authority: religious power and not the state is the source of law.

This kind of split between religious and political power has different implications to that of the Islamic world, since the superior and inferior levels of a hierarchic order are conceived as being interdependent rather than antagonistic. Nevertheless, the hierarchic order established by the caste system appears to be capable of existing without state regulation, prompting Hall to model the classical pattern of Hindu India as one in which politics was 'free-floating' above a stable social order organized by the Brahmans (Hall 1985: 71–2). The Brahmans provided law and the religious services necessary for social reproduction, and mediated where disputes arose between or within castes, but the caste system had a self-regulating quality. Establishing a new political rulership was easy, since the conqueror merely had to set up court and allow society to go on governing itself. Thus Hall characterizes the state in India as a 'custodial state', which could be of variable size and duration, but had little to do because the Brahmans organized society totally and 'penetrated' it to an extent which made further central state intervention redundant. He points out, however, that Indian society was not completely cellular and localistic. The geographically mobile Brahmans possessed a translocal organization more capable of binding 'laterally insulated' peasant communities together than the translocal organizations of rulers and warriors (ibid.: 75). By withdrawing from politics and concentrating on religious control of society, the Brahmans succeeded in limiting the power of the state and other elite groups to transform that society.

Hall cites Geertz's (1980) model of the 'Theatre State' in Bali as a paradigm for the 'custodial state' in Indic civilization in general, arguing that the state was a device for the ritual enactment of the cosmic basis for this-worldly status in hierarchic principles, its 'sound and fury signifying nothing' (Hall 1985: 76). He concedes that Brahmans did, on occasion, have to fight for control of society and play politics. In the third century BC, Buddhism presented a particularly strong challenge, backed by the Mauryan emperor Asoka. Normally, however, they did not oppose political regimes, or possess the power to do so. Their position rested on the hierarchic model in which the superiority of the Brahmans was expressed in their power to legitimate political rulership and the continuity of the hierarchic order as a whole depended on the complementary and mutually supportive relationship between the castes as providers of services. Nevertheless, Hall argues that the instability of political rulership in India resulted from the superiority of Brahmanical power over that of kings, and the level of Brahmanical control over society.

Although Hall is critical of Dumont on some points, he does not challenge his fundamental ideas about the encompassment of political power by religious status. As I noted earlier, however, some anthropologists have argued that even in India power affected cosmic-ritual status, and that the Dumontian model of caste represents an over-coherent, ahistorical representation of an ideology distant from the realities of political practice. On the basis of an ethnohistorical study of the small kingdom of Pudukkottai in Tamil-speaking south India, Dirks argues that caste was 'embedded in the political context of kingship', and had less to do with Dumont's opposition between purity and pollution than with 'royal authority and honor and associated notions of power, dominance, and order' (Dirks 1987: 7). He suggests that the detachment of caste from politics was actually the work of the British colonial order, which found removing the politics from colonial society not merely convenient, but necessary in order to rule an 'immensely complex society by a variety of indirect means' (ibid.: 8). Dirks suggests that the role of the Brahman reached new heights under British colonial administration. When colonialism stripped kings of their power, the Brahmans were left to develop new models of caste centred on the obsessions with purity and pollution which figure so prominently in the *ethnographic* realities of the caste system which influenced the models of Dumont and others.

Dirks's analysis also bears on the 'Theatre State' model of the Indic polity developed by Geertz and cited with approval by Hall. Geertz attempts to provide a non-eurocentric approach to thinking about the Hindu-Buddhist states of South-East Asia, including Thailand, Burma and Cambodia. He uses his work on Bali to argue that no state in the region can be analysed adequately in terms of Weberian concepts of feudalism or patrimonialism (Bakker 1988). Geertz argues that the 'exemplary centre' at Klungkung had merely ceremonial significance, and that 'the state' consisted of an acephalous band of sovereigns for whom political competition meant disputing an equally ceremonial order of precedence. Myth tells of a decline from a classical model of perfection, but Geertz argues that the 'centre' and the myth of its glorious past is of essentially symbolic significance within the local cultural logic of status and hierarchy, and should not be taken as embodying an historical truth. It is clear, however, that we would expect the Princely State to be reduced to a ritual shell for dramatically enacting an essentially fictional power once kingship had been stripped of any real basis of power by colonial rule.

Geertz is not alone, however, in seeing pre-colonial South-East Asian polities as relatively decentralized. Tambiah (1976, 1985) describes them as 'galactic polities', in which cosmic rulers rule through a coalition of powerful lineages over an ethnically diverse mass of subservient lineages, castes and villages. The periphery of such polities consisted of a more or less autonomous set of small 'kingly' or 'chiefly' domains, and their boundaries were unstable and shifting. Tambiah's model, however, does not necessarily lead us to Geertz's account of Indic politics as pure superstructure or theatre.

In the first place, the principle that power can affect status is hardly controversial in the Hindu-Buddhist world outside India. In Buddhist Sri Lanka, the location of castes in the hierarchy was clearly determined by their relationship to the king, and Dumont himself conceded that the pure–impure opposition was less significant (Kapferer 1988: 20). Nor are analysts critical of Dumont's formulation of the hierarchic relationship of status and power such as Dirks attempting to reverse the argument and suggest that 'political' and 'ritual' forms of power can be sharply distinguished and separated on Western lines. Both Hinduism and Sinhalese Buddhist ideology present the state as symbolized by kingship as encompassed by religion: *artha*, the sphere of force and self-interest, is encompassed by *dharma*, universal order. It is the job of rulers to ensure that the principles of cosmic harmony are upheld. Political revolts become symptoms of the fragmentation not merely of the kingdom, but of the cosmos itself, a failure of rulership to maintain control over the forces constantly threatening fragmentation and conserve the 'society' constituted by hierarchy. In Sri Lanka, kings can be benevolent restorers of hierarchic order or manifest a demonic, destructive power, when the ordering cosmic principles of hierarchy break down (ibid.: 13). There is clearly no question here of the state being deemed irrelevant to the reproduction of 'society'.

Dirks is, however, arguing a second, stronger thesis. His point is that even in India under pre-colonial conditions states did organize and reorganize society in significant ways, distributing land grants, symbols of power and titles, endowing temples and organizing warfare. These centre–periphery relations were more than ritual and symbolic in nature:

> In many of the smaller states in eighteenth century Tamil Nadu between sixty and eighty per cent of all cultivable land was given away to military chiefs, retainers, temples, Brahmans, village officers, priests, servants and artisans. Lands were given away in central and peripheral areas of the state. When insufficient cultivable land was available for such grants, the king gave grants of forest land to be brought under cultivation or embarked upon predatory warfare for honor, fame, booty and new lands. (Dirks 1987: 53)

Dirks therefore challenges the entire notion that political power had a superficial or simply predatory impact on a village society which was largely organized by the holders of religious power.

In Geertz's model, power seems only to exist in its symbolic and ideological manifestations, leaving us dangerously close to the Orientalist 'stationary' model of Asian societies. Relative political decentralization and instability do not necessarily imply that class and property relations and patterns of social reproduction are unchanging or that political power is merely a ritual-ceremonial superstructure without any impact on social life. What these anthropological analyses do suggest, however, is that it is important to conduct in-depth studies of how pre-colonial non-European agrarian civilizations actually functioned, to look at the content and cultural meaning of the relationships of power and domination on which they were based – and to understand them as truly *historical* societies. We cannot understand them adequately simply by asking how their organizational principles differed from those of Western societies of either the modern or pre-modern period, since one of the most important things we must try to understand is how Western domination changed them.

Colonialism did not simply reduce indigenous forms of power to a theatrical shell of what had gone before. It also redefined 'society' in fundamental ways, forcing people to attach new meanings and practices to old identities, such as 'caste' and 'ethnicity'. If failure to identify these transformations impedes our reconstructions of the pre-colonial world, it becomes doubly problematic when we try to understand the contemporary, post-colonial world. Distinctive cultural structures inherited from the past leave traces in the present, but colonialism also produced strong discontinuities and a restructuring of established institutions, practices and beliefs, the subject of the next chapter.

4 THE POLITICAL ANTHROPOLOGY OF COLONIALISM: A STUDY OF DOMINATION AND RESISTANCE

An exclusive emphasis on the transforming power of Western colonial domination can be another way of denying Europe's 'others' a role in history. Indigenous resistance shaped the development of colonial societies, and this is important for understanding differences between post-colonial societies. However, as Roger Keesing pointed out, the topic of 'resistance' is a minefield of conceptual problems (Keesing 1992: 6–10). 'Resistance' at one level frequently seems ultimately to reproduce the 'categorical and institutional structures of domination', and it is often difficult to decide whether to label particular actions by individuals or groups as 'resistance' in the first place. Keesing does regard 'resistance' as a valuable notion, providing it is taken as a rich metaphor, not a precise concept. It illuminates facets of power relations which are easily overlooked because the actions in which relatively powerless people engage are different from the dramatic confrontations that attract the attention of historians and journalists. Such acts of resistance have often been ignored precisely because they are not obviously 'political' in the sense of the term understood by colonial and post-colonial states.

Keesing's work contributed to a larger reaction against both conservative social science and orthodox Marxist models which dismissed various forms of popular struggles as 'millenarian' and 'pre-political' or simply ignored them. Other important contributions come from political science (Scott 1985, 1990), the 'Subaltern Studies' school's writings on the Indian peasantry (Guha 1983), and from the work of diasporic literary critics working in leading universities in the United States, such as Edward Said (1978, 1993), Homi Bhabha (1994) and Gayatri Spivak (1988, 1996, 1999). This latter type of 'post-colonial criticism' or 'cultural studies' writing[1] is relatively unattractive to many anthropologists. Its ideas derive from a variety of fashionable Western theorists (Foucault in the case of Said, Lacan and Bakhtin in the case of Bhabha, and the deconstructionism of Derrida in the case of Spivak). Post-colonial criticism seems more concerned

---

1 For a sample of writing by important figures in the field, including Frantz Fanon and Chinua Achebe, see, for example, Moore-Gilbert *et al.* (1997).

with 'Western knowledge systems and identity' than 'with current local knowledge of the cultural politics of everyday life in post-colonial hinterlands' (Werbner 1996: 6). Although Spivak spends part of each year in India, not only lecturing, but training rural language teachers, her prose style remains a challenge to even the most self-confident reader of English, and her 'positioning' that of a Western feminist. Nevertheless, these diasporic intellectuals from the former colonial world have played an important, and in my view, positive, role in forcing anthropologists to be more self-critical about how we have represented that world.

Spivak, in particular, has offered important reflections on how any academic (irrespective of nationality) can present the viewpoint of 'subalterns' and make their experience known without distorting it and replicating the same kinds of power relations implicit in the colonial regime's claims to 'speak for' Indian women in prohibiting *sati* (the burning of Hindu widows) (Spivak 1988). One can object that Spivak's argument leaves her in the doubly difficult position of both repeating the gesture for which she berates others – speaking for the mute Indian subaltern, and even interpreting her actions (Ortner 1995: 189) – *and* principally addressing the Western intellectual, using a language and theory which is a product of Western intellectual culture. Yet her deconstructionist method leads to a very important point of principle. The colonial and post-colonial 'subaltern' can become an heroic and one-dimensional surrogate through which Western intellectuals fantasize about 'liberation' from capitalism, bureaucracy and imperialism. As Spivak (1996) notes, the 'subaltern studies' writers assumed that there was some kind of pure and authentic 'subaltern consciousness' that was unaffected by colonial discourses and practices. As anthropologists such as Keesing have shown, such completely 'autonomous' subjects do not exist, and the idea that there are spaces of subaltern social life that are completely uncolonized by power relations is also a fatal weakness of James Scott's theories.

Within anthropology itself, some writers, including Keesing and Jean and John Comaroff (1992), have appealed for theoretical inspiration to the heterodox Marxism of Antonio Gramsci (Hoare and Nowell Smith 1971). The extent to which some anthropological references to 'hegemony' reflect Gramsci's own ideas as distinct from those of Raymond Williams, whose version sits more comfortably with the traditional anthropological concept of 'culture', has, however, been questioned by Kurtz (1996). Roseberry (1994) has also demonstrated the potential advantages of a closer reading of Gramsci in a discussion which rejects James Scott's interpretation of 'hegemony' as 'false-consciousness' or 'mystification'. There are, however, older works within anthropology itself which anticipate some aspects of the contemporary debates about colonial domination and resistance. One major contribution which I discuss later is Worsley's pioneering 1957 study of Melanesian cargo cults, republished as an extended second edition in 1968. This rich text hardly deserved the castigation as an orthodox Marxist tract it received from Lucy Mair (1958) simply because it argued that the economic impact of colonialism had significant social consequences. It was also distinguished from many subsequent analyses because it viewed what the Melanesians were doing as a meaningful form of *political* action rather than a product of 'anomie' or cultural 'break-down'.

That studies of 'resistance' had a growing impact in anthropology through the 1980s reflected the discipline's progress towards reflecting on the colonial experience and exploring its history in depth. By the end of the 1990s, ideas had developed considerably as simple oppositions between the dominant and the dominated, and the notion of a unitary 'resisting subject', gave way to more sophisticated formulations. What anthropology might contribute to other perspectives was, Sherry Ortner suggested, the ethnographic 'thick description' often found wanting in cultural studies: this would not only improve our grasp of the meanings of action from the actor's point of view – something we might expect to change in the course of the experience of 'struggle' – but offer a better possibility of understanding the politics of action within its social context (Ortner 1995). It will be useful, however, to begin with a broader, historical-structural perspective. Western colonialism itself has a history, the impact of Western domination on particular regions of the world is related to its timing in terms of this larger history, and anthropological thinking itself needs to be contextualized in terms of specific historical moments of the 'colonial encounter'.

STRUCTURAL-FUNCTIONALIST POLITICAL ANTHROPOLOGY AS A CHILD OF ITS TIME

As Talal Asad pointed out, even anthropologists from the 'left-leaning' Manchester wing of the British school, like Victor Turner, proved 'strangely reluctant' to take stock of the power structure within which their discipline had taken shape. If it was simplistic to dismiss anthropology as a 'handmaiden of colonialism', as some intellectuals in post-colonial countries were doing in the 1960s and early 1970s,[2] it was naive or disingenuous to assume that the 'professionalism' of the community of anthropological 'participant observers' guaranteed the objectivity of anthropological knowledge, as Turner had suggested (Asad 1973a: 15–16). However sympathetic they might be to the 'native', anthropologists were part of a larger colonial power structure, and that affected their analyses.

Structural-functionalist anthropology depicted the relationship between the rulers and the ruled in African political systems in terms of consensual government, reciprocal obligations between government and people, and

---

2 See, for example, the analysis of the 'morbid perversion' of much of Africanist anthropology' offered by Onoge (1977).

'checks and balances' inhibiting the arbitrary exercise of power (Asad 1973b: 104–5). Such accounts generally described local African political structures without reference to the political fact that the African chief was subordinated to European coercive and administrative power. At best they produced an 'ideologically loaded constitutional history of African states prior to colonial rule' (Asad 1973b: 109). Even when anthropologists *did* begin to refer to the colonial regime as part of the local structure:

> they generally did so in such a way as to obscure the systematic character of colonial domination and to mask the fundamental contradictions of interest inherent in the system of indirect rule. The role of new political-economic forces brought about by European colonialism (labelled 'Social Change') were usually not thought to be directly relevant to understanding the dynamic of *African* political structures. (Asad 1973b: 109, emphasis added)

This vice was not peculiar to Africanists, since precisely the same problem arises in the study of politics and caste in India. What is most illuminating about Asad's critique, however, is his explanation for why the structural-functionalists depicted African polities in the way that they did. European 'Orientalist' accounts of the Islamic world projected a quite different image of the other, focusing on the repressive nature of the relations between rulers and ruled. Asad argues that structural-functionalist political anthropology in Africa was the objectification of an era of 'routine colonialism'. The now professionalized anthropologists set about their work within an already long-established, and apparently stable, colonial regime, which most found it relatively easy to view as essentially benign. The foundations of modern Orientalist images of Islamic civilization, in contrast, were laid towards the end of the nineteenth century, when Western powers were still engaged in a protracted colonial penetration of the Islamic world, and needed to dele-gitimize the Muslim rulers they were displacing.

Since most British anthropologists were conservative, the majority's acceptance of the positive nature of the 'Pax Britannica' is not surprising. The issue is not, however, simply whether British colonialism was really more vicious than most anthropologists at one time painted it, but about why it is not adequately present in their analyses and the implications of this absence for the models they produced.

This becomes clear if we take the example of Max Gluckman, whose work deals in a self-evidently critical way with the apartheid regime in his native South Africa, recognizes the way 'traditional' authorities were coopted to serve colonial interests, and suggests the need to see changing African urban identities as a consequence of capitalist transformation. In *Analysis of a Social Situation in Modern Zululand* (1958) Gluckman uses the apparatus of structural-functionalist political anthropology – in particular the notion of 'cross-cutting ties' – to show how routine practices in daily life allowed the reproduction of a regime premised on racism, by mediating the 'dominant cleavage' between Black and White. His analysis undeniably made a useful contribution to understanding the mechanisms of domination in South Africa, since it is not immediately obvious how such a patently unjust and exploitative system could maintain itself over time. Yet it remained trapped within the same boundaries as work of the era which is less critical, because it takes the colonial status quo as a structure which is stable. The difference is that Gluckman felt that this stability was paradoxical enough to require explanation. His perspective still deflected attention from forms of action among Black South Africans which could be described as 'counter-hegemonic' resistance to domination and remained a partial vision of social reality.

Although anthropology now claims to have decolonized itself, many of the issues raised by the contributors to *Anthropology and the Colonial Encounter* (Asad 1973c) at the start of the 1970s remain live ones. Anthropology continues to be professionalized and anthropologists continue to be involved in power relationships with the people they study, whether they are from the West or products of the higher educational systems of non-Western countries. I review these issues in more depth in Chapter 9.

THE COLONIAL PROCESS AS AN OBJECT OF ANALYSIS

A focus on colonialism as a system of economic exploitation has been central to anthropological approaches influenced by Marxism, dependency theory and world-systems theory. It is immediately apparent from this perspective that we cannot treat Western colonial expansion as a single process in either time or space. There are differences in terms of political economy between the kind of colonialism represented by the Spanish conquest of the Americas, which establishes a tributary empire and is associated, like early Portuguese and Dutch expansion, with a 'world economy' integrated by merchant capitalism, and the nineteenth-century 'scramble for Africa', which occurs after metropolitan capitalist industrialization. As the 'articulation of modes of production' approach of the French Marxist anthropologists suggests (Foster-Carter 1978), Europeans began to transform African societies through the slave trade even before they implanted direct colonial rule. The same point has been made by Wolf (1982) in his comprehensive analysis of indigenous reactions to the expansion of global commodity trading networks. Wolf emphasized that the 'peripheral' populations incorporated into the European world economy played an active role in shaping the new systems and could not be regarded merely as passive victims, as I noted in the previous chapter.

Even within a single region a variety of different kinds of colonial economic system emerged. On a moral scale of barbarities, it might be possible to draw distinctions between the operation of Belgian colonialism in the Congo of Joseph Conrad's *Heart of Darkness*[3] and the British in East Africa. Yet such

---

3 Taussig (1987) offers a modern anthropological analysis of a South American equivalent of the horrors recounted in *Heart of Darkness*, the case of the Colombian Putamayo.

comparisons simply lend themselves to apologetics and are best avoided in favour of drier categories. In Africa, we can distinguish areas where colonial states left exploitation in the hands of private concessionary companies from those where they regulated the process of exploitation more directly (Wallerstein 1976). The latter were subdivided into zones where European settler agriculture became important, those where indigenous agriculture remained predominant and those where European enterprise focused on extractive industries drawing on indigenous migrant labour. Some areas, however, not only mixed economic regimes, but combined them in a systematic way.

The transformation of South Africa's political economy into the form associated with apartheid involved, first, state interventions to limit African farmers from competing commercially with Whites, and second, the forced removal of Blacks to the so-called 'homelands' where poor agricultural conditions forced them into wage-labour migration (Wolpe 1972, Legassick 1977). This political economy perspective is an obvious advance on the anthropological models of the 1940s and 1950s. It reveals both the systematic nature of colonial economic exploitation and the less benign side of colonial politics. The South African example shows how the politics of the dominant White stratum of colonial society contributed to the deteriorating economic position of Blacks since this was in part the result of pressure from poor Whites on the White elite within a political system from which Blacks were excluded. Starting analysis of the colonial world with the local structure of economic exploitation does however, obscure the way economic exploitation of the colonies was shaped by international political factors.

Political struggles in Holland, for example, played an important part in determining how Indonesia was to be exploited. A system of forced cultivation and forced deliveries of cash crops by the indigenous population continued for decades in the face of opposition from liberals advocating an extension of Dutch-owned plantations (Kahn 1981). World-systems theory explains such differences in terms of the dominance of different factions of capital within the metropolitan and/or colonial state, but it seems difficult to explain why different class factions are hegemonic in different national states without a broader analysis of their politics. This would include analysis of the role of non-elite classes and the balance of power between regional and national elites, but political oppositions not reducible to conflicts of economic class interests might also be relevant to shaping state policy.

Differences in the administrative regimes implanted in the colonies themselves may also not be explicable simply in terms of the needs of a particular type of colonial economy, and there were broad differences between different European countries' colonial policies. France, for example, delegated little control over policy to colonial administrators on the ground in comparison with the British. The French ensured that their colonies did not develop economic sectors which would harm metropolitan enterprises and that they covered the full costs of their administration from local taxation, even if those costs were increased by the need to put down rebellions against colonial head taxes (Scott 1976, Murray 1984). Nevertheless, all colonial states, irrespective of nationality, were military-administrative units, reliant not simply on Western-style bureaucracies and professional military forces maintaining internal pacification, but on the strong security services of which anthropologists occasionally fell foul. Since colonial regimes were by nature authoritarian, interested in coopting local elites but not in consulting them about policy, their 'penetration' of civil society remained limited. In certain aspects of daily life, the colonial state interfered greatly, even in indirect rule systems, through modern apparatuses of surveillance, yet it excluded the bulk of the population from direct participation in the political system and defined them as a special type of 'colonial citizen', generally on explicitly racist lines.

This way of looking at the colonial order has radically different implications from the view implicit in the work of anthropologists during the colonial era itself. In many cases, the political legacy of colonialism was a formal state apparatus weakly linked to civil society and enjoying little popular legitimacy because it was designed by bureaucrats, authoritarian in style and orientated to domination rather than government by consent. Yet the experience of European colonialism was not identical for all subjects of European empires. In the first place, some had been subjects of other empires previously, whereas others had not, and, in the second place, some strata of the colonized societies were more integrated into the colonial system than others. European colonialism created new classes, new bourgeoisies, new types of commercialized peasantries, and urban working classes. Later European colonialism's growing need for a bureaucratic infrastructure produced not simply a Western-educated native elite but hordes of school-teachers, clerks and other minor functionaries. These developments shaped the political legacy of the colonial era, but they also reinforce the point that the colonial systems of nineteenth-century industrial capitalist metropoles had distinct transformative effects linked to the 'modernity' of their power infrastructures.

Although the transformation of indigenous class structures and property relations is one of the most important dimensions of nineteenth-century colonial transformations, Western colonial bureaucratic and educational systems also had a crucial impact on subsequent political developments. The policies of the colonial state transformed indigenous elite culture in ways which subtly linked such things as religious affiliation to the colonial class and bureaucratic order, and as Anderson (1991) has shown, Western domination changed the nature of discourses on 'culture' by bringing with it the print-capitalism that was the vehicle for the propagation of popular nationalism in the European context. Each of these dimensions of the colonial impact deserves further comment.

The 'new empires' forged by industrial capitalist powers generally sought to develop commercial agriculture on the basis of private property relations.

Even in societies that had long historical experience of landlordism, the implantation of a colonial capitalist model had traumatic social consequences, as Scott (1976) demonstrates for the case of Indochina. Peasant tenants had been used to an agrarian system in which landlords were flexible about the rents due to them in years when harvests were bad and families faced a subsistence crisis. Indigenous landlords now faced pressures from the world market, as colonial regimes opened up local regional markets to rice imports. Those who displayed traditional 'flexibility' towards tenants faced ruin, and ceased to do so. Peasant communities around the world found that their rights to use landlord resources like pasturage and forests were curtailed as these resources now had a commercial value. Such changes greatly reduced the ability of the peasant household to maintain itself without recourse to participation in wage labour off the farm. The transformation of landlord agriculture was therefore intimately related to processes which turned peasants into 'semi-proletarians', even if there was no reduction in peasant access to land through the conversion of village 'common land' into private property. Furthermore, there was less the peasantry could do to resist landlord power than in the pre-colonial past. Landlords now enjoyed the backing of a more powerful colonial state actively sponsoring socio-economic transformation.

Nevertheless, colonial capitalism did not, by and large, produce 'modern' capitalist class structures dividing society into bourgeoisie and proletariat. In many cases, even the coercive power of the colonial regimes could not carry through a process of mass proletarianization on the scale required and the implantation of a generalized system of wage-labour-based capitalism was seldom even deemed necessary or desirable in the short term, since the prime economic objective of colonialism was to supply the mother country with cheap food and industrial raw materials rather than to develop an integrated modern economy on metropolitan lines. The later nineteenth century saw an increasing emphasis on improving the efficiency of sectors such as mining and sugar production, but both continued to rely on migrant labour drawn from rural hinterlands based on peasant subsistence agriculture.

Such systems could be based on 'internal colonial' relationships within independent national states. The dictatorial liberal government of Guatemala in the 1870s, for example, reintroduced colonial labour draft laws to force migrant labour out of Indian villages down to the coastal coffee plantations, and backed up labour contractors with a modern system of surveillance and military policing designed to ensure that peasants did not escape their debts and work obligations (Dunkerley 1988). Such systems, which mixed 'contractual' forms with coercive enforcement and surveillance, might be organized by local planter oligarchies (as in El Salvador) or by the state itself, but all rested on coercive transformations of agrarian structures and property relations which forced wage labour out of what remained overwhelmingly agrarian populations. In the periphery the processes of class formation were everywhere affected by the fact that industrialization was limited in scale and mainly restricted to basic utilities, transport and light industries. More urban people worked in services than industry, and large numbers of people were caught in an ambiguous status between peasant and proletarian as migrant workers in mines and plantations. These class dimensions of colonial transformation had an impact on political development when colonialism ended.

The bureaucratization created by the colonial state laid the basis for the later emergence of new class factions and political leaderships among the indigenous population. This theme is central to Benedict Anderson's analysis of the origin and spread of modern nationalism. His primary thesis is that it is premised on the 'imagined community' of people who can define their common identity with other people with whom they do not have a face-to-face relationship. The medium of its spread is print-capitalism, but even in the period when national identities were proliferating in Europe, the mid-nineteenth century, almost half the population of even Britain and France remained illiterate. What Anderson terms 'the rising middle strata of plebeian lower officials, professionals and commercial and industrial bourgeoisie' were therefore the key actors in the process. The expansion of the civil and military bureaucracy of European states drew in persons of far more varied social origins than previously (Anderson 1991: 76). Since, however, print-capitalism made it possible for people to form common identities and solidarities on an imaginary basis, this development transformed political life everywhere.

The French Revolution was a complex historical event, but it now became a 'thing' capable of serving as a key symbol in polemical political debates across national boundaries. Different political cultures produced different interpretations of the symbols, but Anderson argues that the logic of the paradigm acquired a certain force of its own which constrained interpretation. The liberator of South America, Simón Bolívar, was a plantation owner who was embarrassed by his own dark complexion and feared that the end of slavery would prompt a Negro revolt. Yet once creole leaders accepted a general 'model' of independent national 'modern' republican society diffused through print, institutions like legal slavery had to go because they were too incompatible with that model (ibid.: 80–1).

English imperialism sought to use English educational systems to create an indigenous colonial elite which would be culturally English. Yet the official nationalism propagated by the English state did not lend itself to the integration of the empire. Neither Anglicized Indians not Anglicized Australians were allowed to occupy the commanding heights of imperial administration outside their homelands (ibid.: 93). Though they became culturally alienated from their own society, they remained excluded from real admission to the society of the metropolis. Nevertheless, however artificial the colonial demarcation of territorial units may have been in relation to pre-colonial conditions, the administrative organizations of the colonial states created the basis for articulating new national units based on imaginary communities formed by these indigenous functionaries, communities which corresponded to the administrative domain of the highest administrative centre to which they could be assigned. This effect was reinforced with the vast expansion of the bureaucracy in the colonial world after the mid-nineteenth century. Anderson shows how this hypothesis helps us to understand Indonesia's continuing unification after independence in contrast to cases such as French Indochina.

Colonial educational facilities in Indochina were concentrated in Hanoi and Saigon up to 1917. After 1915 the regime ceased to accept Confucian education as a qualification for entry into the bureaucracy, fearing influence from Sun Yat-Sen's nationalist movement in China. This prompted the Vietnamese elite to place their children in French *lycées*, provoking protests from French colonists which led to the creation of a separate Franco-Vietnamese educational structure, based on instruction in Vietnamese in the lower grades. This excluded Indochinese from Cambodia and Laos and led to the development of a separate educational structure in Phnom Penh. Since Vietnamese were also given preference by the French in appointments to administrative posts in western Indochina, these developments fuelled Khmer nationalism (and antagonism to Vietnamese). Colonialism therefore created nationalist political leaderships by creating an indigenous bureaucracy educated in the values of Western nationalism but subject to discrimination. Its need for school texts provided European or vernacular print-languages through which such nationalisms could be invented and diffused (ibid.: 133–4).

European global expansion also produced new nationalisms in other ways, illustrated by the Japanese formulation of their own 'official nationalism' under the Meiji (ibid.: 94–9). Anderson argues that the aggressively imperialist character of Japanese nationalism reflected Japan's long isolation and unbroken dynastic tradition. The Japanese elite produced an interpretation of what had made the Europeans superior and what Japan needed to do to make herself a great nation. Yet both official and popular nationalisms outside Europe were forged under conditions created by European expansion and propagated themselves through similar mechanisms, even if they embodied distinct social and political ideologies. The culture of nationalism was the most universal legacy of the West to the colonial world.

The colonial state and its bureaucratic apparatus transformed indigenous social organization in fundamental ways not considered by Anderson. It turned previously flexible 'ethnic' categories into fixed criteria for the bureaucratic identification of groups. It incorporated caste into the workings of the colonial state in India and Sri Lanka by treating caste communities as autonomous groups. Yet this bureaucratic redefinition of the caste system ironically also provided subaltern groups with means for engaging in political resistance (Guha 1983). It is now time to look at such resistance in more depth.

CRACKS IN THE STRUCTURES: THE ANTHROPOLOGY OF RESISTANCE

A focus on 'resistance' to domination may, as I remarked earlier, draw our attention to practices which are often overlooked. James Scott's (1985) analysis of 'everyday peasant resistance' argues that confrontational forms of 'class struggle' or mass mobilization behind the banners of political oppositions are generally not perceived as viable options simply because they are too dangerous, given the repressive power of modern agrarian dominant classes and the states which back them. Dramatic forms of conflict which mobilize large numbers of rural people in violent attacks on the 'system' typically occur only when the structures of repressive power are perceived as weakened or disorganized. Nevertheless, the poor in Malay villages did not take growing social differentiation and insecurity linked to commercialization and technological changes lying down. Beneath the tranquil surface of rural life, machines were broken but the culprits proved hard to identify. Labourers engaged in a whole series of even less overt forms of 'foot-dragging' resistance in a continuous effort to mitigate the impact of change on their welfare.

Such practices have also been documented in contemporary transnational capitalist industry. One example is the women workers in the offshore assembly plants (*maquiladoras*) established on the Mexican side of the US–Mexico border in the second half of the 1960s, who resisted management attempts to speed up the assembly line by coordinating their own work rhythms (Peña 1987). These tactics have some impact on the way capitalism works but they seem to pose little threat to the capitalist system as such. Against the criteria of revolutionary class struggle, 'foot-dragging' in the production process seems a feeble form of resistance, premised perhaps on yearnings for the lifestyles of a doomed agrarian society. Lenin (1967) decried even trade unions as a spontaneous first step in working-class organization which would merely habituate the workers to capitalist relations without the intervention of professional revolutionaries who could lead them beyond 'economism' and 'trade union consciousness'.

Scott is not impressed by Lenin's argument. He argues that far from being an obstacle to revolution, 'trade union consciousness' is 'the only plausible basis for it' (Scott 1985: 318). Part of his case rests on rejection of 'false consciousness' theories of lower-class abstention from collective acts of rebellion and an interpretation of Gramsci's concept of 'hegemony'[4] as the thesis that

---

4 In my view, and that of Roseberry (1994), this is a bad reading of Gramsci, who defined 'hegemony' as a dynamic process of 'establishment of unstable equilibria' which is shaped in significant ways by the actions and reactions of the subaltern classes (Forgacs 1988: 205–6; see also Hoare and Nowell Smith 1971: 158–68, 175–85, 210–18 and 279–318). Gramsci argued that *both* ruling and subaltern classes are 'historical blocs', *fragile* coalitions of diverse social forces. Their unity needs to be built by hegemonic *practices*, which include real politics and its dirty deals as well as cultural and ideological dimensions. The political revolution which created the modern Italian nation state was what he termed a 'passive

78   *Power and Its Disguises*

the lower classes internalize a 'dominant ideology' imposed from above. Scott argues that lower-class people are not 'mystified' in this way and form perfectly sound understandings of the way exploitation works without the intervention of political leaderships from outside their class. The understandings embodied in everyday resistance are what make rebellions possible. His position also rests, however, on the argument that the power commanded by the dominant in modern societies is so substantial that more overt forms of popular resistance tend to constitute a fatal misreading of the real prospects for emancipation, whilst radical political leaderships recruited from the urban intelligentsia, like the Bolsheviks, tend to betray the lower-class groups they mobilize (Scott 1990: 79).

The kind of 'realism' about power structures which Scott commends here has an affinity with the ideological pessimism of our times. It could lead us to downgrade the study of organized popular movements, and to denigrate all attempts to unite different segments of the lower classes into broader 'political' coalitions (the major focus of Gramsci's politics). Scott's theoretical approach is in danger of postulating mechanical relationships between social class position and forms of consciousness by arguing that lower-class politics is basically concerned with 'bread-and-butter issues' (Scott 1985: 296). Learning from experience of struggle and the repressive reactions of the dominant seems to me to be an important part of the dynamic of many forms of 'resistance', even if it is dangerous to assume that people are passive simply because they are 'mystified'. Finally, economic class identities may be less important in particular contexts of action than other kinds of non-class identities. Nevertheless, although Scott's brand of realism is open to various challenges (Roseberry 1989, Gutmann 1993), it is useful to start discussing 'resistance' in a sceptical frame of mind.

Returning to the example of the Mexican *maquiladoras*, we find that in the 1980s the workers organized themselves into unions independent of the

---

revolution': a change in political regime which involved no fundamental reordering of society. Garibaldi, the most radical political leader, failed to mobilize the peasant masses to carry through a more radical social reform and destroy the power of the Catholic Church, professional army and the landlord elite. So the state created by the Piedmont bourgeoisie was ultimately incoherent. Discontented peasants and workers could not mount a direct challenge to the regime: a *war of movement*. The only realistic strategy was a *war of position*, in which communist cadres and progressive intellectuals would conduct a slow and protracted campaign to win the hearts and minds of the masses. Yet since passive revolution did not establish an effective bourgeois government, whilst the communists had not succeeded in establishing their hegemony over other disgruntled social classes, the latter turned to Fascism. Gramsci's approach emphasizes the way subaltern groups are divided in many ways – by economic interests and their conditions of life, and by regional or ethnic differences – which are, in turn, *constructions* of identity which can be manipulated politically by elites. Many different sorts of alliances are therefore possible between different segments of the social elites and different segments of the subaltern classes. Hegemony, for Gramsci, is a *dynamic process*, and as Roseberry suggests, may be more usefully used as a tool to understand 'struggle' rather than 'consent' (Roseberry 1994: 360–1).

official trade union organizations which the post-revolutionary state created to control the working class. The state's response was, however, the characteristic one of arresting independent union leaders and supporting a further reduction in worker rights in a bid to encourage the flow of foreign capital south, so the immediate fruits of a more collective form of struggle were not positive. Furthermore, traditional Marxist notions of what a more adequate form of resistance to capitalism would be, centred on the notion of 'proletarian class consciousness', seem less plausible today than they might have done earlier in the history of capitalism. The peasant-proletarian migrant workers created by colonial capitalism have not turned out to be a historical anomaly or a phenomenon of transition, but precursors of a more general pattern in which the uprooting of the peasantry from the land has not led to 'classical' forms of proletarian existence. A certain renewal of the capacity of some rural people to 'resist' capitalism today owes much to the global environmental movement and a new global politics of indigenous rights, but most rural people live by a combination of farming and other activities which may include urban or rural small-scale commercial activities as well as migrant wage labour (Kearney 1996, Gledhill 1997).

Urban working-class families in the Third World also typically combine different ways of getting an income. A growing number of people not only find themselves excluded from the social role of a full-time, stably employed, wage labourer able to feed a family from the weekly pay-packet, but may never enjoy any form of official 'employment' at all, though they too are bombarded with images of a model modern lifestyle centred on the nuclear family unit and the 'culture of consumerism'. The contemporary growth of such 'social exclusion' adds salience to Jean Comaroff's historical-anthropological study of the Tshidi branch of the Twsana peoples of the South Africa-Botswana borderland.

The Tshidi were first brought into the orbit of capitalist 'civilization' by Methodist missionaries in the 1830s, were subjected to British overrule in the Bechuanaland protectorate in 1885, transferred to Cape Colony under the pressures of mining interests in 1895, incorporated into the Union of South Africa in 1910 and de-incorporated into the 'homeland' of Bophuthatswana by the apartheid regime in 1977 (Comaroff 1985: 23–39). They were consigned by the apartheid state to participate in a labour migration system in which lone males from diverse ethnic backgrounds congregated in urban centres in which they had no permanent place, whilst their families remained in the homeland[5] in poverty. Since the wages of migrant workers were purposely set below the level needed to meet minimal family subsistence costs, the Tshidi Twsana remained in the position of being an extreme type of 'peasant-proletarian'. Their marginalization was

---

5 Unless women themselves entered the world of the Whites as migrants independently of their husbands, as some did.

enhanced by the racist basis of their exclusion from 'South Africa' and ultimate 'inclusion' in what a majority saw as the illegitimate 'homeland' society of Bophuthatswana. Their response to growing alienation was a shift away from orthodox Methodism and the dissenting forms of Protestantism which were the precursors of African political nationalism,[6] towards the 'fundamentalist' Zionist Church.

Zionism originated among the urban poor of Chicago at the end of the nineteenth century. Although the meaning of Zionism and its practices to the Tshidi congregations must be understood in terms of the specific sociocultural forms which constitute it as a religion, it is of great significance that the image of Zion is a product of a *transnational* historical process, a diffusion 'from English nonconformity, through American fundamentalism, to the shantytowns and villages of the Third World' (ibid.: 254). Comaroff suggests that South African Zionism can be seen as part of a second, counterhegemonic global culture, part of a larger movement of symbolic orders which share an opposition to bourgeois liberal secularism and promise to subvert the divisive structures of colonial society. Each individual case is different, the product of contingent historical conjunctures between 'external agencies and specific local systems under particular circumstances' (ibid.). Nevertheless, broadly similar contexts produce a repetition of broadly similar developments, though they are not *precisely* identical, even within South Africa (ibid.: 256–7). This leads us, however, to the question of where, if anywhere, these supposedly counter-hegemonic movements lead. In the opinion of many Black intellectuals, the Zionist churches are 'utopian' sects which substitute for 'real' forms of struggle against class exploitation and racism and actually reproduce the material and symbolic forms of a neo-colonial system. They also sought accommodations with the apartheid regime.

Like Scott, Comaroff argues that the 'coded' nature of such forms of popular resistance reflects the 'realpolitik' of oppression,[7] and she denies that

---

6 The development of an African Independent Church movement is explicable in Benedict Anderson's terms. Methodist missions created a literate Black laity and a print culture in African languages through their Bible translations. This group could also advance socioeconomically as a class, within the severe constraints imposed by racist exclusion. The Independent Church movement developed in the early years of the twentieth century. Its offshoot in the Ethiopian Church combined 'the symbolism of a biblically-indexed millennium with an evolving African nationalism, itself cross-fertilized with the neatly overlapping ideology of Marcus Garvey – that blacks were the dispossessed of Ethiopia' (Comaroff 1985: 175). Although the discourses of the Independent Churches had some appeal to the proletariat, they did not 'contest the structure of the colonial order' but 'debated the place within it of the aspiring Black protestant elite' (ibid.: 176). With the development of the struggle around segregation and the Natives' Land Act, this elite focused on developing a 'secular' nationalist movement, but remained strongly influenced by *liberal* Christian ideology, stressing multiracial integration and free enterprise.

7 The mine compound, with its strong surveillance apparatus of police, spies and physical discipline, was not conducive to 'uncoded' forms of resistance. The apartheid system, with its tight control over Black movement in White areas, routinized diffuse forms of everyday repression to which diffuse responses were most appropriate (Comaroff 1985: 196).

they represent an 'apolitical escapism' for two basic reasons. Firstly, utopian movements frequently clash violently with secular political authorities, and this can have significant long-term implications for the stability of existing power structures. Comaroff notes that dismissal of such movements as 'utopian' and 'symbolic' reflects conventional Western divisions between politics and religion and thought and action, divisions which obscure the way that ritual practices, particularly those orientated towards healing the body, *can* promote a thoroughgoing rejection of dominant values and ideologies. This leads her to a second contention, that Tshidi Zionism constitutes a counter-culture which is the basis for a *kind* of 'working-class' oppositional consciousness. This is the consciousness not of a 'classical' working class, but of a large sector of marginalized people. It is therefore a *modern* form of consciousness which should not be seen as 'primitive' or 'pre-political' relative to another, more 'effective', politically and socially transformative, type of consciousness.

Sociological approaches to popular religion tend to be uninterested in their religious and ritual content since the existence of 'sects' is explained in terms of broad sociological processes like the 'dislocations' caused to 'traditional' social organization by urbanization. They are therefore often reduced to forms of group organization and identity-re-establishment concerned with 'adaptation' to a changing world. Similar views were also advanced by structural-functionalist anthropologists such as Mayer (1961) who shared sociologists' ideas about 'social order' and 'social change'. As Comaroff points out, other anthropological approaches have followed the idealist and intellectualist paths set by Weber, but such approaches fail to set the movements in any kind of meaningful politico-economic and cultural context (1985: 169).

It is important to analyse the content of such popular 'practices of resistance' in order to see what *kind* of impact they have on power relations, accepting that they do not pose an immediate threat to the stability of existing forms of social and political domination. Indeed, it is crucial not to think about these issues in terms of stability versus totalizing 'revolution', even where we are dealing with a counter-hegemonic culture whose tone is apocalyptic. After all, even 'real' social revolutionaries like Lenin and the Bolsheviks did not succeed in creating the societies of their imagination.

Zionism represents a phase in a longer history of relationships between religion and capitalism and politics in the region, which began with the entry of Methodist missionaries before the period of British overrule. The Methodists could to some extent be incorporated into the indigenous political system, but the missionaries blundered their way into inducing major political and social transformations by introducing the plough and digging wells for agricultural as well as domestic use (Comaroff 1985: 139). Since rain-making was central to indigenous chiefly authority, the missionaries' campaigns against the rituals engendered conflict between the mission and the indigenous political authorities which persisted until the office of chief was denuded of its remaining temporal as well as spiritual power by the colonial state.

The missionary project went deeper than simply converting the 'natives' to Christianity. Following E.P. Thompson (1967), Comaroff argues that the cultural logic of Protestantism 'mediated a protracted transformation of European social and productive systems' towards capitalism, and that Methodism was orientated towards inculcating a set of values and disciplines specifically associated with industrial capitalism (Comaroff 1985: 131). The missionaries dedicated themselves to instilling the regimentation of industrial capitalist civilization in the layout of the mission settlements and the fields, and in the timetabling and scheduling of both religious and secular activities. Yet they believed an agrarian route to civilization was more appropriate to the Tswana and promoted a commercialized peasant model of economic development which was ultimately to be undermined by colonial mining interests, the rinderpest pandemic of 1896, changes in transport systems and market networks and the Natives' Land Act of 1913. From the start, however, the new agricultural model changed Tshidi society. Men took on the role of drivers of plough teams, displacing women to a secondary place in agricultural production which reduced their influence over distribution of the product. 'Feminization' became an image of male social debasement as class differentiation increased (Comaroff and Comaroff 1992: 143). Production of commercial surpluses for the diamond fields by some farmers was accompanied by growth of clientage relations, proletarianization and land concentration, processes in which aristocratic families predominated (Comaroff 1985: 35–6, 148).

The impact of the missions was contradictory. The attempt to impose the cultural system of capitalism conflicted with indigenous principles, producing an opposition in Tshidi consciousness between *sekgoa* (the way of the white man) and *setswana* (Twsana tradition). The literate lay Tshidi elite associated with the mission identified itself with *sekgoa*, but it too objectified the elements of its new world-view in terms of concepts which resonated with pre-colonial ideas (ibid.: 144–5). Yet it was the confrontation between world-views that led the Tshidi to become *conscious* of the distinctive features of their own cultural order and *objectify* them in the category *setswana*. The indigenous political leadership found a way to resist mission control and encompass the evangelists within its own political order, yet this strategy created a minority which identified with the mission in opposition to the chief. The mission's impact on the local political economy both undermined politico-ritual mechanisms which reproduced allegiance to the centre and strengthened existing centrifugal tendencies in indigenous society (ibid.: 146).

The ability of the Tshidi to resist 'missionary imperialism' was undermined by the fact that the chiefs were forced to ally politically with the missionaries to secure British protection against annexation by the Boer Republic or the Cape Colony. The missions came to favour formal colonization to deepen the conversion process, whilst the Twsana chiefs sought it as a defence mechanism against still more profound changes. Both parties were rapidly overwhelmed by the superior power of other factions within the colonial regime. Commercial agriculture did not collapse entirely, but the combination of subsistence agriculture on eroded land coupled with labour migration replaced the missionary dream of a prosperous yeomanry. With the transition to 'the development of underdevelopment', personal experience came into sharper contradiction with the content of the Methodist ideological model, partly because of its sanctification of inequality and bourgeois interests, but also because of its spiritually unsatisfying ritual practice (ibid.: 166).

In particular, the new Churches centred on healing and the ritual reconstruction of the body, and parodied the insignia of Western protestant orthodoxy. In his analysis of the extended resistance of the pagan Kwaio of the Solomon Islands, Roger Keesing argues that parody enabled the Kwaio to use the semiology of European domination to frame a counter-hegemonic discourse based on 'emulation without deference':

> We find a sort of parody at two levels. First, running through the Kwaio texts, we find parody in a strict sense, a more or less intentional imitation of the semiology of the rulers, deployed as a sardonic mode of resistance ... Second, we find what is not really parody in a strict sense, but appears as such only in the eyes of the (Western) beholder: as where Malaitans, often Christian scribes acting on behalf of pagans, write documents they intend to be taken with legal seriousness in what they take to be legalistic language ... When I advised Folofo'u that the claim was not valid in terms of European or international law, his response was 'It's valid in terms of *our* law!': but Kwaio *loa*, so conceptualized, is constructed in opposition and correspondence to the law that has historically been invoked to end Malaitan autonomy. (Keesing 1992: 234)

The Kwaio were first incorporated into the British colonial world as plantation labourers taken to Queensland, Samoa and Fiji. The pivotal event of their colonial experience was the massacre of around a thousand Kwaio men, women and children by the 'punitive expedition' sent to avenge the killing of District Officer William Bell in 1927. Remaining obstinate pagans in a world where everyone else had converted to Christianity, the Kwaio nevertheless came to conceptualize their pagan-ness in terms of *Christian* discourse. A Kwaio priest, for example, adopted the sobriquet of 'Peter Satan'. The Christian Churches defined the people's ancestors as manifestations of the Devil, the old pagan world as one of darkness, and conversion as a process of rebirth, so the Kwaio fought that cosmology of Christian power by accepting its categories but inverting their meaning.

Jean Comaroff argues that the same 'irreverence' characterizes the Tshidi Zionist transformation of orthodox symbolic schemes in South Africa. The opposition between Zionism and orthodox Protestantism corresponded roughly to an illiterate peasant-proletarian/literate bourgeois-petty bourgeois class divide. Tshidi conceptions of social differentiation are not, however, couched in Marxist class terms – differential control of means of production – nor in purely economic terms. This is hardly surprising since education, literacy and race, as well as wealth, influenced life-chances (Comaroff 1985: 190). Nevertheless, the practices of one of her case studies, the Full Witness Church, do include attempts to reverse commoditization through the ritual processing of outside products and, through dance and divine healing, to realize a collective integration which defies the enforced personal and social differentiation imposed by the hegemonic structures of the outside world (ibid.: 218–19, 233).

The Church has a 'collection' of money, used to support the leader's domestic expenses, but the bulk of such support is provided in labour and foodstuffs. The ritualized deposition of coins in the jar suggests a negation of the commodity role of money (ibid.: 236). None of this removes the contradictions imposed on the congregation by the larger political-economic forces which compel them to live in a world in which social relations are negatively influenced by commoditization, but the ritual process does seem to express a desire to subvert the actual. Other Zionist Churches actually own and operate means of production collectively, but even the Full Witness Church goes some way towards countering individuation and privatization by encouraging pooling of assets. This assertion of collectivism is not, however, a return to the pre-colonial order. The organization of the Churches and their ritual practices constitute a *bricolage* of elements. What is most 'non-Western' about Zionism is the way the healing of the body is the healing of society and reconstitution of its relations. Comaroff argues that this process is counter-hegemonic in the sense that pre-colonial metaphors and images of bodily affliction were reworked to address the effects on the person of the social changes wrought by capitalism and the apartheid state (ibid.: 202). Yet core symbols of redemption and apocalypse derived from Christian traditions and both pre-colonial and colonial symbols were 'recycled' to create something new.

Similar principles apply to indigenous Catholicism in Latin America, which incorporated elements of European popular culture (Ingham 1986, Brading 1990). The *cofradías* (religious brotherhoods) were introduced by the Church as an instrument of spiritual conquest, but multiplied in an extra-official manner through indigenous initiative. The Indians used the images of the saints as oppositional symbols, denying the clergy control of them and asserting that they had belonged to the community from 'time immemorial'. The public ritual procession of saint images by Indians had more in common with popular European than indigenous pre-colonial practices. The ritual was used, however, to establish and defend frontiers between Indian and Spanish society (Gruzinski 1990), in just the same way as the Kwaio use colonial symbols and categories to build an 'invisible wall ... to defend and preserve a space within which the ways of the ancestors can be followed'

(Keesing 1992: 226). Dominated groups do not simply appropriate the symbols of the dominant order but subject them to powerful inversions.

Inversion, as Keesing points out, is not the same as 'strategic obliteration' of the semiology of colonialism, as when the Algerian revolutionaries suppressed the colonial 'ethnic' distinction between 'Arabs' and 'Berbers' or when Gandhi donned homespun to symbolize his counter-hierarchical style of leadership (ibid.: 238). Keesing's chosen examples in fact seem to demonstrate that even radical rejection of colonial semiology in oppositional discourse does not necessarily secure a transformation of social practices, since the old divisions and old styles of leadership were subsequently reactivated. Yet difference in subversive potential is clear and inversion without 'strategic obliteration' is certainly more subversive than Keesing's third possibility, 'reproduction in opposition' of the categorical structures of domination, as I can again show with a Latin American example.

Franciscan missions implanted European apocalyptic and millenarian visions into indigenous societies in Latin America. Yet the redemption which Andean peoples sought in eighteenth-century rebellions was one in which the Spanish and their allies amongst the indigenous elite were transformed (through symbolic inversion) into the Anti-Christ, to be swept away in a cosmic renewal which combined indigenous notions of cyclical time and world renewal with Christian traditions (Szemiński 1987). The Indian underclass would inherit the earth as the truly Christian community of suffering. Such examples may seem archetypal 'millenarian', 'pre-political', reactions to colonialism. Keesing argues, however, that although Melanesian cargo cults were millenarian in content and doctrine, they embodied a political analysis of European wealth and power (1992: 223), a point echoed by the Comaroffs (1992: 259–60). By these criteria, Andean rebellions were consciously 'political'. They aimed to destroy the colonial state and restore an indigenous socio-political order. They failed to achieve their goal, but left a legacy in historical memory and fed a counter-hegemonic indigenous historical consciousness which changed over the centuries and could manifest itself in the form of participation in more conventional political and class-based organizations in recent times.

This brings us back to Worsley's classic analysis of Melanesian cargo cults. Like Comaroff, Worsley argued that these millenarian movements were 'objectively' politico-religious movements (whatever the actors' conscious will and purpose) because they brought the participants into a clash with institutionalized authority (Worsley 1970: 312–13). In his reflections on theoretical criticisms of his original analysis, Worsley was careful to emphasize the variability of the cults, whilst standing firm against models that based themselves on concepts of 'cultural breakdown' without any reference to exploitation, oppression and indigenous senses of 'relative deprivation' (ibid.: 336–41). He suggested, however, that millenarian movements tended to give way over time to secularized nationalist movements in colonial countries and to class-based political organizations

elsewhere, since he saw them as essentially movements of the poor and marginalized (ibid.: 233). As the evolution of secular politics proceeds,
millenarian cults become both secondary in importance and change their
content. They become 'religions of the afflicted', orientated to the problems
of the individual (ibid.: 319). Comaroff, however, argued that Zionism had
counter-hegemonic significance precisely because it *was* a kind of class
movement, of the marginalized.

Even Melanesianists sympathetic to Worsley's approach have argued that
his evolutionary argument is invalid because a simple progression from cults
to a more inclusive nationalist movement was deflected by new forms of differentiation within the emerging national political community. Gerritsen,
for example, argues that poorer peasants develop communal groups
practising a politics of protest on the basis of an ideology of egalitarianism,
and suggests that these are closely connected to earlier cargo cults (Gerritsen
1982, cited in Rimoldi and Rimoldi 1992: 9). As Rimoldi and Rimoldi have
pointed out, however, this argument depicts 'the political rationality of
community as a development corresponding to a phase of political change
initiated by the state' (ibid.: 9). It cannot account for the specific cultural
practices through which people, as historical agents, respond to the contradictions they experience. In their view, the historical development of social
movements on Buka reveals neither a different set of rationalities charac-
terizing early and later movements nor a simple continuity of a general
'culture of resistance' because the actors have meaningful disagreements
amongst themselves about what to do in response to particular situations.
What Bougainvillians do have in common at any particular moment of time
is a shared historical experience and 'political commitments linking them to
past practices and to each other' (ibid.: 12).

The secessionist movement on Bougainville is a serious conflict, which
has cost thousands of lives. Nevertheless, the concept of 'resistance' in
general remains problematic. As Keesing reminds us, it is easy for the
observer to romanticize 'acts and stances which may have an oppositional
element' but which have other motives of personal gain and political
ambition (Keesing 1992: 216–17). Such motives are present among leaders
of even great 'millenarian' acts of defiance, and the leaders of 'revolutionary' movements do not necessarily (or even usually?) share their followers'
world-views.

Keesing argues that it is important that the *political* force of the kind of
resistance discussed by Comaroff for the Zionist cults is 'at least partly hidden
from the consciousness of the adherents', like the 'Devil' worship Taussig
(1980) describes as resistance to capitalism in the Bolivian tin mines. He
suggests that Kwaio resistance has passed through three dominant modes,
armed struggle and violent confrontation in the period before 1927, a phase
of ancestral revelation and religious cultism through the 1930s, and political
confrontation from the mid-1940s onwards. The third phase follows Kwaio
contact with US troops during the war, some of whom were people of colour

who were shocked by the racist brutality displayed by the British towards the Kwaio as a colonial people and plantation workers.

Although the 'religious' dimension focused on the ancestors remained an inseparable component of Kwaio 'political' action throughout, Keesing sees the 'religious' cultic phase as a *displacement* of the struggle, resulting from the impossibility of overt resistance (1992: 212). He views the Zionist cults as another example of deflection of resistance into religious forms, and argues that a broadly defined 'political' mode of resistance must be based on the existence of a 'subculture of subalternity, a collective code in which strategies for opposing domination and exploitation are communicated, shared, themselves represented ideologically' (ibid.: 214). Other modes of resistance have an impact on power relations, even if they are not based on a conscious analysis of systems of domination, but Keesing argues that only forms of resistance sustained by subaltern subcultures have the potential to 'radically transform' the structures, categories and logics of colonial discourse even as they seem to be internalizing them.

It does seem problematic to argue that forms of action which become 'political' because the state chooses to classify them as 'subversive' and represses those who participate in them have the same implications as movements which articulate a more direct and sustained counter-hegemonic politics. Yet as Keesing concedes, much oppositional thought is *reactive* (ibid.: 237). As Roseberry notes, parodic or not, 'the forms and languages of protest *must* adopt the forms and languages of domination in order to be registered or heard' (Roseberry 1994: 363–4). Structures of domination constrain the ways in which the dominated and oppressed *can* resist their condition. In the case of the Kwaio, the institutions of the colonial state had a powerful influence on the way subaltern groups could define their identities. Kwaio now try to control resources, patronage and political power as *Malaitans*, a social unit and ethnicity that did not exist in pre-colonial times, and they do so in opposition to a series of other pseudo-ethnicities. They also internalized Christian ideas about good and evil, light and dark, in relation to ideas about 'race' that introduce significant ambiguities into their 'subaltern culture of resistance'. 'Blackness' can be opposed positively to 'Whiteness' in a discourse of emancipation but it also figures as derogatory racist imagery applied by the Kwaio to non-White rivals and enemies.

Such processes often seem to be concerned with defending spaces of relative autonomy and dignity *within* oppressive social orders. Scott argues that even everyday and individualized forms of resistance have significant consequences for the way systems of domination are structured. It is true, for example, that the flight of Indians from indigenous communities towards towns and Spanish estates to escape the colonial labour draft had a significant impact on class structures and colonial state policy in the Andes (Larson 1988). This form of 'resistance', however, did not change the fundamental balance of class and ethnic power in the long term in a direction which was favourable to Indians and peasants. Chazan *et al.* (1992) argue that the political fabric in Africa is slowly being undermined by a plethora of forms of 'popular confrontation', many of which fall into Scott's 'everyday resistance' category. Again, however, this 'undermining' may ultimately merely provide the scenario for the replacement of one elite by another, more effective, dominant group. It is important to recognize the existence of 'hidden' processes of resistance, but it seems impossible to say anything useful about their consequences in isolation from a broader analysis of power relations.

Keesing's concept of 'subaltern subcultures' of resistance is attractive, and he emphasizes the way 'old forms acquire new meanings' in the practice of resistance. Yet the Rimoldis' analysis suggests that the historical reproduction of communities of resistance through practice involves moments of tension where a change of course is conceivable. Shifts generally occur in the world-views and consciousness of those doing the resisting as they pursue their struggles. In seeking terrain on which domination can be contested, as Keesing concedes, the evolving strategies of subaltern strata are shaped by the structures created by the dominant to implement their hegemony. This has several important implications.

Firstly, the production of a 'counter-identity' on the part of subaltern groups in the face of oppression may express *antagonism* but elites may be able to manipulate such reactive oppositional discourses to their own advantage. I discovered that the resident workers on a landed estate in Mexico represented themselves as the real base of the enterprise, and expressed a thinly veiled contempt for the administrators and foremen (Gledhill 1991: 84–5). This dignified their productive efforts in conditions of physical abuse and social humiliation, but involved a profound form of self-alienation, in which the hacienda appropriated the peons as much as the peons appropriated the hacienda. The majority of these estate workers opposed the revolutionary land reform.

Secondly, as Matthew Gutmann suggests, self-conscious acts of outright rebellion may have unintentional system-conserving qualities (Gutmann 1993: 85). Among the examples he cites is Eckstein's analysis of how everyday defiance of the law by citizens 'rationally rejecting authority' may enhance the stability of undemocratic regimes which thrive on corruption (Eckstein 1977).

Thirdly, it seems impossible to reduce power relations to a simple opposition between the dominators and dominated, as James Scott tends to do. In *Domination and the Arts of Resistance* (1990) Scott argues that all sub-ordinated groups create a 'hidden transcript' that is a critique of the dominant, but spoken behind their backs in places which are beyond the reach of their surveillance – in slave quarters or places where only poor people come to eat and drink, for example. In public interaction, the subordinate are constrained to talk to the dominant in a way that appears respectful of their power. By and large, observers therefore get a false perspective on subalterns that makes them seem to be passively accepting their place. Scott argues, however, that even in the public transcript we can find a kind of muted, disguised resistance in what subalterns say, which is about dignity and justice. Yet Scott's efforts to build a general theory of domination and resistance raise fundamental difficulties.

The first is that he erases all differences between different kinds of subaltern groups and situations: the same theory is supposed to apply to members of Indian scheduled castes, eighteenth-century plantation slaves in America, Maya Indians in Chiapas, and workers in US factories (Gal 1995: 415). There are enormous differences in the way such diverse groups were dominated, their experiences and their identities. There seems to be little space in this formulation for culture, history or, indeed, the 'internal politics' of subalterns (Ortner 1995: 177). As the Kwaio case illustrates, members of one subaltern group may invest considerable energy in differentiating themselves from other subaltern groups. In the case of the Caribbean, not only did Blacks differentiate themselves from Asians and vice versa, but island-born Blacks taunted new slaves arriving on the docks as 'savages' in a process of micro-differentiation in which all members of oppressed groups strove to carve out what spaces of dignity they might within the framework of White domination, giving rise to a pigmentocratic hierarchy of status in which distance from Blackness was the organizing principle (James 1993). This casts doubt on Scott's assumption that the 'hidden transcripts' emerge in an autonomous space where power does not enter, simply as a product of face-to-face interaction within subaltern communities. In this sense, Scott is more of a romantic than a conservative, wilfully ignoring the substantial body of evidence that shows that real subalterns resist some things whilst accepting others, and that resistance at one level can be accompanied by repressing other people.

As Susan Gal (1995: 420–1) points out, Scott uses a simple representational theory of language, in which the world and its realities are already there, unmediated by the structure of language itself. Yet various 'truths' about our world are already naturalized in the specific languages we need to use to talk about it. In English, for example, we have to make a real effort to say 'he or she' to avoid gender bias in talking about 'people' in general. As I have stressed, even direct protest is impossible without subalterns adopting certain categories originally imposed by dominant groups as a basis for struggle. No human situation or relationship exists independently of the meanings we ascribe to it and we need a more complex theory of meaning production than Scott offers.

This last point is underscored by Sherry Ortner's critique of the simple opposition between 'domination' and 'resistance'. Since the meaning of acts to actors changes in the course of their experience of struggle, Ortner argues that it is not important if actors are ambivalent about what they are doing and why they are doing it (Ortner 1995: 187). As the Comaroffs stress, much of what goes on within power relationships has this 'murky' quality (Comaroff and Comaroff 1992: 259). Quite clearly we need to avoid two kinds of conceptualizations about 'the resisting subject' which would be empirically and theoretically naive. Firstly, we have to recognize that subalterns are not a homogeneous group of people, but have their own politics and internal power relations. Not only do some subalterns dominate or brutalize other subalterns, but even small-scale local social movements often display internal conflicts and the very important category of people who do not participate in resistance movements are not necessarily collaborating with the dominant (Ortner 1995: 179). Secondly, it follows from this that individual subalterns do not display unitary senses of their own identity and uniform types of consciousness. Yet it is also clearly true that individual identities are shaped by various kinds of social and cultural processes, including categories that dominant groups seek to impose on people and which they *may* accept.

Spivak and some of the other writers that Ortner discusses have concluded from this that what we should be studying is how individuals accept or reject 'subject positions' assigned to them, and how they shift from one possible 'subject position' to another. The problem is that this shifting subject appears to have no agency, does not learn, develop or create anything. Ortner argues convincingly that what we lose sight of here is how people construct projects that *transform* who they are through social action and thus do gain a voice and in some ways change history.

As Brackette Williams (1991) demonstrates in a study of post-colonial Guyana, people cannot change history entirely in a manner of their own choosing. The Guyanese have built a post-colonial national identity in a way that reflects the efforts of different ethnic groups to retain their own specific identities. The post-colonial politics of cultural struggle in Guyana reflect a legacy of Anglo-European hegemony, and the struggles of individuals and groups to build new identities re-create ethnic and racial stereotyping, along with religious and class divisions. A colonial culture of domination remains a 'ghostly constraint' on contemporary Guyanese identity formation (Williams 1991: 257–8). Systems of shared meanings that divide Guyanese are reproduced in everyday social practice and even by political leaderships that claim to be struggling to get rid of the colonial legacy. Yet at the same time, Guyana and the Guyanese do, in other senses, 'move on' and no one group has succeeded in imposing a single framework of shared meanings on the post-colony.

Thus, although there is a clear logical difference between 'resistance' which is merely concerned with improving the terms of oppression and that which strives to implant a new socio-political order, only further analysis of an ethnographic kind can determine how far conscious projects of radical rejection actually transform structures and practices of domination. This is also true of less consciously radical forms of resistance which have unintended consequences because the state reacts to them in a repressive way. It is therefore ultimately undesirable to try to privilege the analysis of one kind of counter-hegemonic activity over another a priori. The argument cuts both ways, since privileging 'everyday resistance' may lead us to ignore the way actors can gain new confidence and horizons of struggle from the experience of defying the dominant by overt collective rebellion on a limited issue. The real issue is not one of deciding what is or is not 'real' resistance. We must analyse both the possibilities and limitations of individual acts and collective movements within particular historical contexts and larger fields of power relations.

5   POST-COLONIAL STATES: LEGACIES OF HISTORY AND PRESSURES OF MODERNITY

In this chapter, I focus on post-colonial states or the state systems of countries of the 'South'. To analyse any state structure, we need to look at how the actors in political systems exercise power. This entails closer examination of the relationship between class power in society and political power, and of political parties and other organizations, including the military, which may contest power in the 'high politics' of what I will later define as the 'official state' associated with the formal institutions of government. As we shall see, there may be other kinds of power relations hidden behind the formal facade of the 'official state'. It is difficult, however, to exclude 'the masses' entirely from the discussion. Not only may popular forces resist elite power in various ways, but elite groups may also mobilize support from below to compete with each other. Here it seems possible to make a distinction between elites which mobilize lower-class support through particularistic, local or regional, clientship ties, and those which mobilize a mass base in national society, either by appealing to the 'citizenry' in general or to a particular social class, most notably the working class. Such distinctions can, however, be deceiving.

Regimes that claim to be 'democratic' may still harvest votes through patronage and the distribution of material bribes in return for electoral support. The Indonesian Communist Party (PKI) under Sukarno proclaimed a class-based, revolutionary theory, but recruited members in the countryside through 'traditional' patronage relations between peasants and landlords (Scott 1976). Downwardly mobile children of the old mandarinate provided much of the communist leadership in China and Vietnam (Wolf 1969). As we shall see in the next chapter, the whole notion that political life develops on the basis of the 'representation of class interests' is questionable. Although the development of the British Labour Party, for example, was related to the growth of an industrial proletariat, from the start the party combined affiliating workers through their trade unions with individual membership, in a bid to draw in middle-class people. The 'working class' is as much a *product* of political representation as the reverse, and working people do not necessarily identify with the parties which claim to represent them.

In Britain, what Tony Blair redefined as 'Old Labour' did at least develop out of popular struggles and many working people saw the party as a crucial step towards consolidating their rights. In Brazil, however, a 'workers' party' (the Brazilian Labour Party, PTB) was created 'from above' by the populist dictator Vargas in 1945, as a means of preserving the authoritarian state and preventing working-class organizations disrupting capitalist development (Cammack 1991).

'Populism' is an important concept in the analysis of politics in Latin America and many other parts of the world. It contrasts the kind of political representation of the 'working class' represented by the PTB in Brazil, Peronism in Argentina or the APRA (American Popular Revolutionary Alliance) in Peru, with a supposedly more 'authentic' form of working-class political representation that develops 'from below'. Populism is based on middle-class leadership that builds a mass base by promising working people jobs and social benefits, using a discourse that tends to be patriotic and anti-imperialist. Bryan Roberts explains the development of populism in Latin America as follows:

[Populist] regimes solve the problems confronting capital at a particular stage of its development. This stage occurs at a time when industrial interests are becoming predominant in the economy, but when their power is not sufficiently consolidated to enable them either to incorporate other groups through economic benefits or coerce them through control of the state apparatus. (Roberts 1978: 68–9)

Roberts's aim here is to explain the links between populist politics and the development of 'official' trade unions in cases like Brazil. The Vargas regime sought to industrialize Brazil and end dependence on export agriculture. It concentrated on organizing industrial workers rather than the economically marginalized. Roberts's model does not, however, seem appropriate for regions like the Middle East, where 'populist' regimes did appeal to the urban poor, mobilizing them through anti-Western or Islamic revitalization ideologies urging the need for cultural, national and political reconstruction (Gilsenan 1982, Chehabi 1990, Abrahamian 1991). As we will see later, populism in Africa also needs a different explanation.

Even in Latin America, we should see populist leaderships as independent political actors with their own agendas rather than as problem-solvers for a weak industrial bourgeoisie. They emerged from the middle sectors of the social hierarchy which were denied a share of power and recognition as social equals by established elites but possessed some autonomous power. This is why the army has provided so many populist leaders. Since the export-orientated economy was the basis for the power of the old elites, change to a nationalist economic model based on industrialization and political control over the working class made purely political sense. There were, however, differences between the strategies for economic 'modernization' pursued by different populist regimes, which reflected the role of lower- as well as upper- and middle-class actors in shaping politics. Between 1934 and 1940, Mexico's President Cárdenas, for example, aimed to create a dynamic commercial agriculture through state-backed peasant cooperatives rather

than large-scale capitalist farming. Cárdenas also pushed forward industrialization and brought workers' organizations under state control, but
Mexico's populism drew heavily on the support of peasants as well as the
urban working class, whereas Vargas made no attempt to reform the
agrarian sector.

   We can, however, relate the rise of populism in Latin America to economic
change in a different way. Cammack (1991) argues that export-orientated
oligarchies were unable to cope politically with the social changes produced
by the export-orientated model of development. By the end of the 1930s,
even countries like Guatemala had developed a significant urban political
opposition (Dunkerley 1988). As Roberts suggests, they had weak industrial
bourgeoisies. Given the entrenched power of landowning and mercantile
dominant classes, the state would generally prove the main vehicle for
economic restructuring. Yet different paths of political development were
possible. In Guatemala, an alliance of businessmen not tied to the export
trade, artisans, professionals and workers, brought a reformist government
to power in 1944, to be overthrown by a CIA-backed coup ten years later,
after it embarked on a land reform which threatened the interests of the coffee
growers and the American United Fruit Company.

   Finding populism too vague a concept, other analysts have labelled Latin
American regimes 'bureaucratic-authoritarian' and 'corporate' states
(O'Donnell 1986). Yet typologies need to be complemented by other styles of
analysis if they are to help us to understand variation and change, as I will
demonstrate by discussing a survey of African state forms. Chazan *et al.* work
in the fields of political science and international relations, but their
theoretical framework draws them closer to the interests of anthropologists
in the sense that they adopt a 'political interaction' approach in which the
relationship between state and civil society is central (Chazan *et al.* 1992:
22–3). By modelling political process in terms of power transactions
involving a diversity of other actors, ranging from individuals to multina-
tional companies, they raise useful questions about the dynamics of change
in African politics, though many of the answers they offer may still be
challenged from an anthropological perspective.

REGIME VARIATION IN POST-INDEPENDENCE AFRICA

Chazan *et al.* define six 'major types' of state-regime. Some states have
belonged to different categories at different moments in their history, and
the types themselves do not represent a developmental sequence. All typol-
ogizing provokes arguments about which boxes are most appropriate for
particular cases, but here I want to focus on the concepts underlying
the boxes.

Administrative-hegemonic Regimes

These have existed at one time or another in most African countries. The leader and his close advisers make the main policy decisions, but such regimes do not entirely exclude ethnic, regional, class and other leaders from the decision-making process. The military is controlled politically, the bureaucracy is allowed to make technical decisions, and bureaucracy and judiciary maintain a certain autonomy vis-à-vis each other (ibid.: 137–8). Thus, the personal power of the leader is predominant, but exercised in an *inclusionary* way. In Kenya, for example, Kenyatta brought into his cabinet leaders of ethnic-regional groups other than his own, the Kikuyu, and allowed factions to bargain with each other within the cabinet and ministerial structure. The carrot of judicious allocation of public resources to different interest groups was, however, balanced by the stick of threatening repression against disaffected groups that expressed outright opposition to decisions.

Kenyatta's successor, Daniel arap Moi, shifted to a less inclusionary strategy in the 1980s, favouring his own close associates at the cost of offending major regional leaders. Moi's regime thus had to rely more on repression. Although he survived violent protests to be re-elected for a fourth term at the end of 1992, after conceding demands for a return to multi-party politics, and remained in power at the end of the decade, Amnesty International continued to accuse the Kenyan government of direct complicity in ethnically based political violence which killed 15,000 people and displaced more than 300,000 between 1991 and 1994.[1]

Cameroon provides another example of how ethnic and religious divisions can be handled pre-emptively by incorporating regional elites into the regime. The authoritarian and northern Muslim President Ahidjo selected Paul Biya, a Catholic from the centre-south, as his prime minister. Biya then chose a northerner as his own successor when he succeeded Ahidjo as president (Bayart 1980). This attempt to alternate supreme power between regions did not work smoothly: conflict between Ahidjo and Biya led to a coup attempt in 1984. Nevertheless, although Biya treated the coup leaders severely, he persevered with the policy of coalition and inclusion.

The material basis for this kind of politics is the construction of patron–client networks and distribution of state resources and offices to the different leaders incorporated into the regime. Loyalty is secured through the way participation in the regime bolsters leaders' personal wealth and local power. Administrative-hegemonic regimes actively encourage foreign investment, but prove capable of bargaining over the terms of foreign capital's penetration of their economies. Any advantages secured for 'the nation' by such bargaining are, however, mainly restricted to the elite groups

---

1 *Kenya: Abusive Use of the Law: Koigi wa Wamwere and Three other Prisoners of Conscience on the Trial for their Lives* (AI Index: AFR 32/15/94).

'managing' the state, whilst workers and small farmers receive few concessions (Chazan *et al.* 1992: 140). Not only does this generate 'development' with a class bias, but, as we shall see, the possibility of practising such a politics deteriorated in many parts of Africa during the 1990s.

Using economic resources to foster elite cohesion may promote political stability, but has its disadvantages. Not only are national leaders and privileged cliques accused of squandering foreign aid and the tax revenues generated by foreign investment for personal ends, but even the competence of ministers is compromised when each faction has to be assigned its portion of power according to strictly political criteria.

Pluralist Regimes

Pluralism is an intensely problematic concept. Chazan *et al.* identify pluralist regimes with the preservation of a notion of separation of powers between the executive, legislature and judiciary, 'checks and balances', multi-party political institutions and 'fairly vibrant representative structures'. They suggest that although pluralism in this sense was tried and failed in most African countries immediately after independence, it resurfaced in the 1990s. Chazan and her co-authors conceded, however, that even the con-temporary regimes that they saw as best exemplifying their pluralist type – Senegal, Botswana and Gambia – remained 'elitist'. Gambia in fact suffered a military coup in 1994, not returning to civilian rule for four years. The shock waves of the Gambia coup were felt in neighbouring Senegal, whose governments have also continued to face defiance from a separatist movement in the southern province of Casamance through the 1990s. Within 'pluralist' regimes, resource allocation underpins patronage structures and protects the position of the dominant. Although parliamen-tarians and political 'big men' in government remain dependent on their constituencies and are subject to periodic popular scrutiny, mechanisms for overseeing bureaucratic behaviour are underdeveloped. The countries which have best approximated pluralism in the past have been small and homogeneous. 'Pluralist phases' have not endured in larger countries because any group which tries to incorporate larger segments of the population into the political process faces severe problems in controlling rival elite factions (Chazan *et al.* 1992: 141). This is a pluralism without a substantial non-elite participation, a less centralized way of conducting the intra-elite bargaining process in a system held together by sharing out spoils.

Party-mobilizing Regimes

Regimes such as Ghana under Nkrumah, Guinea under Sekou Touré, Tanzania under Nyerere, Zimbabwe under Mugabe and Algeria under

Boumedienne are grouped in this category. They differ from administrative-hegemonic regimes in that power is centralized around a leader heading a party of the state associated with an ideology. The party permeates the bureaucratic apparatus and legal system, and the system is more exclusionary. Elites and groups not included in the party may even be attacked and eliminated. Greater domestic elite dissent is countered by mobilizing popular support for the regime by appeals to socialist and/or nationalist ideologies, coupled with repression. Chazan *et al.* suggest that the weakness of party-mobilizing regimes in Uganda and Ghana lay in the difficulties of sustaining a monopolistic ruling coalition, while Tanzania's less traumatic experience of a voluntary change in leadership in 1985 reflected Nyerere's skills as the leader of a one-party system which allowed unusual scope for competition (ibid.: 142).

The role of the leader is not, however, the whole story, as I can demonstrate with the case of Algeria. Boumediennism was, as Chazan *et al.* point out, of a 'socialist predisposition', but it was also an Algerian version of a Nasserite, anti-colonial nationalism. The 'nation' which Boumedienne defined as the new identity of the territory the French invented was defined as Muslim and *Arab*, that is, as *not Berber*. This provoked a Kabyle backlash that exploded into a general strike and rioting in 1979, a year after Boumedienne's death, which in turn provoked *arabisants* and *françisants* reactions amongst the intellectual elite. That set the stage for the development of the Islamic 'fundamentalist' movement that produced the political crisis of 1992 (Howe 1992).

The FLN was already moribund as a 'party-mobilizing' regime by the time of Boumedienne's death in 1978. Algeria's high rate of population growth, problems of corruption in a heavily state-controlled economy, and public clamour for greater press freedom and removal of the dead hand of the FLN from social life had sealed its fate before Chadli Bendjedid began to dismantle the ossified one-party structure. Nevertheless, Chadli could not reap any benefit from his role. The economic situation worsened as the effects of being caught in the international debt-trap of the 1980s were amplified by the fall in oil prices, and Chadli's purges of the party and military hierarchy provoked antagonism from those who lost their sinecures.

The legalization of multi-party politics brought not pluralism but crisis. The army, increasingly the power broker after 1978, annulled the 1991 elections to block the rise of the Islamic Salvation Front (FIS). It is therefore important to look beyond the skills (or lack of skills) of leaders to understand the rise and fall of regimes of this type. Boumedienne's regime revealed long-term weaknesses general to all such regimes, including those of Eastern Europe, but its specific character influenced the way in which it disintegrated. With the tacit support of Western European governments, led by the old colonial power, France, the Algerian military spent the 1990s waging a low-intensity war against the Islamic movement. Political violence escalated to new heights after voters approved a new constitution in 1996, banned Islamic parties and granted dictatorial powers to retired general Zeroual, following his re-election as President the previous year. The turn-out was a suspicious 79 per cent, higher than in Algeria's first democratic elections. By the end of the decade, some progress had been made towards a political system in which different non-Islamic parties could compete for power, and modest gains had been made in making government institutions and politicians more accountable. Yet violence continued, and the military retained substantial power behind the scenes. What changed most profoundly was that the government could declare 1999 'the year of privatizations'.

Party-centralist Regimes

Chazan *et al.* distinguish these from the 'party-mobilizing' type by virtue of their stronger centralization and intervention in the organization of civil society and economic life. They subordinate the administrative apparatus more profoundly to the party and frequently depend on the backing of the military, itself controlled by the party in cases such as Angola (1992: 145). Such regimes generally refuse to bargain with opposition factions in their regions (as witness, in particular, the case of Ethiopia), but both Angola and Mozambique faced intractable problems of external support for armed opposition movements, which forced accommodations with South African regional power. In the case of Angola, economic problems brought accommodations with transnational capital as well. In Ethiopia, regional armed opposition wore down Mengistu's army and produced the regime's collapse.

The case of Angola does not, however, fit the analysis offered by Chazan *et al.* too well, since it is a case where a transition from one 'type' of regime to another is undertaken by the ruling party itself. The dos Santos government, now deprived of support from Cuba and the Soviet Union, proved it enjoyed substantial popular support in elections generally judged 'free and fair'. It also moved away from party-centralism and a state-run economy, only to face a revival of military opposition from Savimbi's UNITA after the latter failed at the polls. Yet despite the intervention of a UN peace-keeping force in 1994, conflict between UNITA and the government resumed at the end of 1998, reducing the areas outside Luanda to zones of high-intensity conflict. A June 1999 US consular office advisory warned any citizens foolhardy enough to plan a visit to the country that even in the capital 'police officers, often while still in uniform, frequently participate in shakedowns, muggings, carjackings and murders'. This pattern of state transformation is not, as I show later in this chapter, peculiar to Angola (although it is particularly tragic in what was Portugal's richest colony).

The lesson to be drawn from the Angolan case is that problems of 'governability' cannot be laid entirely at the door of party-centralist regimes themselves. The MPLA was given little chance to 'accommodate' an opposition backed by South Africa and the West. The shape of Angolan politics was determined by the particular conditions of that country's late decolonization. Differences in the class basis of the coalitions that came to power in struggles for national liberation in different countries are related to local social and political-economic differences as well as to the policies of the colonial power and the manner of its withdrawal. These differences cannot be grasped in terms of rigid typological categories. This argument also implies that political conflict in countries like Angola cannot be explained simply in terms of the malign interventions of outside forces, but it would be hard to ignore the continuing role of relations with the West in Africa's unfolding political crises.

Personal-coercive Regimes

In personal-coercive regimes, such as Amin's Uganda and Bokassa's Central African Republic, the bureaucracy, political machinery and judicial system were 'subjugated to the whims of the leader backed by military force' (Chazan *et al.* 1992: 147). Even the creatures of the leader may find his affections inconstant. Chazan and her co-authors observe, however, that such regimes tend to be transitory, an exception being Mobutu in Zaire, who 'routinized' his patrimonialism through the creation of a coterie of loyal followers. They also argue that a style of leadership that patrimonializes and privatizes the public arena and its institutions tends to provoke civil discontent in Africa wherever it develops. This is certainly evident, for example, in the images of such rulers in popular political satire, which tend to stress the linked metaphors of over-indulgence of the stomach and sexual appetites, explicitly confronting an ideal of a sound public administration and government with the deformations of patrimonialism (Toulabor 1993). We should also note, however, that such patrimonial African leaders have frequently enjoyed the personal support of leaders of European democracies.

Populism in Africa

Populist regimes in the Chazan *et al.* typology include Ghana under Jerry Rawlings, Qaddafy's Lybia and Thomas Sankara's Burkina Faso. 'Populism' here has slightly more positive connotations than in Latin America. It has not only been associated with attempts to incorporate non-elite groups, such as professionals and technocrats, into the political process, but with greater scrutiny of public administration by popular organizations like Ghana's people's defence committees and workers' defence committees (Chazan *et al.* 1992: 148). These changes did not, however, displace existing patron–client networks and factional alliances. Leaders like Sankara and Rawlings were military men from outside the traditional party-elite structures. They found it difficult to consolidate a broad base of support, and tended to condone abuses by their lieutenants (ibid.: 166). Although populist regimes brought new organizations recruiting students, young working people and the rural disadvantaged onto the political stage, they did not empower them sufficiently to institutionalize a new political order.

The material basis for unifying national states in Africa has been the patron–client networks forged by elites. World recession and the imposition of structural adjustment policies by the World Bank and IMF have made it more difficult to keep these systems functioning. Chazan *et al.* argue that central control has weakened where local leaders controlling non-state resources find themselves able to offer more than the central elite is now able to offer (ibid.: 182). Nevertheless, central power may still respond by increasing coercion (Rowlands and Warnier 1988) and reductions in state-controlled resources may simply alter the way patronage systems work. Populist political challenges may undermine elite cohesion without altering the basic mechanisms for building and consolidating power relations. Chazan and her co-authors suggest, however, that there may be deeper challenges at work, at the level of the 'deep politics' of the relationship between state and civil society.

In insisting that this 'level' is important, Chazan *et al.* reflect a more general trend in Africanist political science, inspired, in particular, by the work of Jean-François Bayart (1986). Africa presents the paradox that the post-colonial state is both 'overdeveloped' and 'soft', strongly authoritarian and yet unable to avert crisis (Geschiere 1988: 35). Bayart argues that this reflects the limitations of the state's hegemony over a recalcitrant civil society (1986: 113), and that we need to look at politics 'from below' to appreciate the active role played by often invisible 'popular modes of political action'. This takes us back to the discussion of 'resistance', and it has reawakened wider interest in what anthropologists might contribute to the study of state formation in Africa.

DEEP POLITICS: THE STATE AND CIVIL SOCIETY

Although they acknowledge the influence of Bayart, Chazan *et al.* use the phrase 'forms of popular protest' rather than his 'popular modes of political action'. These cover a wide range of phenomena: legal and illegal small-scale economic activity beyond the range of state control, job absenteeism and tax evasion, popular arts, religious revivals and anti-witchcraft movements, refusal to vote and clandestine political activity. Chazan *et al.* argue that such forms of 'protest' are largely 'coping mechanisms' and express themselves as much through 'quiet alienation and passivity' as confrontation. Nevertheless, they also feel that they have the objective consequence of wearing down the continent's existing political fabric. States cannot really control such dissidence: it is too disorganized and sporadic to respond to systematic repression, and, in contrast to more organized factional political conflicts, cannot be stopped by buying off leaders (Chazan *et al.* 1992: 207). In the short term, they suggest that popular protest has done nothing more than 'underscore disintegration'. Yet they are also sympathetic to a more positive view of its potential long-term impact, arguing that it reflects the stirrings of an African civic consciousness based on 'customary notions of political obligation such as trusteeship, probity and public accountability' (ibid.).

As Peter Geschiere observes, however, the 'effectivity' of unstructured and 'invisible' forms of popular action is ambiguous. They are harder for the state to combat, but 'less specific in their effects' because 'they lack a consistent organization and are less able to express a counter-hegemonic project' (Geschiere 1988: 37). This kind of argument about 'reactive' forms of popular resistance is already familiar from Chapter 4. Chazan and her colleagues draw no firm conclusion about where African polities might ultimately be headed as a result of 'wearing down of the existing political fabric', and pose only two possibilities – 'rehabilitation of authoritarian state structures' or 'a broader process of democratization'. They see civil unrest primarily as a problem of 'governability' in conventional political science terms, and appear relatively untroubled by working within Western liberal definitions of 'democracy'.

In this respect their perspective stops short even of the position of Bayart, let alone more radical approaches that I consider later in this section. Bayart challenged the idea that we should look for symptoms of awakenings of 'democracy' as it is understood in Western terms in Africa, arguing that state power in the region might be limited by forms of 'political accountability' other than formal democracy. The starting-point of his analysis is the distance between state and civil society in Africa and the 'totalizing' hegemonic project of the state:

Underlying the ideologies of national unity there is a hegemonic imperative which drives the state and the self-proclaimed dominant social groups to seek to control and shape civil society. The first task is to define the basis on which others can gain access to the political system. Most regimes severely restrict such access by preventing the autonomous and pluralistic organisation of subordinated social groups. Instead, rulers either attempt to integrate the various social forces into single movements or set up intermediary and indirect means of control. Their objective is to enlist the dominated social groups within the existing space of domination and to teach them to be subject to the state. The aim is to administer society, even against itself, and to order it according to the explicit, ideal canons of modernity. Thus the African post-colonial state is a 'well-policed' state (*policeystaat*), relatively close in conception to the enlightened despotisms of the seventeenth and eighteenth centuries. (Bayart 1986: 113)

Bayart observes that state coercion in Africa is to be found in more 'pluralist' regimes as well as the most centralized. Irrespective of political ideologies and regime type, the state is the dominant economic agent and channel of accumulation. State accumulation is intimately connected with individual accumulation, directly, since power means wealth, and indirectly, since private businessmen generally need to operate through political channels in order to do business. Both the 'private' and the 'public' sectors are 'instruments of the dominant class striving to establish its hegemony' (ibid.: 116). Bayart also notes that it is far from clear that the principal object of African politics is power rather than wealth (ibid.: 123). Where autonomous indigenous business classes formed (Nigeria, Kenya, Senegal and Cameroon), this did strengthen civil society. Yet the Cameroonian business class supported the coup against Biya in order to conserve the benefits they had received from Ahidjo's 'patrimonial largesse', threatened by Biya's attempts to open up the political system.

Bayart argues that the legacy of colonialism was not simply a tradition of administrative and coercive authority but a heterogeneous and discontinuous civil society. Attempts to unify this heterogeneity in an organized way to challenge existing regimes within the African context simply replace one form of state domination with another because what is at issue is merely access to the state. Authoritarian norms of political organization characterize movements of opposition, and atomization and disunity remain inherent in all such mobilizations. The backbone of all African states – independently of ideologies and regime types – is the bureaucracy. Bureaucracy, by providing a minority with social mobility, has acquired a power to integrate and mediate the state–civil society divide. This is a crucial point for understanding the values that orientate 'civic consciousness' in Africa and many other parts of the world.

We must ask whether people consider it undesirable for officials to help their kin, or use their position to accumulate wealth. That such things can be subjects of popular protest may reflect only antagonism to exclusion and excess, rather than objections of principle. Bayart's position is broadly pessimistic on the issue of the possibilities for formal political democracy. He argues that the creation of small collectives controlled by local urban and rural associations has a greater democratizing potential than parliaments and parties. Since, however, he argues that concepts like class are too analytically rigid for use in contexts like Africa, his notion of 'popular' groups remains vague (Geschiere 1988: 39). This does not help us to identify specific circumstances and groups that might produce more effective counterhegemonic projects.

Populism may mobilize notions of public accountability embedded in popular political culture in Africa. Yet in the light of Bayart's analysis it is even less clear that such movements could eliminate 'corruption' – the practical means of making public life 'work' at all levels – and serve as the basis for new political institutions. It seems unlikely that there could be any simple revenge of 'civil society' over the elitist and authoritarian states that have reinforced the impact of global power inequalities and Western cynicism on the continent's growing miseries.

This theme has been pursued in anthropological studies of a particularly diffuse 'popular mode of political action', witchcraft and sorcery (Geschiere 1988, Rowlands and Warnier 1988). Sorcery accusations are not simply a reactive 'protest' but central to power relations in Africa. As Rowlands and Warnier put it, 'manipulating the threat or reality of sorcery ... is integral to the local strategies for equalizing wealth and making elites honour their kinship obligations' (1988: 131).[2] At the same time, African elites fail to counter this threat by carrying through the sustained kind of anti-witchcraft offensive associated with state consolidation in seventeenth-century Europe, despite frequent official condemnations of sorcery practices (Geschiere 1988: 54–5). Elite attitudes remain ambiguous because elites manipulate sorcery beliefs to strengthen their own power. Village-born urbanized elites in Cameroon invest in a modernized and costly sorcery apparatus which is not simply designed to impress villagers with their immunity from attack, but figures in intra-elite political competition (ibid.: 47–9). Even the mightiest, like ex-President Ahidjo, are 'heavily armed by occult forces' (ibid.: 57).

Sorcery therefore plays an ambiguous structural role: it represents a force menacing elites from below and a force elites turn back on those they dominate. Geschiere argues that this ambiguity reveals the truth of Bayart's claim that 'totalizing' African state regimes have been unable to complete their conquest of civil society. Yet the ambiguity also seems to express the limits of society's capacity to civilize the exercise of power.

POWER RELATIONS IN THE SHADOW STATE

The experience of some African countries, in particular Sierra Leone, Liberia and Zaire (renamed the Democratic Republic of Congo [DROC] in the post-Mobutu era), might suggest that efforts to 'civilize the exercise of power' proved increasingly futile in the second half of the 1990s, and a 'disintegration' scenario increasingly significant. It is true that Charles Taylor's regime in Liberia legitimated itself through elections in 1997 (without securing social pacification), and that the West Africa Intervention Force, ECOMOG, was formed as a regional peace-keeping agency, albeit with controversial results on the ground. Yet Uganda, once a success-story for the restoration of democracy and economic reconstruction, was showing signs of increasing instability by the end of 1998, in part because of its government's support for insurgent forces in the DROC. Nigeria faced continuing problems of civil unrest and low-level regional insurgency and presented visitors with the same kinds of personal security problems as Angola, Liberia or Sierra Leone.

---

2 The most powerful form of sorcery among the Maka is that which comes from inside the 'house' or family and it is this that villagers who have become part of the urban elite (*évolués*) fear most (Geschiere 1988: 45).

Kidnappings of foreigners became more frequent, whilst citizens and visitors alike had to contend with the threats posed by armed bands of police, soldiers and 'bandits' posing as, or operating in collusion with, police or soldiers. Yet neither 'state disintegration' nor 'banditry' (the term favoured by the US State Department and British Foreign Office) give us an adequate purchase on these apparent symptoms of mounting disorder.

Paul Richards's analysis of the Sierra Leonean civil war offers a good example of what anthropologists might say in response to conventional thinking about African politics (Richards 1996). Richards charts the way the 1992 coup by young army officers started well and ended badly, as the occupying forces in the rainforest zone succumbed to the temptations of diamond smuggling and regular troops began to dress as rebels of the Revolutionary United Front (RUF) and plunder impoverished villagers (Richards 1996: 14). By 1992 the full impact of IMF-imposed 'structural adjustment' and shifting donor country priorities in an era of global capitalist restructuring had worked itself out. Elites could no longer construct effective power relations simply by controlling the institutions of the official state, even if they helped themselves to what remained of foreign aid budgets and stole tax revenues to reward their clients. The only place effective power relations could now be built was within a 'shadow state' linked to 'informal markets,' in particular, illegal diamond mining in the case of Sierra Leone. These processes are best seen not as a *collapse* of the state but a *transformation of the forms of state power*, and they were, as Richards shows, a product of Sierra Leone's relations with the North Atlantic powers. Firstly, urban-biased Western development policies destroyed rural subsistence economies; secondly, the withdrawal of De Beers and other transnational mining companies from Sierra Leone did not end their role as price fixers in the international market, which ensured the continuing profitability of diamond smuggling (ibid.: 48–52). Richards concludes that it is pointless for Western powers to seek to rebuild the institutions of the 'official state' under these conditions. Showering further resources on 'democrats' in Freetown (and re-training the army) would not address the real 'development' problems of the Sierra Leonean rainforest zone, whilst the mechanisms of shadow state power would continue to shape the practice of politics 'on the ground'.

The relationship with the West is central to Sierra Leonean history. Western powers have been extracting resources through violence and trade since Freetown was founded in the eighteenth century. The country was created by Black servicemen who fought in the British army in the American War of Independence and wished to be resettled in Africa. As a product of transnational processes, the country has a creole or hybrid culture that reflects its historical place in the 'Black Atlantic' world (Gilroy 1993). Richards provides convincing evidence that the RUF rebels from the rainforest wish to be 're-included' in that 'modern' world in a material sense and are still part of it in an ideological sense, a point I consider in more depth in Chapter 7.[3] The importance of not seeing the current Sierra Leonean crisis as a consequence of contemporary conditions alone has been emphasized even more strongly by William Reno (1995), who offers a detailed analysis of how the foundations of the 'shadow state' were laid in the colonial period.

Reno argues that a 'state-centred' analysis focused solely on recent crisis obscures the long-term relations between control of informal markets and the exercise of political power in a context shaped by the country's place in the global economy. For Reno, the shadow state represents an alternative *institutionalization* of power in which private and political circuits of accumulation reinforce one another (Reno 1995: 183). His approach suggests that we should not expect moves towards Western ideals of 'good governance', that the apparent 're-institutionalization' of a 'democratic' framework in cases such as Liberia may be an illusion, and that systems based on shadow power relations may persist over an extended period. Many of the political actors in the shadow state are striving to accumulate wealth in circuits that are tied to the global economy and their power networks may include foreign companies. This makes them vulnerable to changes in fields of political and economic power far beyond their immediate field of action and control. Yet, Reno insists, against the grain of more optimistic prognoses for Africa's political futures, the local social power of shadow state actors is such as to throw doubt on the capacity of an untainted and romanticized 'civil society' to enforce political reform and accountability.

'DEMOCRATIZATION' IN LATIN AMERICA

Latin America shares Africa's history of 'overdeveloped' authoritarian regimes and crisis. Yet many commentators at the beginning of the 1990s felt that the collapse of military regimes and adoption of neoliberal policies by their civilian successors offered the prospect of a genuine 'democratic transition', based exactly on this kind of 'strengthening of civil society'. Even some of those who remained more sceptical about any shift to formal

---

3 This does not, however, mean that the politics of the rebels is necessarily fully coherent at any level – whether we are talking about the leaders or the young people who are the fighters. It remains unclear whether the rebels want an end to patrimonial styles of government or a return to a more even-handed patrimonialism in which resources are more widely distributed through society. The movement sometimes sounds as if it is advocating radical egalitarianism and direct democracy, sometimes simply the rule of law, better roads and renewed access to public education and social mobility. Sometimes it looks as if the destruction of the state is seen as a kind of catharsis from which a new society might emerge (Richards 1996: 58–9). Any of these projects might seem meaningful to individuals, depending on the conjuncture; different rebels may have different visions, and none of what may seem to us to be mutually exclusive alternatives may be seen in these terms by the actors themselves.

democracy in which the military retained backstage power concluded that peace agreements between the states and guerrilla movements of Central America would open a new chapter for that region (Wilson 1993a, Dunkerley 1994).

Caution seems justified by developments in the second half of the decade. Electoral competition between political parties is now flourishing in most Latin American countries, and there are developments in the field of human rights and indigenous rights politics in the region that should not be dismissed lightly. Civic movements demanding the rule of law and greater accountability are pressing challenges to older styles of governance. Yet movements of the Right are as active as those of Centre and Left, and civic activists and journalists from independent newspapers still face serious personal risks. Another important development is the way in which national non-governmental organizations of various kinds, including indigenous rights organizations, have received increasing moral, media and logistical support from foreign NGOs and UN agencies. The arrest of Chile's former dictator, General Pinochet, in Britain suggested that securing 'accountability' might in future be increasingly rooted in efforts to build a 'public sphere' beyond nation-states. Yet some of the foreign sponsors that offer funding to Latin American groups in the name of 'strengthening civil society and democracy' are also firmly committed to neoliberal free market economics and cuts in public spending (Warren 1998: 4, 203–6). In the discussion that follows, I argue that it is too simple to talk about an unambiguously positive 'transition to democracy' but also important to recognize that Latin American political life is changing.

There is a clear downside to neoliberal economic policies. They have undeniably increased social inequality. Nineteenth-century diseases of poverty have reasserted themselves, whilst the personal security situation in many regions is similar to that I have already described for Africa. As Charles Hale, writing from Guatemala, puts it, an increasing quantity of 'brown areas' reflect the state's incapacity to solve basic social problems (Hale 1998). Yet the political consequences of neoliberalism are not uniform. Social discontent with the effects of neoliberal economics, along with desires to 'break the mould' of national politics by voting for leaders from outside the ranks of established political parties have produced new manifestations of 'populist' politics. Some political 'outsiders', notably President Fujimori of Peru, have demonstrated that both authoritarian rule and firm commitment to neoliberal economics are compatible with political survival. Others, such as Fernando Collor de Mello in Brazil, or Abdalá Bucaram in Ecuador, have been removed from office. In Bucaram's case this was through the intervention of a still powerful military, though his fall also reflected popular fury at his turn to a neoliberal agenda, and civilian government continued. Collor de Mello was replaced democratically, after a period of interim government, by what for a time appeared a successful centrist neoliberal administration. Yet Brazil, like Mexico, was to experience a major economic crash. Brazilian politics then turned in a similar direction to those of Mexico, where some aspirants for the candidacy of the ruling Institutional Revolutionary Party (PRI) in the 2000 Presidential elections deployed the rhetoric of the 'populist' past of the party against the neoliberalism of its leadership. Yet such ideological postures offer little insight into the underlying politics of competition for power, the forces involved or their relationship to popular social movements.

Let me begin a more detailed discussion with the Brazilian case. Military rule began in 1964 when President Goulart abandoned the compromise between the landowning class and the state that had previously kept the government deaf not only to peasant protests but to pleas for a modernization of agriculture from industrialists (Cammack 1991). Although the military did not close Congress, but instead manufactured a new rubber-stamp ruling party and 'loyal opposition', Brazilian politics became dependent on the manipulation of state patronage, electoral machines and deals between different factions (ibid.: 36–7). Although this had long-term implications for the nature of party politics after military rule ended, severe repression encouraged the growth of new organizations outside the formal political structure, including independent trade unions and Catholic Christian Base Communities, along with other kinds of 'new social movements'. The multiplication of diffuse but *organized* sources of popular dissent promoted a general politicization of areas of social activity outside the formal political system and, most importantly, laid the basis for a new leftist political organization, the Workers' Party (PT) (Moreira Alves 1993). As the military became increasingly unpopular, even with Brazilian business, their manipulation of a veneer of electoral politics went badly wrong.

The electorate protested against the system by voting for the 'loyal opposition' MDB (Brazilian Democratic Movement). This eventually became Brazil's principal centre-right party, the PMDB, through a realignment of political forces. As the army's grip on power weakened, Brazilian politics became dominated by efforts to block a victory of the Left and by the problem of finding politicians who were not tarnished by association with military rule or electoral machine politics. The choice of Fernando Collor de Mello as an 'outsider' proved disastrous because he led a minority party which depended on the support of the machine politicians for survival: he was therefore unable to deliver on pledges to reform the system (Cammack 1991). Nevertheless, Collor de Mello's triumph over the PT's candidate, Lula, in Brazil's first truly democratic presidential election for twenty-nine years, reflected the new power of television to influence the outcome of 'free and fair' elections in a significant way (Castañeda 1994: 380–1), and his fall on corruption charges did not leave the field clear for a PT victory.

In 1994, Fernando Enrique Cardoso, an economist once famous on the Left as a theorist of Latin American 'dependency', won a landslide victory as candidate of the social democratic PSDB, offering neoliberal solutions to the problems of stabilizing Brazil's economy. Cardoso's initial successes against inflation and non-involvement in the 'old politics' kept his popularity rating high, until the economic strategy turned sour and financial collapse brought IMF intervention. By 1999, Cardoso's poll ratings had slumped, conservative politicians who had previously backed neoliberal policies were switching to a 'populist' anti-neoliberal rhetoric, and even the centrist PMDB, now a junior coalition partner in Cardoso's government, demanded a tougher stance with the IMF as economic misery deepened. Brazil's agrarian problems remained unresolved. Yet neoliberal economics in Brazil proved so disastrous for commercial farmers that Cardoso's headaches were increased by the PT's lending its support to the UDR, a right-wing farmer's organization, in its demands for more government aid in rescheduling debts. The PT's natural allies are the radical Movement of the Landless (MST), normally the enemies of the UDR. The fact that the latter were willing to restrain their normal condemnations of the MST to make common cause against Cardoso's fiscal prudence was one of the more interesting ironies of the 1990s.

Although civilian political institutions were holding up in most countries at the end of the 1990s, Colombia presents an example of apparent 'state crisis' with the potential to provoke instability in neighbouring countries. The Pastrana government's attempt to broker peace with Colombia's guerrilla movements, the FARC (Revolutionary Armed Forces of Colombia) and ELN (National Liberation Army) stalled in mid-1999, after the FARC continued military operations from the demilitarized zone created in the south of the country and right-wing opposition to a peace process hardened. Colombia has a long history of political violence, but the last two decades of the twentieth century took this to new heights. The drug cartels directly challenged the government in a terror campaign, and the miseries of ordinary citizens were increased by the appearance of right-wing paramilitary death squads receiving covert support from the army. As in Sierra Leone, it became difficult to identify the agents of violence. Up to 12 million Colombians in rural and urban areas participated in demonstrations for peace in October 1999. Yet the United States increased its military aid, whilst the FARC justified its continuing bellicosity by arguing that the first priority in the peace negotiations should be reversal of the social polarization induced by Colombia's pattern of high-growth capitalist development in the 1990s, which reflected both the effects of opening to the world market and the contribution of the violence to displacing rural people (*Latin American Weekly Report* WR-99-43: 508).

Although right-wing paramilitaries and some military figures also have strong links with drug-trafficking, guerrilla movements in several Latin American countries found protecting the trade in narcotics and running processing laboratories an invaluable way to finance war. They sometimes gained support from harassed peasants involved in coca and marijuana cultivation for doing so. This strategy, in turn, enabled their opponents to claim that the movements had shifted from ideology to criminality, providing the pretext for governments to link counter-insurgency operations to the US-sponsored 'War on Drugs' and secure Northern acquiescence in brutal tactics as well as material support. In the case of Peru, the Fujimori regime succeeded in isolating, containing and largely annihilating two important guerrilla movements, and an attempt to build a new guerrilla movement in Mexico, the EPR (Popular Revolutionary Army) had met with limited success four years after its initial appearance in 1996. Yet low-level social violence continues to manifest itself in many different forms in the region.

Eric Wolf argued that 'privatization' of power beyond or behind the state stimulates political violence and is a direct consequence of the shift to neoliberal market economics and the reduction of state's capacity to provide public services:

Everywhere the exercise of public power is being challenged by rising claims of privatization, not only of property and service provision but also of means of violence. In many areas, armies are attempting to expand their economic and political influence, while paramilitary formations, private armies and security forces proliferate. Not infrequently, such groups enter into connections with 'mafias,' able to employ extralegal force in operations that can range from supplying the drug trade to clearing people off land to make it available for alternative uses. All such violence-prone situations favor the emergence of armed entrepreneurs who attract followers and build group solidarity through quasi-military styles of cohesion, preparedness and discipline. (Wolf, 1999: 273)

A distinguishing feature of Wolf's view of power relations and ideology was that it included an emphasis on the need to study agents, organizations and logistics as well as discourses and symbolic constructions. This is an essential perspective for understanding how reconfigurations of national state power are associated with the development of other kinds of 'decentred' powers.

Decentred powers may be linked to formal political networks behind the scenes or may be more autonomous or even 'anti-state' organizations, but all have the common property of exercising a kind of sovereignty over people. Part of this process is linked to the role of transnational companies, whose operations in Latin American countries have expanded in the 1990s as nationalized industries have been privatized and controls on foreign investors have been relaxed. Since foreign investment provides jobs and tax revenue, regional governments have an interest in competing with each other to attract transnational companies to their areas, although the activities of both oil companies and biotech firms may also stimulate local conflicts over resource use and control (Escobar 1998). Latin American elites therefore operate in a political field that is contested by a variety of grassroots social movements. Some of them are linked to transnational movements or are themselves transnational, as in the case of organizations that have developed among Mexican and Central American migrants in the United States (Kearney 1996, Stephen 1997a, Smith 1997). Elites also face pro-democracy movements with a middle-class base and a public culture in which political satire plays a prominent role, though 'speaking truth to power' remains a dangerous activity in countries which also have strong traditions of assassination. Yet Reno's injunction that we remember just how much power actors in the shadow state now hold applies to Latin America as well as Africa. In some regions, actors whose power is based on the 'illegal' second economy are those now most likely to fund local clinics and schools and to offer people livelihoods.

MEXICO: DEMOCRATIZATION VERSUS THE SHADOW STATE AND MILITARIZATION

I will pursue these issues with further discussion of Mexico. Mexico has the distinction of having enjoyed continuous civilian government since the 1920s, admittedly after experiencing a decade of tumultuous revolution. Indeed, post-revolutionary Mexico was always, at least in principle, a multiparty democracy, although the same party, the PRI, has, under different names, been in power since 1929. It remained in power in 1999. Some saw the best hope of defeating it as an electoral alliance between the right-wing Party of National Action (PAN), rooted in Catholic opposition to the post-revolutionary regime and a long-standing advocate of free enterprise, and the centre-left Party of the Democratic Revolution (PRD), which incorporates the old Communist Party along with a growing number of defectors from the PRI itself. This unlikely alliance foundered, however, in part because Mexico's presidentialist rather than parliamentary political system did not lend itself to coalitions.

Mexico's modern political system was consolidated under the 'radical' presidency of Lázaro Cárdenas. Earlier leaders of the post-revolutionary state had used land reform to turn peasants into political clients of the regime, but Cárdenas took the expropriation of the great landed estates (*haciendas*, *latifundios*, or in Chiapas state, on the border with Guatemala, *fincas*) much further. He changed the nature of the reform by giving rights in the land reform communities termed *ejidos* to resident workers on the estates as well as to members of indigenous communities whose lands had been usurped. Although large-scale landholding did not disappear in Mexico, Cárdenas's agrarian reform remained one of the ideological props of the regime after the peasantry was sacrificed to the dictates of industrialization in the decades that followed. It remained an important basis for some communities' loyalty to the PRI even after it embraced neoliberalism (Stephen 1997b). Although the neoliberal government of Carlos Salinas sought to bring land redistribution to an end by amending the constitution in 1992, the rebellion of the Zapatista Army of National Liberation (EZLN) in Chiapas in 1994 demonstrated that agrarian reform remained a live issue and triggered further land invasions.

Until Cárdenas, the final shape of the post-revolutionary state remained uncertain. Regional agrarian movements retained a degree of autonomy, although they became tied to individual revolutionary 'chieftains' (*caudillos*). Cárdenas himself used one of these movements as a springboard for his own ascent to national power (Gledhill 1991). His great political achievement was to bring popular movements under state control by incorporating local peasant and worker organizations into national confederations. Yet Cárdenas did not succeed in creating a highly centralized 'corporate state' (Rubin 1990, 1996). Some regional bosses retained autonomous power, forcing the centre into protracted processes of negotiation and compromise.

Nevertheless, the basic shape of the 'system' that has governed Mexico since the 1940s was mapped out in the Cárdenas administration, which began by 'bureaucratizing' the military. The Mexican army has traditionally taken its orders from politicians in return for prestige and opportunities to acquire private wealth – a principle that took on a new significance in the 1990s as 'narco-politics' came together with the counter-insurgency war in Chiapas. A major problem that Cárdenas did not resolve was state–Church conflict. This had posed a major threat to the survival of the post-revolutionary state in the period 1926–9, when attempts to impose secular education followed by the closing of Catholic churches provoked a massive popular backlash in the form of the *cristero* rebellion (Meyer 1976). The conflict smouldered on through the 1930s and early 1940s in the *sinarquista* movement, a Mexican variant of fascism (Gledhill 1991). Nevertheless, the heat was taken out of it after 1946, when the regime turned its back on Cárdenas's social policies but retained its grip on power through the institutions he created.

The post-revolutionary political elite had provincial, urban petty-bourgeois social origins. The *caudillos* turned on the rural popular movements that temporarily captured both the capital city and the state in 1914, and murdered their leaders, Villa and Zapata (Gilly 1983, Knight 1986). Their project was the construction of a 'modern' national state and 'modern' capitalism, although the way the project was implemented reflected historical particularities of Mexican society and culture. In some respects, the Cardenista state appeared to be acting 'autonomously', against dominant class interests, but as Nora Hamilton (1982) has shown, this 'autonomy' was more apparent than real. The Mexican Revolution did not break the social power of the bourgeoisie domestically and could not break the power of international capitalism.

The revolution also renewed Mexico's social elite. It brought 'new men' of dubious origin into its ranks as possessors of wealth who could resuscitate family fortunes, a process brilliantly captured in Carlos Fuentes's novel *The Death of Artemio Cruz*. The political leaders of the post-revolutionary state also joined it. The old elite conserved its coherence as a status group, but post-revolutionary ideology left the business class on the margins of its new model of society based on corporate 'peasant', 'worker' and 'popular' sectors.

The official trade unions acknowledged interest conflicts between capital and labour in their constitutions and pledged themselves to fight for workers' rights, through the state apparatus and the ruling party, of which all were declared members. In practice, leaders dedicated themselves to maintaining the 'pact' established between the state and private sector on the limits of working-class rights (Trejo Delarbre 1986), but they also operated as a faction within the state, seeking benefits for their 'sector' in the interests of their own power.

The Mexican elite is therefore not monolithic. Political competition at the top has sometimes been pursued by controlled mobilization of popular forces. The state could clash with the bourgeoisie. Although Mexican capital was largely satisfied by the support and subsidies it received from the state until the 1980s, the powerful industrial elite of the northern city of Monterrey mounted a successful challenge to the Cárdenas government that secured it considerable autonomy (Saragoza 1988). The administration of Luis Echeverría in the early 1970s responded to growing rural mobilization with a new round of populist measures, which included expropriation of agribusiness concerns (Sanderson 1981). Echeverría then embarked on an ambitious programme of state intervention. He created a huge para-statal enterprise sector. The federal bureaucracy and public employment expanded massively. This provoked a backlash in the 1980s, drawing more businessmen into politics and towards the right-wing PAN. The ruling PRI was forced to respond politically in the 1990s. Business was offered a new role in the ruling party's affairs, within a citizen-based rather than 'sectoral' state, and government committed itself to economic policies that maximized the opportunities for big capital to prosper in an international free market framework (Bensabat Kleinberg 1999). Connections within government also proved useful to businessmen for other reasons, as the scandals surrounding the efforts to turn the private losses of some of Mexico's richest families into public debt in 1998 were to demonstrate.

The period of 'statization' under Echeverría and his successor López Portillo (1976–82) brought greater political centralization but also highlighted the role of intermediaries in the power structure (de la Peña 1986, Lomnitz-Adler 1992). The relations between the Mexican 'people' and the state that ruled in its name had long been mediated by local and regional brokers known as *caciques*. Under Echeverría *caciquismo* changed its character. Rural and urban community leaders became closely tied to state bureaucratic agencies. Managers of state enterprises could acquire economic power not simply comparable to, but even menacing that of private businessmen in the regions. Many Echeverrista *caciques* had close personal ties to the president, and such individuals often became major regional power brokers. Nevertheless, there are also underlying structural continuities in the phenomenon of *caciquismo*.

The 'local boss' was an instrument of rule by *caudillos* in the period of decentralization of power that followed independence. *Caciquismo* was integral to the weakly institutionalized centralization of power achieved by the dictator Porfirio Díaz in the period 1876–1910, and became an instrument for consolidating the post-revolutionary 'mass-incorporating' national state. Again the history of the period of Lázaro Cárdenas is instructive. Cárdenas made unprecedented attempts to incorporate the Mexican masses into a national political order, tirelessly visiting the most distant regions of the rural heartlands, talking to the people and dispensing patronage and resources. Yet *Cardenismo* proliferated *cacicazgos* (Gledhill 1991, Rus 1994, Rubin 1996). The group of violent village bosses whom Paul Friedrich calls 'The Princes' in his ethnography of the village of Naranja, in Cárdenas's home state of Michoacán, provides an example of the kinds of actors through which this 'reforming' state consolidated its political networks (Friedrich 1986).

De la Peña argues that the creation of a formal structure of mass repre-sentation in state institutions was not sufficient to overcome the social segmentation of a highly regionalized country which already had a population of 18 million in 1940 (de la Peña 1986). In general terms, the *cacique* can be seen as a local leader linked to political patrons at a higher level, who maintains his own power by winning resources from above for the communities he represents. He can enrich himself in the process, provided he wins sufficient resources to sustain a substantial clientele. *Caciques* may be corrupt and repressive, but only within bounds consistent with maintaining political order, or they lose the backing of their patrons. There are, however, different forms of *cacique* power, which Claudio Lomnitz-Adler explores through models of regionally specific 'intimate cultures' of class domination and ethnographic study of the dynamics of state penetration of a regionally diversified national space.

Lomnitz-Adler argues that the persistence of *caciquismo* reflects a dialectic in which *caciques* provide avenues for the state to penetrate local intimate cultures and in time establish a bureaucratized institutional structure for their management. The *cacique* is incorporated into the bureaucratic apparatus and eventually promoted or displaced, detaching him from his original constituency. This transformation eliminates local people's personal links with the state through their ties to the *cacique*. As access to state resources becomes increasingly a matter of personal wealth, a popular indif-ference to state institutions develops, associated with what Lomnitz-Adler terms 'state fetishism': contact with the figure of the president standing above the selfishness of ordinary politicians becomes the only guarantee of justice (Lomnitz-Adler 1992: 307–8). The coherence of the old intimate cultures of power breaks down, the government's bureaucratic apparatus and discursive practices cannot control new local organizations which develop to contest the existing distribution of resources, new *caciques* emerge as leaders of these constituencies, and the cycle renews.

This is a modified version of the 'hegemonic centre' model of national state formation that I discussed in Chapter 1, noting the way it has been criticized as an account of the creation of political 'modernity' in Peru by David Nugent (1997). Popular liberalism was also associated with provincial areas outside the old colonial centre in Mexico (Knight 1992: 121–2), although, in the fullness of time, the Mexican post-revolutionary state achieved a far greater capacity to 'penetrate' everyday life than the Peruvian state. Lomnitz-Adler emphasizes the way the 'national' is built up through interactions between the political centre and regional spaces characterized by differences in political culture. Yet his account of the dynamics of *caciquismo* still separates and polarizes 'centres' and 'peripheries', allowing the latter to oscillate between 'incorporation' and 'resistance'. This approach does not fully satisfy those who emphasize the way that localities shape the nature of state institutions themselves, as national discourses and symbols are locally *re-appropriated*, and rule is *negotiated* in this highly regionalized nation (Nugent 1993, Joseph and Nugent 1994, Mallon 1995, Rubin 1996, Aitken 1997).

Lomnitz-Adler's analysis does, however, highlight the tension between 'rational-bureaucratic-democratic' practices and practices founded on particularistic principles such as friendship, kinship and personal loyalties (1992: 297). Since Mexico's political elite does not correspond precisely to the social and economic elite, it can be defined as a 'political class' based on its own mechanisms of recruitment and for maintaining cohesion despite factional conflicts. The elite reproduces itself through a structure of cliques (*camarillas*) associated with past presidential figures (Camp 1996). Individuals owe their ascent to political alliances with those who dominate these cliques at a particular moment. As the clique structures evolved over time they created chains of social solidarity that broke down regional barriers and made the political class more unitary and less truly 'regional', even if particular families continued to dominate the politics of their home states. The *camarilla* networks organized the allocation of public offices and division of the spoils of office. They therefore acted as the deep social structures of power behind the formal state apparatus. The political class was competitive and factionalized, but proved extremely solidary when it came to defending the 'system', up to the 1990s.

The PRI is not a 'political party' in the democratic liberal tradition but a party of the state formed to consolidate the power of the victorious revolutionary *caudillos*. It was a vehicle for that state's hegemonic project of remodelling civil society by authoritarian means – through imposing secular education, for example – but also for responding, flexibly, to the resistance this process provoked. It maintained itself in power through an electoral process that was persistently marked by fraud as well as by manipulation of the electorate and exchange of resources for votes. Mexicans accordingly tended to define their 'democracy' in terms of freedom of speech and the press, whilst recognizing that the basic rule of the system was that the PRI wins. Although the PRI was actually losing elections for state governorships to candidates of both the PAN and the PRD in the second half of the 1990s,[4] the vices of the old system have proved persistent, and have not been restricted to the PRI itself.

It is often argued that repression was only used as a 'last resort' in the Mexican political system, because cooptation of dissidence was done so successfully in the years when the post-revolutionary state's mass organizations provided the basis for an extensive system of state clientelism. The neoliberal state consolidated by Carlos Salinas de Gortari (1988–94) progressively dismantled the corporate organizations. The resources they commanded dwindled further as a result of the 1994 economic crash. Salinas did, however, smooth the transition by a selective process of clientelism targeted at the more important social movements – including some movements with an indigenous social base and cultural politics – that had supported his rival in the disputed presidential elections of 1988 (Harvey 1991, Mattiace 1997). That rival was Cuauhtémoc Cárdenas, son of the great reforming president of the 1930s, whose myth was still a powerful popular mobilizing symbol (Gledhill 1991, McDonald 1997). Salinas deployed a social development programme that was supposedly targeted at the poorest members of society and backed by the World Bank, the National Solidarity Programme, in ways that were astutely politically calculated (Dresser 1991, Moguel 1994). Yet despite the continuing importance of this mode of exercising rule in Mexico, political behaviour has been influenced in direct and indirect ways by a pervasive threat of violence, especially in rural areas (Gledhill 1995).

The threat is premised on the practical impunity of the judicial police and military and the inadequacies of a justice system in which money and political influence talk. The regime can even make use of anxieties about violence by issuing propaganda with an ambiguous message – is it the opposition that is violent or is the implication that violence will be meted out by the state to those who support the opposition? Although these problems have been addressed in Mexican political discourse for a century, and administrations have made repeated promises to improve the human rights situation, after 1994 denunciations by international monitoring organizations of routine human rights violations by police and military security units increased rather than diminished. Reduction of the resources available to practise state clientelism forced the regime to rely more on the military as a means of containing opposition.

---

4 Under Salinas the PAN was allowed to win gubernatorial elections in the north of the country, but only through a process in which the executive negotiated the surrender of power with its own party machines in the states concerned. The PRD was not allowed to gain victories until the administration of Ernesto Zedillo (1994–2000). After the December 1994 crash, there was growing internal dissent within the PRI itself, and political conditions changed to the point where *priístas* denied their party's nomination were willing to run for the PRD in states such as Zacatecas.

In terms of electoral democracy, major changes appeared to be taking place under Salinas's successor, Ernesto Zedillo, whose own election (once again standing against Cuauhtémoc Cárdenas, who came third, after the PAN's candidate) was deemed legitimate.[5] Cuauthémoc Cárdenas himself was finally rewarded for his patience by a landslide victory in the first direct elections for Mayor of Mexico City in 1997. Yet Zedillo's victory came in the wake of disturbing signs of systemic transformation. January 1994 brought the EZLN rebellion, a development to which the government initially responded with violence, and although it hastily changed to tactics of negotiation, it subsequently became clear that the military were asked to plan and implement a low-intensity war from the outset of the conflict. In March, the PRI's presidential candidate, Luis Donaldo Colosio, was assassinated in Tijuana, to be followed by former President Salinas's brother-in-law, a minister and former governor of the state of Guerrero. Carlos Salinas's brother Raúl was eventually convicted of intellectual authorship of the latter crime in 1999, in a manner which left the case subject to as many obscurities as the Colosio affair. Both the crimes themselves and the conviction of Raúl were symptoms of breakdown in the solidarity of the political class. This also became manifest in bitter in-fighting within the PRI for the presidential succession, although Zedillo's stage managing of a public reconciliation betweeen the ultimate winner and his principle opponent – a politician who proved popular in opinion polls despite past accusations of criminal links and electoral malpractice – suggested that the political class was eager to settle its differences to retain its grip on power.

Continuing caution about Mexico's 'democratic opening' is necessary for three structural reasons. Firstly, shadow state relationships penetrated as deeply into the respectable heart of cabinet government in Mexico during the period of Salinas de Gortari as in the case of the contemporary Samper government in Colombia. As the scope for enrichment through traditional forms of political corruption based on plundering the public purse declined, Mexican politicians appear to have become increasingly tied into the world of drug-trafficking and money laundering. The purchase of banks and currency exchange houses for the latter purpose ties in well with the 'legitimate' activities that free market policies have promoted, through the privatization of state enterprises and encouragement of investment in tourism, transport and consumerism. The cores of important political cliques, such as that headed by a former school-teacher turned multi-millionaire, have become powerful transnational economic family corporations, important enough clients of US banks to merit total confidentiality and

5 For an anthropological analysis of the roots of Zedillo's victory in the 'politics of everyday fear', see McDonald (1997). The aspersions cast on the electoral process at the time focused on the PRI's habitual use of public resources for electoral campaign purposes. The political infighting of 1999 led to claims that Zedillo's campaign also received funds from an entrepreneur within Salinas's circle involved in drug dealing and money laundering.

technical assistance in financial operations some would judge dubious. It is encouraging that these facts are widely discussed in the public domain in Mexico. Yet these groups retain a formidable power to influence the course of Mexican politics.

Secondly, Mexico's opposition parties have their own internal divisions and ideological positions are often quite secondary to the dynamics of competition for power. The clique structures themselves cross-cut party and ideological divisions. The generation of politicians known as *neopanistas* are businessmen who do not share the world-views of the traditional social bases of the old PAN. Many of them have been protegés of PRI politicians and are involved in ongoing business relations with *priístas*. Since the PRD is increasingly made up of PRI defectors, the scope for compromise is equally great at the other end of the political spectrum. Furthermore, at the local level party political labels may prove quite meaningless where developments are driven by factional struggles, an issue on which ethnographic evidence can be extremely instructive.

As an example, we can take the *municipio* of Zinacantán in Chiapas. The shock-waves of the EZLN rebellion promoted a move towards a more representative and accountable administration in Zinacantán in 1994, along with a *rapprochement* between Catholics and converts to Evangelical Protestant churches, who had previously been subject to expulsion from the community (Collier 1997). A group of PRI bosses whose past power arose from their control of trucking was removed by a citizen group that included militants of the PRD and the PAN as well as PRI supporters hostile to the *caciques*. Yet a year later both the local and state PRD were split by competition over political leadership. Local factional conflict also gravitated around charges of misuse of resources received from the federal social development programmes (Collier 1997: 22–3). The EZLN had, by 1995, advised its supporters in the state to abstain from voting for the PRD (Viqueira 1999). The disaffected PRD faction also refused to support the party's candidates in the October 1995 elections (Collier 1997: 23). The result of this disunity among the opposition was that PRI bosses retained power in many municipalities on the basis of the votes of minorities of non-abstaining electors. This set the stage for a subsequent escalation of violence by frustrated PRD supporters and counter-violence by bosses, increasingly tied to the emergence of paramilitary bands. This process culminated in the massacre of women and children from a peaceful diocesan group in the hamlet of Acteal, at the end of 1997 (Viqueira 1999: 96).

In Zinacantán, the PRI rebuilt its power more peacefully, by using the social development funding it received as a strategic bastion of political control in the central highlands to demobilize most of its former PRD opponents. By 1996, however, the old trucker *caciques* had re-emerged politically as yet another *perredista* group that also claimed Zapatista sympathies and support (Collier 1997: 24–5). The old bosses now reversed their previous position of insisting on the expulsion of the Protestants. Yet the mainstream, including other PRD leaders, withdrew from participation in the wider regional movement to focus more strongly on Zinacanteco ethnic particularity and 'tradition', which also prompted a renewal of calls to expel religious dissenters.

Collier suggests that disillusion with the Zapatistas was not simply a result of government measures to deal with the conflict, but of the growing difficulties ordinary people faced in 1995 after the economic crash. Neoliberal economic policies continued to provoke collective resistance in the form of massive street demonstrations, as in the case of the opposition to privatization of the electricity supply industry in 1999, which coincided with a new Zapatista national 'consultation' on indigenous autonomy legislation. Yet their everyday impacts also encouraged individuals to seek what immediate solutions they could find to their everyday problems, which ranged from migration, through participation in the 'second economy', to accepting political bribes in the form of social development funding. Whatever the outcome of the 2000 elections, it will not be easy to 'break the mould' of the way rule is accomplished in Mexico.

A third reason for caution about 'democratization', is the militarization of internal security, a significant development in a country that has traditionally had one of the world's smallest armies in relation to population size (Grindle 1987). This reaches beyond the dirty war in Chiapas, with its deployment of paramilitary violence[6] and more subtle tactics of fostering religious and social divisions within communities that supported the EZLN uprising. Not only are other rural regions increasingly devastated by neoliberal economics subject to counter-insurgency operations, but the major cities have also seen major campaigns against popular organizations (Gledhill 1998).

That these developments have attracted little academic commentary is symptomatic of weaknesses in the way political change has been conceptualized. Petras and Morley (1992: 160) argue that studies of dictatorship focused on violation of human rights obscure the way military regimes implemented a form of class domination ultimately tied to North Atlantic interests. The political framework of neoliberalism continues to impose a model of capitalist development sponsored by the North through different (though often still authoritarian) mechanisms. There are such substantial

---

6 Some paramilitary groups are run by PRI politicians and registered as 'social development organizations'. Like all paramilitary organizations used as proxies in counter-insurgency campaigns, they offer the state the opportunity to deny its involvement in repression and to dissociate itself from 'excesses'. The Acteal massacre gave the government a pretext to send in more troops, reinforced by further detachments in 1999, after the army began to force its way into more of the 'autonomous' Zapatista rebel communities and denied access to journalists and human rights activists. These included communities located in the biosphere reserve, rich in timber and biological resources of interest to pharmaceutical companies and a major asset for eco-tourism development.

variations between political regimes in different countries that we clearly need to explain them in terms of specific national histories, which would include the distinct social histories of different Latin American armies. Yet the value of rights to vote in free and fair elections may seem limited in conditions under which families face increasing impoverishment. The 1948 UN Universal Declaration on Human Rights included a series of articles on 'socio-economic rights' which are far from being satisfied in Northern societies today, let alone in Latin America or Africa (Gledhill 1997).

For some this is an argument *against* welcoming the new politics of indigenous rights and autonomy that have emerged in countries such as Mexico and Guatemala. Yet the indigenous rights movement is one of the most potentially 'mould-breaking' developments in Latin American political history, and adds a distinctive 'post-colonial' dimension to 'democratization' in Latin America.

INDIGENOUS PEOPLES AND THE STATE IN MEXICO AND GUATEMALA

Indigenous rights politics is linked to neoliberalism in two ways: through international pressures on Latin American states to concede civil rights and through the increasing resource pressures that indigenous communities face. The latter reinforce the value of efforts to make special claims on states and the international community for services and aid (Warren 1998: 9). To anthropologists, some styles of indigenous identity politics appear alarmingly essentialist (Hale 1994, Warren 1998: 21, 35–6) and indigenous rights can come under fire from both the Left and the Right. It can be argued that there are no clear boundaries between 'indigenous' and 'non-indigenous' peoples in post-colonial cultural systems that are essentially hybrid (Warren 1998: 10). A politics of indigenous rights may not only fail to address the problems of poor people who cannot claim indigenous identity, but can be manipulated by elites eager to exploit social divisions to their own advantage (Gledhill 1997). The Mexican government has found it convenient to accuse the indigenous autonomy movement of threatening the break-up of the nation, promoting separatism that could foster Balkan-style ethnic violence. Yet the Zapatistas, like Guatemala's Pan-Mayanist movement, reject this charge, arguing that they are advocating 'unity in diversity' (Warren 1998: 13).

In Mexico, 'Indians' are a 'minority', at only 12.4 per cent of the population according to official classifications, though Mexico has the largest absolute number of citizens professing an indigenous identity, at 10.5 million (ibid.: 8). In Guatemala, in contrast, just over half that number of people make up 60.3 per cent of the population, and indigenous citizens are 71.2 per cent of Bolivia's population (ibid.: 8–9). There are, however, also important historical differences between the places these indigenous citizens occupied in the political construction of the 'nation'.

Peru, for example, was constituted in terms of a political and cultural opposition between an 'Indian' rural hinterland and 'White/mestizo' urbanized coast, leaving the mestizo as a kind of intermediary between White and Indian society identified with the dominant (White) side of the divide (Mallon 1992: 36–7). In colonial Guatemala, *ladinos* were originally either Hispanicized indigenous people who ceased to live in indigenous communities or persons of mixed race, mestizos in a biological sense, both distinguished from Spaniards and Guatemalan-born creoles (Warren 1998: 10). Both *ladinos* and Indians remained politically marginalized and impoverished in the colonial period, but this changed as the nineteenth-century plantation economy developed and *ladinos* were used as labour recruiters and functionaries in the Western Highlands, acting on behalf of the creole elites that dominated national politics: *ladino* became a synonym for 'non-Indian' (ibid.: 11). In Mexico, concentration of the indigenous population in the colonial centre and intense social interaction between Europeans and Indians led to a different political construction. A mestizo-peasant centre was opposed to an Indian periphery through what the Mexican anthropologist Guillermo Bonfil (1990) called a 'de-indianization' of the centre. Mestizo identity is the core of Mexican identity in official nationalist culture, with the Indian part of the mestizo valorized in that culture as folklore and archaeological sites. Contemporary Indians enjoy diminished social, economic and human rights, within a society in which skin colour continues to be related to social prestige.

In a sense, the Mexican 'people' is an invention of the Mexican state. The post-revolutionary state's model of national society as a corporate structure based on peasant, worker and 'popular' sectors represented a rejection of nineteenth-century liberal principles in favour of a modernized version of the colonial model of society as a hierarchic order of castes. The national community represented by the state was based on the complementarity of 'sectors', but the valorization of the mestizo in post-revolutionary ideology combined continuing commitment to the principle that 'progress' meant 'whitening oneself' with nationalist rejection of subordination to *gringos* (Lomnitz-Adler 1992: 278–9). In the 1940s, mass media, such as the cowboy films starring Jorge Negrete, reinforced this idea of the mestizo nation in opposition to the *gringo* North, celebrating the masculine virtues and cultural traditions of a new nation forged by revolution (Gutmann 1996: 228).

The Mexican 'people' (*pueblo*) is not, however, simply an official or media invention. Mexico has long-established traditions of popular resistance and community cultures of opposition (though, as I have stressed, these are of the Right as well as the Left). The peasant (but also 'Indian')[7] movement led

---

7 It must be stressed that contemporary ethnic labels such as 'Tzeltal', 'Purhépecha', 'Zapotec' or 'Nahua' are largely products of later twentieth-century indigenous movements. Even today many indigenous people in Chiapas and other indigenous regions prefer not to

by Zapata in the 1910 Revolution articulated its own political vision of a national state assigned its powers by 'free municipalities' based on participatory democracy (Warman 1988) and the theme of accountability has remained strong in Mexican civic culture. By opting for a socially exclusionary economic policy, neoliberalism re-creates spaces for civil resistance even if economic difficulties also encourage individual accommodations with the world as it is. The failures of Mexico's neoliberal economic model remain capable of producing a popular nationalist backlash against elites. It is common for provincial people to express their social alienation from the national elite by observing that its members are foreigners. Such metaphors achieve new salience in an age in which transnational class interests are transparent determinants of government policy, but Mexico's elite faces the particular problem of trying to have done with a revolution whose unfulfilled promises dominated the rhetoric of the state for 60 years.

The Zapatista uprising brought indigenous rights more firmly onto the national agenda, but combined this with the symbols of the popular nationalist and revolutionary tradition. By offering a politics of indigenous identities that argued for 'unity in difference', Zapatismo threatened the official nationalist ideology based on *mestizaje*. The Zapatistas suggested ways in which Mexican national identity could be rebuilt from the bottom up (Stephen 1997a: 93). They simultaneously demanded a development model that helped the poor and sought to form a coalition with a diverse range of social movements that were divided in terms of class and ethnicity, but united in opposition to neoliberalism. They thus posed a threat to the national regime's model of capitalist accumulation that was far greater than they posed to any economic or political interests in Chiapas itself.[8] That is

---

see themselves as Maya and may even prefer to be Chamulas or Zinacantecos rather than see themselves as part of a wider ethnic community defined by one of the Maya languages such as Tzotzil or Tzeltal. In the nineteenth century, people in indigenous communities focused on the local identity of their village and still used the language of the ethno-racial hierarchy of *castas* to define their relationships with non-Indians.

8 The situation in Chiapas has been misrepresented in some academic analyses and the press. It is not true that Chiapas remained untouched by the revolutionary land reform: its agrarian structure is complex and heterogeneous. In Chapter 9, I stress the importance of middle-sized and small ranchers, who have grievances that would need to be recognized in pacifying the state through negotiation. It is also not the case that the Chiapaneco elite remained independent of the national state, although it is convenient for the federal government to perpetuate this fiction in order to deny the impact of national policies and past interventions on the situation that produced the rebellion. There is a substantial history of peasant organization in Chiapas that precedes the EZLN rebellion, and many different perspectives within these organizations, which have fragmented further since 1994 as a result of internal splits. The rebellion itself is the product of a specific social situation in the Selva Lacandona, where multi-ethnic communities were formed by peons from the highland plantations who had begun to colonize the area sixty years before the rebellion. For further analysis see, for example, Stephen (1997a) and Harvey (1998). Readers of Spanish should also consult Leyva Solano and Ascencio Franco (1996) for an ethnographic account of the Zapatista base communities.

why the Zedillo government proved willing to spend far more pursuing a military solution to the conflict than it would have had to spend to satisfy the material demands of the peasants supporting the EZLN.

In comparison with Guatemala, the Mexican state may appear historically relatively benign, although there are parallels between the development of plantation economies in Chiapas and Guatemala (Rus 1983). Guatemala became notorious for its human rights record after the 1954 coup against Arbenz (Adams 1970), but the country plumbed new depths with the military regime's genocidal attacks on the indigenous communities of the Western Highlands in the 1980s. In January 1986, Guatemala returned to civilian rule. After a period of continuing political uncertainty in which the army repeatedly threatened to take back direct control of the state, a peace treaty was finally signed with the URNG guerrilla movement a decade later. Although it still appeared irreversible, the 'peace process' received a setback in 1999 after 81 per cent of registered voters abstained in a government-backed referendum on constitutional change. This delivered the Right an unexpected 'no' vote against constitutional reforms giving legal status to the treaties signed in 1996, which recognized the country as a multicultural society in which the rights of indigenous people would be considerably enhanced.

As far as the issues of class interest on which Petras and Morley focus are concerned, the facts seem to speak for themselves. By the mid-1990s, employment in export-processing zones constituted 77 per cent of total industrial employment in Guatemala. The highest figure for any Latin American or Caribbean country, it is not unrelated to the fact that Guatemala was bottom of the league table of wages per employee by a very wide margin (*Caribbean and Central America Report*, RC-99-04: 4–5).

Although the power of the army was apparently reduced in the 1990s, the extent to which the military constitute an autonomous power invites further reflection. Dunkerley (1988) argues that the origins of the repressive apparatus of the military state in Guatemala can be traced back to the coffee boom of the 1870s. In contrast to El Salvador, where the coercive apparatus that controlled plantation labour and dispossessed peasants was in the hands of the oligarchy at the local level, Guatemala's coercive machinery was always more centralized in organization. Nevertheless, despite the coercion used to control plantation labour, until the 1980s Guatemala's elite had only limited ability to control Indian communities in general. The state, run by a tiny elite priding itself on its Spanish descent, had only weak penetration of a very fragmented civil society lacking unifying national symbols (Smith 1990: 35). From 1983 onwards, the military embarked on a radical reorganization of civil society in the Highlands, resettling people who had fled violence in compact 'model' village communities alien to traditional dispersed settlement patterns (Wilson 1991, 1995). Populations from different communities were mixed together in the new settlements to inhibit organized resistance, living under the surveillance of civil guard units. This marked a new phase in the development of the militarized state in Guatemala.

The militarization of Guatemala after 1954 was linked to US involvement in the region and the expansion of the international arms trade. The presidency of General Ríos Montt, established by a coup in 1982, was also backed by North American Protestant evangelical organizations. After Carter's arms embargo of 1978, however, the Guatemalan military became disenchanted with their US patron, and, despite Reagan's more sympathetic attitude, rejected US protests about human rights violations and began to define themselves in nationalist terms. The High Command was recruited mainly from the (non-White) middle classes. This, Carol Smith argues, reinforced a growing cleavage between the military and an oligarchy which the army accused of being too selfish to promote the national interest (Smith 1990: 13). Against the wishes of a 'modernizing' faction of the oligarchy, which saw the costs of financing an overblown military apparatus as money badly spent, the army sought to create a militarized state capitalism intended not to displace, but to dominate the private sector and produce the resources needed to sustain the military apparatus.

Smith argues that the Guatemalan case indicates that modern military states can develop the infrastructures for reshaping civil society needed to implant such a model. The economic restructuring process in the Western Highlands was not uniform through different sub-regions, any more than the preceding phases of repression and reorganization of social life by the military pacification campaign was uniform. Some areas remained relatively uninvolved in the violence, dominated as they were politically by Indian mercantile elites linked to conservative parties (Carmack 1995). Smith argues, however, that the broad thrust of the restructuring process was to reduce peasant landholdings and rural incomes, and to destroy the subsistence farming, artisan production and indigenous marketing systems on which the relative autonomy of Highland indigenous communities had been based, leading to a massive increase in proletarianization. This paved the way not only for growth of capitalist agriculture, but also for the development of the export processing activities to which I referred earlier (Smith 1990: 33). At the same time as the Highlands were turned into a labour reserve for capitalist development, with a corresponding need for policing by an expanding internal security apparatus, other state agencies and institutions increased their local presence, reorganizing local politics around state-sponsored development projects. Although anti-military and anti-state sentiment remained strong, Smith argued that local political protest was at a low ebb in the period of her study (up to 1987). People were not simply cowed by intense repression, but preoccupied with economic survival.

Although the economic changes that Smith anticipated did take root, and Wilson argues that the army was perfectly happy to hand over rule to civilians in 1986, since it retained 'undiminished domination of society'

(Wilson 1993a: 132), her analysis assumed too much about the capacity of the military to control indigenous people. As Wilson (1993b, 1995) has shown, even the most sophisticated strategies of ideological manipulation failed to achieve their goals. The generation of community leaders who took their communities into the guerrilla movement (and who were largely eliminated by the violence) consisted of lay catechists who were mostly better-off peasants, spoke Spanish and had a strong 'developmentalist' ideology, antagonistic to celebrating Maya culture. Yet the generation that took over embraced a new politics of indigenous identity. In the past communities identified themselves with local mountain spirits (*Tzuultaq'a*), which, in accordance with the duality of Mesoamerican thought, were both male and female, kind but capricious, and, above all else, authoritarian figures who often took on the appearance of White German plantation owners. In the camps, the military sought to identify themselves with the mountain spirit symbols, to establish their own claims to ultimate power. Yet people did not forget who actually killed their children and neighbours, and struggled to have the army withdraw.

In community after community, the civil patrol system the army set up was either abandoned or put in the hands of more acceptable community authorities. Given that it had the backing of the Catholic Church, the catechist movement was in a strong position to recover, but it now focused on an agenda in which indigenous rights and rebuilding Indian culture were central. In again looking towards mountain-spirits as a symbol of their identity, the villagers no longer saw them as white-skinned Germans or mestizo army officers, but as dark-skinned Maya (Wilson 1993b: 134). Although many of today's ethnic revivalist leaders are the children of 1970s catechists, the ethnic identity they are celebrating today is different from the local village identities that were the principle expression of 'ethnicity' amongst their grandparents. This reflects the way traditions with some anchors in the past have been reworked by an emergent pan-Mayanism (Wilson 1993b: 124, Warren 1998).

Noting (correctly) that contemporary concern with 'Maya' identity represents a break with the past, and arguing (more controversially) that Guatemala's guerrilla movement enjoyed little support from indigenous people, David Stoll (1999) contends that the violence of the 1980s was prolonged by the support that a defeated guerrilla movement received from foreign academic sympathizers. The latter mistakenly saw the guerrillas as the authentic expression of a post-colonial struggle by indigenous peoples, seduced, in particular, by the testimonial volume recounting the experience of Nobel laureate Rigoberta Menchú, whose veracity as 'the voice of a voiceless people' Stoll challenges. Stoll's polemic might have made a useful contribution to exploring the complexities of 'grassroots mobilization' had it been handled in a different manner. Yet his attack on Menchú ultimately obscures more than it reveals about the history of the Guatemalan guerrilla movement, agrarian structures, political economy and the causes of rural poverty and, in particular, the development of indigenous activism, before and after the violence.[9]

As Kay Warren shows in her analysis of that activism in rural as well as urban contexts, although the development of the Pan-Maya movement is linked to both transnational forces and changing national politics, it also responds to inter-generational tensions and the dynamics of community leadership (Warren 1998: 191). 'Cultural revitalization' has found diverse historical and contemporary forms, and there is no consensus amongst indigenous Guatemalans around a Pan-Maya agenda. Yet we do need to highlight *activism*. The older generation of catechists who attacked traditional folk Catholicism could turn organizations such as Catholic Action that elites had designed to depoliticize Indians into vehicles for struggling against racial discrimination (ibid.: 182).

There is certainly no necessary affinity between either the old or new community leaderships and left-wing politics. Many Guatemalan rural people may have mistrusted non-indigenous guerrilla cadres, although Stoll's efforts to discredit the guerrillas need to be set against the fact that the Guatemalan Commission for Historical Clarification found the army responsible for 93 per cent of the killings. Neither the Nicaraguan nor Salvadorean experiences suggested, at the time, that armed struggle was futile. Arguing that the Guatemalan guerrilla movement was particularly weak makes it even harder to explain why Guatemala's officer corps saw it as necessary to destroy so many lives and communities, including lives and communities in areas where the guerrillas had not been active. It is also important that much of the violence was committed by indigenous soldiers and members of civil patrols against other indigenous people (Warren 1998: 120). Stoll's analysis stops well short of what is needed to understand how state violence induces a culture of terror that leads neighbour to denounce or kill neighbour, a theme to which I return in Chapter 7.

What can we make of the politics of Stoll's contention that the legitimacy as a Maya voice of 'the man with a large family who owns three worn-out acres and wants me to buy him a chain saw so he can cut down the last forest more quickly' equals that of Rigoberta Menchú (Stoll 1999: 247)? It combines a blaming the victim approach to rural poverty with putting to one side his own evidence that many indigenous Guatemalans identify with this story told by a Maya woman from a country where neither Maya nor women have found it easy to speak for justice. Yet the greatest danger of all in Stoll's polemic is that of perpetuating a view of indigenous Guatemalans as victims without agency. Despite the variety of their projects of resistance, the non-confrontational nature of many of these projects, and the fact that many of them have been led for generations by people whose lives were lived

---

9 For detailed critiques of Stoll, see the contributions to *Latin American Perspectives* 109, Volume 28, Number 6, 1999, a special issue of the journal dedicated to discussion of his book.

on the interface of Indian and non-Indian society, what is most remarkable about Guatemala, given the scale of the suffering, is that a new kind of activism did emerge in its aftermath. The fact that indigenous communities are often locked in conflicts with each other, today as in the past, does not make the appearance of new forms of indigenous politics less significant for changing the political face of Guatemala. As Warren puts it, despite its hybrid and internally contested nature, the Pan-Maya movement can offer us 'lessons about non-violent options for rethinking political marginalization in multi-ethnic states that seek democratic futures' (1998: 210); and so can other manifestations of continuing popular activism in rural and urban Guatemala.

We have seen that anthropological studies interest political scientists because they can provide insights into the 'deep politics' of civil society's resistance to authoritarian states. Anthropologists, in turn, recognize the need to look at organized movements pursuing conscious projects and to develop analyses of national political culture and the 'intimate cultures' of regional power systems. I have already given examples in this chapter of how understanding 'the local' can reveal that politics on the ground is not what it might appear at first sight. In the next chapter, I take this further with a more detailed examination of how anthropologists have used the study of local-level processes and micro-mechanisms of power to illuminate the paradoxical and non-obvious in human affairs.

6 FROM MACRO-STRUCTURE TO MICRO-PROCESS: ANTHROPOLOGICAL ANALYSIS OF POLITICAL PRACTICE

Since most anthropologists have done fieldwork, most could write something about politics at the local level. Although whole cities are too large for anthropologists to study by 'participant observation', much urban anthropology is based on studies of particular neighbourhoods using traditional fieldwork methods. Anthropologists find themselves dealing with local actors such as community leaders campaigning on issues of importance to the residents, as well as representatives of the bureaucracy and national political parties. Most rural communities have local authorities, and even pastoral nomads have leaders who mediate between the group and sedentary society. Village politics around the world involves contests between different factions for offices and perhaps conflict between different local office-holders, such as religious and secular authorities. Conflict is partly about parochial issues, and understanding what sometimes seem byzantine manoeuvres over little of significance demands local knowledge of who the actors are, what their background is and what the issues represent in the eyes of those involved.

I can illustrate this with material from my own fieldwork in a village in Mexico. In the mid-1980s, the priest staged a kind of *coup d'état* by mobilizing the community's women through Catholic lay organizations to vote for him to take over administration of the drinking water supply. The previous administrator was a peasant farmer and past migrant to Mexico City who had a reputation for cattle rustling. He secured the job of installing the system by convincing the village assembly that he and two friends not only had the technical knowledge required but could acquire the materials unusually cheaply. This was true, since they obtained them from friends in Mexico City who pilfered them from building sites on which they were working.

The system worked well in technical terms, but it soon became apparent that the administration was lining its own pockets. An attempt was made to depose it in a public assembly of aggrieved users. This move was only successful in the short term, since the former administrator used his technical knowledge to sabotage the pump. He was reinstated by the women, against male protests, on the grounds that having no water at all was worse than being robbed. At this point, however, the priest began his moves to take over

127

control, using his influence over the women to counter the pragmatic basis for their reluctant backing of a return to the status quo. The priest's intervention produced a new reaction on the part of some of the men who had previously argued against the reinstatement. They now read the situation in terms of the region's long history of violent struggle between clerical and secular power and the Church's supposed manipulation of 'ignorant and fanatical' women in its campaign against land reform. A whole historical discourse of radical agrarianism and anti-clericalism was reactivated to justify opposition to returning to the priest some measure of non-religious influence in community life.

One must bear in mind that in years gone by priests in this village had subtly incited members of Church organizations to assassinate peasant leaders associated with agrarian radicalism. Yet it was also clear that some men resented the fact that the women had displayed a degree of autonomy in village politics as a group. They saw it as symptomatic of a general threat to male patriarchal authority posed by other kinds of social change and a situation of economic crisis. The male faction that presented itself as champion of a struggle against a return to reactionary theocracy appealed to the official discourses of the post-revolutionary state to legitimate its position. It succeeded in securing a new secular administration of the water, following a meeting in which the outgoing administrator was publicly humiliated and deserted by even his closest associates. The incoming group were professionals, mostly working for federal agencies, but their position was fragile. Such persons were associated with corrupt bureaucratic practices and manipulation of state clientelism for political ends. The priest continued his campaign remorselessly, skilfully playing on anti-state discourses. Eventually he secured a majority, and began exercising his control in an increasingly authoritarian way once the secular opposition was divided by the political changes provoked by neoliberalism.

The study of such micro-political processes can, therefore, both illuminate particular local situations which might otherwise remain somewhat obscure, and contribute to an understanding of how processes at the local level not only reflect larger political processes and national-level conflicts, but may contribute to them. Nevertheless, there are dangers of failing to see the larger wood for the local trees. Michael Gilsenan brought out this problem effectively in a critique of the thesis that Mediterranean societies are 'based' on patron–client linkages (Gilsenan 1977).

The thesis is premised on two ideas: firstly, that civil society is fragmented because the state has limited reach at the local level in rural areas, and secondly, that there are also weak horizontal linkages between local communities, which patron–client relations are said to reproduce. The existence of mediators between local and higher levels is thereby 'explained', in teleological fashion, as the result of a 'gap' between levels of social and political organization which has to be filled if society and polity are to function. Anthropologists working in local communities observe that the social relations of most villagers are limited to face-to-face contacts, but often fail to ask the question of what determines *who* fills the gaps in relations with the larger system and *how* this 'filling' is carried out. It is here, Gilsenan argues, that 'a wider and more sociologically crucial set of relations and structures' come into play, which ensure that the 'gap' is *always* filled. We need to explain what particular kinds of social agents fill the gap and how they do so. The Sicilian Mafia, for example, emerged from nineteenth-century transformations of agrarian structure which gave the armed guards of the old estates the chance to insert themselves as intermediaries between the peasantry and the wider society. The PRI bosses of indigenous communities in Chiapas at the start of the 1990s were often the heirs to a generation of bilingual school-teachers and other young people aspiring to challenge the power of village elders who received the backing of the Cárdenas government in the 1930s (Rus 1994). Others, such as the bosses of Zinacantán who were deposed in 1994, achieved power by exploiting the new sources of wealth produced by economic 'development' and forging close relationships with the federal bureaucracies that played an increasingly important role in the region from the start of the 1970s (Cancian 1992, Collier 1994). In the neighbouring municipality of San Juan Chamula, famous for its hostility to non-Indian outsiders as well as for its expulsions of Protestant converts, a small oligarchy of families has retained an iron grip on power by maintaining the closest of ties with the PRI apparatus in the state and unconditional political loyalism (Gossen 1999). As Gilsenan notes, emphasis on the predominance of 'vertical' patron–client ties over 'horizontal' class ties among the *lower* classes obscures the fact that 'horizontal' relations among the *dominant* classes may be strong. It obscures the way changing structures of intermediation can be associated with political centralization forged through elite solidarity or cooperation between elite factions in developing new patterns of class domination. The study of local-level politics should therefore be embedded within wider perspectives on the structures of class domination and other forms of elite power, although, as I stressed in the previous chapter, the local appropriation of the symbols of the state and negotiation of the manner in which rule is effected in its turn shapes patterns of 'vertical' domination.

In this chapter I review various styles of anthropological analysis of 'micro-political' processes. Analysis of micro-mechanisms of power also forces us to return to the issue of how power is grounded in everyday life. As we have already seen, a particularly influential contribution to this discussion has been provided by Michel Foucault.

Foucault defined power in a distinctive way, by refusing to reduce it to negative control of the will of others through prohibition. He argued against treating dominant forms of social knowledge merely as ideologies legitimating oppressive relations. Foucault contended that such forms of knowledge could only underpin 'technologies of domination' over people because they could define a field of knowledge accepted as truth. The production of these 'regimes of truth' is the positive dimension of power. It is positive in the sense that power relations construct human subjects who act and think in a certain way which cannot be reduced to 'false consciousness'. Foucault argues that we need to understand how regimes of truth are produced before we can understand how they might be subverted in social practices. Starting by judging them and trying to subvert them through a rationalist 'critique' short-circuits that necessary analytical task.

Foucault also argued that micro-level power relations – within the family and the school, for example – cannot be reduced to an extension into the domestic realm of the power vested in the state. They have 'relative autonomy' from state and class power:

For me, the whole point of the project [*The History of Sexuality*] lies in a reelaboration of a theory of power ... Between every point of a social body, between a man and a woman, between members of a family, between a master and his pupil, between everyone who knows and everyone who does not, there exist relations of power which are not purely and simply a projection of the sovereign's great power over the individual; they are rather the concrete, changing soil in which the sovereign's power is grounded, the conditions which make it possible for it to function. The family, even now, is not a simple reflection or extension of the power of the State; it does not act as the representative of the State in relation to children, just as the male does not act as its representative with respect to the female. For the State to function in the way that it does, there must be, between male and female or adult and child, quite specific relations of domination which have their own configuration and relative autonomy. (Foucault 1980: 187–8)

Foucault's studies of the disciplining of the body in institutions such as prisons and mental asylums have inspired some anthropological analyses in a direct way, and his influence as a pioneer in the analysis of 'discourses' remains pervasive throughout the discipline. There are, however, other routes through a more conventional anthropological interest in symbolism into some of the areas which Foucault's work tackles, though different theoretical positions should not be conflated. I will begin, however, by surveying some earlier, and conceptually very different, anthropological approaches to the micro-level in political anthropology, all of which retain some salience today.

GETTING AT STRUCTURE THROUGH EVENTS

Within the British anthropological tradition, one of the most significant developments was Victor Turner's analyses of unfolding 'social dramas' (Turner 1996 [1957], Swartz *et al.* 1966). This type of analysis uses crises surrounding key individuals as a way of looking at 'a limited area of trans- parency on the otherwise opaque surface of regular uneventful social life' in order to explore society's basic value systems and organizational principles (Turner 1996: 93). Of course, the ethnographer has to be fortunate enough to witness such 'critical moments' during fieldwork, but Turner used this method to great effect in exploring the political life of the Ndembu and it continues to be widely used today.

In a way that epitomized the Manchester School's attention to the wider context, Turner showed how a long-standing contradiction in Ndembu society, between virilocal residence and matrilineal descent, was exacerbated by the colonial state's model for capitalist development. *Schism and Continuity* is populated by local leaders who are migrant workers in the Copperbelt and by women who prostitute themselves to passing truckers. Larger forces made the contradictions of Ndembu social life increasingly difficult to resolve and were propelling that society towards more radical change. But what Turner focused on was how the Ndembu themselves responded to the forces of change, as individuals pursued their interests, ambitions and conscious goals. In this he was ahead of his time, anticipating Pierre Bourdieu's theory of 'practice', discussed later in this chapter. Turner argued that individual responses to change were in part constrained by their culture, but that social action, or social practice, modified existing normative patterns and produced new forms of social life.

A central figure in Turner's Ndembu writings is Sandombu. He made money as an urban wage-labourer and foreman of Public Works Department labour gangs outside the village, but was not one of a younger generation of men spearheading a capitalist transformation of Zambian society. He wished to convert his money into a traditional status position and become a village headman. In the fourth chapter of *Schism and Continuity*, Turner describes how Sandombu publicly challenged the existing headman, Kahali, and left the village in a welter of mutual threats of sorcery, to visit another village where a famous sorcerer, Sakasumpa, lived. A few days later, Kahali fell ill and died. Sandombu was accused of killing him by sorcery, but not driven out of the village, because the people were too frightened of colonial government intervention to employ a diviner to determine his guilt and Sandombu was also an important source of job opportunities (Turner 1996: 114). Nevertheless, he was denied succession to the headman's position. The elders of the three dominant village matrilineages agreed that the succession should go to Mukanza Kabindi. Turner shows how this train of events reflects both Ndembu cultural values and practical matters of political competition. In doing so he explores the relationships between norms and practice.

Sandombu's initial challenge to the headman was a breach of expected behaviour by younger men towards their elders, but he also belonged to the same matrilineage, and succession to the headmanship within the same lineage was not the Ndembu norm. Sandombu's sister was barren. This had both negative cultural connotations – it suggested sorcery – and immediate practical ramifications, since it reduced the number of matrilineal kinsmen Sandombu could call on for support (ibid.: 108). He himself only had one daughter, and the general feeling was that she was not his child: people thought that he had been made sterile by gonorrhoea contracted when he had worked in a town in 1927. Sterile men were also seen as sorcerers, and Sandombu beat his wife for not bearing children, which added to his dark reputation (ibid.: 107). His candidacy was therefore blighted, but he continued to prosper economically. He was able to rebuild his reputation subsequently by being generous in his patronage towards other villagers, making use of the money that he earned outside the village economy. He tried to overcome his lack of a kin following by establishing a clientship network among stranger lineages; later in Turner's story we find him living in a modern brick house with a bizarre set of clients, including accused witches, a mad child and a woman of easy virtue (ibid.: 153–4). This enabled this essentially marginal figure to continue to dream of becoming a headman, if not of Mukanza village then at least of a new community centred around his farm.

Sandombu comes out of the next two social dramas Turner describes in a relatively strong position, although Mukanza village itself seemed to be heading for fission. This was reflected in the jockeying for position of two other leaders, and expressed the way an underlying logic of matrilineage division after three generations was working itself out, providing a good example of how Turner tried to relate structure to process (ibid.: 99). In the end, Sandombu's own ambitions were again thwarted by a coalition of rivals, but the result was not a foregone conclusion. As Turner shows, norms governing succession to high office within the same matrilineage were breached when a different balance of forces prevailed, and sorcery accusations could be launched in any direction. They stuck to particular individuals only when they reflected a majority consensus reached on other grounds (ibid.: 144–5).

Turner situated his actors within what the Manchester School termed 'social fields': arenas of social and political practice in which actors are seen as manipulating 'norms' which are neither consistent nor fully coherent, as they pursue their ambitions and personal interests. This approach did not entirely dispense with the model of societies as equilibrium systems, but Turner's equilibria were transitory and unstable. When the actors provoke crises, this leads to a realignment of forces and a new, but equally provisional, equilibrium. Turner's study of an ongoing sequence of 'social dramas' (the 'extended case' approach) therefore offers us an ethnographic method for studying historical change, at the micro-level, as it happens.

The idea that critical situations can make manifest latent possibilities which enable us to see how a given society may develop in the future can be illustrated by another analysis in the Manchester tradition by Chandra Jayawardena (1987), who also pays careful attention to the way past historical experiences structure present patterns of behaviour. The events in question took place in Acheh province in Indonesia in the 1960s. They were inadvertently triggered by Jayawardena himself, when he heard that Sufistic devotional singing sessions, anathema to modernist Islam, were being organized by youths in local men's houses.

Jayawardena hoped to record the *rateb* and put out feelers for an invitation. He was residing in the house of a leading modernist *ulama*, Tgk Suleiman, and felt obliged to tell his host of his plans. This provoked no great offence and he was told to go ahead providing Tgk Suleiman was seen as having nothing to do with his activities. Yet word got out, and he received a letter from the headman, Khairullah, ordering him not to attend. This was interpreted as a calculated insult to his host. Tgk Suleiman still took the position that it was up to Jayawardena to decide what to do, though he now advised him not to go. Jayawardena eventually decided not to attend, but the session went ahead.

Shortly afterwards, Jayawardena was approached by Daud, one of the leaders of the proscribed event. Daud offered to organize another session if Jayawardena promised to attend and therefore, by implication, joined in with the youths' defiance of the headman. Again, Tgk Suleiman consented to him going, though other villagers expressed concern that the youths were adopting an openly defiant posture towards the headman. The *rateb* was held, attended by people from different villages and, Jayawardena noted, even by close associates of Tgk Suleiman, suggesting that modernist Islamic hostility to the *rateb* was overlain by another kind of antagonism towards the headman. Despite secrecy, the headman did make an appearance and ordered the performers to stop, retiring with threats after they refused. Subsequently Daud was arrested.

The arrest proved problematic, however. The local police sergeant was reluctant to do it, and the sub-district chief had to intervene. Daud was shortly released, and the villagers interpreted this as a humiliation for both the headman and the sub-district head. They also argued that the headman should not have relied on the police but respected that of the traditional authority responsible for men's house affairs. Nevertheless, the sub-district chief rearrested Daud and two other dissidents. This provoked a picket of the headman's office by a large crowd. Daud was released again after signing an undertaking not to incite further resistance to government policies, but villagers considered the release a vindication of the dissidents.

A few months later, Jayawardena was leaving. The people decided to hold a *rateb* in his honour, not in the men's house but in the place Tgk Suleiman used to impart religious instruction. This had the connotations of a sanctuary in which the government could not legitimately interfere. On this occasion, Tgk Suleiman himself presided, despite his outspoken condemnations of Sufistic practices. Although not holding the *rateb* in the men's house appeared to be a concession to the opposition of the headman and sub-district chief, the arrest and release of Daud was followed by other forms of local opposition to the government, over a new land tax and an instruction from the central government that prayers should be offered for the well-being of President Suharto.

Any anthropologist confronting a sequence of events such as these, in particular the puzzling role of the modernist Tgk Suleiman, has to ask how far the conflicts reflect contingent clashes of personalities and petty local squabbles unconnected with wider issues, and how far they are manifestations of deeper social cleavages. Jayawardena adduces two major sets of (interrelated) background events in the past which underlay the 'major lines of social fracture' he observed, and a third ongoing process which was producing a reaction.

The first is the schism between modernist and traditional Islam. The Achehnese resisted Dutch colonialism militarily. Defeat drove their leaders into the mountains, from which some returned with a project for balancing acceptance of colonial rule with rehabilitation of Achehnese Islam on modernist lines. This provoked conflict not merely over 'folk practices' such as the *rateb* but with traditional *ulama*, whose religious schools now faced modernist competitors. The village community in which Jayawardena lived was deeply divided by conflicts between modernist and traditional Islamic leaders over the construction of a school which inculcated not simply modernist doctrines but elements of the Dutch school curriculum. Although the main family of traditionalist *ulama* left the area, some of their kin continued in residence. Others returned subsequently, after the 1953–61 Darul Islam revolt in Acheh, which is the second major historical factor in Jayawardena's analysis. The kin of the leading modernist had also mostly left the village by the 1960s, but again a kinsman remained in residence, and so the fault-lines of the original conflict were preserved.

Grand issues of faith were, however, underpinned by more mundane political conflicts. The *kampong* unit administered by headman Khairullah was divided into three named sections. One had petitioned to become an independent *kampong* with its own headman. As a reprisal, Khairullah ordered its people to pay a religious tax directly to him at the mosque, rather than at their own men's house to a representative of religious authority, as was the custom. The mosque itself was a source of conflict between the headman and the modernists. The *imam* (prayer-leader) the headman appointed was the son of a school-teacher belonging to the traditionalist *ulama* family. Khairullah wanted to use the mosque as his power base, but he was unpopular because of the way he had achieved office and people who disapproved of this withdrew his usufruct rights to their ricelands. The headman responded by selling lands donated to the mosque to complete the construction, provoking further criticism. The dissident section defied Khairullah by refusing to pay their tax at the mosque, and modernists like Tgk Suleiman would have nothing to do with it because a traditionalist had been appointed *imam*.

Khairullah came to power after Suharto's coup in 1965. All existing office holders were ordered to join the new government party, Golkar. The existing headman was deposed for refusing to do this, but Khairullah himself had previously been associated with the modernists and a member of the PSI (Partai Saraket Islam). The modernists had opposed the Sukarno regime in the Darul Islam revolt, and the national party the rebels had originally supported was banned in 1957 after a revolt in northern Sumatra. They switched allegiance to the PSI, which continued to operate as an opposition party under Suharto despite restrictions. Another twist to the story was provided by the background of the sub-district head, who backed up Khairullah on all points. He had been a guerrilla commander in the Darul Islam revolt and enjoyed close personal relations with the modernist faction. Under Suharto, however, he too supported Golkar, and became politically opposed to his former allies and reliant on Khairullah for support.

Jayawardena argues that the modernist–traditionalist cleavage underpinned modernist defiance of the sub-district chief despite his past record of modernist militancy. Ostensibly the dispute was about suppression of a Sufic practice. Modernists ought to have applauded this on religious grounds, but reacted differently because the dispute was about village autonomy and the sub-district head now represented the imposed Golkar and restrictions on dissident modernist politics. The village autonomy issue also reflected opposition to extension of bureaucratic domination under the Suharto regime, which harked back to earlier experiences under the Dutch. The headman proved arbitrary in his dealings with village sections. He ignored the views of village elders and the customary religious leaders responsible for men's house affairs. The headman had not come to power on the basis of community consensus but through reliance on the external power of the state (and was a political turncoat to boot).

The forces of opposition drew back from total confrontation by deciding to hold the *rateb* in honour of Jayawardena outside the men's house in an area accepted as sanctuary. Yet what is interesting about the case is how the modernists, advocates of the creation of a modern national state, came to oppose that state, used practices of which they did not approve to express that opposition and then embarked on other forms of opposition which were presaged by the 'latent' opposition revealed in these seemingly minor village squabbles.

Jayawardena's analysis suggests that individual political actors are drawn towards certain stances by a variety of conflicting commitments and historical conditions. The logic of one dimension of commitment – religious principles and modernist ideology in this case – can be overridden by the position of members of opposed factions in the political structure. Both underlying logic and historical contingency play a role here. Some types of analysis in political anthropology, however, have gone so far as to treat politics as a relatively autonomous process with a structural logic deriving from the 'rules of the game' in political terms.

POLITICS AS THE ACTIVITY OF 'POLITICAL MEN'

Another way of escaping the functionalist straitjacket of seeing social behaviour simply as the enactment of fixed 'norms' by actors who are assigned equally fixed roles was the 'transactionalist' theory of Frederick Barth (1966). Transactionalism explains the regularities of social organization in terms of the strategizing behaviour of social agents interacting with one another. It is one of a series of methodological individualist theoretical approaches which echo Weber's focus on 'social action'[1] as distinct from Durkheim's view that the key to understanding individuals' behaviour lies in analysing social structure and the rules of social order.

Transactionalism is based on the specific metaphor of individual 'economic men' striving to maximize value in exchange with like motivated actors. The notion that economic actors seek to maximize value seems a useful way of looking at any kind of human behaviour based on rational calculation. There is no reason why the value sought in such behaviour should be economic: it could equally well be power (Blau 1964). Thus the notion that the 'economic man' of neoclassical economic theory provided a conceptual approach to looking at human social behaviour in general (Schneider 1974), could easily lend itself to a concept of 'political man' based on the same theoretical premises.

Such an approach might be dismissed out of hand as ethnocentrism, and in practice transactionalists seem able to explain very little without describing structural constraints which shape actors' behaviour, a problem to which I return in the next section. There is, however, another way of developing this perspective. Contemporary political life in the West might convince us that formal politics is an essentially pragmatic business in which immediate political returns and staying in power count for more than long-term goals, and ideologies count for even less. From this standpoint, there is scope for looking at underlying similarities between the logics of political action on a cross-cultural basis. This was what F.G. Bailey (1969) offered in an analysis of politics based on the metaphor of a competitive game. Bailey argued that rules and goals beyond the pursuit of power *per se* are defined in culturally specific ways, but that all political systems can be analysed in terms of the basic notion of a rule-governed game, whether or not the participants are fully conscious of the codes which regulate their actions. Bailey drew inspiration from Barth's earlier analyses of Swat Pathan politics (1959a, 1959b), and in particular from his flirtation with the formal theory of games developed by John Von Neumann and Oskar Morgenstern (1953). He cheerfully confessed, however, that all this mathematical stuff was beyond him and developed a less formal approach.

---

1 Weber (1978: 4) defined sociology as a science concerned with the 'interpretative under-standing of social action'. Social action entails the individual attaching 'subjective meaning to his behaviour' which 'takes account of the behaviour of others and is therefore oriented in its course'. This definition is foundational for the 'methodological individualist' position that 'social structure' does not 'exist' over and above actors, whose interactions in terms of meanings and expectations shape the 'structures' (regularities) of social life.

Bailey distinguishes between (culturally determined) normative rules and pragmatic rules. The latter are the 'real' rules of the political game, the rules of 'how to get things done'. An environment may contain rival political structures that compete in the absence of an agreed set of rules and make up a 'political field'. As an anthropologist, Bailey is particularly interested in colonial situations in which one type of political structure gets encapsulated by another, more powerful one and how the emergence of intermediaries or 'brokers' might be related to the survival of such encapsulated structures. There are, however, also *arenas* where teams that accept the same rules of the game attempt to build support and subvert that of their opponents.

Competition may move from one such arena to another, or groups in one arena may unite temporarily against a common external threat. Regular competition for power depends on the teams in question being more or less equal in strength. For Bailey, the game of politics as practised in these arenas is defined by rules, although breaking the rules and cheating is a possible political strategy. 'Teams' may be divided into two types: 'contract' teams, where the relationship between leaders and followers is based on material benefits alone, and 'moral' teams based on a shared ideology. Bailey argues that leaders of moral teams have the security of knowing their followers will not readily defect to another team when things go badly. However, they are also constrained by the need to adopt strategies consistent with the normative values of the group. Leaders of both types of team have to engage in a calculation of the political expenses of decision-making. Proceeding by consensus costs least in terms of potential follower recalcitrance, but may give an impression of leadership weakness. Authoritarianism, however, can prove disastrously costly if things go wrong.

Bailey's analytical apparatus sounds like a useful approach to under-standing the pragmatic dynamics of political competition and for looking at some of the structural regularities underlying such competition. His examples range from the Mafia through colonial India to African tribal societies. It is, however, an analysis based on an extended series of metaphors and commonsense observations which are not always valid as empirical gen-eralizations. The distinction he makes between 'moral' and 'contractual' teams would have helped us little in understanding the events in Acheh discussed in the previous section. Actor-orientated approaches of this kind may break out of the structural-functionalist straitjacket, but they imprison us in a new one. What actors do is seldom easily explained without reference to wider relations of force, structures and processes of which the actors themselves, and particularly local actors, frequently have no direct knowledge or consciousness. In some contexts, there is scope for arguing that what actors do is determined by immediate considerations of maintaining political power and the logic of the political situation. Political strategies at this level may have a certain autonomy from deeper objectives, and from the wider social forces and specific cultural structures which will influence the development of the 'game' in the longer term. Yet making that the centre of political anthropology scarcely seems productive, since it leaves the most significant causal factors in political process outside the field of study (Silverman 1974). We will usually only be able to make sense of what political actors do by resorting to deeper analysis of the specific social and cultural frameworks of their actions.

There is, however, another line of analysis which compares the kind of formal political process associated with modern party systems with a game which has a logic of its own. Pierre Bourdieu's theory of political representation (Bourdieu 1991) also addresses the question identified in the last chapter as a crucial one for a critical analysis of Western democracy and class politics. At first glance, Bourdieu appears to have much in common with Barth and Bailey. His theoretical exposition makes extensive use of the 'economic' metaphor of capital. He argues that social fields and practices which are not themselves 'economic' nevertheless obey a broader kind of economic logic, that of increasing some kind of 'capital' – symbolic or cultural, political or linguistic – and maximizing 'profit' in the form of honour or social prestige. He therefore assumes that social action is structured by the pursuit of 'interests' by human agents, although the content of those interests is always determined culturally, and may not be 'material' or 'economic' in the narrow sense. Indeed, the artistic community, for example, may actually enhance their social prestige by professing a complete disinterest in the monetary value of artistic productions: 'art for art's sake' (Bourdieu 1984). This systematic distancing of the world of 'high art' from the mundane world of commodities and economic value could, however, be seen as a disguise which actually allows elite consumers of art to have their cake and eat it: to accumulate objects which have a higher market worth because they belong to the rarefied aesthetic world of high art, and at the same time enjoy the social prestige of being aesthetes who appreciate art for its own sake.

The argument that self-interested social actors pursue 'non-material' scales of value is not, in itself, distinct from the position adopted by transactionalists, but Bourdieu does not subscribe to a methodological individualist position. He stresses the connections between social fields in which the accumulation of symbolic or other non-economic forms of capital is predominant and the accumulation of economic capital and class structures. Class is a central concept in Bourdieu's sociology. Bourdieu also differs from Bailey by directing our attention to the symbolic practices surrounding power relations.

THE AUTONOMY OF THE POLITICAL FIELD AND ITS SYMBOLIC PRACTICES

Bourdieu's original critique of the dominant approaches of social theory was equally antagonistic to the kind of 'objectivist' models of society offered by Lévi-Straussian and other brands of structuralism and the 'subjectivism' he associated with the existentialism of Jean-Paul Sartre and interactionist and transactionalist theorists (Bourdieu 1977).

Structuralist objectivism tries to explain social behaviour from the point of view of the observer. It 'explains' behaviour by constructing a model of rules, much like a computer program, which can 'generate' the actors' observed behaviour or a set of 'transformations' representing all possible permutations of behaviour. Structuralism tended to locate 'structuring structures' in the unconscious mind, and appeared to leave no scope for human strategizing or the unintended historical consequences of conscious human actions. It seemed incapable of tackling history and change. Sartrean theory, on the other hand, left social actors more or less unconstrained by 'structuring structures', as free agents. Neither it, nor models based on the individual strategizer of the kind Anglo-Saxon social theorists favoured, seemed capable of accounting for the systematic nature of social behaviour. Behaviour evidently is systematically structured in ways that cannot be derived directly from social interaction, since social interaction is already structured. We become locked in an explanatory vicious circle.

Bourdieu's resolution of the problem was to argue that social agents are imbued with dispositions to think and behave in certain ways by the action of historical social forces. They are like musicians whose improvisations are neither predictable in advance, a product of conscious intent, nor simply a 'realization' of a structure which already exists in the unconsciousness. This is Bourdieu's concept of the *habitus*, 'a system of durable, transposable dispositions, structured structures predisposed towards acting as structuring structures' (1977: 72). As 'the durably installed generative principle of regulated improvisations', the *habitus*:

produces practices which tend to reproduce the regularities immanent in the objective conditions of the production of their generative principle, while adjusting to the demands inscribed as objective potentialities in the situation, as defined by the cognitive and meaning structures making up the habitus. (ibid.: 78)

According to this theory, systems of domination will be reproduced over time because the way the actors understand their world, the cognitive and meaning structures of the *habitus*, has been shaped by the workings of relations of domination which produce those 'structured structures'. The collective practices produced by the *habitus* in turn reproduce the historical conditions which shaped those cognitive and meaning structures in the first place. Change is, however, possible, because objective political and economic circumstances change – ruling elites suffer military reverses and social groups experience economic problems. This can influence social actors' dispositions if it has an impact on the positive discourses of power and silent 'taken-for-granted' assumptions through which the power of dominant classes is reproduced.

Bourdieu defines the field of taken-for-granted knowledge as *doxa*. The importance of taken-for-grantedness is that there are some subjects which are never discussed, and certain questions which are never raised, in social discourses relevant to power and domination. This is one of Bourdieu's most important ideas. Political or economic crisis can provoke confrontations between groups. Yet this may go no further than opening up what Bourdieu terms the 'field of opinion' (that which is talked about) to a heterodox discourse, which is distinguished from, but still structured by, an 'orthodoxy' defined in terms of the positively expressed aspects of dominant class ideology. Radical critique and fundamental change demand a questioning of what is not normally questioned (ibid.: 168). To secure emancipation from existing modes of domination, the dominated classes have to go beyond offering a competing heterodox discourse in the 'field of opinion' to question the wider field of *doxa*, the 'taken-for-granted' domain of social thought on which orthodox and heterodox discourses are equally *silent*.

Bourdieu's theory therefore locates social actors within 'objective' circumstances beyond their immediate control, but stresses the way their reactions to changes in those circumstances are mediated by symbolic meaning structures. The strategies individuals pursue in social action are structured in a way which normally reproduces structures of domination. The collective *habitus* produces a collective order behind individual strategies and constrains them to improvisation on a theme. The problem here is the mechanism that generates the *habitus* shared by all individuals in the same group or social class.

Bourdieu argues that the homogenization of *habitus* within the group can be understood in terms of Leibniz's notion of 'windowless monads'. If we consider two clocks that always strike in unison, we could explain this in three ways: in terms of communication between the clocks, in terms of the intervention of a workman or regulator (God), or in terms of the precision of their original construction – each clock is so perfectly made that the two keep perfect and synchronous time for ever, solely as a result of their 'internal' laws (ibid.: 80–1). The 'construction' of the individual in society is a matter, for Bourdieu, of socialization. He develops this point in his analysis of the Kabyle house, which he compares to a school book inculcating the worldview of Kabyle society to children as it is 'read with the body, in and through the movements and displacements which make the space within which they are enacted as much as they are made by it' (ibid.: 90). The house and the activities which take place in it are structured in terms of symbolic oppositions which the child learns through practice: 'all actions performed in a space constructed in this way are immediately qualified symbolically and function as so many structural exercises through which is built up practical mastery of the fundamental schemes' (ibid.: 91).

The individual thus internalizes objectified structures and all individuals in the same group or class acquire the same *habitus*. Accordingly, collective mobilization 'cannot succeed without a minimum of concordance between the *habitus* of the mobilizing agent (e.g. prophet, party leader, etc.) and the dispositions of those whose aspirations and world-views they express' (ibid.).

The problem with the analogy between people and Leibnizian monads is, however, that it leads to a one-sided view in which social agents are, once again, programmed through socialization and the role of communication between them in action is downplayed. It is surely important that there is communication within social groups about the extended experience of 'being-in-the-world'. Human beings are not, in fact, windowless monads, even if the *habitus* plays a crucial role in structuring the meanings social collectivities ascribe to changing experience.

How do we account for the unusually persuasive nature of the 'messages' of certain prophets and party leaders at particular moments in time, and for the fact that the same community (say French industrial workers) can be mobilized by communists in one period and racists and fascists in another? Bourdieu's concept of the *habitus* seems more useful for explaining reproduction than for explaining change. We might accept that the capacity of the fascists to mobilize workers ultimately rests on a concordance between fascist discourse and the dispositions and meanings embodied in the *habitus* of the French working class. We might also accept that the shift in political loyalties is linked to the existence of ethnically stigmatized immigrants within a working-class social world experiencing economic crisis. Yet the problem is that even if working-class socialization always contains a latent possibility to foster racist xenophobia, this only becomes central to practice at certain moments.

Bourdieu's work does, however, offer us additional insights into questions of this nature. Firstly, although 'class' is central to his analyses, he offers a different account of class to that offered by Marxism. Bourdieu argues that Marxist theory produces analyses of what he calls 'classes on paper'. We define the position of social groups in terms of an objective account of their place in the socio-economic structure and then *infer* their *probable* actions in terms of the 'material interests' this objective model defines (Bourdieu 1991: 231–2). We define forms of 'consciousness' appropriate to material interests defined in terms of economic position, and can therefore talk about the political work of 'consciousness-raising', encouraging workers to adopt 'correct' forms of consciousness. The problem is, however, that social identities and systems of social distinction are not based solely on people's relationships to economic capital. The *actual* rather than *theoretical* consciousness of members of a class is the product of practical historical experiences of living-in-the-world. This involves all the different dimensions of power relations and not simply the economic ones.

Throughout his later work, which has focused on dimensions of European elite culture such as art and higher education (Bourdieu 1984), Bourdieu has stressed the way societies consist of a series of differentiated social spaces distinguished by differences of lifestyles. Cultured elites have a distinct social position compared to people who possess economic capital but can be denigrated as vulgar parvenus by those who hold symbolic capital in fields where 'cultivation', 'education' and perhaps 'breeding' count. Systems of social distinction constitute a vision of society's divisions that certain agents succeed in imposing. The key to being able to control systems of social classification is to acquire the authority to name and confer titles. A 'professor' acquires symbolic capital firstly through the official recognition of the university institution and secondly through the recognition the state gives to the university as a structure authorized to place individuals in a hierarchy of grades of social distinction.

Labour leaders and workers' parties are individuals and organizations authorized to speak in the name of the working class. This 'power to speak' on behalf of a group turns the group from a collection of individuals into a political force. The fact that working classes are widely deemed to exist is based on their political representation by political and trade union apparatuses and party officials 'who have a vital interest in believing that this class exists and in spreading this belief among those who consider themselves part of it as well as those who are excluded from it' (Bourdieu 1991: 250). The political field cannot be reduced to a reflection of the structure of 'classes on paper'. In fact, the logic of the political field determines which 'classes on paper' will actually be represented politically:

The interests of the unorganized sub-proletariat have no chance of gaining access to political representation (especially when that sub-proletariat is made up of foreigners without the right to vote or of stigmatized racial minorities) unless those interests become a weapon and a stake in the struggle, which, in certain states of the political field, sets two things against each other: on the one hand, spontaneism, or, up to a point, revolutionary voluntarism, both of which are always inclined to favour the least organized fractions of the proletariat, whose spontaneous action precedes or goes beyond the organization; and, on the other hand, centralism (which its adversaries label 'bureaucratic-mechanistic'), for which the organization, that is the party, precedes the class and its struggle. (ibid.: 188)

Bourdieu's analysis of 'political representation' stresses that the political field is professionalized and that political capital has historically tended to be concentrated in few hands. Since members of subaltern classes do not possess either leisure time or cultural capital in abundance, Bourdieu suggests that they have little choice but to cede their power to a political party, a permanent organization which will represent their class and give it continuity. Ironically, therefore, political capital is most concentrated in parties whose aim is to struggle against the concentration of economic capital in the name of the workers (ibid.: 174).

This is what gives the logic of the political 'game' its relative autonomy. Political parties have to find ways of mobilizing the largest number of citizens, subordinating the production of ideas about the social world to maximizing votes. A series of professional skills are developed to control the base and secure 'mandates' from it, manifest in the complex procedures for constructing motions at party conferences. Professionalized leaderships generate an 'esoteric culture' of political practices, a specialized cultural world of politicians from which 'ordinary people' are excluded (ibid.: 184).

This does not mean that party politics or government itself becomes completely detached from economic and social forces, but simply that the dependence of the political field on these forces is matched by the impact political activity has on them 'via its control of the instruments of administration of things and persons' (ibid.: 182). Furthermore, the positions occupied by different parties within the political field are determined by a structural relational logic. The 'right' and the 'left' of the political spectrum do not stand for the same things at different historical moments. The only constant is the need for a Right and a Left[2] to exist:

The opposition between the 'right' and the 'left' can be maintained in a structure transformed at the cost of a partial exchange of roles between those who occupy those positions at two different moments (or in two different places): rationalism and belief in progress and science which, between the wars, in France as well as Germany, were a characteristic of the left (whereas the nationalist and conservative right succumbed instead to irrationalism and to the cult of nature), have become today, in these two countries, the heart of the new conservative creed, based on confidence in progress, technical knowledge and technocracy, while the left finds itself falling back on ideological themes or on practices which used to belong to the opposite pole, such as the (ecological) cult of nature, regionalism and a certain nationalism, the denunciation of the myth of absolute progress, the defence of the 'person'. (ibid.: 185)

Nevertheless, professional politicians cannot compete for power with each other without mobilizing non-professionals, and differences in party orientation can only be translated into winning political strategies when they converge with the strategies of groups outside the political field itself (ibid.: 188).

This, however, creates further contradictions. Close convergence with a sectional social interest, particularly a minority interest, is likely to lead to exclusion from power or power-distributing coalitions. Yet compromise-based political realism may dilute the party's mobilizing potential. Mobilizing ability may be based on a leader's personal 'political capital', in the form of either charisma or a capacity to dispense patronage. An alternative way of building a permanent apparatus of mobilization is to delegate the party's political and symbolic capital to a bureaucratized party organization. In this case, dispensing jobs within the apparatus becomes more important than winning 'hearts and minds' and policy-making becomes a closed and professionalized affair. Bourdieu concludes that the primary problem facing political organizations designed to subvert the established order[3] is that, given the cultural and economic deprivation of those they represent, they

---

2 The terms themselves originated in a French convention about where Conservatives and Liberals sat relative to the President of the Constituent Assembly.

3 Bourdieu includes trade unions in this category. It is not obvious, however, that trade unions *are* organizations orientated towards subverting capitalism. They might, indeed, be seen as essential to its long-term reproduction as mediating agencies involved in the regulation of capital–labour relations. We can also question whether 'class struggle' between capital and labour *in itself* is a force likely to overthrow capitalism (Therborn 1980).

become more and more apparatuses of mobilization and less and less means for expressing the will of their 'base'.

One implication of Bourdieu's analysis is that left parties which neither succeed in satisfying their working-class supporters' interests nor in engineering intense loyalty based on the perfection of mobilizing apparatuses may fall victim to voter discontent with 'professional' politics itself, when a political 'outsider' appears as a candidate. Another implication is that class struggle is a symbolic struggle, which takes place at two levels, in everyday life, and by proxy, through struggles between professionalized producers of symbols. Symbolic power consists in making people accept an existing or transformed vision of the world, and it rests, in Bourdieu's view, not on the words and slogans as such, but on people recognizing the legitimacy of those who utter them.

In my view, these are important insights, but Bourdieu has little positive to say about the role of the lower classes and their political culture. His theory of political representation stresses the way leaders and parties define their constituencies' ideological horizons. His interests are primarily in the way relations of domination are instituted, legitimated and 'euphemized'. The various forms of social power are not, Bourdieu points out, routinely deployed in everyday life as physical force but transmuted into 'symbolic power' and 'symbolic violence' (Bourdieu 1977: 196, 1991: 170). Symbolic power is based on 'social taxonomies' which subaltern groups 'misrecognize' as legitimate by failing to see them as arbitrary constructions serving dominant class interests. The dominated are thus accomplices in their own domination by symbolic power. Thus, not only has Bourdieu increasingly focused on the study of elites, but his own perspective seems an elitist one, offering little scope for understanding how power relations are also shaped 'from below'.

Consider, for example, the idea that there is a 'popular' vision of the Mexican Revolution that is discordant with the 'official' version. This might be relevant, for example, to understanding the emotive power of political rituals, where crowds are moved by the symbols involved and yet remain utterly cynical about the roles of the civil or military public figures officiating at the ceremony. The emotive power of the figure of Emiliano Zapata for lower-class Mexicans lies in the authenticity of his representation of 'the people'. As a popular leader betrayed and murdered by the political elite of post-revolutionary society, Zapata is not simply someone who did not 'sell out' the people. He stands for their collective betrayal (Powell 1996: 52–3).

The popular 'political imaginary' of what the Mexican Revolution could have achieved in terms of social justice went beyond anything the dominant class in Mexico was ever going to concede. It cannot be seen as something constituted by and through the political representation of the masses. Nevertheless, part of Bourdieu's argument retains its force. The popular imaginary was reduced in potency by the fact that the state gave it limited recognition by incorporating popular symbols into the official iconography of the Revolution. This disposed popular movements to pursue their goals through alliances with 'progressive' factions of the political class and by petitioning the state itself to concede rights to them under the law. Another problem is revealed by Kapferer's analysis of the Anzac day ceremony in Australia. Anzac celebrates and sacralizes the people (embodying the nation) *against* the State. Yet the popular ideology enshrined in the ceremony is also a force for domination. Australian popular nationalism based on egalitarian individualism embodies habitual assumptions that underpin weak working-class solidarity, subordination of women and racism (Kapferer 1988: 180).

Unravelling these kinds of issues has been one of the achievements of semiotic, structuralist and hermeneutic approaches which concentrate on both the content of the symbols manipulated in political life and their underlying logic and deeper associations. As an illustration of the potential of this kind of analysis, I will discuss a case study offered by Marc Abélès (1988) of two French 'political rituals' involving President Mitterrand. One, the inauguration of a new railway station in the town of Nevers, followed by a round of conferring decorations on local personages, is a long-established institutionalized political ritual. The other, the President's annual 'pilgrimage' to the Rock of Solutré, is a personal invention.

The inauguration is a conventionalized performance. All the actors know the scenario beforehand. Acts that follow, like the investiture of Knights of the Legion of Honour, are equally codified, though proceedings are enlivened by unscripted embracings of small children and other touches relevant to the photo opportunity. Yet the pilgrimage itself has symbolic value: the President moves from the political centre to the provincial periphery, and then from the departmental headquarters to outlying localities. Mitterrand was the elected representative for the department of Nièvre for thirty years. The inauguration 'symbolizes in itself the permanence of the exchanges represented by this political man between the abiding countryside, in which he finds the source of his legitimacy, and the capital city, from which it is his task to attract financial means for the betterment of his department' (Abélès 1988: 394).

Mitterrand's discourse throughout the day emphasized return and the reconcilability of national and regional interests. This had a particular conjunctural significance. France was on the eve of national elections that returned a non-socialist executive. Abélès argues, however, that there is another significance to the endless repetition of micro-sequences of bestowing decorations, honouring local worthies, inaugurating new public facilities, listening to school children performing and all the other things that politicians on tour routinely do. Repetition creates a special kind of 'ritual time' and atmosphere, lending the acts a 'quasi-religious' significance. The community pays homage to the President and the President sanctifies the local notables he honours. At one level, then, it is concerned with the bestowal and recognition of symbolic power in Bourdieu's terms.

Yet there is another level and another register. On the train *en route* to the inauguration, Mitterrand was quizzed by journalists on the topic of the legislative elections. He pronounced that he would 'choose whomever he wished' as prime minister, remarking that the premier chosen would have 'every right to contribute to all political debate outside the province of the president' (ibid.: 392). On this matter, he was 'very much in advance of his predecessors'. Abélès suggests that Mitterrand deliberately used a ritual occasion which evoked the representative character of the President as 'the choice of the people' to assert his transcendent authority as Head of State. When he began his speech at the station with the statement 'I am not particularly keen on inaugurations', Mitterrand was really saying: 'See me playing the role of a president in the style of the Fourth Republic! But know well that I will never be confined to such a role!' (ibid.: 395).

This is also, Abélès argues, the key to understanding the President's pilgrimage to Solutré. Mitterrand, an active member of the resistance, took refuge in Solutré after escaping from Germany during the war, and married one of the daughters of the family that gave him shelter. He used the place as a retreat throughout his political life, but, after becoming President, began inviting journalists along.

The ritual has three stages. Firstly, Mitterrand ascends the steep path to the Rock, a prehistoric site offering spectacular vistas over the Saône Valley. The exertion required testifies to the President's health. The ascent is made in the company of an intimate entourage, projecting an image of alliance and loyalty. The President stands on the summit, steeped in history, contemplating the countryside that is a metaphor for the nation. In the second phase, the participants gather in a restaurant for a family lunch, followed by the third phase, a press conference where Mitterrand makes disclosures about future political developments. In 1986 this included insights into his strategy for living with the conservative majority and points on which he would resist legislative changes. The Solutré pilgrimage thus became an important exercise in political communication, but Abélès argues that this was not all it was, and that focusing only on what the President said would impoverish its symbolic content and political effect.

The ascent of the Rock mirrors the President's ascent to meditate in the Pantheon on Montagne Sainte Geneviève on the day of his inauguration. It reaffirms his position in the political hierarchy, at the same time as it 'proves' his continuing physical capacity to exercise supreme power. In Solutré the ascent not merely allows him space to meditate on his great responsibility, but places him in contact with history, the history of France and its greatness, of which both the Pantheon and Solutré are symbols. Again, Abélès argues, the political ritual at Solutré has a religious dimension, but it is not concerned with the legitimacy of an elected representative. It establishes Mitterrand as a mythological hero, a resistance fighter and mediator, on whom depends the historical fate of the nation. The Solutré ritual takes place at Pentecost. Abélès cannot determine whether the choice of this day – which marks the descent of the Holy Spirit and the beginning of a new era – was intentional, but the association between the press conference and enunciation, perhaps fortuitously established, does add to the occasion. He argues that secular France has not effaced a religious dimension from the Republican project, despite the Napoleonic separation of Church and state. Modern political rituals are therefore not totally distinct from those of pre-modern societies.

The comments on Abélès's paper which follow from other anthropologists in the usual style of *Current Anthropology*, include some doubts about whether one should talk of 'religion' where no supernatural forces are involved. The author counters this objection by observing that an explanation of the ritual that omitted the aspect of 'secular worship' of the Republic and Nation involved would impoverish its content. Maurice Bloch argues that the similarity between what Abélès describes and more 'exotic' anthropological cases is, if anything, even stronger than Abélès recognizes: Mitterrand's ascent of the Rock at Pentecost is equivalent to rituals of the symbolic death of a king, involving a temporary acceptance of ageing and shift to a liminal place from which he can return as a strengthened rejuvenator of himself and others. Bloch is inclined to see the stress on innovation and intentional creation in the Solutré ritual as misleading, since the participants are, in fact, following through familiar patterns, though Abélès continues to argue that the ritual is invented, despite its use of symbolic patterns commonly found in other cultures and his own suspicions that some aspects of the performance might address specific symbolic logics within French culture.

Abélès is, however, encouraged by Bloch's reaction to strengthen his resistance to taking the folk categories of modern societies – the kinds of distinctions we make between the religious and the secular and the religious and political – at face value. He argues that the study of political ritual offers a different set of insights into the political process from those offered by conventional institutional models.

However, as Georges Augustins observes in his commentary, although Abélès succeeds in establishing that the rituals involve symbolic discourses about legitimacy, he has not offered much of an explanation of how such discourses arouse emotions in the spectators and participants that lend the symbolic discourses practical efficacy. Abélès's response to this point is a vague nod in the direction of 'psychological mechanisms' (ibid.: 403). This is an issue that is central to Bruce Kapferer's analysis of the roots of ethnic violence in Sri Lanka. He tackles it with reference to Bourdieu's *habitus*:

Broadly, the legitimating and emotional force of myth is not in the events as such but in the logic which conditions their significance. This is so when the logic is also vital in the way human actors are culturally given to constituting a self in the everyday routine world and move out towards others in that world ... Where human beings recognize the argument of mythic reality as corresponding to their own personal constitutions – their orientation within and movement through reality – so myth gathers force and can come to be seen as embodying ultimate truth. Myth so enlivened, I suggest, can become imbued with commanding power, binding human actors to the logical movement of its scheme ... It comes to define significant experience in the world, experience which in its significance is also conceived as intrinsic to the constitution of the person. By virtue of the fact that myth engages such a reasoning which is also integral to everyday realities, part of the taken-for-granted or 'habitus' of the mundane world, myth can change the emotions and fire the passions. (Kapferer 1988: 46–7)

Kapferer insists that we must avoid a 'descent into pyschologism' in trying to account for the emotional appeal of myths and other elements of the symbolic order. Myths carry *ontological* weight: they define 'the fundamental principles of a being in the world and the orientations of such a being towards the horizons of its existence' (ibid.: 79). The same ontology governs the con-stitution and reconstitution of being in some rituals. The cultural universe of Sinhalese Buddhists does not, however, contain only one ontology or mode of being, but a multiplicity, some of which have been introduced through Sri Lanka's incorporation into the modern global system. They include that according to which 'the individual realizes his or her value in the possession of commodities which have value in a capitalist economy' (ibid.). It is particular social, economic and political circumstances that make certain ontologies of overriding importance, as actors organize particular cultural raw materials into relatively coherent ideological schemes, imbuing them with new meanings and new force in the process. At this point, the logic of a myth, ingrained in the habitual practices of everyday life, can, as Kapferer puts it, 'turn the tables on those who use it'.

In Sri Lanka, the new meanings given to established ontologies of evil, power and the state by ethnic nationalist ideology led to a passionate desire on the part of Sinhalese to preserve the hierarchic order of the state, because the integrity of the state was seen culturally as a condition for maintaining the integrity of the person. The Tamils were seen as a threat to individual Sinhalese people because they posed a threat to the state.

I will return to Sri Lanka in the next chapter, but this introduction to Kapferer's analysis suggests ways in which micro-analysis of the symbolic dimensions of power in everyday life can be related to macro-structural analyses. Anthropologists have been trying to develop the insights of struc-turalist analyses in a way which makes it possible to talk about dynamic social processes and transcend the unsatisfactory alternatives of seeing human beings as either free agents creating structures through interaction or automata merely enacting a programme. For Kapferer, as for Bourdieu, it is impossible to analyse the symbolic domain without also discussing class formation, global political economy and geo-political relations, but both see social action as inseparable from meaning and seek to avoid the reduction-ism which leaves 'ideology' as a superstructure floating above some more 'material' reality.

I will conclude this chapter, however, with further discussion of Foucault. Foucault's concept of power takes us more deeply into an exploration of the way power enters into everyday social relationships and the bodies of individuals, and, as I pointed out earlier in this chapter, Foucault's approach is strongly antagonistic to Bourdieu's account of domination as subaltern 'misrecognition'.

INSIDIOUS STRATEGIES OF POWER

I have already made frequent reference to Foucault's work on modern forms of power, which is integral to the work of such otherwise disparate theorists as sociologist Anthony Giddens and anthropologists Aihwa Ong (1999) and Ann Stoler (1995). Stoler's use of Foucault is particularly concerned with transcending his eurocentrism, but she finds his iconoclasm a useful starting-point for pursuing her own explorations of how colonial power relations shaped desire. In his unfinished project *The History of Sexuality*, for example, Foucault (1985) made the argument that bourgeois society's apparent interest in the control of sexuality, hygiene and family morality should not be seen as an effort to repress universal 'natural' urges of the kind discussed by Freudian psychoanalysis. On the contrary, bourgeois interventions in the field of sexuality were *provocations, creating* a specific type of sexual subject and inciting specific desires.[4]

Foucault's rejection of a model of bourgeois sexuality as repression was a logical extension of the theory of power developed in his earlier work, focused on how institutions such as prisons and mental asylums enabled bourgeois societies to replace centralized and hierarchical forms of control based on repression and interdiction with more diffuse forms of 'disciplinary power' or 'governmentality' (Foucault 1979). Disciplinary power works on the individual through the disciplining of the body, creating subjects who *regulate themselves*. Thus, what Foucault called 'biopower' makes direct state regulation of social life through repression less necessary. Social life is 'normalized' through the creation of scientific knowledge that underpins specification of what is 'deviant' behaviour: social problems are 'medicalized', for example, so that deviant people are considered to be sick people who can be rehabilitated by treatment.

Barry Morris (1989) draws on Foucault's work on disciplinary institutions to frame an analysis of the changing relationships between the Dhan-Gadi Aborigines and the Australian state. Morris examines official texts that illustrate the changing nature of constructions of Aboriginality by

---

4 Since Freudian ideas have frequently been used to explain the sexual behaviour and desires of European colonialists, Foucault's ideas offer the opportunity to explain the many anomalies that cannot be explained within such a framework. Stoler demonstrates, however, that 'colonial discourses of sexuality were productive of class and racial power, not mere reflections of them' and that within this 'racially charged field' not all bodies were treated the same, be they White or non-White (Stoler 1995: 176).

the Australian state, and investigates how the local European population's constructions of Aboriginality changed in response to these shifting official discourses. For example, as official thinking turned to view the 'problem' of the Aborigine as a social welfare matter in the second half of the 1960s, and stressed environment as the determinant of the Aborigines' problems, the White reaction was to construct the Aborigines as *inherently* inferior because of their welfare-dependence and argue that this, in turn, was a product of their inherent racial inferiority (Morris 1989: 185–7). Like Kapferer, Morris links this form of racism to the egalitarian ethos of White Australian society. The basic principles that Morris derives from Foucault are that disciplinary power requires the creation of a body of knowledge about the subject group. The Aborigines were turned into an object of specialist knowledge (which has taken various forms historically). Others thereby came to become 'dispensers of truth about the needs and requirements' of Aborigines, and the Aborigines themselves were increasingly called upon to fulfil the constructions of their identity created by those in authority over them. They thus lost control over their communal identity (or more precisely, their ability to define themselves).

Foucault's analysis of the past four centuries of European history draws our attention to the emergence of a whole series of discourses designed to construct programmes for reshaping society, but his work is not concerned purely with 'discourses', at least in principle. He distinguishes between what he terms 'strategies', 'technologies' and 'programmes' of power. Programmes of power define a domain of social reality to be turned into an object of rational knowledge, intervened in and made functional. Technologies of power are techniques and practices for the disciplining, surveillance, administration and shaping of human individuals. Programmes define forms of knowledge and discourses about objects of knowledge. Technologies are apparatuses of power designed to implement that knowledge. Strategies of power are what agencies do in practice in exercising power and in operationalizing programmes and technologies. They develop in response to changing circumstances and are therefore improvisations. Furthermore, the field of strategies also includes strategies of resistance. Foucault sees power relations as present in *all* social relationships, permeating society in a capillary way rather than coming 'down' from a single centre of control such as the state. The first point of resistance to power for Foucault must thus be individual strategies which counter specific forms of domination, even in minute, everyday ways.

Since programmes of power elaborated in discourses must be implemented through technologies that encounter the recalcitrant material of real societies and real people, their practical effects are determined by strategies (of domination and resistance). Foucault points out that prisons, for example, totally fail to fulfil their declared programme, the elimination of crime and the reform of the criminal:

The prison, apparently 'failing', does not miss its target; on the contrary, it reaches it, in so far as it gives rise to one particular form of illegality in the midst of others, which it is able to isolate, to place in full light and to organize as a relatively enclosed, but penetrable, milieu. It helps to establish an open illegality, irreducible at a certain level, but secretly useful, at once refractory, but docile ... This form is ... delinquency ... So successful has the prison been that, after half a century of 'failures' the prison still exists, producing the same results, and there is the greatest possible reluctance to dispense with it. (Foucault 1979: 276–7)

The context of these seemingly bizarre remarks is the pattern of popular 'illegalities' in the nineteenth century. There was not merely an increase in crime, linked to the social transformations of industrial urbanization, but the European elites saw this illegality as politically threatening. The lower orders were seen as essentially criminal and barbaric. The prison's 'fabrication' of delinquency offered a number of advantages: individual members of the barbarous classes could be identified, and perhaps turned into informers. In place of the vagabonds roaming the countryside in the eighteenth century, ready to form 'formidable forces for rioting and looting', those classified as 'delinquents' were a controllable group, now pushed to the social margins, unable to unite with other sections of society, and locked into a life of petty crimes of which the poorer classes were most likely to be victims.

Those branded delinquents were thus isolated from participation in other 'popular illegalities' which might turn 'political'. Delinquents were often used to spy on workers' organizations (ibid.: 280). Delinquency as a 'controlled illegality' could even be profitable for the dominant groups in society. Prostitution in nineteenth-century France was turned into a domain of surveillance, with checks by the police and checks on the prostitutes' health. Brothels were organized into hierarchic networks and delinquent-informers served as intermediaries between officialdom and this subterranean world. Public moralization made consorting with prostitutes a more clandestine and expensive activity, increasing the profits of what legal and moral prohibition had turned into big business. Foucault concludes that: 'in setting up a price for pleasure, in creating a profit from repressed sexuality and in collecting this profit, the delinquent milieu was in complicity with a self-interested puritanism: an illicit fiscal agent operating over illegal practices' (ibid.). The prison failed by the criteria of its original programme and the discourse that gave birth to it, but proved a success in terms of other, improvised, strategies of power.

The eurocentrism of Foucault's work is clearly problematic. He assumes that there is an evolving historical entity that we can call 'Western civilization' that begins in the world of classical Greece and Rome, tracing the genealogies of bourgeois society and culture within that framework alone and never asking himself any questions about the role of Europe's colonial empires in the formation of Western modernity and 'the bourgeois self'. His methodology is rather slipshod. Like Bourdieu he focuses most of his attention on French society and culture, but when unable to illustrate a point with French material, cheerfully substitutes an example from England or another country that fits his argument without regard to possible differences of context. More significantly still, his talk about power inevitably provoking 'resistances' has little real substance. His capillary model of power privileges the 'micro-politics' of resistance, yet his analyses remain 'top-down'. Although he acknowledged that the analysis of discursive constructions of the subject traced genealogically through texts alone could never suffice, Foucault was no ethnographer and made no effort to study human beings in concrete social situations directly. This leaves his account of how 'resistance' might play a role in the constitution of power relations at the level of strategies and improvisations quite underdeveloped. Though different from James Scott's position in other respects, Foucault's argument about the micro-politics of resistance can also lead us to a dismissal of organized popular political action which would be premature, as can Bourdieu's equally 'top-down' view of subaltern 'misrecognition' of domination.

Nevertheless, Foucault's 'capillary' model of power does offer further insights into the processes that influence the horizons and practical results of organized and self-conscious political struggles. His idea that modern forms of 'governmentality' are based on the construction of self-regulating subjects is a powerful one. His work offered new ways of exploring central theoretical issues in this chapter, the relationship between 'structure' and 'agency' and the role of the unintentional in history. We have also seen that analysing change involves understanding the mutual articulations of the micro- and macro-levels of social life. In the next chapter, I turn to the most 'macro' of all levels, the modern global system.

7 POLITICAL PROCESS AND 'GLOBAL DISORDER': PERSPECTIVES ON CONTEMPORARY CONFLICT AND VIOLENCE

After the collapse of communism, George Bush proclaimed US victory in the Cold War and the initiation of a 'New World Order'. It is tempting to parody Bush's rhetoric by focusing on the escalation of 'small wars', civil strife and ethnic and political violence in many parts of the world in the post-Cold War era. Yet we should resist. In this chapter I argue against post-Cold War rhetorics which see crisis as something rooted in the South by which North Atlantic countries remain untouched and for which they are not responsible, other than as the world's policemen driven by purely humanitarian motives. Furthermore, as Benedict Anderson has argued, it makes no sense to describe what is happening as the 'fragmentation' of some more 'orderly' prior state of affairs:

This language makes us forget the decades or centuries of violence out of which Frankensteinian 'integrated states' such as the United Kingdom of 1900, which included all of Ireland, were constructed. Should we really regard such 'integrations' as pathological when we see how calmly the Irish Republic and the United Kingdom have coexisted since the former was established in 1921 – after decades of often violent repression and resistance? Or when we observe the brutal warfare still continuing in 'integrated' Northern Ireland? Behind the language of 'fragmentation' lies a Panglossian conservatism that likes to imagine that every status quo is nicely normal. (Anderson 1992: 5)

Anderson suggests that this fallacy is especially dangerous when the leaders of powerful countries believe it to be true. Three other fallacies accompany it – that only 'big' nation-states are viable in the modern world, that the transnational organization of modern capitalism makes nationalism obsolete and that the 'free market' is instinctively opposed to military violence. Those who have opposed their integration into larger states, such as the people of East Timor, have been branded opponents of rationalism and 'development'. The word for such resistance is usually 'terrorism', legitimating a state terror seldom named as such.

To avoid misunderstanding the world's contemporary ills, we must take a longer view. I have already touched on some elements: the impacts of colonialism on 'traditional' practices, its creation of new class structures and political orders, the relationships between global capitalism and the rise of 'shadow states', and the uprooting of huge numbers of human beings in global migrations. We must recognize the violence of these processes. There is also violence in the way Foucauldian programmes of power rob subaltern groups of their ability to define their own identities. Class violence is explicit in the processes that make it impossible for local communities to sustain themselves without migration to distant places. International displacement is not necessarily permanent, but it may still split families and the very persons of the migrants themselves. They may never be able to secure full incorporation into a host society which practises systematic discrimination against them, but at the same time cease to be fully 'at home' in the everyday life of their communities of origin, even if they continue to identify politically with their home nation. The same class violence tolerates grinding poverty in the midst of consumerism, and may, as Nancy Scheper-Hughes has shown, respond to the symptoms of chronic hunger by dispensing tranquillizers rather than food (Scheper-Hughes 1992: 207).

In this chapter, I focus on more overt manifestations of organized violence in the global order, in particular those perpetrated by states and those labelled 'ethnic conflict'.[1] The study of these forms of supposed 'disorder' can lead us towards a deeper appreciation of class and racial oppression within modern states, including the Western democracies, by revealing their systematic character. First, however, we should explore the dynamics of the contemporary global order as a global order.

EXPANDING CAPITALISM, DECLINING EMPIRES

It has become a commonplace to say that the former Soviet Union was an empire rather than a nation-state. Nevertheless, the empire that Lenin reconstructed from the wreck of the dominion of the Romanovs had a peculiar quality because of the transcendent nature of its official ideology: communism was the future destiny of all humanity, inscribed in the progressive development of history.

Stalin's mobilization of Russian nationalism during the Second World War and the expansion of the communist world revealed the ultimate impracticality of this attempt to supersede the association between political boundaries and nationalist constructions (Anderson 1992: 4). Furthermore, the post-Soviet resurgence of national identities revealed the fragility of an imperial project that remained a Russian project. The Soviet Empire embraced more than a hundred separate nations within its territorial boundaries, although less than half received political recognition from the

---

1 For more general discussions of anthropological approaches to nationalism and ethnicity, see Eriksen (1993) and Banks (1996).

Soviet state, and Stalin intensified their hierarchization by a 'Russification' drive which involved mass deportations. Yet a less state-centred analysis of the empire 'from below' suggests that cooptation of national elites by the centre actually promoted the persistence of national sentiment at the grassroots (Bremmer 1993: 19). Nor did communist ideology inhibit the rulers of the Soviet Empire from pursuing economic development strategies that have parallels in the capitalist world. These were in part products of the leadership's world-view, in part consequences of pre-revolutionary conditions, in part consequences of specific historical conditions associated with the Bolshevik Revolution itself (Carr 1959). At one level of analysis, the Communist Party of the Soviet Union represents simply another 'party of the state'. Yet it seems important not to ignore the peculiarities of communist political culture.

Communist ideology did define horizons of popular social aspirations and historical destiny for the people of the Soviet Union. It thus fulfilled some of the functions commonly associated with nationalist ideologies. With hindsight, it is clearer how these horizons were distinctive: faced with the sufferings and humiliation of economic collapse *and* a fall from great power status, many citizens of the former USSR came to understand both the old regime and capitalism in a different way. Since the Soviet Union was enormously economically, socially and culturally diverse, it would be surprising if post-socialist responses were uniform, even in the way the Soviet era was re-imagined and reinterpreted in the face of the experience of crisis. In her work on the Siberian Buryats, Caroline Humphrey (1998) has shown how indigenous culture offers alternative models for collective economic organization (of a hierarchical rather than egalitarian kind). Yet she also argues that Buryat responses reflect a *habitus* developed during Soviet times that can be compared meaningfully with the post-socialist dilemmas of communities in parts of the former Soviet Union that are culturally very different. She explains these similarities in terms of socialist political culture, in the sense of general political attitudes and collectivist values, ironically securing greater recognition in a moment when 'their achievements are almost overwhelmed' (Humphrey 1998: 492). The political *habitus* of the ex-empire was, however, tied to the practice of power as well as to its official ideology, and Humphrey suggests that there was also an elective affinity between pre- and Soviet-era models of politics in the Buryat case. This now manifests itself in the search for vertical ties with community patrons who are international media and sports personalities with influence in Moscow and, in some cases, Mafia connections – 'idols of the people' – and in the popularity of charismatic but authoritarian political leaders whose wealth is of dubious origin (ibid.: 499–501).

There are parallels between this kind of politics and developments in other areas of the world discussed in Chapter 5. Yet the broader legacy of socialist political culture suggests that it would be wrong to see transformation in Eastern Europe as a simple repetition of the developments produced by the retreat of Western colonial empires after the Second World War. There is, furthermore, enough variation in the latter cases to suggest that history will continue to produce surprises. The ultimate destinations to which post-socialist societies are 'in transition' are not yet clear, but it seems more productive to focus on the new economic, social and political forms being built amidst the wreckage than simply on the symptoms of 'disorder'. 'Crisis' or 'disorder' may be terms that people themselves use to describe their experiences, as economic or physical insecurity weighs heavily on their everyday lives and forces them to seek 'ways out' that they find morally ambiguous or even repugnant. Yet some actors are experiencing change in a quite different way, as access to extraordinary wealth and breathtaking power.

Contemporary patterns of transformation raise questions about the relationships between local and global processes. Historically and culturally contextualized analysis is essential to understanding not merely the causes but also the exact *nature* of contemporary conflict, and even the *meaning* of violent acts to those who perpetrate them. There is, however, still a point to examining the broad picture of global processes. The construction of contemporary 'disorders' as pathological results from inadequate *general* theories of the 'normal'.

In a study of the relationship between the United States and Latin America at the end of the 1980s, James Petras and Morris Morley offered a theory articulating global capitalist development to the emergent social and political properties of the world order, including the rise of new social movements, deracination and routinized state terror. These writers saw declining empire as 'the central over-arching reality that shapes political and social action in the post-modern world' (Petras and Morley 1990: 44). The empire whose decline was central to their analysis was that of the United States. In the Petras and Morley model, the US state is an imperial state because it responds to the interests of capitalists moving capital abroad to pursue accumulation on a global scale (ibid.: 65). The imperial state creates the framework within which transnational capitalist enterprises can function. It is distinct from the national capitalist state because it 'exercises its authority in a field of competing and aspiring sovereigns – competing imperialist states, regional powers, and local authorities' (ibid.: 66). The US imperial state, as Petras and Morley define it, has both economic and military-ideological components. The difference between US imperialism and its Japanese and German rivals lay in the way the former based its hegemony increasingly on the military-ideological agencies, whereas the latter emphasized economic agencies. As a result of this divergence, US global economic hegemony declined.

US emphasis on attempting to control political and social change in the 'Third World' reinforced the dominance of military over economic agencies. Petras and Morley argued that this prevented the kind of economic restructuring necessary for the US to regain competitiveness as a producer of commodities. Although this turned out to be an over-simple view, it is worth pursuing the logic of the argument further, since it helps us to understand why US global hegemony has proved resilient, but also highlights its social costs. During the 1970s, Petras and Morley argue that there was a shift from industrial investment towards financial markets and accumulation of what Harvey (1989) terms 'fictitious capital'. This embraces not merely speculation within stock and commodity markets but also real estate development, sectors at the heart of the economic crisis of the late 1980s and early 1990s. Throughout the Reagan-Bush years, America responded to its declining industrial strength and escalating levels of internal and international debt by increasing dependence on fictitious capital coupled with 'a major refashioning of the political and military foundations for projecting power abroad'. This turned the United States into the world's largest debtor, and led to a decline of basic (non-arms related) manufacturing and take-over of more profitable sectors of the US economy by foreign, and particularly Japanese, capital.

The declining significance of productive capital in the USA led to the rise of new political actors linked to the ideological-military apparatuses of the National Security State. 'Lumpen intellectuals' like Jeane Kirkpatrick, Vernon Walters and Richard Perle produced 'demonological' propaganda designed to legitimate a shift towards illegality in the internal and external practices of the imperial state (Petras and Morley 1990: 46). Activities such as violating international law in mining the entrances to Nicaraguan ports were complemented by building airstrips useful to both the Contras and elements of the Honduran military in their subsidiary role as drug-traffickers. Even after Panama's General Noriega was known to be involved in drug trafficking, George Bush insisted that he be put back on the CIA payroll.[2] The 'informal' links between US subversion and the militarization of external politics, on the one hand, and the international drugs and arms trade, on the other, fitted into the logic of an economy increasingly orientated towards accumulation via speculation. Neo-conservative intellectuals were themselves amoral 'social marginals' who had much in common with their associates in the 'periphery' (ibid.).

Petras and Morley thus see American foreign policy as increasingly detached from the economic interests of US corporate capital, driven by the logic of military strategies aimed at overthrowing regimes considered threatening to American hegemony, directly as in Grenada, or through proxies, as in Nicaragua. Respectable corporate leaders acquiesced in an opportunist alliance with neo-conservative ideologues and military

---

2 Noriega's subsequent demonization served the hidden agenda of the US invasion of Panama, the destruction of the Panamanian Defence Force. The agreement to transfer control of the canal signed by President Carter included removal of US bases. Without an army, Panama would remain susceptible to US interventions justified by 'threats to regional security'. The operation was also a technical rehearsal for the Gulf War.

adventurers simply because that was the way things were. Wrong-doers could easily be disowned if too much became public knowledge.

With hindsight, it is clear that Petras and Morley's diagnosis of the implications of the costs of the Reagan-Bush military apparatus was shared by members of the US political elite, including former Secretary of State Kissinger. The technological fantasy of Reagan's 'Star Wars' defence system ceased to have any purpose with the collapse of Soviet power, and the realignment of the Democrats under Clinton with much of the Republican social policy agenda made domestic economic restructuring possible. The increasing competitiveness of Asian and European capitalism made 'globalization' the language of its political legitimation. US citizens lost industrial jobs exported to Asia and Latin America and costs were trimmed by 'downsizing' at managerial level, yet the result was not mass unemployment but the drawing of larger numbers of women into the labour force as family incomes fell (Susser 1996: 414). Citizen labour was disciplined by job insecurity, whilst immigrants from the South continued to take the worst-paid jobs in an expanding service sector (Nash 1994, Leach 1998, Davis 1999). Welfare was cut or turned into 'workfare'. Inner-city populations forced into the 'second economy' by lack of job opportunities that they did not find socially degrading were dealt with by building more prisons (Bourgois 1995, Fox Piven and Cloward 1997). The Clinton boom remained heavily dependent on the global financial sector, whose growth also generated more low-paid service sector jobs, along with the demand for cheap services provided by the increasing number of working-class families in which both partners worked (Salzinger 1991, Hannerz 1996).

US military intervention abroad did not cease, although the US government was increasingly concerned that the 'international community' and in particular, the European Union, share the costs. As demonstrated by the continued bombing of Iraq and the Kosovo intervention at the end of the 1990s, the North Atlantic powers – increasing locked into bitter economic competition – were still willing to spend substantial sums of money on military means of pursuing of their perceived economic and geo-political interests.[3] There was, however, some change in the way US interests were advanced abroad, especially in Latin America. Neoliberal governments mostly succeeded in converting their economies to a new model orientated away from economic nationalism towards the global economy in a way that satisfied the objectives of US-based transnational corporations. The stresses of this development model have produced a continuing need for military aid

---

3 The survival in power of a weakened Saddam Hussein allowed the Western alliance to avoid the costs of aid for post-war reconstruction, and also helped to keep Israel's natural enemies from regrouping. Even the victims of Saddam who were not annihilated like the Marsh Arabs, such as the Kurds of Northern Iraq, received little humanitarian aid. This situation also reflected the sensitivities of Turkey as a member of the NATO alliance and the Kurds' division into factions that the Northern powers could not control.

legitimated by the 'War against Drugs'. Yet the shift in the kind of political regime that US foreign policy now wishes to reproduce in the region reflects the success of earlier strategies for implanting the neoliberal economic model and securing enough social pacification to sustain it.

Petras and Morley argued that state terror became 'routinized' in the South during the 1970s and 1980s in a way which was related to a global terror network serving as an instrument of US foreign policy (1990: 49). The US provided direct support to forces seeking to overthrow popular regimes threatening US economic interests – as in Chile under Allende – but also offered 'technical assistance' to bolster the counter-insurgency efforts of regimes practising terror against recalcitrant elements of civil society. In particular, it covertly fostered the adoption of techniques for eliminating opposition from which the state could dissociate itself, namely the death-squads. Where public opinion was eventually mobilized against US involvement, as in Central America, the policy was continued through proxies such as Israel and Argentina. Such strategies proved beneficial for extending an internationalized model of capital accumulation by bolstering 'investor confidence' (ibid.: 49).

State terror cannot, however, be reduced simply to a mechanism facilitating economic imperialism. Petras and Morley describe it as forming 'a middle-level linkage between the politics of global hegemony ... and the emergence of social movements and the politics of personal experience' (ibid.: 48). State terror was initially both a means for implanting a model of accumulation associated with transnational capital and a means of securing US hegemony. It then became the means by which regimes responded to renewed challenges generated by the social impact of the neoliberal model and, indeed, by state terrorism itself. Working from this argument, we might conclude that reduction in the deployment of terror in some countries simply reflects the fact that the earlier strategy was successful enough either to annihilate the state's enemies (Peru) or to force them to negotiate a peace and enter electoral politics (Central America). Covert operations or tacit support for repression would therefore continue where conditions were less satisfactory from the US point of view (Colombia). This fails, however, to register the fact that, once deployed, state terror may set in train a dynamic of its own, an important part of Petras and Morley's original thesis, which can be clarified by unpacking that thesis into its component parts.

Firstly, we should consider the new social movements. Petras and Morley conceive of these as democratic popular organizations with grassroots leaders recruited from outside established party-electoral machines. They emerge in opposition to authoritarian states and the transnationalized elites that those states now represent. Their actions go beyond those of older organized labour movements: human and political rights and social dignity are as central as economic demands. They also bring onto the political stage sections of the lower classes not normally represented by organized labour movements (ibid.: 53). The economic crisis of the 1980s broke down much of the control previously exercised over labour and fostered social movement participation. Social movements may present a challenge to repressive regimes, as the Brazilian case suggests. Nevertheless, the civilian political proxies the United States promoted to replace increasingly ineffective military governments could reconstitute a terror apparatus capable of bringing the social movements back under control, if a unified political leadership failed to emerge from the movements themselves (ibid.: 51–2).

Secondly, restructuring of the world order produces deracination, a process more radical than classical forms of proletarianization because 'it involves the displacement and destruction of one's sense of self' (ibid.: 55). Armenians deported from Turkey, Palestinians displaced by the state of Israel, violent youths in the South African townships or the *barrios* of Colombia, all exemplify this kind of deracination. Petras and Morley argue that the terrorism of the deracinated is produced by the brutality of the powerful, mirrors its logic and reproduces a structure of mutually reinforcing violence. Unless the deracinated are returned their sense of humanity, any regime they succeed in establishing will replicate the injustices of its precursor:

Sooner rather than later some of the uprooted learn to be violent – with no moral compunction because no authority has observed moral codes or been subject to any social constraints ... What kind of regime results from the rise to power of the uprooted? It will not be a generous regime particularly for those who are displaced. The victims become the executioners ... (ibid.: 58)

It is not obvious that the mutual reinforcement of state terror and the counter-terror of the deracinated always serves imperial state interests in the longer run. As we saw in Chapter 5, Smith (1990) argued that the Guatemalan military developed an antagonism towards the United States that crystallized into a nationalist project distinct from that of the Guatemalan bourgeoisie. The 'terrorist threat' in this context was a pretext for the elaboration of a local military hegemonic strategy.

Yet Guatemala does now fit the general model of transfer of power to civilians. It is a model citizen of the neoliberal global economic system, even if the military may be ready to redeploy its violence should everyday social disorder – some of which is linked to neoliberal economics and some to the 'downsizing' of the military apparatus itself – escalate (Warren 1998: 197). A more serious problem is the growth of 'illegal' economies and their continuing but potentially contradictory linkages with US hegemonic strategies. US attitudes to 'narco-politics' in Colombia and Mexico have differed in a manner that seems explicable in terms of expediency. The ability to pressure a still far from 'clean' Mexican political class over drug-trafficking helps the US to get its way over trade relations within the North American Free Trade Agreement and on immigration control. Stronger intervention in Colombia in the name of the 'War against Drugs' seems to reflect counter-insurgency concerns, with toleration afforded to right-wing paramilitaries and military personnel involved in the drugs trade. Yet the outcomes of such expedient choices are not predictable. CIA covert operations in Afghanistan during the 1980s led the US to facilitate the training and arming of Islamic forces and made a contribution to the development of the transnational opium poppy industry (Cooley 1999). US security services no doubt came to regret their fostering of international terrorism that targeted US citizens. There are few guarantees that such episodes will not be repeated.

What is clear is that the world arms market created by Cold War military-industrial complexes remains relatively unconstrained by moral considerations (Anderson 1992: 11). As the Blair government's reluctance to suspend supply of Hawk aircraft to Indonesia demonstrated, Britain's new 'ethical foreign policy' was qualified by the country's responsibility for 20 per cent of world arms shipments. Newer suppliers, such as Brazil and Russia, see expanding arms sales as a solution to economic problems. Anderson observes that military officer corps are often recruited from dominant groups defined on 'ethnic' lines and defend profoundly 'ethnicized' power structures. Free markets promise the expanded reproduction of the means of state violence and the clandestine foreign interventions of 'responsible and democratic' governments have helped foster violence as a means of pursuing political objectives. If the world the empires created now alarms them with disorders they can no longer control, such disorders are of their own creation.

Another unintended product of Northern global hegemony is the phenomenon Anderson dubs 'the long-distance nationalist'. Successful emigrants residing in metropolitan countries now fuel local conflicts by par-ticipating in the politics of putative homelands they may never have seen. Attached by emotive bonds to a fatherland created in their imagination but unconstrained by the need to live with the consequences of their actions, the 'long-distance nationalist' is peculiarly susceptible to political manipulation by those who organize local conflicts. Arjun Appadurai (1990) takes this line of argument further in discussing the implications of what he terms 'deterritorialization'.

CULTURAL GLOBALIZATION AND POWER RELATIONS

Appadurai argues that the fact that 'uneven development' has brought foreign migrants into the lower-class sectors of relatively wealthy societies sometimes creates 'exaggerated and intensified senses of criticism or attachment to politics in the home-state'. Deterritorialization fosters 'fun-damentalist' re-creations of cultural identity. Religion is an ideal basis for grounding concepts of self and other in moral terms, and thus religious difference elides into constructions of irreducible 'ethnic' difference backed by historical myth-making, as in the Balkans. Pursuit of secular goals becomes a religious mission. The logic of the market and hegemonic practices of states reinforce these tendencies. Appadurai's argument is worth quoting at length:

In the Hindu case ... it is clear that the overseas movement of Indians has been exploited by a variety of interests both within and outside India to create a complicated network of finances and religious identifications, in which the problems of cultural reproduction for Hindus abroad has become tied to the politics of Hindu fundamentalism at home. At the same time, deterritorialization creates new markets for film companies, art impressarios and travel agencies, who thrive on the need of the deterritorialized population for contact with its homeland. Naturally, these invented homelands, which constitute the mediascapes of deterritorialized groups, can often become sufficiently fantastic and one-sided that they provide the material for new ideoscapes in which ethnic conflicts can begin to erupt. The creation of 'Kalistan', an invented homeland of the deterritorialized Sikh population of England, Canada and the United States, is one example of the bloody potential in such mediascapes, as they interact with the 'internal colonialisms' ... of the nation-state. The West Bank, Namibia and Eritrea are other theaters for the enactment of the bloody negotiation between existing nation-states and deterritorialized groupings. (Appadurai 1990: 301–2, emphasis added)

Appadurai's analysis of the 'sociology of displacement' leads him to argue that cultural globalization exacerbates a tendency towards conflictive relationships between 'states' and 'nations'. States strive to monopolize ideas about nationhood. This may lead to the violent extirpation of groups that stand in the way of such projects and forced 'assimilation' of the survivors, but national elites also employ more subtle strategies for 'domesticating' groups which claim a different cultural-historical identity. A leading Guatemalan politician suggested, for example, that the culture of his country's indigenous people represented a rich 'folklore' that the state should display to the rest of mankind at Disneyworld. Such 'heritage politics' sustains a vision of the Guatemalan nation in which the descendants of the European colonizers are heirs to a civilizing mission that defines core national culture. Indigenous people add a picturesque element of 'local colour' of no profound significance for the central *moral* ideas of nationhood.

Appadurai argues that the transnationalization of media and population diasporas of the modern world reinforce proliferation of a micro-politics of identity which contests state projects. Separatist movements are groups with their own ideas of nationhood seeking to create their own states or carve pieces out of existing states against the projects of national elites. The two sides of the process are linked in an explosive dialectic founded on the contradictions of a global capitalism which keeps countries open to the flow of commodities, people and media images which are the material foundations for the subversion of control over ideas of nationhood and 'peoplehood' (ibid.: 305).

On this view, developments in the global organization of capitalism have contradictory political consequences. States restructure civil societies in order to secure the conditions for a particular kind of capitalist development, but the economic, social and cultural consequences of that development frustrate programmes of regulation. This fosters the emergence of new political actors pursuing other agendas, forcing states to improvise new regulatory stategies to retain control, which provoke further reactions and unintended effects. Even national states with close ties to a hegemonic centre may act in ways that are relatively autonomous and even contradictory to the centre's strategy because all states must adjust their strategies to domestic alignments of forces. Transnational processes of the kind Appadurai discusses enable local actors to articulate themselves to communities located outside the national unit and provide the basis for novel kinds of counter-hegemonic or nationalist imaginaries in both 'peripheral' and 'metropolitan' societies.

The phenomenon of 'long-distance nationalism' operates both ways. Identification with homelands and their distinctive cultural practices can reinforce boundaries between different groups within metropolitan societies and promote new kinds of ethnicization of metropolitan politics. Not only do conflicts in the Indian sub-continent now manifest themselves on the streets of England, but they express themselves in increasingly sharp ways because the identities formed by the metropolitan-born are purged of any nuances which still exist in the regions of origin defined as the homelands. They are 'purified' into increasingly fundamentalist forms. Racism and refusal of full social recognition by the dominant 'ethnic' group can drive even middle-class people of otherwise conservative disposition towards identification with separatist ideologies.

As I pointed out in Chapter 1, transnationalism as 'living life across borders' can also be supportive of the integrative national projects of post-colonial states (Basch *et al.* 1994). In cases such as Haiti, social discrimination in the USA has reinforced a desire to belong to what Glick Schiller and Fouron (1999) term the 'deterritorialized' Haitian nation-state, a desire actively fostered by the Aristide government after the fall from power of the Duvalier family. Yet as these authors show, the Haitian case again illustrates negative dimensions of these new transnational nationalisms. Haitians can take pride in their country's origin in the first successful war of national independence fought by African slaves. Yet the idea of a shared history or culture is less significant than the idea that overseas residents continue to be part of the nation because they share the same substance transmitted by 'blood ties'. The latter establish immutable forms of personal identity that are also forms of immutable difference between human communities. By placing their hopes in Haitians abroad and the informal redistributive networks linked to the remittance economy, poor Haitians at home may be less inclined to press political challenges to domestic elites and their foreign allies, and seek to resolve problems at an individual level through patron–client relations. Those in the United States are less inclined to join larger coalitions to ameliorate their disadvantages, even if they have opted for full citizenship. The Haitian example does demonstrate, however, that political leaderships can still harness popular nationalist energies in a world of mobile and displaced people, irrespective of whether those leaderships enjoy universal popularity or support, and irrespective of the strength, coherence or legitimacy of the state apparatuses that they control. A state's striving to pursue the politics of majoritarianism and homogenization may be undermined by the global culture of consumerism. Bryan Turner argues that the appeal of the 'Islamic state' is not so much dependent on whether people accept religious teachings as rational and coherent, but on how far they prove compatible with changes in everyday lifestyle is brought about by the flow of commodities (Turner 1994: 90–2). As Christine Gailey (1989) has shown, Tongan commoners interpret 'Rambo' movies in a way that is totally at odds with the ideologies of their Hollywood creators. The appeal of kung-fu films to working-class and urban marginal households throughout the world lies in the way they lend themselves to expression of opposition to dominant class values. Yet imported kung-fu films have their greatest popularity among particular sections of the Tongan population, those dominated by mercantile capital and landlord–tenant relations rather than regular involvement in wage labour, in line with 'their romantic glorification of cooperative, non-exploitative production' (ibid.: 27). Local interpretations of transnational cultural products are thus rooted in local conditions of life and specific local histories of relations between elites and subaltern classes. They also vary within particular societies according to the social position of the audience.

Appadurai suggests that martial arts films enable long-standing cultural traditions in Asia to be reformulated to satisfy the fantasy cravings of urban youth. They create new cultures not simply of violence but of masculine violence. Coupled with the global diffusion in both media images and everyday life of the Uzi and the AK-47, such images of violence in turn become linked to 'aspirations for community in some "imagined world"' (Appadurai 1990: 306). This is, however, merely to note a latent possibility without identifying the conditions under which people may actually try to make the worlds of their imagination real. Aihwa Ong (1999) has argued that the ultimate problem with Appadurai's work is that it produces a simple opposition between 'resistant' local cultures and universalizing capitalist forces. It fails to specify the mechanisms of power that shape cultural flows and social imagination, enabling or triggering the mobility of some whilst 'localising and disciplining' others who cannot move, such as the former workers of 'downsized' US industrial giants (Ong 1999: 11). In this respect, Appadurai echoes the even more totalizing approach of Manuel Castells's (1996) account of the 'network society'.

For Castells, 'resistance' (of the kind supposedly embodied in Islamic 'fundamentalist' movements, for example) is viewed simply as a reaction to 'exclusion' from global networks of capital and information flows. Such reactive resistance to 'the global' embodies no autonomous or constructive project of its own, other than that rooted in an atavistic local 'tradition'. This would be an unfortunate framing of some Islamic fundamentalist movements given the role of the CIA in their development noted above. More significantly, however, it fails to register the differences between movements labelled 'fundamentalist'. Not only is 'Islamic' evidently not a valid synonym for 'fundamentalist', given the existence of Christian fundamentalisms, but the 'Islamic state' is a contemporary project that is not really rooted in the past (Ayubi 1991). Fundamentalisms are also 'modern' in their employment of mass communication technologies and often mirror the organization of left-wing groups (Marty and Appleby 1993).

Kung-fu films and the original Rambo movie, *First Blood*, also play an interesting role in the RUF rebellion in Sierra Leone (Richards 1996: 57–8). Rambo, in the eyes of the rainforest insurgents, is a hero who is victimized by his society's authorities, takes off for the bush, turns the tables and revenges himself on his uncaring persecutors by living on his wits as a fighter. Rambo may also resemble a classic Mende trickster, but the emphasis is clearly on how a global media artefact seems to speak to and for the rebels themselves (ibid.: 103). The RUF rebels are also avid consumers of newsreel footage of war from CNN, which they classify as 'war films' in a way that blurs the distinction between fiction and documentary (ibid.: 109). The cultural terms of reference of the RUF include the Toffler's books *Future Shock* and *The Third Wave*, along with Qaddafy's *Green Book*, which argues for populist participatory democracy against both communist dictatorship of the party and a Western-style democracy in which small majorities can dictate to large minorities (ibid.: 53). Every idea may be given a local reading, but the struggle for meaning in the forests of Sierra Leone clearly involves the interplay of ideas from different parts of the global cultural economy. This is not a closed peripheral situation that has reverted to a thinly suppressed barbarism. The people of the forest simply want to be reconnected to global networks on terms more acceptable than the predation of colonial powers and transnational companies. They may, indeed, be better informed about our world than the citizens of London and Los Angeles, most of whom know absolutely nothing about Sierra Leone.

In Ong's view, Appadurai's insights need strengthening by a firmer grasp of political economy and analysis of how power relations remain rooted in particular regions. Her own approach is based on the analysis of transnational relations: horizontal economic, social and cultural processes that stream across spaces but are embedded 'in differently configured regimes of power' that are culturally specific (Ong 1999: 4). In her work, transnationality refers to both cultural interconnectedness and the movement of people, but the emphasis is on how the cultural logics and practices of individuals and states articulate to changing processes of capital accumulation.

Employing the Foucauldian concept of governmentality, Ong argues, for example, that Chinese businessmen moving across frontiers employ the 'flexible citizenship' offered by holding multiple passports to hedge against political risks and deflect state 'disciplining' whilst localizing their wives and families as 'the disciplinable subjects of familial regimes'. Asian states have responded to economic globalization by subjecting different sections of their populations to different regimes of valuation and control, outsourcing state functions to private enterprises in some cases, so as to produce 'zones of graduated sovereignty' involving the deployment of different forms of disciplinary power which evolve and adapt in a way that reflects the exigencies of the global economy (ibid.: 20, 217). Since Ong is interested in the cultural specificities of global processes, she considers, for example, how the Beijing state, the overseas Chinese diaspora and the governments of Malaysia and Singapore, produce ideologies that express models of 'Asian capitalism' and 'Asian modernity' that emphasize difference and moral distance from 'the West'. Yet although collective identities are grounded in the same racial essentialism as transnational Haitian identity, Asian states also strive to create conditions in which liberal market societies can flourish, transnational companies can be encouraged to invest and a culture of consumerism can prosper.

Asian states thus ultimately play by the rules of neoliberal orthodoxy, in marked contrast to the assumption of Samuel Huntington's[4] 'clash-of-civilizations thesis', which holds that 'Western values' have failed to penetrate Asia (ibid.: 186–7). Ong is also interested in how mobile Chinese male businessmen achieve an agency that satisfies their aspirations for status, wealth and power. Transnational social fields pose them a variety of problems, ranging from the politics of race and Anglo anxiety in California to the popular hostility towards rich foreigners and an intrusive state that they encounter in China. The agency that they do achieve is ultimately at the expense of others. In its focus on different levels of governmentality, Ong's analysis differs sharply from Appadurai's view of the relationship between 'cultural globalization' and the imagination.

Recent anthropological approaches thus attempt to mediate two equally unsatisfactory positions. One is an exclusive focus on the local roots of disorder and violence that echoes post-Cold War ideologies. The other is a perspective on global processes that sees the only alternatives for localities as

---

4 Huntington has been an important figure in US foreign policy since the Vietnam War. A member of the National Security Council, he was an architect of the forced resettlement programmes in Indochina. He argued that South-East Asian countries with large peasant populations could not reproduce European models of political development spontaneously, since the disruptions caused by socio-economic 'modernization' would inevitably lead to revolution ('modernization breakdown'). He therefore advocated US support for authoritarian intervention to stamp out 'traditional' agrarian society and institutionalize 'modernity' through 'political and social engineering' (Poole and Rénique 1991: 136), a paradigm to which anthropologists such as Clifford Geertz sought to make academic contributions (Ross 1998). Poole and Rénique argue that 'modernization breakdown' theory inspired the early work of the 'Senderologists', discussed below. Huntington's more recent 'clash-of-civilizations thesis' contends that 'Asian culture' cannot be obliterated by enforced Westernization and advocates accommodation with China. Yet it is equally supportive of authoritarianism and represents just as totalizing a reading of cultural difference as his earlier position.

subsumption or 'resistance'. Without adequate contextualization of particular situations, we cannot understand why global forces continue to produce uneven development and heterogeneity. In order to explore these issues further, I will consider the *Sendero Luminoso* (Shining Path) movement, which seemed to threaten the continued existence of the Peruvian state until its founder, Abimael Guzmán, was captured, along with other principal leaders, in 1992, setting in train a process of decline that seemed terminal by 1999. I will highlight some similarities between the *Sendero* phenomenon and the RUF rebellion in Sierra Leone. I then turn to 'ethnic' and political conflicts in Sri Lanka. Aspects of the Sri Lankan case parallel the other two. The main purpose of this example is, however, to stress that understanding local cultural logics helps us to see why global processes which have similar consequences throughout the world only trigger extreme violence when they intersect with particular state and national orders.

FROM THE FANTASIES OF 'SENDEROLOGY' TO THE ROOTS OF POLITICAL VIOLENCE IN PERU

After the Cold War, the political imagery of the United States shifted from a vision of a world threatened by rational subversion organized by the communist bloc towards what Deborah Poole and Gerardo Rénique characterize as 'a world made up of *sui generis* madmen and terrorists, warlords and drug barons, charismatic leaders and fundamentalist mass movements' (Poole and Rénique 1991: 160). Like Petras and Morley, Poole and Rénique point out that these 'pathologies' are consequences of US hegemonic strategies. It is, however, essential that they should be constructed in post-Cold War political discourse as *non-systemic*, problems of an irrational periphery separate from a rational centre represented by the United States. To see them as systemic would be to:

unveil the unutterable connections (or 'linkages') between centre and periphery, between drug economies and the international capitalist economy, between Third World debt, metropolitan banks and financial institutions, between Third World dictators like Saddam Hussein and the military industrial complex. (ibid.: 191)

Poole and Rénique's arguments resonate well with Paul Richards's critique of 'The New Barbarism Thesis', associated with writers such as Robert Kaplan (Kaplan 1994, Richards 1996: xiv–xvii).

New Barbarism theorists present economic crisis is Africa as a 'natural' Malthusian catastrophe, deepened by a legacy of tribalism and other forms of 'cultural backwardness' that weakened state machineries are no longer able to contain. Violence is thus the result of conditions *inside* 'peripheral' countries and 'excluded regions'. It cannot be seen as *rational* or *meaningful* and cannot be stopped by reasonable methods of diplomacy or conciliation. As Richards shows, not only do we need to challenge the idea that the West is not responsible for African crises, but we also need to take on the argument that violence is meaningless. I have already indicated how RUF rebels meaningfully locate themselves within a global cultural system, and Richards provides evidence of the banal rationality of some forms of terror perpetrated by relatively small and poorly equipped military forces (ibid.: 6). The RUF leadership did not want to stay in the bush, and their violence was a means of reclaiming a space for themselves in the cosmopolitan urban society to which they felt they belonged.

Richards finds several parallels between the RUF and the Peruvian Shining Path. Their leaderships were embittered intellectuals who felt that they had not found the place in society that they deserved, whilst the movements appealed to young rural people who were 'modernized' but had few prospects of continuing education and social mobility by empowering them through education in the arts of war (ibid.: 27–8). Both movements were intensely didactic, a reflection of their leadership by pedagogues (ibid.: 28). Embittered intellectuals are prominent in the recent annals of violence. Radovan Karadzic, Serb leader in the Bosnian war, falls into this category, along with several of his associates. The role of young people as fighters is also important. In the case of Sierra Leone we are talking about very young people, many of whom were forced into the ranks of the RUF and given crack cocaine to help them through the brutal acts that they were trained to perpetrate.[5]

One possible misinterpretation of the Sierra Leonean civil war arises from the pervasive assumption that all African civil conflict is 'tribal' or 'ethnic'. Misinterpretation was equally rife in the case of *Sendero Luminoso*. A group of American political scientists whom Poole and Rénique (1991) dubbed the 'Senderologists'[6] doubly misconstrued the case (and missed its distinctive features) by assuming that any armed movement in the highlands of Peru must be both a 'peasant rebellion' and an 'Indian' uprising. Both contentions have unfortunate consequences.

Whether by accident or design, 'Senderology' served to legitimate the repression of opposition to the neoliberal development model and US intervention throughout the Andean region. It was not simply that the 'Senderologists' misrepresented *Sendero* itself. Their exaggerated focus on Shining Path distorted the broader picture of a diverse range of popular organizations resisting the economic and social project of the Peruvian state and bourgeoisie and the racial oppression in which class in Peru is entangled (Poole and Rénique 1992). *Sendero*'s violence was directed as much at other

---

5 Richards suggests, however, that capture by the rebels fitted into local cultural traditions, beginning with the Poro secret society rituals (in which young males were taken off to the bush) and continued in the colonial schools, which were also seen as taking young people away. The schools were mostly closed by the time the RUF began its rebellion, and the movement did offer its recruits an alternative form of education (Richards 1996: 30).
6 Their primary targets are Cynthia McClintock (1989) and David Scott Palmer (1986).

organizations of the Left as at the state. Yet the menacing image of a hungry Indian peasant horde isolated from national political culture advancing on the urban enclaves of Western civilization, inflamed by exotic symbols from the time of the Incas, helped to construct all forms of resistance to neoliberalism as backward-looking opposition to global progress. There may, however, be more than legitimation of imperialist strategies to take into account here. The deepest roots of the images of the dangerous and irrational 'periphery' constituted by the Andean indigenous peasant world may lie in American society itself.

American society was founded on immigration from Europe, but it was also founded on slavery and the use of military power to annex territory from Mexico. After the Civil War, Blacks in the South and former Mexicans trapped in the south-west fell victim to internal colonialism, and the subsequent development of the US economy involved continued recruitment of ethnically defined underclasses from the South. American treatment of would-be immigrants is hardly even-handed: Cubans once enjoyed unrestricted access as 'refugees' whilst Haitians were repatriated, often to their deaths. Nevertheless, the reproduction of an immigrant underclass and continuing discrimination against American Blacks has created structural contradictions. American society has become increasingly *self*-segregating, as Blacks in particular have reacted to the failure of White society to deliver general social and economic equality, despite the admission of Blacks to the political elite and growth of a Black middle class.

American national ideology is constructed on the basis of both egalitarian individualism and valorization of European origins and traditions, with skin colour a primary marker (Forbes 1992). The combination of an Anglo-Saxon model of national identity with an extreme individualist ethic, ingrained practices of racial discrimination and ethnically segmented labour markets, is deeply contradictory. It sustains racist explanations of the causes of social inequality, reinforces feelings of non-incorporation in groups subjected to discrimination and promotes segregationist responses from all parties. This is why various forms of Black nationalism and separatism have continued to play a significant role in the United States, whilst their ideologies have tended to take the form of an inversion of the foundational mythology of White nationalism. Even major academic works like Bernal's *Black Athena* (1987) reflect that pattern of inversion, as, indeed, does Said's critique of 'Orientalism' (Said 1978). It also explains why demonizing of the underclasses by Anglo society is so deeply historically rooted. Today it is institutionally manifest in the world-view of agencies of internal pacification such as the Los Angeles Police Department (Davis 1990). LAPD officers live in segregated communities outside the city, dividing its population taxonomically into 'normal' people and 'assholes' – the latter defined as members of 'ethnic' underclasses, whose essentialized lack of affinity with the values of the nuclear holy family of Anglo society generates both reproductive incontinence and innate criminal propensities.

A homology thus emerges between the discourse that defines America's view of centre–periphery relations and that which surrounds processes of internal pacification. In both ethos and organization, the LAPD has the quality of an army of occupation. Poole and Rénique note the way that:

[The Senderologists'] recourse to the ethnocentric and ultimately racist, dichotomization of a rational centre versus an irrational or traditional periphery lends them an obvious utility in an age of both xenophobic foreign policy, and a domestic situation of class and racial polarization *whose structural and discursive features mimic those of imperial centre and colonial periphery*. (Poole and Rénique 1991: 173, emphasis added)

My own argument is, however, that the interdependence is deeply rooted in the historical structural processes which have constituted the 'United States'. The construction of an 'external enemy' is integral to attempts to define the unity of the United States, as witnessed by the 'invention' of Saddam Hussein to occupy this structural position after the Soviet Union abandoned it. Furthermore, it seems necessary to consider the precise nature of the developing internal social crisis of the United States in order to understand the nature of recent constructions of the periphery, as not simply barbarism but a site of irrational disorder and social violence. The crisis of the centre is projected onto the periphery. This is not simply an imperial centre–colonial periphery discourse, but one in which Peru and Los Angeles are cognized through homologous metaphors of order versus disorder and civilization versus barbarism which become fatefully ingrained in the consciousness of ordinary Anglo-Americans. Today, such metaphors have also gathered force again in Europe.

It is against this background of ideological construction that we should evaluate the work of the 'Senderologists'. Amongst the claims that they made was that *Sendero*'s growth reflected the way the organization had a more 'organic' relationship with the indigenous peasantry than the guerrilla movements of the 1960s. Led by alienated urban intellectuals incapable of distinguishing between the Cuban Sierra Maestra and the profoundly distinct 'indigenous' world of the Peruvian Highlands, the old guerrilla activists were unable to gain the confidence of these more 'exotic' peasants (ibid.: 142). *Sendero* thus supposedly shared an ideological and symbolic universe with the indigenous peasantry (ibid.: 143), and this indigenous peasantry remained unaffected by the forces of modernity. The discussion of Chapters 4 and 5 already suggests that this assumption is implausible, but the evidence on Shining Path directly contradicted the basic hypothesis. *Sendero*'s leader, Abimael Guzmán, once a philosophy lecturer at the University of San Cristóbal de Huamanga in Ayacucho, displayed a predilection for inserting lengthy quotes from Shakespeare into his political statements. His organization condemned 'Andean culture' as 'folklore' and 'magical-whining nationalism', an archaism that the revolution aimed to purge from Peruvian society.

Such discrepancies went unnoticed by Senderologists because Shining Path was assumed to be the authentic political expression of a mass peasant response to subsistence crisis under conditions of modernization which left rural people in a 'betwixt-and-between' situation of possessing 'traditional' values incompatible with the new world that awaited them. Yet the discrepancies mount when we consider the socio-economic profile of Ayacucho, the province in which the movement originated. Although Ayacucho is a poor region, it was far from isolated historically (Degregori 1985a) and had the *highest* rate of migration to Lima in the country. Many of the rural communities that supported *Sendero* at the outset of its development in Ayacucho were relatively prosperous by local standards.[7] Peasant perceptions of *Sendero*'s military and political agenda and the nature of the 'support' they gave the organization were not uniform even in Ayacucho, much less in different regions. There were different kinds of rural grievances. Some peasants were dissatisfied with the organizational structures created under the agrarian reform programme of the military regime[8] rather than facing the kinds of subsistence insecurity problems that enabled Senderologists to present the movement as a uniform 'traditional' peasant political response to modernization. The violence of *Sendero* was explained by the argument that peasants could not express their grievances in any other way. This process of decontextualization glossed over differences in peasant political cultures within regions and the role of more pacific organizations in contesting the terms of capitalist development and national state penetration (Poole and Rénique 1991: 147–8).

The Senderologists' vision was not incompatible with support for pre-emptive state terror. 'Hungry peasants' were likely to support *Sendero* because this was supposedly a structural consequence of their socio-economic and cultural situation. The army was first sent into Ayacucho on 28 December 1982, launching a 'dirty war' using the full range of counter-insurgency techniques. The conservative regime of Fernando Belaúnde Terry gave way to what at first promised to be a more reform-minded government of the APRA under Alain García in 1985, but pre-emptive military violence against peasants was renewed under García. The Fujimori regime elected in 1990 intensified repression. Fujimori suspended Congress in April 1992 and

---

7 Degregori argues that the first communities to support *Sendero* were internally socially differentiated and possessed both primary and secondary schools. These communities sent young people to train in teacher-training schools run by *Sendero*. Although some poor communities also supported *Sendero*, Degregori argues that what all early pro-*Sendero* communities had in common was long-standing opposition to the penetration of state control (Degregori 1985b: 6).

8 The land reform carried out by the military in Peru did not redistribute much land to Indian village communities in the Highlands. It focused on landless *hacienda* workers and adopted an increasingly technocratic orientation, based on the creation of large-scale cooperatives managed by non-peasant professionals (Gianotten *et al.* 1985).

governed, with military backing, from a bunker known as the 'Little
Pentagon' (Poole and Rénique 1992: 156–66). The 'grey eminence' behind
the regime was the head of the National Intelligence Service, Vladimiro
Montesinos, and repression of popular movements did not stop after the
capture of Guzmán. The violence of the military towards innocent peasants
had helped sustain *Sendero*'s expansion. In the work of Senderologists this
was simply a question of a 'spiral of violence' provoked by *Sendero*'s tactics
and military 'over-reactions'. Such accounts are unsatisfactory because they
fail to address the long-term role of authoritarianism, racism and systematic
violence in the 'legitimation and reproduction of the hegemonic political
culture which has sustained both elected and non-elected governments in
twentieth-century Peru' (ibid.: 167).

Sendero was not a peasant movement arising out of the long historical
tradition of Andean peasant struggles, but a political party and military organization created in a provincial university town. It was founded in 1970 as
a breakaway from the Maoist 'Red Flag' party, which itself split from the pro-
Moscow wing of the Peruvian Communist Party (PCP) in 1964.[9] *Sendero*
split from Red Flag when the latter opted for qualified support for the land
reform program of the Velasco military regime (Poole and Rénique 1992:
37–8, Degregori 1985a). *Sendero*'s full name was the 'Partido Comunista del
Perú, por el sendero luminoso de José Carlos Mariátegui'. Abimael Guzmán
entered politics as a youth organizer for the PCP when he took up a teaching
post in Ayacucho in 1962.

The PCP-SL and its parent the PCP-BR were quite the opposite of an
'organic peasant movement'. In contrast to many other regions, land reform
was not a central issue in the 1960s in Ayacucho, because landed estates
were no longer a significant issue: the landlord class was in decline, and some
haciendas had actually sold land to peasant communities (Poole and Rénique
1992: 36). Political power at regional level was passing to a new elite of
merchants, bureaucrats and professionals, and the Universidad de San
Cristóbal de Huamanga (UNSCH), opened in 1959, itself became a significant
economic and political force in the region (Degregori 1985a). During the
1970s, bureaucrats of the national state and agents of national capitalism
were to penetrate the region under the auspices of the military regime. In
the relative vacuum of power that preceded these developments, however,
'progressive' academics in the university were able to play a significant role,
not in the countryside, but in the city. The Maoists organized shantytown
residents, artisans, market women and merchants into a 'People's Defence
Front', whilst supra-communal peasant politics remained underdeveloped:

9 By 1985, Peru had around twenty left-wing parties claiming spiritual descent from the
great Peruvian political philosopher, and founder of the precursor of the modern PCP, José
Carlos Mariátegui. Mariátegui's spiritual hegemony over the Peruvian Left lies in his
marriage of Marxism and *indigenismo*, which had previously been harnessed to Creole
nationalist ends.

Peasant resistance to the state and to the dominant culture of the regional mestizo elites was grounded instead in the deeply-rooted community traditions and indigenous authority structures characteristic of Ayacucho's peasant communities. (Poole and Rénique 1992: 37)

Sendero Luminoso began its history without a peasant base at all. When Guzmán's Ayacucho branch of the PCP-BR student organization split, it divorced the nascent *Sendero* from the few peasant organizations the BR had established. The group had achieved control of the UNSCH itself (Guzmán was Provost from 1968 to 1969) but lost ground to New Left parties during the 1970s, as new staff moved in from other regions. By 1975, it had lost control of the student organization, the executive council of the University and the teachers' union. At the same time, its influence in the People's Defence Front declined, and new peasant and worker organizations were developing all over the country in reaction to the changes set in train by the military (ibid.: 39). Other sections of the Left ended up taking over and radicalizing some of the mass organizations the state had created as instruments of control as the hegemony of the military state over Peruvian society waned, but *Sendero*'s strategy left it totally outside this process.

During its period of dominance in the UNSCH, the PCP-SL pursued a relatively pragmatic politics, dedicating itself to the defence of university autonomy (Degregori 1985a: 39–40). Yet its leadership began to adopt an increasingly messianic tone: the rest of Peru was suffering from 'false consciousness' and *Sendero* was the last bastion of correct understanding. The PCP-SL rejected alliances with other parties, defined armed struggle as the only legitimate form of political practice and defined Peru, rather perversely given the situation in Ayacucho itself, as 'semi-feudal'. The Velasco regime was fascist, and all rival Left organizations were reformist, including the CCP (Confederación Campesina del Perú). The CCP not only sponsored peasant land invasions, but also argued that the new cooperatives and collectives created under the Velasco reforms were state-controlled *latifundios*. Nevertheless, CCP cadres became primary targets of *Sendero* violence.

After *Sendero* lost control of the main institutions of the UNSCH, it took over the University's teacher-training schools, but was expelled after eighteen months. Then, in the late 1970s, *Sendero* cadres specialized in youth work were dispatched to other universities and to secondary schools in neighbouring departments, while 'popular schools' were set up in shantytowns. *Sendero* extended its organization by adopting a cellular structure in which individual cadres knew only the adjacent links in the chain. Such a system has advantages in terms of security, but lacks the capacity to develop a participatory mass base. Yet *Sendero*'s leadership did not see this as a problem. They were seeking to create a 'vanguardist' military-political organization rather than a 'popular movement'.

Explaining the initial growth of *Sendero* is therefore a matter of explaining two things. Why did a group of professional intellectuals develop this particularly uncompromising political ideology in a provincial town, and why did it appeal to a particular group of regional social actors? The founders of the movement belonged to a provincial elite whose status was threatened by socio-economic change and the penetration of national state and class structures into the provincial social universe. The 'truth' of *Sendero*'s doctrine lay in its purity and rigidity. The old order must be utterly destroyed, and only *Sendero* had the 'line' that could create the new world. The party could not be compromised by alliances, but must claim absolute pre-eminence in acting as midwife of the new order. The new order itself appeared to be nothing except a cellular society of autarkic communities encompassed by the party. This political ideology is essentially hierarchic and represents a transformation of a 'traditional' provincial elite mentality (Degregori 1985a: 47). It was, however, updated through the creation of a cult of personality around Guzmán as 'Presidente Gonzalo' and by affirmation of the absolute truth of party doctrine as 'Gonzalo Thought' (Poole and Rénique 1992: 46).

Poole and Rénique suggest that the authoritarianism of *Sendero* echoes the provincial political culture of *gamonalismo*. This is associated with Quechua-speaking local landlords who lived with 'their Indians', constructing their personal power around theatrically flamboyant displays of personal charisma, physical violence and a cult of masculinity and anti-state rebellion (Poole and Rénique 1991: 176). Some *Sendero* militants were sons and daughters of local elites from the departments with traditions of *gamonalismo*, and others students at educational institutions dominated by these values. *Gamonalismo* is another variant of patron–client politics, but the particular 'ethnic' dimension of this regional 'intimate culture' is important. Ayacucho's regional class culture reflects the discrimination Ayacucheños face as *cholos* in Lima. *Cholos* are persons supposedly of one-quarter European ancestry, but the term is used to disparage any person of provincial background to whom 'Indian' associations can be attached. The centrality of this form of racism in Peruvian life was starkly revealed in the rhetoric of the presidential campaign mounted by the right-wing novelist Mario Vargas Llosa on behalf of Peru's national elite against Fujimori and his *Cambio 90* alliance (Poole and Rénique 1992: 147–8). Racism makes provincial political cultures oppositional. Yet at the same time there is a shared understanding of the nature of power between *gamonalismo* and military authoritarianism. Coercion and intimidation is integral to both (Poole and Rénique 1991: 177). Much of Fujimori's genuine popularity rested on his successful performance as a 'strong man' who was also non-White.

Sendero's initial expansion was based on the appeal of its ideology to a particular segment of Ayacucho society, male and female adolescents who entered the UNSCH teacher-training programme. Degregori argues that the statistics on secondary education in Peru show that the indigenous people's thirst for education in the Andes was stronger than that of *criollos*. He explains this in terms of Indians' desire to acquire pragmatic tools for liberating themselves from the domination of mestizo intermediaries associated with the dominant White pole of Peruvian society 'to make a place for themselves in the "national society"' (Degregori 1991: 237). At the same time, however, there was a search for *the truth*, shared by peasants as well the urban-popular sectors.

Truth was conceived as something that could liberate Indians from ruling-class dominance, because lack of knowledge enabled the dominated to be subjected to 'trickery and deception'. Peasants saw themselves as ignorant and the truth as something others controlled: they looked for teachers and guides, and responded positively to the absolutism and coherence of *Senderista* ideology in part *because of* its hierarchic quality. Degregori also argues, however, that most of the students who came under *Sendero* influence in Ayacucho were rejecting a 'traditional' Andean world-view and looking for a new one. *Sendero* controlled what the young people had come to see as the source of power and 'getting on' in the world, the 'black box' of education (ibid.: 240–2).

The 'coldness' of *Sendero* ideology – its appeal to 'science' and its rejection of things indigenous as superstition – gave it emotional power and those who embraced it a meaningful new identity. It appealed to Andean youth for the opposite reason to that the Senderologists proposed, because it was not 'indigenous' nor related to old forms of identity, but something associated with 'modernity'. Yet both leaders and followers accepted the hierarchic and authoritarian premises of *Sendero*, and opposed themselves to agents of 'modernization' like engineers repairing electricity pylons, agronomists providing extension services or communist militants organizing peasant federations. These agencies were not created by the party, which alone could teach the people the way of authentic progress. The violence of *Sendero* arose from the organization's need to fit reality to their ideas, which meant stopping all historical movement that did not emanate from the party (ibid.: 244).

Sendero remained a cadre organization rather than a mass political organization. Its development proved uneven. Even before capture of Guzmán, the movement experienced reverses in areas where it initially had success (Degregori 1985b, Gianotten *et al.* 1985). Nevertheless, *Sendero* did succeed in extending its field of combat beyond Ayacucho. Its rural support-base was complemented by support in Lima, although *Sendero* mobilized less support than other popular rural and urban organizations. In the cities, its 'armed strikes' were implemented through violence against small traders and bus and taxi drivers. It established its urban base by assassinating popular community leaders and union organizers belonging to rival organizations. The brutality and limited political effectiveness of these tactics provoked dissent within the organization itself (Poole and Rénique 1992: 92–6).

Much peasant support for *Sendero* was passive rather than active, based on sympathy for what local people perceived as the ultimate goals of the movement. The specific tactics of the PCP-SL changed in line with specific regional circumstances, as the Party learned from earlier mistakes (Poole and Rénique 1991: 169). Nevertheless, its tactics of assassinating rival leaders and fear of military reprisals encouraged many communities to use their vigilante patrols – *rondas campesinas* – to keep *Sendero* out (Poole and Rénique 1992: 70, Starn 1992: 109). This fuelled an escalating cycle of violence which *Sendero* sustained in later years from revenues generated from offering 'protection' in the coca-producing zone of Huallaga (Poole and Rénique 1992: 185–9). Yet Shining Path did not succeed in eliminating more pacific rural organizations and faced competition even as a military organization from the MRTA (Túpac Amaru Revolutionary Movement), formed in 1984. The MRTA pursued a strategy of combined political and military struggle and did not share *Sendero*'s intransigent antagonism to other movements (ibid.: 182–3).

The MRTA attracted international headlines for its seizure of the residence of the Japanese ambassador at the end of 1996. This ended with the massacre of the guerrillas by Fujimori's security forces in the following April, an action applauded by Clinton but condemned by the Dean of Lima's College of Lawyers. The seizure of the residence was to prove a last gesture of defiance by a movement already facing extinction in the countryside. In 1992, now unencumbered by parliamentary democracy, Fujimori had enacted draconian 'anti-terrorist' laws that enabled suspects to be convicted in summary trials by military tribunals. Among those convicted was a young New Yorker, Lori Berenson, sentenced to life imprisonment in 1996 for alleged complicity in an MRTA plot to take over the Congress building. Despite protests from the US government and human rights organizations, and the resignation of a prime minister over the issue in 1998, Fujimori stood firm on Berenson's sentence. The anti-terrorist legislation was even extended to tackle the mounting crime wave provoked by Fujimori's neoliberal economics. As Peruvians contemplated minors receiving twenty-five-year gaol sentences and saw their civil liberties increasingly eroded, their president's popularity fell, but he remained one of the most spectacularly successful authoritarian rulers in Latin American history.

Had state reactions to *Sendero*'s initial successes not been so expressive of the racist ordering of the Peruvian class system, the PCP-SL might have been nothing more than a footnote in the provincial history of Ayacucho. Individuals routinely switch markers of 'ethnic identity' in social practice, and the distinction between 'Indian' and non-Indian does not correspond to clearly defined cultural boundaries, let alone phenotypical distinctions. Yet, as I noted in Chapter 5, 'ethnicity' in Peru is constructed politically in terms of a polarized division between a White/mestizo coastal urban centre and an 'Indian' rural hinterland-periphery. Colonial society dubbed the latter the *mancha india* ('Indian stain'). Thus:

The racist implications of this discourse of polarised and ethnicised class identities have come tragically to the fore in the pattern of collective punishment utilised by the Peruvian army in its anti-terrorist campaigns. Random massacres of 'Indian' peasants by 'mestizo' army personnel and the mass detention of '*cholos*' in Lima's terrorist 'round-ups' clearly reveals the racism latent in Peruvian society. By essentialising the racial and cultural attributes of 'peasants', 'urban slum dwellers', 'migrants' and '*senderistas*', US Senderologists advocate the same racist essentialisms that fuel counter-insurgency campaigns. (ibid.: 176)

State terror gave *Sendero* an opportunity to evolve, and it is tempting to suggest that this had certain advantages from the regime's point of view. The PCP-SL turned its authoritarian violence against other popular movements. The 'terrorist threat' legitimated state repression of other forms of popular action by peasant federations, urban social movements, trade union and church groups. Indeed, it provided a pretext for suppression of constitutional political life. The terror of the state and the terror of *Sendero* thus fed on each other, but it was Alberto Fujimori who proved the more ruthless of the contestants. This provided little comfort to impoverished Peruvians who doggedly pursued their struggles through other kinds of popular action or to more affluent citizens who still courageously defended respect for human rights and the rule of law.

SRI LANKA: CONSTRUCTING NEW ORDERS THROUGH VIOLENCE

The small and beautiful island of Sri Lanka has become a paradigmatic case for the analysis of 'ethnic violence' since the riots of 1983. The city of Colombo ground to a halt during seventy-two hours in which Sinhalese citizens burned and looted the homes and businesses of Tamils, left almost 2,000 dead according to Tamil figures, and turned up to 100,000 into refugees (Tambiah 1986: 22). A substantial part of the island's commercial and industrial base was destroyed and of the 150,000 persons who lost their jobs, a significant number were Sinhalese who wrecked their own places of work (ibid.: 23). The full horror of the riots lay not simply in numbers killed or displaced, but in the fact that violence was perpetrated by Sinhalese against Tamils they knew as neighbours and by poor people upon poor people (Kapferer 1988: 102).

Another disturbing aspect of the violence, which spread to Jaffna, Kandy, Trincomalee and other places, was the role of the army and police, bodies overwhelmingly dominated by Sinhalese. The riots were preceded by the murder of fifty-three Tamils accused of 'terrorism' in Colombo's main prison, an act, reminiscent of events in Peru, which could only have been committed with the collusion of the authorities (Tambiah 1986: 16). President Jayawardene admitted to the BBC that army personnel had in some cases actively encouraged the crowds. In Jaffna, troops pulled twenty civilians off a bus and executed them, in retaliation for the death of thirteen soldiers in a Tamil Tiger guerrilla attack (ibid.: 25).

The 1983 riots did not, however, lack historical antecedents. Tambiah argues that the period after the rise to dominance of 'Buddhist Sinhala chauvinism' in 1956 laid a basis of discrimination and 'sporadically terrorizing' domination. This drew Tamil youth into the increasingly violent response which provided the pretext for the 1983 events, following the 1982 referendum which gave the United National Party under Jayawardene 'invincible majority status' (ibid.: 17–18). State repression had been building up since the SLFP (Sri Lankan Freedom Party) government of Mrs Bandaranaike imposed the State of Emergency that ran from March 1971 to February 1977. Detention without trial became routine, and the Emergency was followed by a Prevention of Terrorism Act. This permitted the army and police to hold prisoners incommunicado for up to eighteen months, giving free rein to human rights abuse. The Emergency was proclaimed shortly before the 1971 'youth insurrection' of the Janata Vimukti Peramuna (JVP). This predominantly Sinhalese and Buddhist movement was based, Tambiah argues, on mobilization of children of the rural poor by an organization 'dominated by educated youths, unemployed or disadvantageously employed':

The insurrection ... showed that there was a malaise of frustrated ambitions among the newly educated youth of a country whose liberal education program was at odds with its insufficient economic expansion. (What if the frustrations in the next round were redirected toward a more defenceless scapegoat, an ethnic minority credited with undue advantages and privileges and manipulations – like the Jews of the European fascist epoch?) (ibid.: 14)

There are again echoes of Peruvian experience here, and the JVP was a cell-based, Maoist organization like *Sendero*. Tambiah's analysis has the virtue of stressing that repression on the part of the Sri Lankan state cannot be seen as simply a reactive 'response' to the security problem posed by the JVP insurrection.

Reflecting on the significance of Sri Lanka for a general analysis of contemporary political violence, Tambiah acknowledges the role of many of the global factors I have already discussed in creating the conditions for violence, but stresses the way the particular facts of Sri Lanka illustrate the principle that 'ethnic fratricide and the demise of democracy are two sides of the same coin' (ibid.: 116). He suggests that ethnic conflict became a convenient justification for the moves taken by successive Sri Lankan governments to incapacitate political opponents – not merely Tamils, but Sinhalese left-wing groups and elements of the press. The capacity for violence amongst certain sections of the Sinhalese population is, he argues, 'tapped, triggered and intensified by political patrons, bosses, politicians and business *mudalalis*,[10] who use it to further their populist causes' (ibid.).

---

10 *Mudalalis* are merchants who 'try to control the retail trade, rice milling, small producers' supplies of cash crops, and local transport services; they are frequently involved

The terrorism of the Tamils is matched by the terrorism of the armed forces. Violence becomes 'theatricalized', as the majority in power is impelled to define and root out its 'enemy', and 'the embattled minority community dialectically produces mirror images of the same phenomena' (ibid.: 117). Tamils respond to exclusion and the propagation of Sinhala Buddhist nationalism by inventing their own mythical histories and 'populist dogmas', turning guerrilla actions into feats as theatricalized as those of the government, and rooting out their own 'collaborators' and 'traitors'. In Tambiah's view, 'ordinary people' were 'caught in the middle' of a systemic violence which became routinized and was organized by adversaries who became increasingly professionalized (ibid.: 119).

Tambiah suggested that ethnic polarization in Sri Lanka would lead to muting of caste, class and regional differences within the majority and the Tamil minority selected for 'scapegoating', to reinforce a simple dualistic opposition. This conclusion turned out to be premature. Major intra-ethnic violence erupted in Sri Lanka at the end of the 1980s, and Kapferer (1994) suggested that the continuing internal fractionalization of both sides of the warring ethnic divide was a major factor in preventing a resolution of the conflict. The JVP had been rehabilitated after the UNP replaced the SLFP in power, and moved into electoral politics, but, having been used as a scapegoat after the 1983 riots, returned to clandestine activity and increased its support after Jayawardene signed the 1987 accord with Rajiv Ghandi (Spencer 1990: 258). The presence of Indian troops in Sri Lanka provoked a Sinhalese backlash against the government. A second JVP insurrection unleashed a new wave of terror from August 1989 until the early months of 1990, causing at least 400,000 deaths before the movement was finally annihilated by the Premadasa government's military and paramilitary forces (Kapferer 1997: 293–4). Although this freed the state to refocus its repression on the Tamil Tigers – no longer even tacitly supported by India after Rajiv Ghandi's assassination – the pattern of violence escalated to provoke new riots between Buddhists and Muslims and Tamils and Muslims.

Kapferer (1994, 1997) is critical of Tambiah, along with other Sri Lankan anthropologists, such as Obeyesekere, for viewing violence as a disorder provoked by frustrations linked to social change. His own argument returns us to the starting-point of this chapter by insisting that 'the disorder of violence does not necessarily reflect a disordered world'.

Acts of violence themselves have a structuring, cultural logic. Extending Tambiah's theme of 'theatricalization', Kapferer shows, for example, how

---

in illegal bootlegging and in opium and ganja traffic, illegal felling and trading of forest timber, and so on. There are networks that connect local politicians, local police, and elected MPs to these *mudalalis*. They enjoy government protection and contracts which are repaid by bribes and election financing, and, most importantly, by their ability during elections to mobilize clients and thugs, unemployed or underemployed riffraff, and to terrorize competitors and adversaries' (Tambiah 1986: 49).

violence turned into the primary metaphor and principal expression of power can play upon the 'symbolic imaginary' of the population and have practical effects, by engaging cosmic metaphors. Crossroads, for example, are places of cosmic danger (as points of conjunction and confluence). Demons roam around them, and shrines are placed at them to keep the demons under control. Where better, then, to place the charred corpses of the victims of state terror, to symbolize the presence of the fragmenting force of the order of the state? The state was, however, itself appropriating aspects of the dynamics of JVP power, just as the latter inverted the ordering power of the state, by, for example, imposing daytime curfews: this attacked the hierarchical order of the state, which imposed curfews at night (Kapferer 1997: 293). The power dynamics of the state and JVP increasing resembled each other, catching the innocent and guilty alike in their 'webs of violence' (ibid.: 294). An execution squad lops off the head of a victim during his own ritual of exorcism, placing it on an offering plate for the demons. A man and his son accused of being informers are killed at a crossroads at midnight, the hour when demonic powers are about to give way to the forces of order. The Ten Punishments of the King are performed on their bodies, the son has his genitals cut off and both have their limbs broken. Burial is denied. The executioners thus establish themselves as 'moral' ordering agents by demonizing their victims, confirming their status as agents of disorder and fragmentation by marking their bodies (Kapferer 1994, 1997: 293).

The non-burial of the dead and public display of their dismembered corpses also victimizes their living relatives, labelled with the same demonic mark. Kin who cannot bury dead relatives are themselves liable to malevolent spirit attack. In this manner, violence strikes at the core of social relations. Yet it is not simply destructive, but a means of (re)ordering and structuring. Kapferer argues that both intra- and inter-ethnic violence produce deep splits in social relations. Yet more Sinhalese died in the few months of the second JVP insurrection than in the ten-year Tamil–Sinhala war that followed the 1983 riots, and government forces killed more people than the JVP, as the conflict gave birth to an increasingly powerful and paranoid state order (Kapferer 1997: 296).

If we recall Geertz's analysis of the precolonial Hindu-Buddhist 'theatre state', there is a grotesque historical irony here. A hierarchic conception of the Cosmic State was transmuted into a theatrical terrorization of society, employing the same metaphors, and forging an ever more centralized political order, crushing all forms of opposition. Myths and symbols were converted into ideologies of ethnic nationalism via elite political strategies and these ideologies entered into the consciousness of 'ordinary people' and fired their emotions, turning neighbours and fellow victims of class domination into demons (Kapferer 1988).

Kapferer (1994) argues that one important factor conditioning the development of violence in Sri Lanka was the shift in the country's political economy inaugurated by the accession to power of the UNP in 1977. The

UNP moved away from the protectionist-statist policies of the SLFP towards an export-led model of development. This is a global shift, but in the specific case of Sri Lanka, the establishment of Free Trade Zones was accompanied by the formation of a new bourgeois class fraction distinct from the economic and political elites which emerged under British colonial rule. The latter tended to be English-speaking and culturally alienated from those they dominated. The new class of the 1970s, in contrast, was not alienated from the rest of civil society in this way, and pursued its competition for political and economic power through elaborating a 'discourse of culture'. This is common to all modern nationalisms, but Kapferer argues that in Sri Lanka it reflected a fractionalizing of elite groups and a contest for control of the state.

Economic openness and the dismantling of what had been a substantial welfare state apparatus sharpened class conflict. Although left and trade union politics in Sri Lanka were not immune from populist tendencies, or even from appeals to ethnic chauvinist sentiment, they did, Kapferer argues, ameliorate class tensions and dampen tendencies to anti-state or inter-ethnic violence. The JVP represented a populist reaction of disenchanted youth drawn from poor rural families towards the established left parties, whose leaders were often drawn from the urban and rural bourgeoisie. The 1971 insurrection was, however, delayed for a time in order to see whether the SLFP would promote reforms. The accession of the UNP and transformation of the political economy of Sri Lanka not only provoked greater economic class polarization, but disturbed the linkages between left organizations and the government. The UNP and new class politicians set about disrupting the personal patron–client networks of political rivals as part of an attack on trade unions and left parties which might challenge the implementation of their new economic model. They thus destroyed established institutional channels for class interest to express itself as class interest, at the same time as they relied increasingly on religion and ethnic nationalism as mobilizing political ideologies to control the tensions of class division.

The new political discourses of the 1970s fuelled popular hostility to Tamils in a variety of ways, including encouraging popular Sinhalese beliefs in the existence of Tamil privilege in access to education, medical care and public employment. Such propaganda played on personal anxieties and the aspirations of the upwardly mobile. Despite the growth of the private and transnational sectors of the economy, Sri Lanka remained a heavily bureaucratized country in the 1970s. The crisis of the 1980s made secure government employment even more attractive. Jobs were distributed through patronage, and the continuity of the UNP in power prevented redistribution of public sector jobs to supporters of other parties. In practice, however, English remained the primary route to advancement within the state apparatus even after Sinhala was privileged over Tamil. This perpetuated the frustrations manifest in the JVP's attacks on both SLFP and UNP governments, but antagonism was deflected away from the state as the fires of ethnic nationalism were fanned by the discourse of culture of the new class.

Kapferer argues, however, that the conditions for conflagration were shaped by colonial bureaucratic transformations. By enshrining ethnicity as an administrative category within the colonial state, the British turned a labile pre-colonial identity into a spurious distinction between 'communities', making membership of such communities pragmatically relevant to a range of life-situations. Sinhala-speaking populations found themselves pursuing economic and political competition by reflexively constructing historical legitimations for the present in terms of the frozen categories created by colonial definitions of the 'caste community'. This engaged all Sinhalese in an intense process of constructing Sinhala ethnic identity to which Tamils were irrelevant. They were thereby exteriorized from the Sinhalese social universe in a way that was not true of the ethnic distinctions of the pre-colonial era.

Class formation processes also shaped the direction of Buddhism's evolution. The British conquest of Kandy in 1815 destroyed the hegemony of the ruling chapters of the Buddhist monkhood. Buddhist organization became decentralized and subject to the control of leaders of caste communities. The Sinhala urban-based bourgeoisie was drawn – like similar strata within other religious traditions – to 'modernist' readings of Buddhism in which 'traditional' practices such as exorcism were denigrated. This, however, opened up the possibility of a plethora of Buddhist practices being used in rhetorics of power by different groups. Each declared its practices 'pure', 'authentic' Buddhism. Small businessmen, for example, revived practices and 'traditions' precisely because these were anathema to elite groups. An endless debate about what it meant to be a Sinhala Buddhist became integral to conflict between class fractions and to the formation of all other identities and associations.

The clients of political patrons and neighbourhood gangs alike defined themselves in ethnic and religious terms. Rioting over a completely trivial incident now brought these principles into play. Sinhalese sought out Tamils to kill in the 1983 riots in regions where the only resident Tamils were a few impoverished estate workers completely marginal to the social lives of their assailants. The link between Buddhism and Sinhala nationalism legitimated a politics of identity in which the pursuit of secular goals became a religious mission, and religion became secularized. Monks became active in politics. The fractionalization evident on both sides of the 'ethnic' divide after 1983 is thus, in Kapferer's view, a product of underlying conflicts in several registers (class, caste, village and political patron–client structures). At the same time, it reproduced the ordering principles of violence. The powerful mobilized cosmic rhetoric and myth as ideologies in constructing their power and materialized this symbolism in violent practices. Those who resisted them responded in like fashion.

The state and its bureaucratic processes create ethnic categories and attach them to 'communities' in all modern societies. In Western democracies we think about such actions as being concerned with promoting 'equality of rights' or even 'affirmative action' to counteract social disabilities suffered by minorities in the absence of positive state intervention. As Kapferer (1988) has shown, the hierarchical logic of 'cosmic states' and the symbolic practices of everyday life in Sri Lanka do not lead to a 'balancing of interests' but an inegalitarian practice of enormous destructive potential.

The apparently egalitarian practices of supposedly 'neutral' bureaucratic control in Western societies can, of course, also serve as instruments of ethnic and class domination. Certain categories of citizens may have their rights severely restricted in the name of the interests of the majority. Sri Lanka, however, developed a political culture in which the 'ethnic other' defined by the self-construction of the post-colonial Sinhala Buddhist nation was seen as a fragmenting, demonic threat to the integrity of the state in which that nation was embodied, and thereby to the integrity of the person. Difference must be subordinated. If it refuses such subordination – as it must while it shares the same cultural premises – the symbolism of destructive and regenerative power will continue to be the motivating force beneath a politics of violence which cannot be reduced to the work of a minority of activists, populists and terrorists empowered by the social dislocations of modernization.

8 SOCIETY AGAINST THE MODERN STATE? THE POLITICS OF SOCIAL MOVEMENTS

I have already made several references in earlier chapters to late twentieth-century social movements, and discussed movements focused on indigenous rights and identities in some detail. In this chapter I focus on a long-standing debate about the political impact of social movements.

Social movements might provide an alternative to a kind of politics in which many citizens of Northern liberal democracies have lost faith – the electoral games played by professional politicians and party machines in the age of the 'sound bite'. They seem to develop at the grassroots, as a spontaneous rising from within civil society of groups seeking social justice, rights or protection from victimization. Yet one of the difficulties in producing a general theory of social movements is their heterogeneity. Sometimes people from different social classes join together in a common cause, whereas other movements are more anchored in a particular kind of social identity and a particular kind of person. It is true that the situation is not static, and that movements that begin as 'middle-class' concerns can become more 'popular'. 'Green' politics, for example, has had an increasing impact on poorer people in Latin America, in part due to the role of the media and environmental NGOs, and in part because such people are engaged in struggles to defend access to, and local control of, resources. 'Ecology' is now part of the everyday vocabulary of a large number of people. Yet the goals social movements pursue remain diverse. Some social movements are orientated to a single issue, although this can change if pursuit of that issue brings repression that leads to questioning of wider frameworks of power and rights.

Yet social movements do not always lean to the left. Some pursue goals that most of us find frightening, and with methods we find repugnant. Women struggling for defence against rape and domestic violence represent social movement politics. Yet so do pro-lifers who murder doctors working in abortion clinics, right-wing militias in the United States who are prepared to kill innocent people to keep the federal government off their backs, and cultural nationalist movements that perpetrate violence on a demonized other. A striking feature of some historical movements, such as the right-wing *sinarquistas* and left-wing agrarian reform movements in Mexico mentioned in Chapter 5, is that they appear in so many respects to be mirror images of each other.

Thinking about social movements has changed during the 1990s as exaggerated expectations of the transformative role of social movements in modern politics have given way to more sober assessments. Most contemporary analysts recognize the difficulty of seeing social movements as something entirely separate from the rest of the political domain, immune from the influence of the state, and they also recognize the ambiguity and contradictions within the movements themselves. It is, however, necessary to begin with a brief review of earlier thinking, which was based on the idea that there was a global development of 'new social movements' (NSMs) from the 1970s onwards.

SOCIAL MOVEMENTS THEORY: THE NEED FOR SCEPTICISM

Foweraker (1995) argues that social movements theory developed in response to both a disenchantment with existing theories of popular mobilization and the emergence of new forms of mobilization outside the framework of conventional politics – the movement against the Vietnam War in the USA, the May 1968 student movement in Europe, and the green and women's movements on both sides of the Atlantic. There were, however, two distinct theoretical trajectories in this early work.

One, resource mobilization theory, is a product of mainstream US social and political science and follows the methodological individualist paradigm. As an instrumentalist approach, resource mobilization theory ignores the questions of meaning, actor consciousness and social identity that anthropologists tend to emphasize. It does, however, pose other questions that it seems very important to ask, such as why do some people join social movements while (many) others do not, why do individuals join one social movement rather than another, how do social movements get organized, how does their leadership structure work, and why do most of them go through a *cycle* of mobilization and demobilization? The other stream of theorizing is concerned with issues of identity and consciousness and fits into a broader panorama of European post-structuralist thinking. Important figures include Alain Touraine (1977, 1981, 1984), Alberto Melucci (1989) and Ernesto Laclau (1985).

The Europeans' interests in Latin American social movements might be explained by developments in Europe itself. The NSM literature emerged in a period in which European communist parties were in decline and traditional class-based politics seemed incapable of changing society. Many European leftists found a new source of political optimism in the wide variety of movements that were mobilizing people on environmental issues, anti-nuclear issues, and civic and women's rights issues. Judith Hellman (1992) suggests that the study of Latin American social movements attracted disillusioned European intellectuals because:

The study of the Latin American movements is a page out of their own political auto-
biography; it permits them to relive a satisfying experience or rework an unsatisfying
one from their own youthful days of militance in anti-authoritarian movements in
Europe. (Hellman 1992: 54)

There was, however, an upsurge of popular movements in Latin America at
the same time as European politics was changing, even though the contexts
were very different. In Latin America the political problem of the previous
decades had been military governments, although that region also had left-
wing parties that seemed incapable of gaining power. The Sandinista
revolution in Nicaragua offered a brief exception to that rule, but in the end
only seemed to confirm the historical failure of the Left. There was, however,
considerable mobilization of lower-class grassroots organizations. Some of
them, like popular organizations in shantytowns fighting for land regular-
ization and public services, could be seen as pursuing basic 'material'
demands. Yet others, like the mothers demanding that the military reveal
the fate of their 'disappeared' children, seemed to be setting in motion broader
campaigns for human rights and democratization. The 'new' movements
were not simply the personal followings of middle-class populist leaders and
appeared to be trying to keep their distance from the state. They had not just
emerged independently within 'civil society', but brought previously
'marginal' social groups into the political process. Many of them were
concerned with a new kind of politics of identity. This included new
movements of Black people as well as 'indigenous groups' (Wade 1995,
1997), but feminism (Stephen 1997c), and in the fullness of time, gay and
lesbian politics,[1] also began to make some headway in Latin America.

The NSMs in Latin America thus came to be seen as 'new actors', distinct
from established political parties and bureaucratized trade unions. Many
inferred from this that their internal organization was also democratic and
participatory, so that their members achieved the 'empowerment' that other
organizations denied those they mobilized. Yet the very heterogeneity of the
new movements raised questions. What meaningful comparisons could
really be drawn between Europe and Latin America, given the obvious
differences in social structures, political cultures and socio-economic
conditions? What did middle-class feminism have in common with the
struggles of poor women in the *barrios*? Were 'motherist' groups simply
reproducing patriarchal ideologies by attempting to shame conservative
regimes into honouring their supposed commitment to the sanctity of
motherhood and the family? Independent workers' and peasants' organizations, Liberation Theology-inspired Christian Base Communities, and some
of the indigenous movements, often appeared to be pursuing 'classical' social
objectives, provoking a lively debate on whether 'new' movements were

---

1 For discussions of social attitudes to same-sex relationships, see Lancaster (1992) and
Gutmann (1996).

genuinely distinct from 'old' ones (Gledhill 1988b, Knight 1990, Campbell 1993). Struggles for civic rights, for example, have a long history in Latin America, whilst other movements continued to make material demands for land, services and jobs that did not, in themselves seem novel. Others debated the value of imputing common characteristics to such heterogeneous movements, in particular 'autonomy' from the state and democratic 'internal' organization (Escobar and Alvarez 1992).

It could be argued that the 'new social movements' are both a political construction and a fiction and it is this issue I will explore first. The maturing literature has shown that early optimistic assessments of the likely contribution of social movements to a more socially just and democratic world were little more than romantic fantasies. Yet the study of Latin American social movements has deepened our understanding of the dynamics of popular political action and certainly does not support the conclusion that nothing ever changes. Later in this chapter I will illustrate these positive developments through case study material, but I will begin by clearing the theoretical ground a little more.

Noting the ways in which the shift of Latin American states towards neoliberalism mirrors global trends, some theorists have argued that the comparison between Latin America and Europe can be based on the idea that social movements respond to a general 'crisis of modernity' and global shift to a condition of postmodernity (Escobar 1992). The attempt to find an overarching framework is not, in my view, a meaningless undertaking. Many of the obvious objections to postulating similarities in the development of social movements in Latin America and Europe are better viewed as objections to lumping together social movements of different class composition than as arguments against comparing similar kinds of social movements in the North and South. The danger in refusing any kind of comparison is that it can reproduce old dichotomies between 'the West' as the source of 'modernity' and its backward colonial 'others'. Eurocentrism has dogged much of the literature on the rise of new social movements as a global process associated with postmodernity, and it is important to transcend such perspectives.

The *doyen* of European social movements theorists is Alain Touraine, whose work is widely taught in Latin American universities (Touraine 1977, 1981, 1984). Touraine's arguments are based on the notion that the societies of Western Europe have entered a 'post-industrial' phase of development. His perspective is, as Escobar points out, 'not free of a certain teleology and rationalism', because he argues that the explosion of 'social movements' as he defines them is conditional on a society reaching a certain stage of development not yet reached in 'dependent' peripheral countries (Escobar 1992: 408). Social movements in Touraine's view are forms of social mobilization which involve a contest over the cultural models which govern social practices and the way societies function, a struggle over normative models of society. They can be distinguished from 'conflictual actions' which are simply 'collective defensive behaviour' in the face of exploitation and oppression, and from 'social struggles' which are simply about the distribution of economic resources, particular policies or control over decision-making processes. In Touraine's words, social movements are 'the work that society performs on itself' and conflict is ultimately about control of 'historicity', defined in terms of cultural orders which delimit not only where society has been but where it might go to in the future.

Touraine argues that what is at stake in most social mobilization in Latin America is not historicity but greater participation in the state (social struggle). On this score his argument echoes Bayart's contemporary emphasis on the centrality of the state to the social as well as economic development of African countries, but it is underpinned by the problematic assumption that self-reflective historical consciousness is only possible in fully 'modernized' and 'developed' late capitalist societies.

This seems implausible since, as we saw through the Comaroffs' work, colonialism draws colonized peoples into the process of 'objectifying' their traditions, and therefore spreads this particular characteristic of Western 'modernity' at an early stage of the process of incorporation. Furthermore, as Escobar points out, the form of self-reflection on social life found in the modern West does not appear to be the only possible form found in human societies (1992: 404). The obvious lesson to be learned from the New World is that the meeting of European and non-European cultures provoked an indigenous working of the Europeans into *their* cosmologies and visions of history at the conceptual level as well as the reverse. I would judge the Mexican *campesinos* with whom I have worked over the years to be considerably *more* given to reflections on their historical identities, the meanings of their history, and differences between societies as cultural and normative universes, than Europeans of similar social background are. This is unsurprising given the intensity of the struggles over the shape of 'modernization' which afflicted their lives for more than a century and the relatively transparent systems of social and political domination to which they have been subject.

Readers of this book should already have noted ample evidence that Latin American social movements often do negotiate with states, although this does not necessarily entail permanent cooptation.[2] They are also increasingly closely tied to the transnational politics of NGOs, and have plenty of internal politics of a kind that suggests that the early NSM model of

---

2 A good example is the Committee for Popular Defence (CDP) in Durango, Mexico (Haber 1994). Salinas secured the defection of the CDP from the coalition supporting Cuauthémoc Cárdenas, since its leadership calculated that accepting federal resources was the best way to advance the interests of their supporters in the short term and to win local political power for themselves. The CDP was the original base of the PT (Labour Party), whose development was facilitated by the Salinas government as a means of splitting the left vote. Yet by 1998, the PT was fighting elections against the PRI in coalition with the PRD.

'autonomous' and intrinsically democratic social movement practice is a poor fit with Latin American experience. Hellman (1992) argues that the problem with European theorists is a set of preconceptions about 'good politics' that should be questioned. Why she asks, did European theorists get equally depressed when the outcome of a social movement's action was the partial or total fulfilment of its demands by some agency of the state, its cooptation into the following of some populist leader, or its incorporation into a broader political struggle led by a political party or coalition of parties (Hellman 1992: 55–6)? The search for something 'pure and wonderful', an incorruptible kind of 'autonomy', seemed to reflect more about the analysts' world-view than the world. Their failure to acknowledge the qualitative difference between these three possible outcomes of social movement activity was quite perverse.

The failure makes sense, however, if all political activity is seen as inevitably leading to pathologies of 'political representation' through movement bureaucratization under an 'iron law of oligarchy' (ibid.). Yet if the only desirable product of social movement activity is the multiplication of 'counter-cultures', the reproduction of alienation and oppression seems more or less guaranteed. 'People' do not, in practice, seem satisfied with the kinds of solutions offered to them by what Hellman aptly terms a 'fetishiza-tion of autonomy' that denies the capacity of political parties to learn from historical experience or be influenced by the experience and strategies of their 'bases'. This is why the first two outcomes of social movement activity she mentions, cooptation by the state or populist oppositions, remain prevalent, though far from universal.

Where the leaderships of social movements have sought to prevent their supporters from entering into a compromise with officialdom, to secure legal titles to urban land they occupy, for example, such movements have tended to disintegrate rapidly. Ann Varley (1993) argues that urban movements aiming to regularize land tenure are inevitably drawn towards a compromise with the state in the fullness of time. Indigenous movements also need to have their special rights recognized by the state in constitutional provisions. It is clear that representation by political parties can be a problem for 'people' irrespective of their political colour. Sectarian political conflict on the Left can have a catastrophic effect on popular urban organizations, as the problems of the *pobladores* movement in Santiago de Chile in the Allende period demonstrated (Castells 1982). Yet this same case is a good demon-stration of the way 'new actors' may also disappoint.

Focusing on the autonomy of informal shantytown organizations and the role of women and youth within them, many commentators saw the *pobladores* as the most promising form of resistance to the Pinochet dicatorship. Yet, as Salman (1994) shows, collective shantytown mobiliza-tion declined after the protest cycle of 1983 and 1984, and the *pobladores* ultimately exercised little influence on Chile's 'democratic transition'. Older men who had been political activists dropped out as young men's protests became more violent (ibid.: 22). Women's participation did not, in this case, lead to any obvious tendency towards empowerment in the political field, even if women's consciousness was changed (ibid.: 17). Only 25 per cent of shantytown residents participated in *any* kind of organization, and in talking about the role of 'women' and 'youth' we are not talking about *all* women and young people or even identifying social categories which were basic to shantytown social life, since 'heterogeneity goes beyond gender and generation' (ibid.: 23). Studies during the 1960s showed that shantytown residents in Latin America were socially heterogeneous, with factory workers and clerical employees living alongside recently arrived rural migrants and people earning their livings in street-trading, casual work in construction and the 'second economy' (Roberts 1978). Whilst neoliberalism has had a downwards-levelling effect, it is, as we will see later with other examples, essential to recognize that 'the poor' themselves remain socially differentiated. We also need to recognize the role of NGOs as well as state agencies and political parties in their unfolding strategies. Like Hellman, Salman stresses that social movements' failures to meet 'expectations born of euphoria' (1994: 26) does not mean that the actors' changing senses of themselves are not significant for the future shape of political life. To be disappointed is to be 'post-modern in the worst sense of the word' (ibid.), blaming the victim and refusing to recognize that flesh and blood actors have to cope with structural forces of inequality, impoverishment and repression and make complicated *choices*.

Hellman argues that the incorporation of social movements into broader political movements in a loose alliance does not invariably mean that they fail to influence the way such movements develop (Hellman 1992: 59). These observations are relevant to the work of another leading theorist of social movements, Ernesto Laclau, a disillusioned Althusserian Marxist of the 1968 New Left vintage who now declares himself a post-Marxist (Laclau 1985, Laclau and Mouffe 1985). Laclau's position is an example of a tendency among radical social theorists in the 1980s that Ellen Meiksins Wood (1986) defines as 'the retreat from class'.

Like Touraine, Laclau explains the decline of socialist politics and trade unionism in Western Europe as a consequence of transition to a post-industrial phase in which the working class is shrinking along with the decline of manufacturing as a source of employment (Gledhill 1988b). On the basis of this argument, Laclau contends that a politics centred on the opposition between 'the bourgeoisie' and 'the working class' can no longer orientate political life in general, subsuming all other struggles. Contemporary social movements represent a more compartmentalized and pluralist response by different social sectors – women, workers, students, greens, peasants – to broader impacts of the hegemonic order which Laclau rather vaguely defines as 'commodification', 'bureaucratization' and 'cultural massification' (Laclau 1985: 38).

Part of the interest of what Laclau has to say lies in his critique of traditional theories of social revolution. It is important to recognize that this critique is just as applicable to neo-modernization theories as it is to traditional Marxist approaches. Such models interpret conflict in terms of oppositions between categories of people defined by their 'objective' positions in social structure, what Bourdieu termed the 'classes on paper' approach. Conflicts are related to some view of the necessary movement of history: they correspond 'objectively', it is said, to the 'penetration of capitalist relations'. The consciousness of the actors is not important, since it simply reflects the necessary underlying movement of history. The theory itself is based on an underlying *teleology* of universal historical stages. Laclau argues, with good reason, that this universalism is spurious and eurocentric. In classical Marxist theory, the actors involved in social conflicts are also defined in economic terms. Where their struggle becomes politicized, and involves a struggle for the control of the state, then it is seen in terms of the 'representation of interests'. The political project is one of reshaping the whole society in accordance with those interests. It is thereby assumed that social struggles will eventually produce some new 'totalizing' model of society, to be imposed by the victorious group. Laclau develops three basic lines of objection to this kind of theorizing.

Firstly, capitalist development on a world scale is too complex and heterogeneous a process to be reduced to any kind of universal formulation. Secondly, it is impossible to read off the identities of particular social movements from the actors' places in the economy. 'Third World' social movements often unite people whose class position defined in terms of relations of production is hard to define, since the work done by members of households is heterogeneous and changes over the development cycle (Connolly 1985, Benería and Roldán 1987, Deere 1990). Furthermore, there is no necessary connection between the problems posed by living in an urban residential area created by land invasion, one's political rights in an authoritarian regime and what one does for a living. Laclau's main argument is, however, that social identities are always discursive constructions in Foucault's sense: social subjects and their practices are constructed through discourses, on ethnicity, gender and, indeed, politics.

In Laclau's view, 'hegemony' rests on those constructions. Gender and ethnicity as principles of subjugation cannot be reduced to mere epiphenomena of class. This seems valid enough. People can clearly be highly 'class conscious' in the sense of having an antagonistic identity vis-à-vis other classes, and yet support fascist and chauvinist populist politics rather than socialist politics. Laclau insists that this cannot be seen simply as 'false consciousness' produced by upper-class ideological manipulation, and follows Foucault in arguing that even the most 'totalizing' hegemonic discourses provoke micro-strategies of resistance.

Laclau's view of power and ideology is crucial for his third contention about modern social movements. As I have already noted, he takes the view that post-industrial society brings with it increasing commodification of social life, authoritarianism and bureaucratization. Even comfortable rural middle-class people can be shaken out of their conservativism when they discover what the state is willing to do to thwart resistance to nuclear waste-disposal programmes. Small demands linked to specific social problems can, Laclau suggests, have just as radical a politicizing effect as the grand revolutionary manifestos of the nineteenth and early twentieth centuries. They are really *more* radical, because they constitute demands for a more open and democratic society against deepening tendencies in the opposite direction. They are also more *universal* in the sense that they are demands for civil rights in general and not bound to the defence of particular sectional interests. After all, workers may have an interest in preserving jobs in the nuclear and arms industries.

This last observation gives us a clue of what may be wrong with Laclau's position, since the particular positions any group of workers adopts seem to be less a matter of discursive constructions than of their pragmatic problems as social agents in a capitalist economy. Laclau is not simply arguing that the material interests of workers do not translate themselves into political action in an unmediated way, and that there are other things besides economic class position that shape identities and consciousness, a proposition hardly anyone, including most Marxists, would find controversial. His argument is that all social identities are politically negotiated and therefore 'open and indeterminate'. As Meiksins Wood points out, this leads him to deny that any common orientations can be imputed to social actors by virtue of their sharing a common life situation and, in particular, that the relations between capital and labour have fundamental consequences for the structure of social and political power. For Laclau, common interests only exist in the form of discursively constructed ideas about them: 'The ultimate conclusion of this argument must be that a caveman is as likely to become a socialist as a proletarian – provided only that he comes within hailing distance of the appropriate discourse' (Wood 1986: 61).

The first mistake here is to assume that if no simple, mechanical and unilinear relationship exists between two phenomena, absolutely *no* relationship exists between them. Laclau argues that the political positions of particular groups, and any alliances formed between them, are based on a *contingent* 'articulation of discourses'. There is nothing about the NSMs which makes them inherently 'progressive' in socialist or liberal terms: any potential they may offer for advance towards 'freer, more democratic and egalitarian societies' depends on 'the articulation ... set up among the different democratic demands' (Laclau 1985: 33). This leaves us with the question of who or what will do the 'articulating'.

As Wood points out, if the answer is 'no one' (or everyone), we are left with an indeterminate 'popular force' made up of a 'plural subject' constituted by discourses. This is at best a circular answer, which it is difficult to distinguish from much older formulations of the notion of 'plural societies'

(Wood 1986: 63). Alternatively, the answer might be an external agency imposing a unified hegemonic discourse from above. Laclau's position often smacks of a model in which intellectuals are producers of unifying discourses, an elitist and rationalist stance that hardly seems compatible with the idea that social movements are the harbingers of radical pluralist democracy.

Such deconstructionist theorizing leaves politics without roots in social forces. Laclau strives to anchor his belief in the democratizing potential of NSMs in the vague 'objectivities' of reaction to commodification, bureaucratization and state authoritarianism, but has little theoretical justification for doing so. In previous chapters I have shown how the production and inner logic of discursive constructions can be related to historical processes and how the selection of particular constructions over others can be understood in terms of the practices of everyday social life. Whatever its other limitations, Bourdieu's insistence on the mediating role of the *habitus* provides a corrective to the explanatory deficiencies of theories which leave 'identities' as free-floating discursive constructs. Laclau's theory gives us no reasons other than faith for concluding that contemporary popular struggles are more likely to be articulated with 'democratic' than with 'anti-democratic' discourses (1985: 74–5).

It is true that Laclau offers us theory at a high level of abstraction, but the limitations of such decontextualization are apparent in the contrasts Laclau and Mouffe (1985) draw between 'advanced' countries and the Third World. They argue that Third World political struggles remain less plural and more orientated towards a straight confrontation between 'the ruling class and the people', because social and economic conditions remain more precarious. What they term the 'hegemonic form of politics' depends on 'the democratic revolution' passing a certain threshold (Escobar 1992: 406).

The first problem is what this contrast assumes about the nature of 'advanced' countries. Laclau's notion of the 'democratic revolution' of the eighteenth century (marked by the American and French revolutions) is an astonishingly ahistorical construct. It reproduces a liberal-democratic ideology that expunges relations of domination by defining society in terms of relations between free and equal individuals. A serious account of Western political culture should begin by distinguishing 'democracy' conceived as direct rule by the people from 'liberal democracy'. The latter is concerned with the liberties of citizens who are 'equal under the law' and is based on the formal separation of the political and economic in capitalist ideology (Wood 1996: 67–9). Universal suffrage was not even on the agenda of seventeenth-century liberal anti-monarchical politics anchored in possessive individualism. Even the 'socially progressive' John Stuart Mill was still arguing for the exclusion of illiterates and those dependent on parish relief from the right to vote in the *nineteenth* century (Gledhill 1997: 84). Civil liberties, independent judiciaries and the rule of law are worth fighting for, and are, as the case of Fujimori's Peru demonstrates, still being eroded. Yet the 'rights' enshrined in liberal democracy are rights assigned to, and constitutive of, individuals. In the case of an indigenous rights politics orientated around mutual respect for 'difference' within the pluri-cultural nation and the defence of the cultural and material resources of indigenous communities, the collective rights and legal personalities expunged by liberal constitutions in nineteenth-century Latin America come back on the agenda (ibid.: 90, Escobar 1999). Furthermore, as Neil Harvey notes, 'although the struggle for rights appears to distinguish recent popular movements from their predecessors, we cannot assume any universal meaning of rights to which these movements appeal' (Harvey 1998: 24). When Mexican popular movements seek to 'make the constitution real', what they struggle to secure are the specific social as well as democratic rights enshrined in the revolutionary constitution of 1917 (ibid.).

A second problem with Laclau's perspective is that 'popular democratic' and 'popular liberal' political cultures were already present in regional social movements in Latin America in the nineteenth century, as I emphasized in Chapter 5. He argues that the last twenty years in Latin America have broken the older patterns represented by liberalism and populism, with the advent of popular mobilizations no longer based on a model of 'total society' divided into two camps. He accepts, however, that return to civilian rule could 'lead to the reproduction of the traditional spaces, based on a dichotomy which reduces all political practice to a relation of representation' (Laclau 1985: 42). This takes us back to the problem of the 'fetishization of autonomy' and its potentially unradical political implications. 'Popular' social movements have different visions of the 'good society'. These visions are still, in part, related to apparently contradictory 'material interests' – such as those between farmers wanting subsidies and urban consumers wanting cheaper food. Despite its imperfections, the 'old' politics of political parties seeking to win power by bringing diverse movements together and working to find mutually acceptable compromises to solve their different problems should not be dismissed so lightly.

Striving to mediate the polarities established by Touraine and Laclau, Escobar suggests that Latin America oscillates between two forms of politics: 'a logic of popular struggles in a relatively unified political space (against oligarchies, imperialism and developmentalist states); and a logic of "democratic" or autonomized struggles in a plural space' (1992: 407). Yet this resolution reproduces the polarity in another form and may inhibit a line of analysis that Escobar himself advocates: the investigation of how the practice of democracy in social movements might translate itself into a broader democratization of society's political practices and institutions. This is precisely the point at which the optimistic prognostications enshrined in the NSM literature tend to be confounded by reality. Many of the problems that turn political parties into organs of representation rather than participation also afflict social movements.

As a first example, we can consider another aspect of developments in Mexico since 1988. Local leaders of the Party of the Democratic Revolution

(PRD), successor to the Democratic Front which crystallized around the candidacy of Cuauhtémoc Cárdenas and received support from many 'independent' social movements, made genuine efforts to get poor members to act as delegates at state-level party congresses. These foundered, however, because the membership could not sustain the constant need to 'cooperate' financially to pay for fares and the cost of lodgings. People were happy to accept 'volunteers' who were better able to subsidize political activity out of their own pockets, particularly if they seemed better 'prepared' for such a role by dint of education and literacy. The same kinds of problems beset social movements that kept their distance from the PRD, such as the Unión de Comuneros 'Emiliano Zapata' (UCEZ) in Michoacán.

Participation is also a problem in Christian Base Communities (CEBs).[3] As Burdick (1992) shows, people who are illiterate, have 'heavy and inflexible labour schedules', married women facing domestic violence and people who identify themselves as *negros* (Blacks) tend to find Pentecostalist churches a more congenial and appropriate environment than the CEBs in Brazilian cities. The CEBs bombarded their members with literature, downgrading those who could not learn through these media and provoking alienation on the part of those who felt excluded. Those who could not 'participate' in the intensified religious and lay activities of the CEBs because of the demands of their work were subject to the same kind of marginalization that Bourdieu argues generates the 'professionalization' of popular representation. As far as women's issues were concerned, the CEBs emphasized wider social causes of problems in the domestic sphere, in particular the way Brazilian capitalism produced high rates of male unemployment. They conceded little 'relative autonomy' to domestic relations. Catholic discourse did not undermine 'pigmentocratic' selection of people for leadership positions, because it reproduced racist stereotyping, such as the association of *negros* with 'devil-worshipping' syncretic cults like *umbanda*. Even CEB campaigns to empower *negros* faltered because the literate, light-skinned leadership remained in charge of such campaigns (Burdick 1992: 179–80). Pentecostalism, in contrast, actually built on *negros*' own notions of their 'spiritual specialness' through its valorization of practices like speaking in tongues and casting out demons.

There are wider lessons to be learned from the CEBs. The magical transformation of 'social movements' into 'the people' in NSM literature was accomplished by abstracting from the relations between participants and non-participants and from 'a whole universe of social processes' relevant not only to the 'internal' relationships of the movements but to the larger arenas and fields of social relationships within which social movements exist:

In shifting our focus from movements to the arenas in which they exist, it therefore becomes crucial to also shift our focus to clusters of people, whose identity and sig-

---

3 The abbreviation is of the Portuguese and Spanish names, *Comunidades Eclesias de Base* and *Comunidades Eclesiales de Base*, respectively.

nificance should emerge from an ethnographic grasp of local social relations. Thus, we should begin not by examining a particular social movement but by considering how, for example, women, youth, the unemployed, blacks or the formal proletariat (the list can be as long and varied as are social relations) encounter a field of ideological, discursive and practical options. Only then, I suggest, can we identify the processes by which people become involved in some options and not in others, as well as the circumstances under which they desist and distance themselves from a given movement – a process that is perhaps just as common as participation itself. (ibid.: 183–4)

What Burdick offers here, from an anthropological perspective grounded in ethnography, is recognition of the importance of the issues posed by resource mobilization theorists of social movements, but from a position that also focuses on actor meaning, consciousness and identity.

ALTERNATIVE MODERNITIES

Escobar emphasizes the way those subjected to domination 'effect multiple and infinitesimal transformations of dominant forms' through what Michel de Certeau (1984) describes as the 'popular tactics' which operate in the practices of everyday life. This returns us to the theme of 'everyday resistance' and to Foucault's theory of power. For Escobar, however, it is the *collective* character of the practices expressed in social movements, and their articulation of alternative 'cultural possibilities', which makes the study of social movements important (1992: 408). This claim cannot be rejected out of hand. 'Communities of resistance' do exist. 'Cultures of resistance' are historically enduring, despite the ebb and flow of mobilizations, crushing defeats and periods of temporary quiescence. What we should avoid doing is transforming social movements into unitary 'actors' devoid of internal contradictions and contradictory tendencies, and isolating them from the larger social, cultural and political fields within which they experience their ebbs and flows.

These points are well brought out in an anthropological study of a rural social movement in northern Peru that Escobar cites with approval, Orin Starn's analysis of the *rondas campesinas* (Starn 1992). Starn expresses considerable scepticism about the NSM literature's tendency to 'present anything less than total antagonism toward the state as "dirty", a falling off from the purity of uncompromising opposition' (Starn 1992: 105). He suggests that this 'all or nothing' view of what constitutes 'good politics' simply reproduces an orthodox Marxist view of revolutionary politics in another form. He also criticizes the way postmodernist social theory's rejection of model-building and 'master narratives' encourages a jettisoning of modernist concerns about 'how and why' questions and a preoccupation with 'identity' at the expense of the tactics, strategy, interests and organization of people who are driven to act by 'often quite elemental matters of scarcity and survival' (ibid. : 93–4).

Starn recognizes the multiple and often contradictory tendencies which exist in popular movements. He restricts himself to demonstrating how people can, under certain conditions and up to a point, secure a degree of autonomy from the state and pursue their 'alternative visions of modernity' in a practical way on the basis of their own popular political cultures. The other lesson to be learned from the *rondas campesinas* is, however, that less 'progressive' outcomes are possible.

The *rondas campesinas* (literally 'peasants who make the rounds') developed out of peasant vigilante patrols formed to deal with the deficiencies of the official justice system. Throughout Latin America, peasants are accustomed to police and judges who can be paid off by wrong-doers, often participate in criminal activity themselves, and practice systematic extortion based on bogus 'fees' and 'fines' (ibid.: 97). Deepening economic crisis from the mid-1970s onwards not only increased the scale of rural crimes like cattle-rustling in northern Peru, but made the fingers of judges and policemen even 'stickier' than before, as they sought to maintain their lifestyles on incomes eroded by inflation. The peasants' response was to take justice into their own hands, but it was not entirely spontaneous.

The Catholic Church promoted the development of *rondas* in some areas. Peasant catechists trained by priests inspired by Liberation Theology were prominent as early *ronda* leaders (ibid.: 98). Catechists also led indigenous community resistance to the military state in Guatemala and played a central role in the Zapatista uprising in Chiapas (Leyva Solano 1995, Harvey 1998). As we saw in Chapter 5, the Guatemalan catechists were originally a 'modernist' group sharing some of the core values of the *ladino* oppressor. Yet their rejection of traditional religion also undermined respect for landlord and government authority and they were effective mobilizers because they could translate 'the doctrine of political revolution into understandable local terms' (Wilson 1991: 37). The modernist dimension of the *rondas* is also apparent in areas where their development was influenced by teachers and lawyers affiliated to the Maoist Red Homeland party. Maoist involvement in turn produced a reaction by the APRA (American Popular Revolutionary Alliance), which sought to form its own federation of *rondas*.

As Starn repeatedly emphasizes, the peasantry of northern Peru could not be seen as a 'traditional' peasantry untouched by modernity. They participated in a larger social world through migration, the diffusion of political and cultural messages, and the impact of state intervention in the countryside in the period of military government. This leads him to reject the 'Subaltern Studies' school's assumption of an 'autonomous' domain of 'peasant consciousness'. Peasants may rework influences they receive from national society through evangelization and state-run education into their 'own special idioms', but: 'multiple interconnections between city and countryside also create partial continuities between rural outlooks and those of other social strata. Peasant politics may be distinctive but it is never autonomous' (Starn 1992: 94).

Starn also exposes the futility of drawing tight distinctions between the 'old' and the 'new' in analysing contemporary movements. The regional landlord class had obliged resident estate workers to participate in 'anti-thievery' patrols. Vigilante groups called *rondas* were set up by the army to fight *Sendero Luminoso*. Not only was the organizational prototype for the *rondas campesinas* part of a dominant-class strategy for controlling the peasantry, but the *rondas* formed by peasant communities themselves borrowed procedurally from both the military service system and state bureaucratic traditions. Yet Starn argues that they did not simply reproduce these structures but integrated the practices of oppressive institutions into an 'original and more democratic system'.

From the start most *rondas* were under the authority of the peasant community as a whole (ibid.: 101–2). They passed from being simply concerned with problems like rustling to handling other kinds of internal disputes, such as those over land. The *rondas* therefore became a generalized peasant justice organization. The procedures for dealing with 'cases' were modelled on official practice, but *rondas* imparted justice in a way which involved the participation of large numbers of people and an appeal to community sentiment. The president quite frequently asks the assembly or 'majority' for its opinion. Those who go against such opinions may find themselves out of office. *Ronda* officials are often elected by secret ballot and the breadth of participation in the judicial process is of particular importance in a country that does not have a jury system. As well as introducing dis-tinctively 'peasant' practices of justice, the *rondas* generated a new spirit of cooperation in public works projects. Their formation underpinned the emergence of alternative models for 'development' at community level. This new form of community organization also promoted larger-scale protests against changes in state policy towards the *campesino* sector. Independent identity was strengthened and political dependence on the state reduced. Yet this new rural political culture was not, as Starn stresses, utterly divorced from established political practices and power relations and this was not the only respect in which there was only a partial break with the past.

The *rondas* brought some changes to women's lives. *Campesinas* took the brunt of the tear gas hurled at peasant protesters, because they marched at the front. Women therefore became more involved in 'public' politics, and their domestic lives benefited from the fact that the *ronda* assemblies provided them with a space to denounce male violence. Yet men who beat their wives might not be punished, since the notion that women might 'deserve' to be beaten did not disappear from male world-views. Men still dominated the organizations. Only men went on patrol, only men were elected *ronda* presidents or vice-presidents and female activism was restricted to 'women's committees'. Women's participation in assemblies tended to be restricted to complaining about male abuse. Those who asserted themselves more faced censure as men took this as a challenge to their authority and control over the public domain (ibid.: 106).

Starn also notes that while 'peasant justice' did not usually replicate the 'gratuitous sadism' of routine use of torture by the police and security forces, it used moderated versions of these practices. The violent potentialities inscribed in the *rondas* were harnessed to 'bossism' in some communities, where rotation of *ronda* leaders in office was not maintained, and favouritism towards friends and kin became the dominant principle. The leaders of competing regional federations of *rondas* expressed this tendency towards *caudillo* or *gamonal* politics particularly strongly, especially in the city of Cajamarca, where the organizations were commonly referred to by their leaders' names (ibid.: 105–6). Particular circumstances may thus enhance the authoritarian potential of the *rondas* and turn them from organizations dispensing communal justice into instruments of personalized domination, particularly when extra-communal forces lend weight to a particular faction.

Even in the absence of boss rule, community justice may seem rough justice. In Chiapas, some communities that decided to support the EZLN rebellion expelled residents who opposed the 'communal consensus' based on the will of the majority in village assemblies and deprived them of their rights to land (Gledhill 1997: 94), in a context in which there are strong pressures for leadership itself to remain deferential and collective (Gossen 1999: 261). Yet both the Chiapas and northern Peruvian cases support the idea that peasant communities can forge their own political cultures and 'alternative modernities'. *Campesinos* today know how power works and understand how 'development' can affect them adversely. They have an interest in trying to maintain control over the resources they possess and over those who represent them as they negotiate with the state. To some extent, they can challenge the state's control over them. The *rondas* illustrate the way people can contest established ways of doing things, without necessarily seeking the total overthrow of 'the system' or liberating themselves from all forms of oppression, including those embedded in peasant social life itself. The 'peasant community' is the site of internal conflicts and factionalism. Yet such conflicts are not always won by the bosses and those who manipulate *campesinos* in an authoritarian fashion for their own ends. The achievements of social movements should not be judged in terms of illusory absolute standards of democracy and autonomy. More modest achievements in the field of popular empowerment in society and making life better than it might otherwise be are worthwhile in themselves and may have a cumulative impact on the more narrowly 'political' field in the longer term.

CULTURAL POLITICS AND POLITICAL CONSTRUCTIONS OF CULTURE

A focus on social movements encourages us to look at the politics of culture as a process by which groups in 'society' construct or reconstruct identities for themselves in their struggles and negotiations with dominant groups and the state. As we have seen, such processes are never entirely free-floating and may involve no radical rejection of the semiology of domination. Furthermore, the state and dominant groups actively strive to impose their classifications on the structure of a 'civil society' that never exists independently of such hegemonic processes. Even if practices of domination never eliminate the spaces within which counter-hegemonic discourses and practices emerge, they still influence the forms taken by counter-hegemonic movements and their capacity to articulate together to mount a challenge to existing power-holders.

An example of the role of the state in the politics of identity is the revision of US census categories during the 1970s. People from Cuba, Mexico and Central America, the Dominican Republic and other Spanish-speaking areas were all now classified as 'Hispanics' (Forbes 1992). This category did not correspond to any coherent set of distinctions of race, ethnicity or nationality, but proved a useful political tool. It disguised racial distinctions of great importance for the way US society works.

Valorization of European origin perpetuates the valorization of a pale complexion. It not only suppressed the Native American antecedents of the vast majority of mestizo Mexicans, but also the African element in Latino populations. At the same time, it suppressed discussion of the bases of discrimination in the US, including the question of examining the relationship between social mobility and skin colour. There are other explanations of the differential rates of social mobility between Cubans and Mexicans and Central Americans (Portes and Bach 1986), but Mexican migrants I have interviewed themselves feel that skin colour is central to discriminatory practices in the North. It is also significant for understanding patterns of discrimination *within* the Mexican and Chicano worlds (Forbes 1992: 64–5, Lomnitz-Adler 1992). The policies and politics of the American government have therefore added another level to historically rooted systems of social distinction. Furthermore, this has happened with the complicity of political representatives of the social segment constructed by the official taxonomy.

Power and resources accrued to 'Hispanic' leaders both on the basis of the game of numbers and on the basis of the image produced of the political 'value' of the social base they represented: dangerous *chicanos* were converted into respectable, hard-working, self-realizing Hispanics. The pay-off for the dominant was a notable Republican victory in one of the great centres of Mexican-American population, Chicago. This is a paradigmatic case of the way metropolitan societies politicize ethnicity.

The official classification of Mexican-Americans is contested by Mexican-American organizations that choose to emphasize the 'Mexican' over the American. These include migrant farm workers' organizations which opted for a populist-*campesino* identity in the incongruous circumstances of the North by identifying themselves with the symbol of Lázaro Cárdenas, whose son drew many thousands of people out onto the streets of California before and after the elections of 1988. This forced the Mexican government to develop new policies towards its diaspora north of the border and introduce dual nationality provisions. The Mexican state worked hard to insert itself into the 'transnational public sphere' created by cross-border migration and settlement (Smith 1997). In some cases, transnational migrant organizations used their mobility to circumvent the national state's repressive power and remain political critics of the regime. This is the case with the Oaxacan Binational Indigenous Front (FIOB), which has pursued a strategy of trying to overcome the traditional ethnic factionalism of indigenous politics in Oaxaca by drawing in people from different ethnic groups (Stephen 1997a: 83). The FIOB also clashed with authorities in the United States in the course of labour struggles in California. Yet despite its character as an oppositional movement, it has been offered resources from Mexican government programmes designed to reinforce links with the diaspora and encourage its members to invest in Mexico. The Mexican consulate in Los Angeles made efforts to minimize the bad publicity caused by conflicts in Oaxaca by attending to FIOB delegations. Relations with migrant organizations linked to other regions, such as Zacatecas in the North, are more cordial (Smith 1997). More prosperous migrants who can invest in small businesses back home fit better into the neoliberal development model, and their organizations have considerable bargaining power to gain federal sources for their home states.

Although migrants from Zacatecas are largely contented with their identity as non-Indian mestizos, there is some interest in rethinking the 'indigenous', non-European side of 'being Mexican' among young Mexican-Americans in the universities. They wish to distance themselves from older 'Chicano' politics as well as the new 'Hispanic' politics and attain the kind of recognition achieved by Black Studies within the academy. It would be foolish to equate these different manifestations of the contemporary politics of cultural difference. They correspond to different social and institutional settings and the actors involved in them are pursuing different objectives and agendas. Yet political consequences of significance could follow from their 'articulation', if it encouraged the reformulation of Mexican national identity from the 'bottom up' in the manner envisaged by Lynn Stephen or promoted a vision of the Mexican nation as 'unity in difference'.

Florencia Mallon (1992) also argues that a 'popular nationalist project based around indianness as an organizing principle' within Latin American societies offers an alternative to the racism and authoritarianism embedded in *criollo* and mestizo political culture. Her analysis begins with the contrast between the way 'ethnicity' has been politically constructed in Mexico and the Andean region (which was discussed in earlier chapters of this book). Mallon argues that the polarized political construction of ethnicity in Peru reflects the Peruvian state's past failures to 'penetrate' the social life of the hinterland. Bolivia represents an intermediate case between Mexico and Peru because of the historical weight of the Cochabamba region. In Cochabamba,

Indian flight from communal villages to Spanish *haciendas* and towns where textile production developed created a situation more like that of Central Mexico (Larson 1988). Images of *mestizaje* and class struggle already predominated in Cochabamba by the eighteenth century, but the rest of Bolivian society repeated the dualistic Peruvian model.

Given these differences, the role of 'Indians' in the national political cultures of Mexico, Peru and Bolivia has also differed. In Mexico, both scholarly analyses and social and political movements tended to focus on class issues by internalizing the politically constructed division between the mestizo centre and indigenous periphery. Developments since 1994 have brought indigenous rights more centrally onto the national agenda, but many would still prefer to see indigenous issues as part of a larger 'popular' struggle over development and democratization (Díaz-Polanco 1992, Hale 1994). A majority of Mexicans still have difficulty identifying themselves subjectively with indigenous people. I found this to be true even of members of the radical UCEZ in Michoacán who came from villages that were 'de-indianized' in the liberal reforms of the nineteenth century. These activists belonged to a movement that put encouraging all poor Mexicans to re-identify themselves as 'Indians' at the top of its ideological agenda, and had risked their lives standing alongside people who did retain their indigenous identities in land invasions and struggles against local bosses. Yet they could still refer to their neighbours by the disparaging diminutive '*inditos*' and utilize the language of the colonial ethno-racial hierarchy in reflecting, quite spontaneously in casual conversation, on how they were essentially different from the Indians as '*gente de razón*' (rational people) rather than '*naturales*'.

In Peru, the failure of both the military development project of the 1960s and the electoral Left encouraged a rediscovery of the Andean utopia and the pure and idealized 'Indian' (Mallon 1992: 38). As we have already seen mestizo political culture in Peru remains authoritarian, and Mallon argues that Mexico and Peru are similar in their reproduction of 'authoritarianism with a neocolonial base' (ibid.: 51). She suggested, however, that Bolivia could offer an alternative. The Bolivian revolution of 1952 at first sight appears to be simply a repeat of the Mexican experience. Urban middle sectors took the lead, in an alliance with mine workers and mestizo and Quechua-speaking peasants from Cochabamba. The revolutionary project was capitalist development via state intervention and agrarian reform. The MNR (Movimiento Nacional Revolucionario) used the Cochabamba peasants as shock troops. Once the revolution was consolidated, it disarmed them and coopted their grassroots leadership. By the 1970s, however, mestizo hegemony in Bolivia was unravelling. Autonomous peasant and communal groups organized in the *altiplano*, and there was a renaissance of Aymara culture among students and urban intellectuals resident in La Paz (ibid.: 39, 47). Violent repression of the Cochabamba peasantry in 1974 derailed Bolivian populism, opening the space for the emergence of a counter-hegemony defined in ethnic terms: *Katarismo*. The movement is named after

Túpac Katari, Aymara leader in the rebellion of 1781–2, who prohibited his followers all things European, including use of Spanish. The modern Túpac Katari Revolutionary Movement (MRTK) celebrated the indigenous traditions of resistance of the Aymara plateau, but also argued for a broad multi-class, multi-ethnic alliance of workers, peasants, students and intellectuals (Albó 1987).

Mallon argues that *Katarismo* differed from other counter-hegemonic projects because it fused the positive elements of the 1952 revolution – its class politics – with the notion that Indians are the national majority, with their own political culture around which other classes and ethnic groups should align. A politics that stresses indigenous identity can raise questions class-based politics cannot, exposing the racist and neo-colonial relations that overdetermine class relations. Demands that the colonizers recognize the rights of the colonized can capture the public political imagination, as legal judgements in Australia over indigenous rights to resources and efforts to redress such past barbarities as the removal of lighter-skinned children from aboriginal families have demonstrated, despite the 1990s backlash against aboriginal rights (Whittaker 1994). Global processes are not only producing a proliferation of new forms of cultural politics, but some genuine 'articulation of discourses' as local movements learn to relate their particular demands to wider themes such as bio-diversity conservation and 'sustainable development'.

It would, however, be dangerous to be over-optimistic, as developments in Bolivia in the 1990s demonstrate. In 1993 Gonzalo Sánchez de Lozada of the MNR was elected president on a minority vote but with sufficient backing to complete the programme of public sector privatization begun under the Paz Estensorro government at the end of the 1980s, despite popular protests. In August 1997, the country elected the former dictator General Hugo Banzer to head a coalition government that pursued a coca eradication campaign in the face of peasant mobilization without delivering economic compensation for the growers' loss of livelihood. The coca growers had been one of the remaining bastions of popular radicalism in Bolivia after the collapse of the world tin price and IMF pressure on the Paz Estensorro government to close state-operated mines destroyed the livelihoods of the country's miners. Yet by mid-1999 their capacity to resist seemed to have crumbled in the face of authoritarianism.

The fate of the miners themselves is instructive. Organized in a powerful union, the FSTMB (Federation of Tin Miners of Bolivia), and backbone of the Bolivian Workers' Central (COB), they were a major force in national politics (Nash 1979, 1994). Yet as Lesley Gill (1997) shows, even in the glory days the movement was not devoid of contradictions. Not only were there factional struggles for control of the union, but deep cleavages based on gender and the correlation miners made between ethnicity and social status (Quechua- versus Aymara-speakers) (Gill 1997: 297). Limited unity was engineered by the leadership using tactics that were seldom democratic, although the miners were able to stand together heroically in the face of state repression. After the mines shut, some ex-miners migrated to coca-growing zones and continued their traditions of militancy in a new context (Nash 1994), but many were forced to seek livelihoods in the shantytowns of the big cities, where the outcome was very different. Poor people already living in the shantytowns were generally hostile to ex-miners, seeing them as people who had once been privileged. The old solidarity and collective organization disintegrated rapidly, as individuals pursued survival strategies as individuals. As Gill shows, this individualization even pitted men against women in the urban environment and destroyed families (1997: 302).

The miners could, theoretically, have used their existing organizational skills to participate in urban social movements or to build new ones, but this was not their initial response. They looked instead for patrons who could help them out materially. They supported mainstream political parties that exchanged handouts for votes in the slums – including the MNR – switching allegiance in accordance with the inducements offered (ibid.: 307). They also built relations with NGOs promoting community development projects, many of which were para-statal institutions actively advancing the neoliberal agenda (ibid.: 308). The picture is thus, at first sight, one of individualization, fragmentation and surrender to clientelistic politics – on the part of people who once defied aerial bombardments in challenging the state. Gill suggests, however, that even though the old basis for the miners' identity, a class solidarity model, was gone, and the urban slums remained riven with social divisions, some unity could be built against common enemies, such as politically connected land speculators. As they were drawn into broader urban social movements, former union militants had a chance to reinvent themselves, building on their old traditions of struggle as they forged a new political identity more appropriate to the new social setting (ibid.: 310). Yet it remains unclear that succumbing to clientelism versus a more confrontational collective politics of protest are *alternatives* rather than strategies that ebb and flow according to circumstances.

'Counter-hegemonic' movements exist, but much of the world's population is not participating in them. Most of the world's people are now familiar with the notion that they have 'human rights', but many continue to be denied them on a daily basis. Challenges to racism and authoritarianism continue to be blunted by the practices of different oppressed people towards each other. New kinds of low-level social antagonisms emerge to limit the scope of 'popular alliances'. In conditions of great social stress and hardship, individualistic responses often seem more viable than pursuing collective utopias. In the case of Latin America, a focus on social movements does still encourage the view that other futures are possible, that the political field has been changed by the politics of rights and identities, and that mass mobilization is resilient, despite its ups and downs. Yet to date the challenge that popular forces have been able to mount to the remorseless progress of the neoliberal agenda and authoritarian patterns of political life has remained limited.

POPULAR POLITICS AND THE POLITICIZATION OF GENDER

Social movements research has highlighted the growing 'visibility' of women in the public arena. In Latin American societies, the general anthropological debate about whether the distinction between the 'public' and 'private' sphere as gendered spaces is cross-culturally valid seems *prima facie* irrelevant given the centrality of patriarchal ideologies which assign women to a domestic role (Jelin 1990: 2). In a historical sense, however, questions should be posed about the development of patriarchal structures in Latin American societies. Although the patriarchal family as such has a long history, the particular construction of women's role in the domestic sphere associated with the term *marianismo* needs a more specific historical explanation.

The association of women with the figure of the Virgin might be represented as a cult of female spiritual superiority. Some writers have interpreted *marianismo* as allocating women a dominant role in the domestic sphere and providing them with a source of power, since women might be able to influence public life through their domestic influence on men. Others have argued that women manipulate the Marian role for pragmatic ends. Yet the main thrust of *marianismo* in male patriarchal practices is to assert the need to confine women to the domestic sphere and to reinforce sexual control over women, particularly those who go out to work, who are often represented as in a state of sexual danger (Ehlers 1990). Arrom (1985) contends that *marianismo* was a Latin American version of Victorianism, designed to deal with the problem that the nineteenth-century liberal constitutions should have abolished traditional patriarchal authority and given women equal rights and opportunities under the law. The principle of women's equality was undermined by the principle that women were spiritually 'different' from men.

On this view, *marianismo* limited the gains of middle and upper class women from modernization. Working-class urban women in nineteenth-century Mexico City were not strongly affected by the ideology at first. They were forced to work outside the home and often had no home in the middle-class sense, living in tenements where relations with other women were often more central than relations with men. Yet the ideology could diffuse downwards through society just as English versions of what were originally models of urban bourgeois womanhood diffused among the urban working classes as changing socio-economic conditions made female domesticity practical. In provincial towns and villages, it frequently became practical for men to view domesticity and motherhood as the ideal destiny of their partners. This was not because female contributions to the family economy were insignificant, but because the economic contributions women made as workers and household managers could be classified as belonging to a 'domestic' sphere.

It has not, however, been easy for men to maintain a completely successful defence of these containers under modern conditions in regions where transnational capitalism has been drawing women into the labour force as migrant workers in agribusiness, local urban agro-industry and industrial plants. Some 'traditional' patterns of female participation in work outside the home, most obviously domestic service, remain consistent with patriarchal classifications. Newer developments have extended the range of domestic outworking women perform for mercantile and industrial capital in both rural and urban areas. Much of the salaried work women do is done prior to marriage and the tendency for older women to be participants in the 'informal' sector is, in part, a reflection of gender ideologies. Nevertheless, such ideologies have come under increasing stress in recent decades, not merely because of changes in the economic roles open to women (and women's own responses to those changes) but because capitalist restructuring has made it more difficult for men to fulfil the role of 'provider'. In some contexts, this has produced a situation in which the possible disadvantages of women-headed households (in terms of income-generating capacity and care of children) are outweighed by the disadvantages for women and children of nuclear family forms in which males are present (Chant 1997: 59–60).

As Gutmann (1996) demonstrates, the image of the Mexican male as a *macho* is a stereotype (with a twentieth-century history that is linked to the relationships between Mexico and the United States, as I noted in Chapter 5). The people of the Mexico City neighbourhood of Santo Domingo not only recognize it as a stereotype, but negotiate their gender relations around it in a way that has complex results. There is no a simple story of progress towards female emancipation in Santo Domingo, since one of the things to emerge from Gutmann's study is that women's 'empowerment' may be associated with a rising tide of violence towards women in the family (Gutmann 1996: 210). Yet Gutmann's insistence that we consider the role of men as fathers, and distinguish actual practice from upper-class images of the lives of the lower classes, suggests that simple generalizations about men and women have to be replaced by more complex accounts of a diversity of changing gender identities. These changes vary by region as well as by social class, and there are no simple correlations to be made between socio-economic change and changes in gender relations.

The increased participation of women in the labour market, heightened by periods of crisis, but also showing sustained long-term growth, has led to some re-negotiation over household work and parenting responsibilities in the case of a popular neighbourhood like Santo Domingo. Santo Domingo was created by 'parachutists' (squatters) in the 1970s. Women became prominent as community activists, and men came to accept this as a normal part of women's social role. In this case, it does seem possible to talk about the development of 'grassroots feminism'. This has not stopped all men from drinking, beating their wives or committing adultery, but it has forced them to reflect on what they are doing in a new way, and, in particular, to reflect on what 'being a man is'. Few want to be seen as *machos*, though they are equally keen not to be seen as *mandilones* (hen-pecked) and are not always fully conscious that they are responding to North American images of superiority founded on the assertion that *machismo* (as brutality towards women) marks the (racially coded) inferiority of Mexican men (ibid.: 232–5). Women themselves are anxious that their husbands should not be seen as *mandilones*, since this would reflect badly upon them. Yet women are becoming less tolerant of male abuse, and organizing against it collectively (ibid.: 206–10). Fewer women now stay with a man who is persistently abusive, so separation rates are rising, although most women start new relationships with other men (ibid.: 140–1).

Mexican gender relations are bound up in a complex way in the relationship with the United States. 'Cultural globalization' provides new images of women and men, yet US negative images of Mexicans also impact on the way Mexicans respond. The imposition of neoliberalism and the restructuring of the Mexican economy through the North American Free Trade Agreement have placed stresses on working-class families and gender relations within them. Gutmann argues that there is, nevertheless, real change, even if it is not of a unilinear kind, and that it is also a change in terms of conceptions of sexuality. In the old order, women's sexuality was denied, and masculinity was defined in terms of the role of penetrator, so some kinds of homosexual practice were consistent with the old image of 'manliness' (ibid.: 128). Homophobia has not disappeared, but Gutmann shows that there is a growing acceptance of the idea that people *have* sexualities, and that this is something separate from gender roles. The cultural boundaries of acceptable sexualities now embrace bisexuals and lesbians, and young people are less concerned with these boundaries than their parents were (ibid.: 125).

A greater participation of women in the public sphere does not always entail erosion of patriarchal domination within the popular organizations through which they participate nor in the family itself. Many women who become activists face hostility from their partners, especially when, as often happens in agrarian grassroots movements, women start protesting and picketing in the state capital and abandon their homes for days (Stephen 1997c: 48). The women themselves may, however, be strengthened in their determination to resist pressure to stay at home simply because they enjoy this new freedom (despite its dangers) and feel 'empowered' by action. One important issue is the extent to which female activism is itself contained within a construction of specific 'women's interests' that are defined by men. Male leaderships have often seen the development of women's organizations within social movements simply as a matter of combating female 'false consciousness' and detaching women from the grip of rival influences, in particular the clergy. The area of 'women's politics' is one in which it is particularly important to emphasize the way subjects and identities are constructed.

The issue here is how women come to be treated as a 'minority' and the other implications of defining 'women's politics' as a special sphere of the political. Class-based politics can be pursued by female actors and the leaders of any social movement could be female. One of the most significant things women may do in entering political arenas in which only men previously participated is question the male practice of politics in general and the male visions of society embodied in those practices. There is mounting evidence that women do begin to pose such questions when they become active in their own political spaces (Stephen 1993, 1997c).

A considerable amount of women's participation in the public sphere is motivated by the need to adapt to the displacements caused by the transformation of rural societies and migration to the cities. Cecilia Blondet's study of women migrants to Lima establishing a family life through land invasion provides pointers to the various levels of women's engagement that arise from their situation as newcomers to city life. Once the land was invaded, women's 'survival strategies' were no longer a purely individual matter, since the home – in physical terms, a shack and a plot of land – had to be fought for. Obtaining community services involved collective endeavours. Women took the leading role in both activities and saw themselves as taking risks and bearing burdens that their men escaped by going off to work (Blondet 1990: 29). They began to pose questions about the validity of male claims to 'head' a household they did so little to establish. They also formed mutual support networks, based on the 'spiritual kinship' bonds of ritual co-parenthood (*compadrazgo*). These allowed them to leave the house for expeditions to the city, secure help with childcare and cope with crises like illness.

Beyond this, women were drawn into public marches aimed at defending tenure of the land and forcing the authorities to perform civil engineering works to prevent flooding, as well as securing basic services. Here, however, women's participation did not generally take the form of assuming leadership roles, which remained in male hands (ibid.: 31). The activity in which women took the lead was organizing the work involved in constructing roadways and laying out pipes and cables within the neighbourhood. Here the field of action could be seen as an extension of domestic space, thereby violating none of the ideological precepts underlying divisions between male and female roles.

The next stage in the evolution of the urban neighbourhood involved replacement of makeshift housing with a more durable home. The domestic unit became the central focus of women's activity, and as children were now old enough to look after themselves, the women could enter the labour market, generally as domestic workers in private households or as street vendors of prepared food. Mutual support networks became less important in daily life. Neighbourhood organizations began to disband, having achieved most of their goals. At this juncture, the period before the military overthrew the first government of Belaúnde in 1968, the Church and the political parties moved into the neighbourhood, introducing clientelistic practices and new organizations. The key development for women was the 'mothers' clubs', aimed at garnering support for political parties.

This development 'from above' reinforced the individualism of the family and the domestic definition of the female role. It also offered club leaders an avenue of limited social mobility and reinforced tendencies towards socio-economic differentiation, since only women who did not go out to work were in a position to become leaders (ibid.: 35). The mothers' clubs involved women in another kind of political process. Women competed against women in factional struggles for control of the clubs and clubs competed for access to the resources provided by patronage networks. In the early 1970s, the mothers' clubs declined, as Velasco's military regime promoted other forms of popular participation, but the crisis of the second half of the 1970s revived them in a new form.

As male unemployment increased, women needed to increase their contribution, but women in their forties and fifties were now too old to gain employment as manual workers or domestic servants. The mother's clubs became channels for distributing food to the poor under social welfare programmes, but women were obliged to perform physically taxing community work. The clubs also acted as agencies for recruiting homeworkers for Lima sweater manufacturers. All this changed the nature of the women's participation in the clubs.

Individuals switched from one club to another in search of better returns to their labour and clubs would only survive if their leaders proved adept at extracting resources from state agencies and the private sector. Over time, however, the women began to demand more of a say in decision-making and the opportunity to acquire real training and skills. The clubs came to be seen as organizations through which collective work could provide solutions to the problems posed by economic crisis. New types of collective organization emerged, such as popular kitchens, as women renegotiated their relationships with outside agencies. As these new collective responses took hold within the community, women began to build links with trade unions, political parties and social movement umbrella organizations such as the Federation of Young Towns. Their relationships with these organizations could become conflictive, as the women reacted to the manipulative practices of political groups and discovered that the men dominant within them had a tendency to disparage mothers' clubs and other women's organizations (ibid.: 43). Nevertheless, Blondet argued that developments since the mid-1970s were positive. Organizations once grounded in clientelistic and 'top-down' practices gave way to collectivities with a more 'bottom-up' orientation. Women reconceptualized themselves by stressing solidarity and collective self-help. They were not merely participating in wider organizations but challenging the principles according to which they operated.

As Lynn Stephen argues, it is necessary to question the extent to which women have ever been fully excluded from the public sphere in Latin American societies, either economically or politically. The way they have participated in politics has often been affected by male domination, not least in left-wing parties. Yet the public–private dichotomy has frequently obscured the role that women have long played in political life, including the role they have played whilst physically located in 'domestic' spaces (Stephen 1997c: 272). This issue is highly germane to the Bolivian experience. The Bartolina Sisa Federation of Peasant Women, closely linked to the *Katarista* movement, politicized gender within the broader popular movement. One of the bases for this development lay in the way that Aymara peasant women of the Bolivian *altiplano* had very specific economic interests outside the domestic sphere, as the main protagonists in rural markets (León 1990: 138). They were also the bearers of a combative ethnic consciousness forged in a context of discrimination and exclusion. Aymara peasant consciousness played an important role in the earlier stages of the Federation's development, but the ethnic discourse of the organization was replaced by a feminist discourse in the 1980s, as it began to link itself to other women's organizations representing socially distinct constituencies (ibid.: 143).

The immediate background to the emergence of the Federation was the struggle against the Banzer dictatorship, which intensified after the 1974 massacres in Cochabamba and generalized persecution of peasant leaders. As in urban Peru, peasant women emerged onto the public stage through women's organizations like mothers' clubs, but the women of the *altiplano* had already proved their activism by participating in hunger strikes, protest marches and road blockades. Their militancy grew after the democratic elections of 1978, which brought a return to the clientelist practices of the established political parties and a determined effort by the MRTK and its allies to resist a repeat of the experiences of the period of MNR rule. The First Congress of Peasant Women, held at the start of 1980, was sponsored by the MRTK[4] and the major militant peasant organization, the Sole Trade Union Confederation of Bolivian Rural Workers (CSUTCB). The male leaderships saw the organization of women as a means of building up grassroots support and the creation of separate unions for women as a means of sustaining the activism women had recently displayed, given the barriers to participation they acknowledged women faced in male-dominated organizations.

4 Bartolina Sisa was the partner of Túpac Katari, and the logic of the 'traditional' cosmology the *Kataristas* sought to draw on here was that of hierarchized gender parallelism or complementarity. This worked itself out in unreconstructed form in the practices of the male-dominated parent body of the Federation: the leadership suggested that women's leaders at Congresses should be responsible for the cooking (León 1990: 147).

The Congress was dominated by the *Kataristas*, whose emphasis on Aymara ethnic identity as a complement to class consciousness reinforced the basis for female militancy provided by a deteriorating economic situation. Aymara women were in the majority. The Congress was organized in a top-down fashion. Many delegates from less politicized regions seem to have been passive participants, looking for a lead. This came initially from the CSUTCB's male leadership, and the Congress's demands followed the line of that organization without formulating a coherent set of demands centred on gender (ibid.: 141). Nevertheless, peasant women who participated in the Federation's political life rapidly put the issues of male abuse onto the agenda.

Initially, the Federation was a national body lacking an organizational structure at provincial level. In building such a structure, it did not restrict itself to drawing in people who already belonged to formal organizations, but attempted to link itself to traditional forms of association between women via kinship and solidarity networks. This had important implications. Bolivia suffered another coup six months after the Federation was founded, and popular organizations were again forced to operate clandestinely. Women's organizations played an important role in solidifying popular resistance, through both active resistance to repression and the formation of mutual help groups and cooperatives. In particular, the peasant women's organizations supported women's organizations in the mining communities. As 'the domestic erupted into the political arena', the entire peasant movement benefited from the strength of rural mobilization against the regime. This gave the CSUTCB leadership a commanding position within the popular movement as a whole (ibid.: 145). With the return to democracy and victory of Democratic and Popular Unity front in 1982, however, the political and ideological consensus within the Federation rapidly collapsed. Political differences emerged amongst its leadership, the membership began to raise questions about participation, and various political organizations and factions attempted to hijack the women's organization.

This brought about a transformation of the Federation's structure. Departmental federations were set up to mediate between the grassroots organizations and national leadership, setting the stage for a more politicized internal debate at the Second Congress of Peasant Women in November 1983. The La Paz leaders continued to follow the line of the parent organization, the CSUTCB, whereas the Federation General Secretary, Lucila Mejía de Morales, argued for the autonomy of the Federation from the CSUTCB and the political party with which the La Paz leadership were aligned (the Nationalist Revolutionary Movement of the Left). In doing so, she allied herself with the women miners' leader, Domitila Chungara. Both sought to build a woman's movement beyond the boundaries determined by the CSUTCB's attempts to define the nature of women's participation in the broader popular movement. Mejía was re-elected, and this marked the beginnings of a shift in the Federation's posture away from *Katarismo*.

The Federation now began to condemn some of the forms of rural women's organization which gave birth to it and had sustained women's capacity to resist in periods of repression, in particular the mothers' clubs (ibid.: 148). At the same time, it stressed the 'sisterhood' of poor urban women and miners by emphasizing the historical peasant origin of other groups. This was reinforced by an internationalist discourse emphasing the role of women in the Sandinista revolution in Nicaragua. The ideology of the Federation thus redefined itself around gender, although it did not embrace a generalized feminism detached from class and continued to emphasize the centrality of peasant women to the struggle for emancipation.

As I have already shown, developments in the 1990s were not favourable to the popular movements of the Andean region. The dynamics of women's movements mirror the complexities and contradictions of the larger societies and political systems in which they are located, as Lynn Stephen stresses in her comparative study of a variety of movements in El Salvador, Mexico, Brazil and Chile (Stephen 1997c: 286). Women activists are involved in broader social struggles with a multiplicity of goals. In these broad fields of action, they continue to face the problems created by structures of gender inequality maintained by powerful institutions such as the Catholic Church, and also by everyday social practices. It might seem that women's subordination to men would make them natural allies of social movement internal democratization. Yet Stephen's case studies show that it is not easy for women to democratize their own organizations (ibid: 279).

Political action has to be negotiated *within* women's movements in a way which comes to terms with the heterogeneity of the women who are participating: they will have different levels of political experience, be different in age, and may also be divided by class, ethnicity and sexuality (ibid.: 276). As in the case of the Bolivian tin miners, unity is likely to be constantly re-negotiated and partial, and may only be achievable if participants can agree to disagree. Women's movements cannot therefore be based on an organic common identity of women as women. Yet Stephen also rejects the idea that women themselves have the kind of divided experience suggested by the public–private dichotomy, and with it the distinction often made between women's 'strategic' activity against female subordination and their 'practical' interests in terms of immediate commitment to their families' survival. She argues that women's mobilization normally involves action on both fronts simultaneously, so that pursuit of 'practical' feminine objectives does not simply reinforce 'traditional gender roles' (ibid.: 273–5).

This leads her to contest the negative interpretations of the 'motherist' movements in Argentina and El Salvador mentioned at the start of this chapter. Tactically, the women played on the supposed respect for motherhood in Latin American culture as a way of making a challenge to the military in public to reveal the fate of their loved ones. Yet as the case of the COMADRES in El Salvador shows, even if motherhood was the starting-point, the actions of the women confronted male power-holders in a way that they found deeply threatening: women detained were routinely raped, 'for not behaving as proper mothers'. This response triggered an escalation of the political significance of women's activism. The COMADRES became a human rights organization challenging the Salvadorian regime head on, as well as the legal codes that made it impossible for any Salvadorian woman to prosecute her husband for domestic violence or any man for raping her (ibid.: 275).

We should therefore conclude that there is still movement at the grassroots. Although it seems even less likely to produce any instant utopias in today's harsh economic climate than it did ten years ago, it is having an impact on the way politics is done and who it is done by.

9 ANTHROPOLOGY AND POLITICS: COMMITMENT, RESPONSIBILITY AND THE ACADEMY

At first sight, it seems self-evident that anthropology cannot avoid engagement with 'political' issues. Many anthropologists choose to work with indigenous peoples who are demanding that states and transnational capitalist enterprises recognize their rights and make restitution for past injustices. As 'experts' on 'non-Western cultures', anthropologists are drawn into legal proceedings concerned with such matters as indigenous land rights and act as expert witnesses in cases involving asylum-seekers and immigrants in the countries of the North. Nevertheless, the commitments of individual anthropologists vary, as do the positions they adopt with respect to the issues involved.

How, for example, do we balance the interests of an indigenous group in Amazonia with those of poor people from other sectors of national society who have migrated into their region in search of a livelihood? They may find themselves worse off than ever if the specific rights of indigenous people are recognized. How do we even decide who the 'authentic' indigenous people are? NGO aid in Guatemala has often been distributed on the basis of how 'Indian' people *look* by virtue of their clothing (Smith 1990). Anthropologists themselves do not necessarily reflect on the 'bigger picture' because of the personal commitments they form with the people amongst whom they do fieldwork. Their world-view often privileges the interests of 'indigenous' groups even if professional self-interest does not enter into their evaluation of the claims of different parties. As Nugent (1993) points out, 'peasants' in Amazonia are 'invisible' in many anthropological constructions of Amazonian society. Where they do appear, on the margins, they may be demonized.

Many anthropologists would not, in fact, want to see their role as a 'political' one, arguing that anthropologists should suppress personal sympathies, beliefs and commitments and participate solely as 'experts' whose testimony can be defended as academic knowledge. Participants in Manchester's 1995 GDAT (Group for Debates in Anthropological Theory) debate were unconvinced by the arguments put against the motion that: 'Advocacy is personal commitment for anthropologists, not an institutional imperative for anthropology' (GDAT 1996). The same year saw *Current*

Anthropology publish a debate centred on a paper by Roy D'Andrade, who argued that 'moral positions' get in the way of 'scientific' work, and a paper by Nancy Scheper-Hughes, who argued that anthropologists' 'ethical responsibilities' obliged them to 'take sides'. Scheper-Hughes's argument provoked some polemical responses, and I will return to this later, but let me begin with some general observations of my own.

The first is that it is not clear that any academic knowledge can legitimately claim 'objectivity' and 'detachment' or that academics can avoid 'taking a stance', even if they remain silent. What was problematic about colonial anthropology was precisely its silences, the reduction of questions of power to a neutral domain of 'administration' kept at arm's length in anthropological writing. We can still choose to be silent, by not dwelling on issues such as human rights violations and corruption in our ethnographies, even where they are part of the fabric of daily life. Yet, as we have seen, at least some modern anthropological research has attempted to engage the most challenging dimensions of contemporary local and global power relations in a non-euphemizing way. Today we must focus less on silence than on the greater dilemmas of speaking.

My focus in this final chapter is on the relationship between academic knowledge and practical, political knowledge. The main form of dissemination of academic knowledge in Britain and the United States is through academic publications read by fellow academics. This is not, however, necessarily true of other countries in which anthropologists participate in an intellectual public culture which disseminates ideas through popular magazines and television programmes that reach a wider audience. Yet academic publishing is not the only form in which anthropological knowledge emerges from field-notes, even in Britain and the United States. Anthropologists who hold university jobs may produce reports for government agencies, NGOs or private companies, and a growing number of anthropology graduates are directly employed by such organizations. Whether we are writing a book or paper that enters the public domain, or compiling a report that is for the eyes of its sponsors alone, we need to ask ourselves for whom this knowledge is produced. Answers to that question are not necessarily straightforward.

THE POLITICS OF ANTHROPOLOGICAL KNOWLEDGE PRODUCTION: SOME INITIAL DILEMMAS

Apparently 'scientific' or 'disinterested' academic writing can sometimes be said to have served the interests of US or British foreign policy and authoritarian regimes – whether or not anthropologists were openly or covertly employed or funded by security agencies. We have already seen how 'knowledge' can be challenged on these grounds in the case of Poole and Rénique's critique of 'Senderology'. Many anthropologists now work for, and are sometimes paid by, indigenous organizations. This might seem a simple way of ensuring that anthropology helps to redress the world's power inequalities and only serves righteous causes, but I have already indicated reasons why things might not be as simple as that.

Leaving aside the issue of whether advocating the interests of some damages the interests of others who might be deemed equally worthy of better treatment, anthropologists often find that the people with whom they are working have problems with what they write about them. When culture is politicized, academics do not necessarily have the last word. They may find that there is a contradiction between what they might otherwise say about 'culture' in a given place and the practical interests of the people concerned in terms of claims to resources in battles with the state and transnational companies. This makes it easy to see why many advocate taking refuge in 'scientific objectivity' and sticking to intellectual convictions (which is not necessarily the same thing, perhaps). Yet there are places in the world where anthropologists could not now do fieldwork without making some concessions to demands to provide some service to the people that they wish to study. We no longer have colonial powers to make the world safe for us.

The relationship between academic knowledge and political practice is particularly problematic for anthropologists because we enjoy face-to-face contact with the people we write about. We do need to think reflexively about our relationships with our subjects, as representatives of the hermeneutic-interpretative and 'postmodernist' tendencies in the discipline have stressed, recognizing that this relationship involves various dimensions of power. Anthropologists have the power to 'represent' through their writing. Representing people simply as miserable victims of exploitation and terror could prove as unsatisfactory a representation, both to the people concerned and in terms of its political impact, as more euphemizing kinds of writing. Yet this is not the only dimension of the power relationships involved in ethnographic research, and there are some senses in which anthropologists may be less powerful than they think, as I will argue in more detail later. Clearly, however, writing about political issues is not necessarily equivalent to political action within the political field in which the people written about are participants. Scheper-Hughes's arguments for an ethical stance in anthropological work are concerned with direct intervention and doing political things *in context* as well as writing and representation (Scheper-Hughes 1995).

The experience of Salman Rushdie suggests that it would be unwise to dismiss writing as a political act that is necessarily always going to be 'safe' because it can be performed at a distance. Even comparatively 'safe' writing should not necessarily be dismissed as politically insignificant. It well may be of political value to the people that an anthropologist studies if something he or she publishes abroad serves to mobilize public opinion behind their cause and leads to international pressure on their government – particularly where international press coverage is scant or non-existent. This is more likely to happen when the anthropologist writes something for a nonacademic publication or provides information the media or campaigning organizations can disseminate. Some anthropologists are, however, reluctant even to bear witness publicly to events for fear of being denied future access to their fieldwork area. Professional self-interest is another issue to be confronted in surveying factors that shape anthropology's politics.

It is tempting to assume that anthropology's 'natural' politics should be radical in the sense of being against Western domination, racism and oppression of the weak by the powerful. Yet many members of the profession hold relatively conservative personal views. There is no compelling reason why an anthropologist should not, for example, have been convinced that the greater good of humanity was best served by counter-insurgency wars to annihilate communist subversion (and some in fact were so convinced). Defences of the Cold War are still appearing, and not simply from the Right. A striking contribution comes from the anti-foundationalist philosopher Richard Rorty (1998), in an argument that advocates a return to US old Left union-orientated politics of labour versus capital as distinct from the new politics of culture and identity. Rorty is unhesitating in his condemnation of the barbarities inflicted on the world in the name of US foreign policy, but not concerned by the fact that left-wingers took CIA money to fight cultural battles against communism (Rorty 1998: 63). He argues that critics who denounced US imperialism undermined the confidence of a generation of young people in the possibility of reforming their country by failing to emphasize other achievements in which 'progressive' Americans might take pride (ibid.: 65–6). Yet it is questionable whether it makes any sense to talk, as Rorty does, of necessary battles against 'evil empires' as if they might have been fought through covert strategies without causing such massive harm to people other than 'mad tyrants' (ibid.: 63). This poses a special problem for anthropologists even if the harm in question does not consist of filling ditches with the victims of US-trained death-squads or peasant children burned to death in napalm attacks.

Can *any* action be ethical that damages people with whom anthropologists enjoyed relations of trust? If not, should the profession employ sanctions against those who practice such behaviour? As we will see, the experience of the Cold War did force professional bodies to introduce ethical codes that proscribed certain forms of behaviour and these codes continue to evolve. The Association of Social Anthropologists of Great Britain and the Commonwealth has recently revised its ethical guidelines to make the principle of 'informed consent' central to the relationships established between researchers and their subjects and to decisions about what can be done with information obtained in the field.[1]

---

1 Both the old and new ASA 'Ethical Guidelines for Good Practice' can be accessed on the World Wide Web at http://lucy.ukc.ac.uk/ASA/index.html. The American Anthropological Association also publishes its ethical code, with additional material on ethics and links to other disciplines' codes, at http://www.aaanet.org/ethics.htm.

The existence of ethical codes does not, however, guarantee that anthropologists will not behave in ways that violate the ground rules laid down and get away with it. Nor do ethical codes necessarily satisfy all anthropologists' visions of what an ethical practice should be, since they are essentially consensual documents. More significantly, matters of personal moral and intellectual conviction are not all that is at issue here. There have always been pressures on the discipline from outside the walls of academia from the state, as well as internal pressures linked to career advancement and the power of the mighty to block the advancement of those who step over the line. Today, these pressures are stronger than ever, despite the apparent proliferation of 'radical' and 'critical' perspectives in the discipline from the 1970s onwards, particularly those associated with Marxism, feminism and post-colonial cultural studies.

It does not seem exaggerated to suggest that even the *ideal* of the 'liberal university' as a supposedly autonomous institution dedicated to the detached pursuit of knowledge is threatened by the demands of government that market principles take on a greater role in determining the scope of higher educational provision. How far the 'liberal university' has ever existed in practice is debatable. Private rather than state funding does not necessarily mean that academic objectives are more compromised (in some cases the reverse might be true). Yet the dangers of present trends are already apparent. Driven by funding exigencies, anthropologists are more than ever becoming interested in selling their services to private and public agencies that have very particular practical agendas, especially in the field of social policy. In Britain, the explosion of 'audit' culture, imposed by the state in the name of enhancing 'quality' and guaranteeing students and taxpayers 'value for money', subjects all academics to pressures that constitute a new form of governmentality in intellectual life (Strathern 1997, Shore and Wright 2000).

Much of this is simply an extension to the public sector of forms of managerialism already established in the world of business, but the implications of self-regulation may prove profound. Individuals are forced to ask themselves whether a given project will further their careers in an increasingly competitive environment in which the quantities of money attracted for research are another 'performance indicator'. The squeeze on state funding is accompanied by emphasis on performance according to criteria focused on 'national and social needs'. Economic competitiveness in the global economy and containment of domestic 'social problems' are at the top of this list. There is a powerful incentive for us to demonstrate our 'relevance' in terms of criteria that are not of our choosing. Professional academics have always been constrained by institutional structures, but if the constraints are now becoming tighter, there would appear to be a prima facie case for vigorous defence of university autonomy and the capacity of academic institutions themselves to set the research agenda. Yet even this is not as straightforward as it looks. University institutions are social institutions with their own cultures, power relations and connections with other power structures.

Great private institutions such as Harvard have played important roles as shapers of public opinion. A noteworthy Harvard effort lay in providing a justification for the use of atomic weapons against Japan (Bird and Lifschultz 1993). Harvard's Russian Research Centre was an important weapon in the Cold War, headed by an anthropologist, Clyde Kluckhohn (Price 1998). Much of Harvard's 'research' focused on propaganda intended to undermine Soviet rule. Anthropologists had already been drawn into this type of work during the Second World War, when their knowledge of cultural difference was seen as useful for psychological warfare against the Japanese. Many saw the Cold War as an extension of this earlier patriotic task, and the culture and personality paradigm lent itself particularly well to this vision. Margaret Mead and Ruth Benedict allowed their research to be funded by organizations such as the RAND Corporation that they knew were 'private' extensions of the US security apparatus. Other projects, notably George Peter Murdoch's Human Area Files, received covert CIA funding because the intelligence community thought that studying other cultures would be useful for US interference in other parts of the world (Price 1998: 396).

Kluckhohn was particularly central to the networks that linked anthropological research to figures inside and outside the academy that played a role in shaping US global strategies, and he also advised the FBI. Even if the involvement of these scholars was driven purely by value commitment, there are still strong ethical objections to their activities: work for the National Security State turned ethnographers into spies and produced knowledge that could be used to physically harm other human beings (Wolf and Jorgensen 1970). The power of these anthropological collaborators of the National Security State also made them complicit in the victimization of some of their professional colleagues during Senator Joe McCarthy's 'Un-American Activities' witchhunt. In collaborating in these persecutions, some of them resorted to tactics that most people would regard as unethical under any circumstances (Price 1998: 408–13).

There were, however, yet more insidious processes at work. Stephen Reyna (1998) has argued that Clifford Geertz's work on Indonesia supports a 'regime of truth' in which blame for the 1995 massacre of communists is shared equally between the communists themselves and the Indonesian army. His attack on Geertz is not a denial of the 'ethical relativism' that entitles us all to our beliefs, but an attack on a form of relativism that refuses to accept that moral judgements have to be *grounded* in evidence. In his semi-autobiographical work *After the Fact* (1995), Geertz uses powerful rhetorical devices to seduce us into believing that both sides were equal in power and that the PKI was capable of seizing state power by force. He ignores what Reyna suggests is a considerable body of evidence to the contrary. Geertz also avoids dwelling on the role of the US security services in turning the Indonesian army into the monster that it was to prove itself, yet again, after the fall of Suharto, in the tragedy that followed the East Timorese independence referendum. Geertz's hermeneutics makes the whole question of evidence and grounds for judgement seem irrelevant, but ultimately legitimates the propaganda 'truth' of the Indonesian army and CIA (Reyna 1998: 436).

Eric Ross takes the discussion of Geertz further by arguing that his early work on rural and urban Indonesia (Geertz 1963a, 1963b) shows a strong affinity with the 'modernization breakdown' paradigm and the 'social and political engineering' such a perspective advocated (Ross 1998: 488–92). Geertz is again perfectly entitled not to share the views of Marxist critics on capitalist development in Indonesia and has, indeed, debated these issues vigorously. Nevertheless, Geertz offered an explanation for Indonesia's rural poverty that deflected the blame from power structures associated with US interests and placed it squarely on the Dutch colonialists, putting post-colonial capitalist development in the positive light of 'modernization'. Such writing was extremely gratifying to power-holders within the university system with strong national security apparatus connections, and as Ross shows, raises important questions about how intellectuals are socialized within institutions.

Geertz was mentored in the Harvard Department of Social Relations by some deeply conservative social scientists, notably the Russian anti-communist emigré Pitirim Sorokin and Talcott Parsons. Both were heavily involved in practical Cold War politics, including the programme to provide refuge for ex-Nazis in the United States (Ross 1998: 484–6). Ross poses some interesting questions about how the social background of a scholar such as Parsons might have shaped his attitudes on race, and about how the mentoring and rewards structure of elite university departments might shape the output of protégés whose own social backgrounds are different. This is not to suggest any mechanical relationship between ideas and social background. It is, however, to point to the importance of linking individuals' careers and the ideas they produce to the politics and socialization processes of university institutions. As William Roseberry (1996) shows, in an analysis of the formation of 'schools' around a series of centres in US anthropology, networks not only promote individuals but also exclude them: part of the politics of academic production is effected by not hiring people.

Even more 'progressive' ideological developments within the university institution reflect the dynamics of academic politics. Paul Rabinow notes that the political field in which 'contemporary anthropological proclamations of anti-colonialism' emerged is clearly not that of the actual colonial world of the late 1950s, but the academy of the 1980s (Rabinow 1996: 49). Arguing that such proclamations 'must been seen as political moves within the academic community', he concludes:

My wager is that looking at the conditions under which people are hired, given tenure, published, awarded grants, and feted would repay the effort. How has the 'deconstruction' wave differed from the other major trend in the academy in the past decade – feminism? How are careers made and destroyed now? What are the boundaries of taste? Who established and who enforces these civilities? Whatever else we know, we certainly know that the material conditions under which the textual movement has flourished must include the university, its micropolitics, its trends. We know that this level of power relations affects us, influences our themes, forms, contents and audiences. (ibid.: 50–1)

June Nash's answer to Rabinow's questions is that the 'involution of anthropology into cultural critique' was the work of metropolitan white males defending their privileges (Nash 1997: 22). There are, however, other political virtues in 'systematic epistemological doubt' from the point of view of powerful people outside the academy. There are also other critiques that can be made of Northern anthropology from the perspective of anthropologists who live and work in the South (Krotz 1997).

We must therefore ask whether it makes sense to talk as if what anthropologists do is simply the result of a community of free and equal intellectual agents reaching consensus. I think the answer is that it makes no sense at all. Anthropological work is enmeshed in academic power structures which have differing configurations within particular countries but are in turn enmeshed in larger national and international power structures. Financial considerations alone ensure that the voices of some anthropologists are heard much more loudly at the international level than others. We can appreciate the enduring significance of these problems by reviewing a past moment of crisis in the discipline's development, when a group of anthropologists in the United States challenged their professional association to take a stand on the Vietnam War.

ACTING ON THE BASIS OF KNOWLEDGE

In November 1966, the annual business meeting of the American Anthropological Association (AAA) passed a resolution condemning 'the use of napalm, chemical defoliants, harmful gasses, bombing, the torture and killing of political prisoners and prisoners of war, and the intentional or deliberate policies of genocide or forced transportation of populations'. It asked 'all governments' to put an immediate end to their use and to 'proceed as rapidly as possible to a peaceful settlement of the war in Vietnam' (Gough 1968: 136).

As Kathleen Gough reveals in her account of the background to the resolution, what was finally passed was a watered down version of the motion originally tabled. The idea that any resolution be put forward at all had been opposed by the president-elect and a majority of the AAA executive board:

The chairman felt obliged to judge the resolution 'political' and hence out of order, since the Association's stated purpose is 'to advance the science of anthropology and to further the professional interests of American anthropologists.' A hubbub ensued at the conference in which the resolution was salvaged when one member suddenly proclaimed, 'Genocide is not in the professional interests of anthropologists!' This allowed the proponent to cite previous 'political' resolutions passed by the anthropologists on such subjects as racial equality, nuclear weapons, and the lives and welfare of aboriginal peoples. A motion to overrule the chair then passed by a narrow margin. Amendments were next introduced that removed an allegation that the United States was infringing international law by using forbidden weapons and transferred responsibility for the war from the United States government to 'all governments' ... The proceedings showed that under pressure, most anthropologists were willing to put their profession on record as opposed to mass slaughter. But most are evidently unwilling to condemn their own government. (ibid.: 136–7)

The reluctance of US anthropologists to criticize their government was a reflection of their personal political positions and an anti-communism that Worsley (1992) shows was not restricted to Americans nor to the period when the Cold War was at its height. More than a question of attitudes was at stake here, however. Both Worsley and Gough are able to recount the more sinister underpinnings of anthropological conservativism through a history of their personal travails.

Worsley shows how research on aboriginal kinship systems in Australia was influenced by the anti-communist witch-hunting of not merely the state but the anthropological establishment itself. At the centre of his account is the persecution of Fred Rose, a committed communist who eventually moved to East Germany. Worsley points out that the stigmatization of Rose's academic work by the anthropological establishment was peculiarly inappropriate given that his rigorous and innovative methods for recording kinship data made it particularly easy for others to reinterpret his findings as they wished, in the confidence that the empirical material was sound. Nor would a dispassionate observer find it easy to demonstrate that Rose's political vision distorted his anthropological vision in some peculiarly pernicious way. Worsley himself was told by seniors of his profession that there was no future for a person with his political record in anthropology and thereafter pursued his distinguished career as a sociologist in Manchester. Yet 'Reds' were not the only victims. Other anthropologists who could hardly be accused of pro-Soviet sympathies, like David Turner, found themselves excluded from the field in Australia in the 1970s by more subtle forms of official obstruction. The reasons for their exclusion were never officially disclosed, in what Worsley describes as a 'terror of indeterminacy', but these events reflected the Australian state's reaction to growing public concern with Aboriginal rights and the Aborigines' own mobilization. Their backdrop was the increasingly devastating social and environmental impact of mining capitalism in the aboriginal reserves (Worsley 1992: 57).

In 1962, Kathleen Gough made a speech condemning the US blockade of Cuba at her university, which enjoyed a liberal reputation. She was instantly vilified and informed that her contract would not be renewed whatever the opinion of her colleagues on her academic merits. As an immigrant from Britain, she was then subject to investigation by the Immigration and Naturalization Service, who questioned colleagues on whether she should be considered a danger to national security. A 1964 grant application to the National Science Foundation was turned down after State Department intervention on the grounds that the proposed research, on why villagers in south India had become Communist supporters, was not deemed in the national interest. This appeared somewhat paradoxical: 1964 was the year the United States Army allocated US$4–6 million to social science research on the factors which gave rise to social revolutionary movements in the Third World, the infamous 'Project Camelot' which was finally cancelled after an international outcry in 1965. Evidently those who might sympathize with revolutionary goals were not deemed suitable researchers into 'insurgency prophylaxis'. Gough eventually managed to fund her south Indian research, partly with her own money; the State Department proved interested enough in its results when she returned from the field (Gough 1968: 152).

Gough was, like Worsley, overtly left wing. She insisted that anthropology had to analyse the world order in terms of neo-imperialism and drew her students' attention to the way capitalist modernization was producing social polarization throughout the underdeveloped world. She saw armed revolution as the alternative to a creeping reimposition of Western domination and made no bones about her sympathies for what she saw as a swelling revolutionary tide. The world of the 1990s is clearly different from the one Gough anticipated in the 1960s, but it is a moot point how dated her writings have become, once we abstract from their over-optimistic assessment of the prospects for 'world revolution' in the ensuing decades.

There are few countries in the world at the end of the 1990s in which a widening gap between rich and poor is not apparent. Nor can Gough be accused of exaggerating the scope of the 'counter-revolutionary' strategies employed by the neo-imperialist powers. The controversial issue of US violation of international law, was, if anything, understated in the light of subsequent developments. Furthermore, most of the issues she posed about anthropology's role in relation to global problems seem to have lost none of their relevance.

Should anthropologists do applied work in the service of governments or other international agencies such as the World Bank? Should anthropologists work in parts of the world which are experiencing social and political ferment, and can they do so without taking sides? How can anthropologists do non-trivial work if we do not recognize the role of force, suffering and exploitation in the processes of social change and the way local situations are influenced by the global distribution of economic and politico-military power? How do we respond to the implications of the fact that anthropologists' salaries are paid by governments, their agencies or 'private segments of the power elite' (Gough 1968: 150), so that the rhetoric of democratic and academic freedoms is continually in danger of being compromised?

In confronting these issues, Gough was able to derive some comfort from the fact that in January 1967, Professor Ralph Beals and the AAA Committee on Research Problems and Ethics put forward a new association policy document. It advised scrupulous avoidance of entanglement with clandestine research activities and agencies, demanded the lifting of government restrictions on foreign research approved by academic institutions and the researcher's professional colleagues, advocated unrestricted dissemination of all aspects of the findings of research projects to people in the host countries, and defended the principle of freedom to publish without censorship and interference. Yet, echoed by other courageous whistle-blowers such as Eric Wolf and Joseph Jorgensen (1970), Gough also noted the way anthropologists had been recruited for work in military counter-insurgency projects as depressing evidence that such principles might not be respected in practice. Her principal hope lay in the next generation of students.

Intellectually and politically, much of what Gough stood for in the 1960s was to be developed in the anthropology of the 1970s and 1980s, but as Joan Vincent has pointed out, the politicization of 1970s anthropology did not lead to a simple paradigmatic renewal. The coexistence of contested paradigms made divisions within the academy more overt but also blurred some of the established boundaries between 'radicalism' and 'conservatism' as reflexive and postmodern approaches undermined the certainties implicit in Gough's perspective (Vincent 1990: 388). In practice, the next generation's susceptibility to radical intellectual paradigms was tempered by its susceptibility to unemployment.

It is important not to oversimplify the dilemmas the contemporary situation is provoking. Let us consider, for example, the issue of 'applied anthropology'. Applied anthropology might be considered a way of enhancing the discipline's commitment to putting its knowledge to work in addressing practical social problems. In areas such as social work and social medicine, an injection of 'knowledge about culture' can ameliorate some of the consequences of ethnocentrism and racism. What is achievable at this level is certainly constrained by larger fields of power relations. It might also be argued that the results of such work are always susceptible to manipulation by those seeking to improve strategies for implementing power/knowledge systems in Foucault's sense, systems that may have a quite different agenda of 'containing' rather than solving people's problems. Yet theoretical and ideological purity is most easily asserted by academics enjoying the salaries necessary to sustain detachment, in publicly or privately funded universities of distinction. Such academics may even be willing to tolerate the casualization of academic labour to defend their own privileged positions, writing 'progressive' works on the suffering poor of the South whilst refusing to support struggles for improved pay and conditions by their own teaching assistants, junior colleagues and other university employees (DiGiacomo 1997).

Yet continuing debate on the ethics of applied anthropological work seems unavoidable. Should anthropologists have participated, for example, in work related to transmigration programmes in Indonesia on the grounds that these things were going to happen anyway, even though they clearly formed part of the Indonesian state's strategy for consolidating its control over a territory expanded through annexation? Filer (1999) has tackled this issue in relation to the work many anthropologists do in supporting or advising indigenous groups fighting against the development of mining in their territories by transnational companies. He points out that mining companies are very powerful agencies, usually enjoying considerable support from the local state, which wants the mining revenue. Indigenous groups are seldom united in their opposition to mining development, and even if a majority wanted to hoist the red flag and create a social and political revolution, they would most likely *fail*. If our analysis of the situation does not encourage the view that 'radical' action *could* succeed, what kind of political stance would it be to advocate it? This line of argument seeks to justify anthropologists working for the mining companies themselves, on the grounds that if we are genuinely committed to the best interests of 'the people' we study, it would be better *politics* to ensure that they get the best deal that they can.

Yet there are clear objections to anthropologists collaborating directly with the companies. The first is the arrogance of what is assumed – that the anthropologist, as a skilled professional, knows what is best for other people in the long run (as well as what is best for his or her personal good as a well-paid employee). This turns anthropologists into gatekeepers who define the 'authentic voice of the local people'. The Shell and Occidental oil companies in Colombia proved adept at finding a handful of urban migrants who could be presented as the voices of communities with which they retained little contact and in which they had no authority whatsoever. This should be a warning that anthropologists may be duped into believing company under-takings that they themselves then 'sell' to community representatives as 'honest brokers'. Even if companies do honour their undertakings to the letter, the community itself may remain divided on the issue, and the anthro-pologist may have to support the repression of minorities.

It may well be the case that the only thing that can often be done with powerful forces is to negotiate the terms of change. Yet it seems less problematic – though not *un*problematic – for anthropologists to participate in this process as adjuncts and helpers to community representatives than as paid employees of the more powerful party. Furthermore, it is quite clear that powerful forces are *not* always unstoppable, and that we need to ask ourselves whether the massive social dislocations caused by dams or mining projects are desirable. To argue that resistance is futile is not only to suspend the need for ethical and political judgement, but also to ignore the fact that there are substantial popular movements around the world mobilizing against development projects of this kind. It is also to betray fellow intellec-

tuals from the countries concerned who are facing the wrath of their own
states and placing themselves in danger by supporting such movements.

The fact that 'development' has been resisted is also germane to the
question of whether anthropologists should work for international agencies
such as the World Bank or for government development agencies such as
the Department for International Development in Britain. Inspired by
powerful critiques of the 'discourse of development' promoted by Western
governments after the Second World War, many anthropologists have
argued that our job is to support grassroots efforts to build 'alternative
development' strategies (Escobar 1995). Yet there have been clear changes
in the official policy positions of most agencies involved in 'development',
with the exception of the IMF, but including the World Bank. It could be
argued that most of the agenda of 'alternative development' has entered
mainstream thinking, especially in UN agencies such as UNDP and UNICEF
(Nederveen Pieterse 1998).

It would be naive to imagine that new rhetorics of 'empowerment' and
'participation' reflect fundamental transformations in global power relations.
It would be even more naive to imagine that such changes were brought
about principally by academics rather than by the failure of old models, and
the resistance and problems of governability that they provoked on the
ground. Yet it is difficult to argue that the changes are completely inconse-
quential for people. It would be possible to write another book about the
limitations of these formal policy shifts in terms of the de facto continuity of
top-down practices of power and the measurement of 'success' in terms of
the logics of development agencies' own 'audit cultures'. Nevertheless, it is
not obvious that non-participation constitutes a more effective way of acting
with respect to these issues and that participation has no impact on reality
other than compromising a would-be critic. Arguments such as those
advanced by Paul Richards about what kind of aid would be 'smart' in terms
of addressing Sierra Leone's real problems seem well worth making not only
in print, but in the corridors of power (Richards 1996: 157–9).

There *are* continuing dangers in allowing organizations to appropriate the
results of research work. Anthropologists who surrender raw data of a
sensitive kind may not be able to control the uses to which it is put, particularly by government agencies. The results of work quoted out of context may
be used to legitimate policies that the researcher actually opposes. There is
also a basic problem of anthropological participation at the project level being
used simply to provide an appearance of study and 'consultation' to
legitimate a process of implementation that has already been decided. Last,
but not least, the agency doing the hiring will usually dictate the terms of
reference of the work performed, and it is often done so rapidly as to be
unconvincing as a serious anthropological investigation, even if its aims are
not controversial.

In the last analysis, it seems difficult to generalize about the desirability or
undesirability of applied anthropological work. It will be clear that my

personal view is that a blanket opposition is unsustainable. It is important that ethical and political considerations are kept firmly in view, that anthropologists continue to do the kind of research that offers a critical challenge to policy-makers, and that they actually press that challenge home. Yet a holier-than-thou attitude of scholarly detachment regarding the transcendental wisdom embodied in a discourse restricted to the academic arena hardly seems a more politically satisfactory position than selling one's conscience for a quick buck.

This brings us back to Gough's challenge to the conservatism and self-serving character of professional anthropology. Given the heat her commitment to socialism generated, it is easy to forget that the starting- and end-point of her critique was not Marx, Lenin or Fidel Castro but *Enlightenment* visions of 'the science of Man': 'How can the science of man help men to live more fully and creatively and to expand their dignity, self-direction, and freedom?' (Gough 1968: 148). Gough's view of the 'anthropologist as functionary' gives short shrift to claims of 'ethical neutrality' and pleads for a renewed consideration of fundamental goals. Anthropologists have, however, found it easier to agree on what is not ethical than establish common ethical goals. It may not be possible to achieve consensus simply because there are fundamental ideological cleavages within the profession at both the national and international levels which cannot be reconciled. Yet the question Gough's intervention still poses for the anthropology of the 1990s is how far we are continuing to evade even clarifying our differences, not out of commitment, but because of an absence of commitment based on the institutional realities of academic knowledge production.

COMMITMENT AT THE GRASSROOTS

At this point we should revisit Nancy Scheper-Hughes's argument for a more interventionist definition of an 'ethical stance'. Scheper-Hughes chose to make it by drawing on her own experience of a black township in the new South Africa. Her argument that anthropologists 'should be held accountable for what they see and what they fail to see, how they act or fail to act in critical situations' (Scheper-Hughes 1995: 437) was not a philosophical generalization. It was directed without ambiguity at the White South African anthropological establishment. Nor did she content herself with the idea that anthropologists as 'witnesses' rather than 'spectators' were 'accountable to history' rather than to 'science' (ibid.: 419) for what they *wrote*. She insisted that taking an ethical stance should embrace *acting* and speaking *for* something in the situation of fieldwork, as she herself had done, first by taking a young recipient of 'popular justice' for hospital treatment and subsequently by addressing a township meeting. Although Scheper-Hughes was invited to speak (in order to explain her actions), she did so as a member of the African National Congress (ANC), in the expectation of reinforcing ANC efforts to replace 'necklacing' and whippings with less brutal forms of punishment.

In responding to her critics, Scheper-Hughes conceded that it might have been better to use others as exemplars of 'ethical anthropology' rather than assume the role of 'anthropologist as hero'. She also backtracked on the necessity for 'action', honouring scholars whose 'morally engaged and politically committed' anthropology expressed itself through the academic text (ibid.: 438). Yet some readers might have been left asking whether such concessions to academic civility did not, at the end of the day, weaken her argument. Did its power not lie in the risks that she had taken personally in the name of 'morality' and her demand for anthropologists to be held accountable for their silences and lack of engagement? In her Brazilian research (Scheper-Hughes 1992), she had been obliged to resume a career of militant partisanship, including campaigning for the Workers' Party candidate Lula in the 1989 elections, as the price of securing the cooperation of the women she wanted to study. Yet nothing had compelled her to put chronic hunger at the foreground of her account of Bom Jesús de Mata or to point her finger so insistently at the pharmacists and doctors who sought to efface its symptoms with tranquillizers and therefore failed in their ethical duty to heal. In her South African work, she made what might have been even more dangerous choices from the point of view of her personal safety, and used the outcome to make uncivil comments about academic colleagues. Perhaps this *is* the price that needs to be paid for taking an 'ethical stance'?

Scheper-Hughes recalls that her words and deeds in Brazil made it impossible for her to enjoy civil relations with elite (and some not so elite) members of the local society. Yet whatever academic consequences that might have had for her research, and however risky it might have been at the time, in the field, it seems to be a risk that can be transcended by career success and professional life. Many anthropologists never revisit the places that form the basis for their successful monograph after the fieldwork period is over. Assuming, however, that fieldwork is survived without physical harm, taking the politics on to the stage of denouncing academic colleagues may also be relatively costless for those whose careers are established. Anthropologist-activists who are 'barefoot' in terms of job security are in a less easy position, unless they encounter like-minded patrons. It is more difficult for them to join a community of 'negative workers' 'colluding with the powerless to identify their needs against the interests of the bourgeois institution: the university, the hospital, the factory' (ibid.: 420). As Scheper-Hughes notes, many academics would prefer not to have their days disrupted by even verbal references to sick people and dying babies. Yet even 'progressive' academics who do wish to hear about hunger and dying babies often have enough sense of self-interest and lifestyle maintenance to make their own contributions to the perpetuation of injustices closer to home, as I noted earlier. Faced with the evidence of our own narrow social worlds, we should be more questioning about the ease with which we can define 'an ethical stance' that is a guide to positive intervention or action.

Scheper-Hughes is quite clear about that in *Death without Weeping* (1992). The cruelty and everyday violence of our world is the result of dominant people and institutions abusing the kind of people anthropologists habitually study. We should 'speak truth to power' and do what we can to undermine the power of the powerful and support the resistance of the resistant. Scheper-Hughes argues that women practise a 'morality of triage' in the social circumstances imposed on them by elites in the Alto de Cruzeiro, which she compares with a hospital emergency room or the 'space of death' in a battlefield or concentration camp. We should not deny the 'disparate voices and sensibilities' of these women by embracing universalizing Western psychological theory but we should, at the end of the day, try to create a world in which women do not have to let babies die. In conducting research here, Scheper-Hughes had problems with maintaining the kind of cultural relativist position to which anthropologists supposedly subscribe. She felt obliged to act against the grain of local practices in trying to rescue a child from death. She also found that cultural relativism simply wasn't *good enough* from the point of view of enabling her to understand why people did what they did in a way that enabled her to empathize with them.

Yet defining an ethical stance to guide action remains difficult in many contexts, because those contexts are full of moral ambiguities. How do we *ground* our ethical judgements, to take up Reyna's theme again? In an essay on human rights issues (Gledhill 1997), I discussed the efforts of the liberal political philosopher John Rawls to produce an account of how political institutions could realize 'justice and fairness' that did not rest on subscription to any particular 'comprehensive idea of the good'. What Rawls leaves us with is either a reliance on moral intuition or (as I suggested) a residual ethnocentrism based on an implicit theory of the inevitable historical transcendence of certain 'forms of life'. He 'solves' the problem of ethics by refusing to discuss ethics in any substantive way (beyond an appeal to history's onward march as a sociological fact). Scheper-Hughes, for her part, is forced to ground her own argument for 'the primacy of the ethical' in the idea that responsibility, accountability and answerability to 'the other' is precultural, in the sense that morality enables us to judge culture. Since judgements about 'culture' are clearly made within specific cultural worlds (by people who challenge or defend dominant practices), a simple-minded relativism about morality – 'This is the way that people in culture X think, so their conduct is unproblematic by their standards' – clearly will not do. Yet it seems difficult to escape the conclusion that Scheper-Hughes invites us to share her moral intuitions as a transcendent and essential 'womanly ethic of care and responsibility' (Scheper-Hughes, 1995: 419) without providing any very strong grounds for us to do so, from either anthropology or philosophy.

Why should 'we' care about 'others' whom we will never meet and whose sufferings may ultimately either be to our material benefit – as a factor in the world market price of sugar, for example – or be of total irrelevance to our own lives? Is it simply that anthropologists do meet some of these 'others' and feel guilty that their sufferings may be the stuff on which careers are built? For Scheper-Hughes the answer is clearly that this is a human experience that is unbearable for her and should not be borne by her 'others'. This does not, however, resolve the problem of what actions are best to end suffering, or the difficulty that there may be competing claims for justice between different groups of suffering, or at least disadvantaged, people, in the same setting.

Many situations are sufficiently complex and ambiguous to make a more generous approach to recognizing competing moral claims seem desirable. As a first illustration of this, I will recount an incident in my own fieldwork that involved the death of a very young child, who thus became an *angelito* or angel baby. The meaning of angel babies is a crucial issue in Scheper-Hughes's Brazilian ethnography. She argues that women in the Alto de Cruzeiro had to be taken at their word when they said that they did not grieve for the dead infants, contrary to the claims of Western pyschology about 'denial' and selves divided between public states and real 'inner states'. This was because their 'culture', shaped by their conditions of life, taught them 'how to feel' (Scheper-Hughes 1992: 431). The idea that small babies who die become angels is common to all Latin American Catholic cultures, but there are distinctive features in how such deaths are handled in Alto de Cruzeiro. There is only a perfunctory ritualization of the wake and burial, and children play an important role in burying the babies, making infant death a part of child socialization. Scheper-Hughes argues that normally this 'works', though her ethnography suggests that it works with tension, not only in the case of an occasional child who cries, but in the case of mature women who display 'inappropriate' emotions in recalling the dead and are scolded by other women for doing so.

Her argument here is that 'abstract' universal moral principles are something that these women cannot afford. The way the women are portrayed by more affluent local families, from a stance of moral superiority that appeals to such values, is essentially hypocrisy which not only fails to register the distinct voices and sensibilities of subalterns, but is complicit in maintaining their suffering. In this account, we are presented with evidence, reading between the lines, of subaltern sensibilities that are subject to stress and tension, but largely conditioned towards uniformity by circumstances. We are given less insight into the moral universe of the elites, because the ethnographer has made up her mind about them.

This may be a mistake, at least as a general recommendation. In 1983, I was asked to photograph an *angelito* in a village in Michoacán, Mexico, by his mother and an aunt. The child had toddled out behind a reversing truck and been crushed to death. In this region, people were less hungry than in Alto de Cruzeiro, but most women lost some children. The angel wake and burial are more elaborate and there is normally a muted display of grief, although it is tempered by the idea that the sinless child has gone straight to heaven. This, however, was an exceptional case. The mother was the youngest daughter of the man who had been the richest peasant in the community and a local boss (*cacique*). His widow, Cruz, had had twenty-one births, from which fourteen children survived to maturity. The daughter who was the mother of the dead child had married a landless fieldhand for love, against the advice of her family. He worked for one of her rich brothers. This was their first and only child.

The truck belonged to the rich brother but was being driven by his sister's husband's brother. The driver was hysterical with guilt as well as grief, but there was, of course, another element in the situation, because the instrument of the child's death was the truck, which symbolized the wealth of other members of the family. What everyone was thinking (but only said with their eyes) was that it was so unfair that the rich brother had taken away the one thing his poor sister had, the child of her love. Muted conversation did suggest that the fact that the father's brother had been behind the wheel added to the moral culpability of the better-off part of the family: they were held responsible for an event that would now haunt *him* for the rest of his life. The rich brother himself did, in fact, feel guilty and, unusually for him, later took to drinking.

In this tragically contingent event, a range of moral issues was unexpectedly exposed. They included issues of social inequality – how some peasants became richer than others. An 'objectivist' answer would consist in explaining the transformation of the political economy of the zone after land reform, which created a new agrarian bourgeoisie outside the land reform communities which needed to find 'insiders' able to mediate their difficult relations with discontented (and now armed) peasants. In terms of local values, however, the former *cacique* was a morally ambiguous figure. People told stereotypical stories about his finding gold under floorboards of a house rented from a poor widow, his cheating a previous *patrón* who was illiterate, and a repertoire of other tales that I heard told in many other places about many other people who had been able to pull their way out of poverty. Yet other stories about Chema, as he was called, suggested that what had made him so successful was his brilliance as a manager of personal clientship relations. He was able to foster the idea that he was, after all, a good *patrón* who looked after people and was, within the limits set by his private self-aggrandizement, caring and socially responsible. It was almost inevitable that none of the sons could match either the charisma or the authority of the father. The son who was best at business was, unfortunately, the least successful in terms of human relations (and the subsequent history of his children, a generation away from the social capital bequeathed by their grandfather, later proved tragic and violent).

Another issue raised by the child's death touched on family responsibilities and whether people had fulfilled them. The normal cultural process for dealing with infant death was of limited help in containing the whole scenario that made this an abnormal event. It simply failed to tell all the parties involved how and what to feel. Furthermore, although the trigger was a specific tragedy, its moral dimensions were observable across a gamut of tensions and conflicts in everyday life. Here, however, it is Scheper-Hughes's approach to inequality and the role of power relations in shaping the terrain of morality that seems of limited help.

Firstly, it is of immense importance for understanding the political and social history of this region to appreciate how people normally related to each other across class divisions within rural communities. Caught between an intensely conservative Catholicism and a disappointing experience of revolutionary land reform, driven to cross-border migration and socially and culturally transformed in the process, the local peasantry had considerable difficulty deciding who to blame for their problems. In the fullness of time they veered in a number of different political directions, yet have lived from 1940 to the present with morally ambivalent ideas about 'exploitation' and 'patronage'. The people themselves worry in a quite spontaneous and self-reflexive way about the apparent contradictions of their feelings.

Secondly, the assumption that the morality of elites is simply hypocrisy is somewhat dangerous. It would certainly be a mistake to assume that elites are homogeneous and that there is no moral contestation within them. I noted in Chapter 7 how lawyers from the upper echelons of Lima society have continued to contest the authoritarianism of Fujimori, for example. Mexico may have become an independent country to rescue the Church from secular reformers in Spain, but even the nineteenth century saw the emergence of a 'Social Catholicism' alongside the conservative forms dominant in western Mexico. This was not simply a pragmatic response to the rise of liberalism and socialism but grounded in a genuine difference of moral orientation, patronizing at one level, but sincere at another. It would also be unwise to ignore the strong sense of moral conviction that can accompany the defence of a religious order of things, at both the top and the bottom of a society in a region like this one, a hotbed of conflict between *cristeros* and agrarian rebels. For elites what is at stake is not simply material privilege, but a whole form of life. To see this simply as self-interested egotism is a barrier to understanding why elites sometimes do not embark on apparently sensible reforms that might, in the long term, have provided them with better guarantees of survival.

A more fundamental problem is, however, the fact that 'societies' of this kind are not simply layered into hierarchically ordered homogeneous strata. In the community where the infant was killed, families that were in equivalent socio-economic circumstances in the 1980s remained divided by legacies of history. These included the role that their forebears played in the days when the region was a vast landed estate, in a workforce which had its own systems of social distinction, still reproduced through marriage patterns long after the reform. Present divisions had also been shaped by the subsequent confrontations between secularizing land reformers and supporters of the Catholic *sinarquista* movement. The latter was, as I suggested in Chapter 8, a mirror image of the agrarian reform movement itself and actually incorporated many disillusioned former agrarian fighters. The root of their disillusion was that the agrarian reform had not lived by its own moral claims. Leaders grabbed land at the expense of other peasants and turned into oppressive *caciques*, quite different in style to the new rich who dominated my study community.

In a local history in which identities had been further complicated by individually variable histories of international migration, micro-differences in socio-economic terms could carry enormous moral loads and impede everyday sociality in unpredictable ways. Furthermore, it would be difficult for anyone equipped with knowledge of the tangled history of land reform to make easy judgements about which actors occupied the moral high ground and how differences might best be reconciled. There would thus be a substantial gap between what might be done in terms of 'speaking truth to power' at a regional, national and international level and charting a course of justice and fairness as a concrete solution to the accumulated problems of decades.

For example, the official rules designed to ensure justice in the allocation of 'land to the tiller' had been widely perverted over a thirty-year period. Yet the outcomes were complex, and relatively poor as well as relatively rich people could be found in illegal possession of land. People who did not possess any land at all might remark on the injustice of this situation, but if they did not have the land themselves, they would prefer those who did have it to be more commercially successful farmers who could offer them work. Furthermore, it was quite difficult to see people who had actually succeeded in becoming small commercial farmers as an 'anomaly' in terms of the expressed goals of land reform, even if they had bought land titles illegally with migrant earnings or a public sector salary. Their semi-proletarianized poorer *compañeros* were neither making a living from the land nor producing the cheap food their urban resident children needed.

These kinds of issues are endemic to rural situations in many parts of the world. Let us briefly consider the case of Chiapas again. As I noted in Chapter 5, the agrarian situation in Chiapas is far more complex than the popular model of a class of rich landowners confronting an impoverished and brutalized Indian semi-proletariat would have us believe. Smaller private farmers have been victims of the development models pursued by national and provincial elites since the Mexican Revolution, yet intractable circumstances now make many of them antagonistic to 'Indians' and supportive of right-wing paramilitary organizations as a 'solution' to the problem of indigenous assertiveness. The paramilitaries themselves are able to recruit young landless indigenous men who see themselves as losers within community status hierarchies. 'Speaking truth to power' in the field would be extremely hazardous in many *chiapaneco* communities, and an anthropologist could do little to explore the complexities of these situations in depth without attempting to find a basis for dialogue with village oligarchs and other agents of 'reaction'. Yet the point I am making is not simply an academic one – that if we do not properly understand a situation, then we cannot hope to produce useful suggestions for changing it – but a moral and political one.

Some of the 'bad guys' are also victims of the power of others, and it would be much easier to improve a desperately bad situation if there was scope for negotiation between different factions. A small rancher whose land has been invaded feels as morally outraged as a landless peasant whose family is hungry: the rancher does not belong to the 'super-rich' and may be having economic difficulties of his own as global free-market economics bite. Neither peasant nor rancher economic strategies may be ideal for promoting 'sustainable development'. There might be other models of development that would make it possible to reconcile their claims to social justice in a way that the actors themselves would accept was fairer and better for all in the long run. On this point at least I find myself in agreement with Richard Rorty, when he argues that a rhetoric of 'no piecemeal solutions' is out of place in the contemporary world (Nystrom and Puckett 1998: 46). Dialogue and piecemeal solutions do not necessarily lead to utopias, but they are surely preferable to continuing violence, and the best guarantee that the ultimate victory will not go to the powers and interests with the weakest moral claims of all. By arguing that a 'good enough ethnography' will do to sustain an ethical stance, Scheper-Hughes (1995: 417–18) is risking failure in analysis of the subtleties and complexities of power relations and the micro-politics of difference. Understanding those complexities is central to thinking about ways of practising a politics that might help the oppressed to improve their position and win, if not everything, then at least something.

FROM KNOWLEDGE TO WISDOM?

This is not a blanket argument against active involvement in the politics of a situation on the ground, but it is an argument for circumspection and humility. In some contexts, it is not even clear whether the anthropologist should do fieldwork in the first place. Consider, for example, the possible implications of trying to interview community activists in a country in which security forces are engaged in the pre-emptive execution of potential as well as actual community leaders. Even the most circumspect enquiries could easily sign someone's death warrant. It is also possible for anthropologists to be unwitting dupes, particularly where they assume that other foreigners they encounter are trustworthy confidants who are what they seem. On the other hand, the argument that anthropologists should avoid working in places experiencing political violence and violation of human rights because of the ethical problems this poses seem dubious. In less extreme situations, study and analysis might indeed be regarded as a duty.

Let us assume, then, that the anthropologist finds him- or herself in a conflictive or potentially conflictive situation. It is unlikely that anyone enters the field so ignorant of local situations as to have no prior sympathies. Yet we may not understand the situation very deeply in advance of research, and once in the field it may take a considerable time to unravel the complexities of local factional politics and individual biographies. We need time to discover who the different actors we encounter really are and what they represent, who they are tied to beyond the study community, and what hidden agendas they might be pursuing. If social and political life were transparent, we would not need ethnography at all. Our view of the situation may change quite radically as our understanding of it increases. Anyone who abandoned a posture of striving to signal neutrality and the priority of academic concerns during the period when this learning process was taking place would be unlikely to realize the goals of a professional study in an optimal way.

In practice, however, anthropologists often find themselves drawn into a closer identification with one side than another irrespective of their intentions by virtue of the fact that other parties are constantly interpreting their behaviour. The simple act of arranging to stay in the house of a particular person can be construed as a political message that it is costly in time and effort to undo. Anthropological writings about the field situation often stress the way the ethnographer, as a person from a metropolitan society or a national from a higher social class, occupies a superior position of power vis-à-vis the people he or she studies. It is true that we hold certain cards: the power of representation through ethnographic writing, and, usually, the possibility of escape. On the other hand, we are likely to be ignorant of much that other actors know about local society, and thereby highly susceptible to manipulation. We will certainly be dependent on the cooperation of individuals from the study community to succeed in our professional goals.

Some of the meta-theory of ethnography that has been developed in recent years exaggerates the anthropologist's mastery of the field situation. Yet there are contexts in which anthropologists can do politically significant things, particularly where they are recognized as figures speaking with authority by virtue of their education or their foreignness or a combination of both. Whether by choice or accident, an anthropologist can lend weight to a particular faction's position vis-à-vis another faction and thereby influence local balances of power. Anthropologists can also, again by accident or design, operate as mediators between conflictive parties. They may even find themselves intervening in relations between the people they are studying and agencies of the state. 'Taking sides' is not the only possible form of action.

Anthropologists may be tempted into practising a duplicitous kind of behaviour if gaining the cooperation of opposed parties is easier when one professes sympathy with their respective positions. Yet blundering about from the outset with one's heart on one's sleeve may be dangerous, both for the anthropologist and those he or she studies. There are, however, usually limits to the degree of duplicity anthropologists can practise successfully. People are inclined to demand answers to questions about one's personal views on social and political matters. Word gets around, and a tactful but not wholly mendacious answer may be the best policy in the long term, particularly if it is underscored by protestations that the job of a researcher is to hear all shades of opinion and to try to understand rather than judge. This kind of answer may not, however, be a totally satisfactory one for the individual or for anthropology in general.

It is not hard to understand why many anthropologists find it morally difficult not to do things that amount to 'taking sides'. Even something relatively trivial, like helping an illiterate friend with some legal paper-work which will help them pursue a dispute with a more powerful kinsman or patron, can amount to quite a large political statement in the eyes of the local community. My point is that we should do our utmost to think about the implications of what we do before we do it, and be able to ground any intervention in the best model we can produce of the larger situation in which we are intervening. Even after the deepest reflection, we may, of course, still get it all disastrously wrong. Nevertheless, many anthropologists working in certain kinds of contexts – such as those involving questions of indigenous land rights – have come to feel that they should switch from the observer role to a participant role, by offering their services as an adviser or go-between in negotiations with higher authorities.

Advocacy can take both defensive and revindicatory forms. It would seem the minimal duty of anthropologists to denounce abuses that violate the laws of the countries in which they work, especially where only anthropologists are in a position to know the facts, and where the people concerned are unlikely to be able to secure wider attention for their problems without enlisting the services of outsiders. There are also many circumstances in which local movements need wider support if they are to advance concrete demands successfully. Here again, the responsibility of anthropologists to the people they study should not necessarily stop at the production of academic writing or even communication with the press. We can also help strengthen local struggles by fund-raising and organizing overseas support groups which can help mobilize international pressure, something which may be particularly valuable when transnational companies are part of the problem in question. It is possible to combine efforts to stop military repression in Chiapas and to secure aid for its victims with politically judged academic analysis emphasizing that the EZLN are only a part of a more complex scenario.

Yet advocacy demands a different kind of commitment than academic writing. It may come into conflict with professional career demands simply because of the time it consumes, aside from any other consequences it might have in terms of future access to the field, the interest of security services and so forth. Furthermore, once we move from actions that defend people from abuse towards actions that support people's aspirations for change, the terms of anthropological engagement become more open-ended. There are certainly causes where a particular anthropological expertise is recognized as having salience, but much of this perceived salience is based on a construction of anthropology as the 'science of the exotic other', raising the 'gatekeeper' issues I mentioned earlier. Anthropologists are likely to be drawn to issues that concern minority groups neglected by other advocates, yet there is no logical reason why anthropological engagement in the political arena should be restricted in this way. Indeed, it might seem preferable for anthropological interventions in politics to be informed by wider reflection on the issues of racism, class and gender inequality, democratization and civil rights. We are therefore back to Gough's Enlightenment agenda and the possible role of anthropology as a socially and politically critical discipline ready not merely to discuss the major issues of our epoch but to produce knowledge that might inform more effective political strategies.

To a great extent, no doubt, the action in which anthropologists should participate as individuals should be pursued outside the academy in concert with other citizens (of their own and foreign countries). Anthropological engagement in social struggles can take a negative and self-serving form which reduces the capacity of 'ordinary people' to maintain their autonomous capacity for action and secure their ends through mobilization in representative organizations. This is essentially only a variant on the more general themes of political representation and problems in the organization of social movements that I have already discussed at length. When anthropologists move beyond the role of offering analysis, technical services, professional advice and bearing witness, to becoming actors within movements and organizations with which they have no organic social links, the legitimacy of their role becomes more questionable. In at least some cases, too much engagement can be as problematic as too little.

In many respects, then, the issue of the political role of anthropology forms part of a broader set of issues concerned with the political role of all intellectuals and academic producers of knowledge. Anthropologists do, however, have a special interest in dialogue with those they study. Thus far the anthropologist has figured largely as the privileged interpreter, the producer of knowledge that might or might not be put at the service of others. Obviously the ethnographic process involves learning by asking questions, but in the final analysis can acquire authority without reference to the conditions of its production in the field and without affording those who are written about any opportunity to denounce the results.

POWER AND ITS DISGUISES

For the theorists of the 'new ethnography' associated with the label 'post-modernism',[2] changing the way anthropologists write is a crucial step towards increasing the political sensibility of the discipline (Clifford and Marcus 1986, Marcus and Fisher 1986). One of the major contentions made by this movement is that ethnographic writing should represent the 'polyphony' present in all cultural settings. What this means can be illustrated by the following quotation from James Clifford: 'there are no integrated cultural worlds or languages. All attempts to posit such abstract unities are *constructs of monological power*. A "culture" is, concretely, an open-ended, creative dialogue of subcultures, of insiders and outsiders, of diverse factions' (Clifford 1983: 137, emphasis added). At first sight, this appears to be true, but the difficulty arises when we move from the polyphony that exists in the world to its textual representation. As Clifford readily concedes, texts can only be representations of dialogue.

Texts usually only give the subjects of ethnography 'their own voices' in a manner determined by the person who coordinates the text as a whole. Some voices are likely to be excluded in the process, and there is little prospect that the full range of power relations involved in the genesis of the dialogue will be laid out in its textual representation. It is, in principle, possible to extend reflexivity about the ethnographer's own reactions to the field situation and particular encounters almost indefinitely, but more difficult to produce a convincing textual account of the other subjects' relationships to the ethnographer in their own words. The participants in the dialogue might rapidly run out of patience if this self-reflexive process was pushed too far, even assuming that meaningful results could be obtained from it. Attempts to capture 'polyphony' through writing may simply encourage literary artifice and a less transparent construction of the subjectivities of others on the part of the writer, particularly a writer who sets out to emphasize the others' 'otherness'.

Nor is it apparent that the kinds of trends presented by these new meta-theories of anthropology represent a move away from an elitist, intellectualist and essentially Western paradigm for academic knowledge production. After all, anthropologists are now being encouraged not merely to learn a whole new series of neologisms, but to explore a wide range of conspicuously Western genres of literary and cultural criticism.

It does, however, seem possible to promote forms of dialogue between anthropologists and those they study which give the represented some opportunity not merely to critique the representations offered but to

---

2 Since most of the leading figures in this movement are unhappy to be branded with the label, on the (I think reasonable) grounds that it is too totalizing and unifying given the diversity of their positions, this form of words will hopefully give less offence.

comment on the anthropologist's silences. Yet academic monographs may not be suitable vehicles for doing this, since they are aimed at a specific type of readership and structured by institutionalized conventions. This clearly says something about the political limitations of academic writing, namely its frequent linguistic and stylistic inaccessibility. This should be a major pre-occupation in tackling the questions of how academic authority and dominant modes of thought can be opened up to greater critical scrutiny. Any normal ethnographic enquiry involves the construction of an anthropological interpretation in dialogue with local informants and interlocutors, but the dialogue is usually closed without the finished product being revealed to those who participated in its creation. We therefore seldom know how adequate it would be judged by different members of the population whose lives and cultures are being interpreted, how its interests and focal points would correspond to those of the people themselves, and where its key silences are from their point of view. In cases where we *do* know something about this – through the critiques of indigenous intellectuals in Central America, for example – we may not draw much comfort from their evaluation.

An equally serious problem is that it is easy to delude oneself into thinking that power can be undermined simply by 'speaking truth' about it. The danger of an emphasis on 'polyphony' is the same as that inherent in the notion of the 'plurality of the social', a neglect of the role of 'structuring structures' and the existence of 'totalizing discourses' in the world. The influence of postmodernism on anthropology seems to have been less radicalizing than many of its exponents hoped. It led to a focus on meta-theoretical issues. The assault on 'grand narratives' diverted attention from the systemic qualities of social and political processes almost completely, not necessarily by denying them salience, but by backgrounding them to questions of representation, construction and deconstruction. As John Hutnyk (1999: 58–60) remarks in discussing some of Clifford's more recent writing, what is the point of 'making space for heterogeneity' in a text by a technique such as collage? Is it a matter of better representing the world? Are 'political and historical juxtapositions' useful if we cannot think of anything to *do* with them politically?

A root problem here is the difficulties anthropology has faced in trying to free itself from the burden of being created by the West as the West established a domination which it is continuing to exert, albeit in a more contested way. Anthropology *is* a Western mode of knowledge, and it continues to revolve around the definition of cultural 'otherness' as non-Western-ness. This makes the centrepiece of anthropology's claims to enlightenment, its commitment to cultural relativism, somewhat problematic. David Scott (1992) has brought this out neatly in examining Geertz's critique of the 'growing atmosphere of ethnocentrism' in the social thought of the United States and Europe.

Geertz (1986) recounts the story of a government medical programme in the south-west USA staffed by liberal doctors from the north-east. The programme offers kidney machines on a first-come, first-served basis. Along comes an alcoholic Indian, who refuses to stop drinking, and thereby monopolizes a scarce medical resource at the expense of other needy patients until he finally dies. As liberals, the doctors cannot refuse the Indian access to the machine. He, in turn, refuses to adopt the doctors' way of looking at things. Geertz concludes that it is difficult to decide whether there was a failure in this encounter, but if there was it was not one which could be resolved by more ethnocentrism (taking the view that the Indian was an ingrate or ignorant) or more relativism (the view that the doctors should have tried harder to see the Indian's point of view), or even more neutrality. Both sides would have had to grasp what it was like to be on the other. Value conflict for Geertz arises out of cultural diversity. Yet as Scott points out, the dilemma Geertz is describing here arises not out of a contingent articulation of two cultural constructions but out of a historical process whereby the power embodied in the Western liberal democratic state historically trans-figured the forms of life of the Indian. These are then 'actively *remade* by the political technology of the modern democratic state in which he has been newly installed as a "free" citizen' (Scott 1992: 384).

Scott observes that the starting-point of Geertz's 'little fable' (subtly displaced by the fable itself?) is the way 'the natives', to whose ways of doing things anthropologists once had to adjust as individuals, are coming 'here' in ever-increasing numbers, raising the question of whether the institutions of metropolitan society should adjust to accommodate them. Geertz's conclusion therefore rests on:

the fairly familiar liberal pluralist [assumption] that things would be a whole lot better if the West's Others – particularly those here – would only accede to its 'democratic' imagination, that imagination according to which the 'other' is marked out as the path to knowledge of the 'self'. (ibid.: 383)

Thus, Scott suggests, the only difference between the apparently opposed positions of Geertz and Richard Rorty (1986), who saw no dilemma whatsoever for liberal institutions in the case Geertz recounted, is that the latter reveals a paternal humanism absent from the cynicism of a West now confident enough in its power to dispense with any attempt to give it a philo-sophical rationale. Geertz's relativism erases the historical constitution of Western power from the argument (along with the anthropologist's own location relative to that power) just as much as Rorty's 'ethnocentrism' does.

This argument takes us back to the starting-point of this book. As Scott points out, anthropology *still* has to struggle to decolonize itself and its modes of thought. Not only is the discipline in danger of hiding its historical, and therefore political, foundations from itself as well as from the world its prac-titioners seek to analyse, but it is heavily constrained in its political impact by the institutional conditions under which academic knowledge is

produced. Nevertheless, I hope that I have illustrated anthropology's ability
to make worthwhile contributions to the comparative study of political life,
and to the unmasking of the manifold disguises of power, both at the macro-
social level and at the level of daily life. Anthropologists have been privileged
to witness some significant episodes in human struggles for economic,
political, cultural and racial freedoms, as well as the violence, mass impoverishment and brutality of past and contemporary restructuring of local and
global systems of domination. Today the 'other' is more than ever in the
midst of the societies of the North. This gives anthropologists enlarged opportunities and responsibilities as public intellectuals. It challenges us to ensure
that the voices of 'others' are not drowned out by the rhetoric of the
dominant in a period when Western power feels able to reassert itself.

Yet the old construction of 'we' and 'the other' will no longer do for an
anthropology which aspires to decolonization. Anthropologists may not like
some of the new definitions of themselves the erstwhile 'others' are coming
up with as they strive to recreate themselves within the societies which
turned them into 'conscripts of Western civilization'. Yet we must be clear
about where the ultimate historical responsibility for the often menacing
shape of our world lies, and worry about the continuing existence of Western
power in disguise in our own discipline's discourse. As Micaela di Leonardo
has demonstrated, anti-modernist anthropological celebrations of the virtues
of non-Western 'others' are just as pernicious as the imperialist construction of the 'nasty savage', although the stance may be a lucrative one if Body
Shop is providing the sponsorship (di Leonardo 1998: 34–5). Like the
'anthropological gambit' of defamiliarizing Western practices through
decontextualized vignettes drawn from the study of 'other cultures', this
restores such others to a safe temporal difference and a different global
system, effacing 'the questions of history and power on both poles of the
contrast' (ibid.: 61). It is the readiness of much of the profession to define its
subject-matter as decontextualized 'cultural difference', di Leonardo argues,
that has limited anthropology's ability to challenge arguments that
America's inequalities and social problems result from the differing cultures
of homogeneous 'ethnic communities', as an invented 'White' ethnicity is
once again juxtaposed to its others, as either 'model minorities' or an
undeserving and degenerate poor.

The Western imaginary has always been based on the assumption that
all humanity could benefit from allowing the West to exercise domination,
reinforcing its case with democratic, capitalist, industrial, scientific and
rationalist imaginaries. Anthropologists are in a good position to appreciate
the limited nature of what has been delivered and the starkness of the issues
this failure poses. We should also be able to appreciate where questions of
value arise and difficult choices have to be made. Engaging with political
issues ultimately means having the courage to stop hiding behind a
paternalist liberal relativism and a stance of academic detachment. Anthropologists should be readier to argue publicly for more inclusionary human

futures, fortified by what they can learn of the range of human experience and by the constant questioning of premises fostered by attention to the multiple and often contradictory points of view of the diverse actors who are making our contemporary history. Yet we cannot do that without engaging theoretically with power, both in history and our own academic world.

BIBLIOGRAPHY

Abélès, Marc (1988) 'Modern political ritual', *Current Anthropology* 29(3): 391–404.

Abélès, Marc (1992) 'Anthropologie politique de la modernité', *L'Homme* 121, January–March, XXXII(1): 15–30.

Abrahamian, Ervan (1991) 'Khomeini: fundamentalist or populist?', *New Left Review* 186: 102–19.

Adams, Richard N. (1970) *Crucifixion by Power: Essays on Guatemalan Social Structure, 1944–66*. Austin: University of Texas Press.

Aitken, Robert (1997) 'Political culture and local identities in Michoacán', in Wil G. Pansters (ed.) *Citizens of the Pyramid: Essays on Mexican Political Culture*. Amsterdam: Thela Publishers.

Albó, Xavier (1987) 'From MNRistas to Kataristas to Katari', in Steve J. Stern (ed.) *Resistance, Rebellion and Consciousness in the Andean Peasant World: 18th to 20th Centuries*. Madison: University of Wisconsin Press.

Anderson, Benedict (1991) *Imagined Communities: Reflections on the Origins and Spread of Nationalism*. 2nd edn. London: Verso.

Anderson, Benedict (1992) 'The New World Disorder', *New Left Review* 193: 3–13.

Anderson, Perry (1974a) *Passages from Antiquity to Feudalism*. London: New Left Books.

Anderson, Perry (1974b) *Lineages of the Absolutist State*. London: New Left Books.

Anderson, Perry (1987) 'The figures of descent', *New Left Review* 161: 20–77.

Appadurai, Arjun (1990) 'Disjuncture and difference in the global cultural economy', in Mike Featherstone (ed.) *Global Culture: Nationalism, Globalization and Modernity*. London: Sage Publications.

Arrom, Silvia Marina (1985) *The Women of Mexico City, 1790–1857*. Berkeley: University of California Press.

Asad, Talal (1973a) 'Introduction', in Talal Asad (ed.) *Anthropology and the Colonial Encounter*. London: Ithaca Press.

Asad, Talal (1973b) 'Two European images of non-European rule', in Talal Asad (ed.) *Anthropology and the Colonial Encounter*. London: Ithaca Press.

Asad, Talal (1973c) *Anthropology and the Colonial Encounter*. London: Ithaca Press.

Asad, Talal (1992) 'Conscripts of Western Civilization', in Christine Ward Gailey (ed.) *Civilization in Crisis: Anthropological Perspectives*, vol. 1 of *Dialectical Anthropology: Essays in Honour of Stanley Diamond*. Gainsville: University of Florida Press.

Ayubi, Nazib (1991) *Political Islam: Religion and Politics in the Arab World*. London and New York: Routledge.

Bailey, F.G. (1969) *Stratagems and Spoils: A Social Anthropology of Politics*. Oxford: Basil Blackwell.

Bakker, J.I. (1988) 'Patrimonialism, involution and the agrarian question in Java: a Weberian analysis of class relations and servile labour', in J. Gledhill, B. Bender and M.T. Larsen (eds) *State and Society: the Emergence and Development of Social Hierarchy and Political Centralization*. London and New York: Routledge.

Bamberger, Joan (1974) 'The myth of matriarchy: why men rule in primitive society', in Michelle Rosaldo and Louise Lamphere (eds) *Women, Culture and Society*. Stanford, CA: Stanford University Press.

Banks, Marcus (1996) *Ethnicity: Anthropological Constructions.* London and New York: Routledge.

Barrington Moore, Jr. (1969) *The Social Origins of Dictatorship and Democracy: Lord and Peasant in the Making of the Modern World.* Harmondsworth: Penguin Books.

Barth, Frederick (1959a) *Political Leadership among Swat Pathans.* LSE Monographs on Social Anthropology 19. London: Athlone Press.

Barth, Frederick (1959b) 'Segmentary opposition and the theory of games: a study of Pathan organisation', *Man* 89: 5–21.

Barth, Frederick (1966) *Models of Social Organization.* Royal Anthropological Institute Occasional Papers 23. London: Royal Anthropological Institute.

Basch, Linda, Nina Glick Schiller and Cristina Szanton Blanc (1994) *Nations Unbound: Transnational Projects, Postcolonial Predicaments and Deterritorialized Nation States.* Langhorne: Gordon and Breach.

Bayart, Jean-François (1980) 'One-party government and political development in Cameroon', in N. Kofele-Kale (ed.) *An African Experiment in Nation-Building: The Bilingual Cameroon since Reunification.* Boulder, CO: Westview Press.

Bayart, Jean-François (1986) 'Civil society in Africa', in Patrick Chabal (ed.) *Political Domination in Africa: Reflections on the Limits of Power.* Cambridge: Cambridge University Press.

Beidelman, Thomas O. (1971) 'Nuer priests and prophets: charisma, authority and power among the Nuer', in Thomas O. Beidelman (ed.) *The Translation of Culture: Essays to E.E. Evans-Pritchard.* London: Tavistock.

Benería, Lourdes and Martha Roldán (1987) *The Crossroads of Class and Gender: Industrial Homework, Subcontracting and Household Dynamics in Mexico D.F.* Chicago: University of Chicago Press.

Bensabet Kleinberg, Remonda (1999) 'Strategic alliances: state–business relations in Mexico under neo-liberalism and crisis', *Bulletin of Latin American Research* 18(1): 71–87.

Bern, John (1979) 'Ideology and domination: towards a reconstruction of Australian Aboriginal Social Formations', *Oceania* 50: 118–32.

Bernal, Martin (1987) *Black Athena: The Afroasiatic Roots of Classical Civilization,* vol. 1, *The Fabrication of Ancient Greece, 1785–1985.* New Brunswick, NJ: Rutgers University Press.

Bhabha, Homi K. (1994) *The Location of Culture.* London and New York: Routledge.

Bird, Kai and Lawrence Lifschultz (eds) (1993) *Hiroshima's Shadow: Writings on the Denial of History and the Smithsonian Controversy.* Stony Creek, CT: The Pamphleteers Press.

Blau, Peter (1964) *Exchange and Power in Social Life.* New York: Wiley.

Blondet, Cecilia (1990) 'Establishing an identity: women settlers in a poor Lima neighbourhood', in Elizabeth Jelin (ed.) *Women and Social Change in Latin America.* London: Zed Books.

Bonfil Batalla, Guillermo (1990) *México profundo: una civilización negada.* México, D.F.: Editorial Grijalbo.

Bourdieu, Pierre (1977) *Outline of a Theory of Practice.* Cambridge: Cambridge University Press.

Bourdieu, Pierre (1984) *Distinction: A Social Critique of the Judgement of Taste.* Cambridge, MA: Harvard University Press.

Bourdieu, Pierre (1991) *Language and Symbolic Power.* Cambridge: Polity Press.

Bourgois, Philippe (1995) *In Search of Respect: Selling Crack in El Barrio.* Cambridge: Cambridge University Press.

Brading, David (1990) 'Images and prophets: Indian religion and the Spanish Conquest', in Arij Ouweneel and Simon Miller (eds) *The Indian Community of Colonial Mexico: Fifteen Essays on Land Tenure, Corporate Organizations, Ideology and Village Politics.* Amsterdam: CEDLA.

Bremmer, Ian (1993) 'Reassessing Soviet nationalities theory', in Ian Bremmer and Ray Taras (eds) *Nations and Politics in the Soviet Successor States*. Cambridge: Cambridge University Press.

Brenner, Robert (1982) 'The agrarian roots of European capitalism', in T.H. Aston and C.H.E. Philpin (eds) *The Brenner Debate: Agrarian Class Structure and Economic Development in Pre-industrial Europe*. Cambridge: Cambridge University Press.

Brumfiel, Elizabeth M. (1992) 'Distinguished Lecture in Archaeology: breaking and entering the ecosystem – gender, class and faction steal the show', *American Anthropologist* 94(3): 551–67.

Burdick, John (1992) 'Rethinking the study of social movements: the case of the Christian Base Communities in Urban Brazil', in Arturo Escobar and Sonia E. Alvarez (eds) *The Making of Social Movements in Latin America: Identity, Strategy and Democracy*. Boulder, CO: Westview Press.

Cammack, Paul (1991) 'Brazil: the long march to the New Republic', *New Left Review* 190: 21–58.

Camp, Roderic A. (1996) *Politics in Mexico*. New York and Oxford: Oxford University Press.

Campbell, Howard (1993) 'Tradition and the New Social Movements: the politics of isthmus Zapotec culture', *Latin American Perspectives* 78, 20(3): 83–97.

Cancian, Frank (1992) *The Decline of Community in Zinacantán: Economy, Public Life, and Social Stratification, 1960–1987*. Stanford, CA: Stanford University Press.

Carmack, Robert M. (1995) *Rebels of Highland Guatemala: The Quiché-Mayas of Momostenango*. Norman: University of Oklahoma Press.

Carneiro, Robert (1981) 'The chiefdom: precursor of the state', in G.D. Jones and P.R. Krautz (eds) *The Transition to Statehood in the New World*. Cambridge: Cambridge University Press.

Carr, E.H. (1959) *Socialism in One Country, 1924–1926*, vol. 1. Harmondsworth: Penguin Books.

Carrier, James (ed.) (1995) *Occidentalism: Images of the West*. Oxford: Clarendon Press.

Castañeda, Jorge G. (1994) *Utopia Unarmed: The Latin American Left after the Cold War*. New York: Vintage Books.

Castells, Manuel (1982) 'Squatters and politics in Latin America: a comparative analysis of urban social movements in Chile, Peru and Mexico', in Helen Safa (ed.) *Towards a Political Economy of Urbanization in Third World Countries*. Delhi: Oxford University Press.

Castells, Manuel (1996) *The Rise of Network Society*, vol. 1 of *The Information Age*. Oxford: Basil Blackwell

Chagnon, Napoleon (1988) 'Life histories, blood revenge, and warfare in a tribal population', *Science* 239: 985–1022.

Chant, Sylvia (1997) *Women-Headed Households: Diversity and Dynamics in the Developing World*. Basingstoke: Macmillan.

Chazan, Naomi, Robert Mortimer, John Ravenhill and Donald Rothchild (1992) *Politics and Society in Contemporary Africa*. 2nd edn. Boulder, CO: Lynne Rienner Publishers.

Chehabi, H.E. (1990) *Iranian Politics and Religious Modernism: The Liberation Movement of Iran under the Shah and Khomeini*. Ithaca, NY: Cornell University Press.

Clastres, Pierre (1977) *Society against the State*. Oxford: Basil Blackwell.

Clifford, James (1983) 'On ethnographic authority', *Representations* 1: 118–46.

Clifford, James and George E. Marcus (eds) (1986) *Writing Culture: The Poetics and Politics of Ethnography*. Berkeley: University of California Press.

Collier, George A. (1994) 'The new politics of exclusion: antecedents to the rebellion in Mexico', *Dialectical Anthropology* 19(1): 1–43.

Collier, George A. (1997) 'Reaction and retrenchment in the highlands of Chiapas in the wake of the Zapatista rebellion', *Journal of Latin American Anthropology* 3(1): 14–31.

Comaroff, Jean (1985) *Body of Power, Spirit of Resistance: The Culture and History of a South African People*. Chicago: University of Chicago Press.

Comaroff, John and Jean Comaroff (1992) *Ethnography and the Historical Imagination.* Boulder, CO: Westview Press.

Connolly, Priscilla (1985) 'The politics of the informal sector: a critique', in Nanneke Redclift and Enzo Mingione (eds) *Beyond Employment: Household, Gender and Subsistence.* Oxford: Basil Blackwell.

Cooley, John K. (1999) *Unholy Wars: Afghanistan, America and International Terrorism.* London: Pluto Press.

Crone, P. (1980) *Slaves on Horses.* Cambridge: Cambridge University Press.

Davis, Mike (1990) *City of Quartz.* London and New York: Verso.

Davis, Mike (1999) 'Magical urbanism: Latinos reinvent the US big city', *New Left Review* 234: 3–43.

De Certeau, Michel (1984) *The Practice of Everyday Life.* Berkeley: University of California Press.

Deere, Carmen Diana (1990) *Household and Class Relations: Peasants and Landlords in Northern Peru.* Berkeley: University of California Press.

De la Peña, Guillermo (1986) 'Poder local, poder regional: perspectivas socioantropológicas', in J. Padua and A. Vanneph (eds) *Poder Local, Poder Regional.* México, D.F.: El Colegio de México/CEMCA.

Degregori, Carlos Iván (1985a) *Sendero Luminoso: los hondos y mortales desencuentros.* Documentos de Trabajo, Serie: Antropología, no. 2. Lima: Instituto de Estudios Peruanos.

Degregori, Carlos Iván (1985b) *Sendero Luminoso lucha armada y utopia autoritaria.* Documentos de Trabajo, Serie: Antropología, no. 3. Lima: Instituto de Estudios Peruanos.

Degregori, Carlos Iván (1991) 'How difficult it is to be God: ideology and political violence in *Sendero Luminoso*', *Critique of Anthropology* 11(3): 233–50.

Diamond, Stanley (1974) *In Search of the Primitive: A Critique of Civilization.* New Brunswick, NJ: E.P. Dutton/Transaction Books.

Díaz-Polanco, Hector (1992) 'Indian communities and the quincentenary', *Latin American Perspectives* 19(3): 6–24.

DiGiacomo, Susan (1997) 'The new internal colonialism', *Critique of Anthropology* 17(1): 91–7.

Di Leonardo, Micaela (1998) *Exotics at Home: Anthropologies, Others, American Modernity.* Chicago and London: University of Chicago Press.

Dirks, N. (1987) *The Hollow Crown.* Cambridge: Cambridge University Press.

Dresser, Denise (1991) *Neopopulist Solutions to Neoliberal Problems: Mexico's National Solidarity Program.* La Jolla: Center for U.S.–Mexican Studies, University of California, San Diego.

Dumont, Louis (1970) *Homo Hierarchicus: The Caste System and its Implications.* London: Weidenfeld and Nicholson.

Dumont, Louis (1986) *Essays on Individualism.* Chicago: University of Chicago Press.

Dunkerley, James (1988) *Power in the Isthmus: A Political History of Modern Central America.* London: Verso.

Dunkerley, James (1994) *The Pacification of Central America.* London: Institute of Latin American Studies.

Easton, David (1959) 'Political anthropology', in Bernard J. Siegel (ed.) *Biennial Review of Anthropology* 1: 210–62.

Eckstein, Susan (1977) *The Poverty of Revolution: The State and the Urban Poor in Mexico.* Princeton, NJ: Princeton University Press.

Ehlers, Tracy Bachrach (1990) *Silent Looms: Women and Production in a Guatemalan Town.* Westview Special Studies on Latin America and the Caribbean. Boulder, CO: Westview Press.

Eisenstadt, S.N. (1963) *The Political Systems of Empires: The Rise and Fall of the Historical Bureaucratic Societies.* New York: Free Press.

Eriksen, Thomas Hylland (1993) *Ethnicity and Nationalism: Anthropological Perspectives*. London: Pluto Press.

Escobar, Arturo (1992) 'Culture, practice and politics: anthropology and the study of social movements', *Critique of Anthropology* 12(4): 395–432.

Escobar, Arturo (1995) *Encountering Development: The Making and Unmaking of the Third World*. Princeton, NJ: Princeton University Press.

Escobar, Arturo (1998) 'Whose knowledge, whose nature? Biodiversity, conservation, and the political ecology of social movements', *Journal of Political Ecology* 5: 53–82.

Escobar, Arturo (1999) 'An ecology of difference: equality and conflict in a glocalized world', in Lourdes Arizpe (ed.) *World Culture Report* 2. Paris: UNESCO.

Escobar, Arturo and Sonia E. Alvarez (1992) 'Introduction: theory and protest in Latin America today', in Arturo Escobar and Sonia E. Alvarez (eds) *The Making of Social Movements in Latin America: Identity, Strategy and Democracy*. Boulder, CO: Westview Press.

Evans-Pritchard, E.E. (1940) *The Nuer: A Description of the Modes of Livelihood and Political Institutions of a Nilotic People*. Oxford: Clarendon Press.

Evans-Pritchard, E.E. (1987) 'The Nuer of the southern Sudan', in M. Fortes and E.E. Evans-Pritchard (eds) *African Political Systems*. First published 1940. London and New York: International African Institute and Kegan Paul International.

Fabian, Johannes (1980) *Time and the Other: How Anthropology Makes its Object*. New York: Columbia University Press.

Filer, Colin (1999) 'The dialectics of negation and negotiation in the anthropology of mineral resource development in Papua New Guinea', in Angela Cheater (ed.) *The Anthropology of Power: Empowerment and Disempowerment in Changing Structures*. ASA Monographs Series 36. London and New York: Routledge.

Forbes, Jack D. (1992) 'The Hispanic spin: party politics and governmental manipulation of ethnic identity', *Latin American Perspectives* 19(4): 59–78.

Fortes, M. and E.E. Evans-Pritchard (eds) (1987) 'Introduction', in *African Political Systems*. First published 1940. London and New York: International African Institute and Kegan Paul International.

Foster-Carter, Aidan (1978) 'The modes of production controversy', *New Left Review* 107: 47–77.

Foucault, Michel (1979) *Discipline and Punish: The Birth of the Prison*. Harmondsworth: Peregrine Books.

Foucault, Michel (1980) *Power/Knowledge: Selected Interviews and Other Writings, 1972–7*. New York: Pantheon Books.

Foucault, Michel (1985) *The Uses of Pleasure: The History of Sexuality*, vol. 2. London: Penguin Books.

Foweraker, Joe (1995) *Theorizing Social Movements*. London: Pluto Press.

Fox Piven, Frances and Richard A. Cloward (1997) *The Breaking of the American Social Compact*. New York: New Press.

Friedman, Jonathan (1994) *Cultural Identity and Global Process*. London: Sage Publications.

Friedrich, Paul (1986) *The Princes of Naranja: An Essay on Anthrohistorical Method*. Austin: University of Texas Press.

GDAT (1996) *Advocacy is a Personal Commitment for Anthropologists, not an Institutional Imperative for Anthropology*, edited by Peter Wade. Manchester: Group for Debates in Anthropological Theory.

Gailey, Christine Ward (1987) *Kinship to Kinship: Gender Hierarchy and State Formation in the Tongan Islands*. Austin: University of Texas Press.

Gailey, Christine Ward (1989) '"Rambo" in Tonga: video films and cultural resistance in the Tongan Islands (South Pacific)', *Culture* IX(1): 21–32.

Gailey, Christine Ward (1992) 'Introduction: Civilization and culture in the work of Stanley Diamond', in Christine Ward Gailey (ed.) *Civilization in Crisis: Anthropological Perspec-*

tives, vol. 1 of *Dialectical Anthropology: Essays in Honour of Stanley Diamond*. Gainsville: University of Florida Press.

Gailey, Christine Ward and Thomas C. Patterson (1988) 'State formation and uneven development', in J. Gledhill, B. Bender and M.T. Larsen (eds) *State and Society: The Emergence and Development of Social Hierarchy and Political Centralization*. London: Routledge.

Gal, Susan (1995) 'Language and the "arts of resistance"', *Cultural Anthropology* 10(3): 407–24.

Gardner, Katy and David Lewis (1996) *Anthropology, Development and the Post-Modern Challenge*, London: Pluto Press.

Geertz, Clifford (1963a) *Agricultural Involution: The Processes of Ecological Change in Indonesia*. Berkeley: University of California Press.

Geertz, Clifford (1963b) *Peddlars and Princes*. Chicago: University of Chicago Press.

Geertz, Clifford (1980) *Negara: The Theatre State in Nineteenth-Century Bali*. Princeton, NJ: Princeton University Press.

Geertz, Clifford (1986) 'The uses of diversity', *Michigan Quarterly Review* 25(1): 263–78.

Geertz, Clifford (1995) *After the Fact: Two Countries, Four Decades, One Anthropologist*. Cambridge, MA: Harvard University Press.

Gellner, Ernest (1981) *Muslim Society*. Cambridge: Cambridge University Press.

Geschiere, Peter (1988) 'Sorcery and the state: popular modes of action among the Maka of southeastern Cameroon', *Critique of Anthropology* 8(1): 35–63.

Gianotten, Vera, Tom de Wit and Hans de Wit (1985) 'The impact of *Sendero Luminoso* on regional and national politics in Peru', in David Slater (ed.) *New Social Movements and the State in Latin America*. Amsterdam: CEDLA.

Giddens, Anthony (1985) *The Nation-State and Violence*. Cambridge: Polity Press.

Gill, Lesley (1997) 'Relocating class: ex-miners and neoliberalism in Bolivia', *Critique of Anthropology* 17(3): 293–312.

Gilly, Adolfo (1983) *The Mexican Revolution*. London: Verso.

Gilsenan, Michael (1977) 'Against patron–client relations', in Ernest Gellner and John Waterbury (eds) *Patrons and Clients in Mediterranean Societies*. London: Duckworth.

Gilsenan, Michael (1982) *Recognizing Islam: An Anthropologist's Introduction*. London: Croom Helm.

Gilroy, Paul (1993) *The Black Atlantic: Modernity and Double Consciousness*. London: Verso.

Gledhill, John (1988a) 'Introduction: the comparative analysis of social and political transitions', in J. Gledhill, B. Bender and M.T. Larsen (eds) *State and Society: The Emergence and Development of Social Hierarchy and Political Centralization*. London: Routledge.

Gledhill, John (1988b) 'Agrarian social movements and forms of consciousness', *Bulletin of Latin American Research* 7(2): 257–76.

Gledhill, John (1991) *Casi Nada: A Study of Agrarian Reform in the Homeland of Cardenismo*. Studies on Culture and Society vol. 4, Institute for Mesoamerican Studies, State University of New York at Albany. Austin: University of Texas Press.

Gledhill, John (1995) *Neoliberalism, Transnationalization and Rural Poverty: A Case Study of Michoacán, Mexico*. Boulder, San Francisco and Oxford: Westview Press.

Gledhill, John (1997) 'Liberalism, socio-economic rights and the politics of identity: from moral economy to indigenous rights', in Richard Wilson (ed.) *Human Rights, Culture and Context: Anthropological Approaches*. London: Pluto Press.

Gledhill, John (1998) 'Neoliberalism and ungovernability: caciquismo, militarization and popular mobilization in Zedillo's Mexico', in Valentina Napolitano and Xóchitl Leyva Solano (eds) *Encuentros Antropológicos: Power, Identity and Mobility in Mexican Society*. London: Institute of Latin American Studies.

Gledhill, John (1999) 'The challenge of globalisation: reconstruction of identities, transnational forms of life and the social sciences', *Journal of European Area Studies* 7(1): 9–37.

Glick Schiller, Nina (1999) 'Transmigrants and nation-states: something old and something new in the U.S. immigrant experience', in J. De Wind, P. Krasinitz and C. Hirschman (eds) *America Becoming, Becoming America*. New York: Russell Sage.

Glick Schiller, Nina and Georges Fouron (1999) 'Terrains of blood and nation: Haitian transnational social fields', *Ethnic and Racial Studies* 22(2): 340–66.

Gluckman, Max (1954) *Rituals of Rebellion in South-East Africa*. Manchester: Manchester University Press.

Gluckman, Max (1955) *Custom and Conflict in Africa*. Oxford: Basil Blackwell.

Gluckman, Max (1958) *Analysis of a Social Situation in Modern Zululand*. Rhodes-Livingstone Paper no. 28. Manchester: Manchester University Press.

Goodman, David and Michael Redclift (1981) *From Peasant to Proletarian: Capitalist Development and Agrarian Transition*. Oxford: Basil Blackwell.

Gossen, Gary H. (1999) *Telling Maya Tales: Tzotzil Identities in Modern Mexico*. New York and London: Routledge.

Gough, Kathleen (1968) 'World revolution and the science of man', in Theodore Roszak (ed.) *The Dissenting Academy*. New York: Pantheon Books.

Gough, Kathleen (1971) 'Nuer kinship: a reexamination', in Thomas O. Beidelman (ed.) *The Translation of Culture: Essays to E.E. Evans-Pritchard*. London: Tavistock.

Gregor, Thomas (1985) *Anxious Pleasures: The Sexual Lives of an Amazonian People*. Chicago: University of Chicago Press.

Grindle, Merilee (1987) 'Civil–military relations and budget politics in Latin America', *Armed Forces and Society* 13: 255–75.

Gruzinski, Serge (1990) 'Indian confraternities, brotherhoods and *mayordomías* in Central New Spain. A list of questions for the historian and anthropologist', in Arij Ouweneel and Simon Miller (eds) *The Indian Community of Colonial Mexico: Fifteen Essays on Land Tenure, Corporate Organizations, Ideology and Village Politics*. Amsterdam: CEDLA.

Guha, Ranajit (1983) *Elementary Aspects of Peasant Insurgency in Colonial India*. New Delhi: Oxford University Press.

Gutmann, Matthew C. (1993) 'Rituals of resistance: a critique of the theory of everyday forms of resistance', *Latin American Perspectives* 77, 20(2): 74–92.

Gutmann, Matthew C. (1996) *The Meanings of Macho: Being a Man in Mexico City*. Berkeley: University of California Press.

Gutmann, Matthew C. (1997) 'The ethnographic (g)ambit: women and the negotiation of masculinity in Mexico City', *American Ethnologist* 24(4): 833–55.

Haber, Paul (1994) 'Political change in Durango: the role of National Solidarity', in Wayne A. Cornelius, Ann L. Craig and Jonathan Fox (eds) *Transforming State–Society Relations in Mexico: The National Solidarity Strategy*. La Jolla: UCSD Center for U.S.–Mexican Studies.

Hale, Charles (1994) 'Between Che Guevara and the Pachamama: Mestizos, Indians and identity politics in the anti-Quincentenary campaign', *Critique of Anthropology* 14(1): 9–39.

Hale, Charles (1998) 'Response to Jeremy Adelman's "Latin America and globalization"', *Lasa Forum* XXIX(1): 14–15.

Hall, John (1985) *Powers and Liberties: The Causes and Consequences of the Rise of the West*. Oxford: Basil Blackwell.

Hamilton, Nora (1982) *The Limits of State Autonomy: Post-revolutionary Mexico*. Princeton, NJ: Princeton University Press.

Hannerz, Ulf (1996) *Transnational Connections: Culture, People, Places*. London: Routledge.

Harrison, Simon (1993) *The Mask of War: Violence, Ritual and the Self in Melanesia*. Manchester: Manchester University Press.

Harvey, David (1989) *The Condition of Postmodernity: An Enquiry into the Origins of Cultural Change*. Oxford: Basil Blackwell.

Harvey, Neil (1991) *The New Agrarian Movement in Mexico, 1979–1990*. University of London Institute of Latin American Studies Research Papers no. 23. London: Institute of Latin American Studies.

Harvey, Neil (1998) *The Chiapas Rebellion: The Struggle for Land and Democracy*. Durham, NC and London: Duke University Press.

Hellman, Judith Adler (1992) 'The study of new social movements in Latin America and the question of autonomy', in Arturo Escobar and Sonia E. Alvarez (eds) *The Making of Social Movements in Latin America: Identity, Strategy and Democracy*. Boulder, CO: Westview Press.

Herdt, Gilbert (1987) *The Sambia: Ritual and Gender in New Guinea*. New York: Holt, Rinehart and Winston.

Herdt, Gilbert (1994) *Guardians of the Flutes: Idioms of Masculinity*. 2nd edn, with a new preface. Chicago: University of Chicago Press.

Hoare, Quintin and Geoffrey Nowell Smith (eds) (1971) *Selections from the Prison Notebooks of Antonio Gramsci*. London: Lawrence and Wishart.

Hobsbawm, Eric and Terence Ranger (eds) (1983) *The Invention of Tradition*. Cambridge: Cambridge University Press.

Howe, John (1992) 'The crisis of Algerian nationalism and the rise of Islamic integralism', *New Left Review* 196: 85–100.

Humphrey, Caroline (1998) *Marx Went Away – But Karl Stayed Behind*. Ann Arbor: University of Michigan Press.

Hutchinson, Sharon E. (1996) *Nuer Dilemmas: Coping with Money, War and the State*. Berkeley: University of California Press.

Hutnyk, John (1999) 'Argonauts of Western pessimism: Clifford's Malinowski', in Steve Clark (ed.) *Travel Writing and Empire: Postcolonial Theory in Transit*. London and New York: Zed Books.

Ikels, Charlotte (1996) *The Return of the God of Wealth: The Transition to a Market Economy in Urban China*. Stanford, CA: Stanford University Press.

Ingham, John M. (1986) *Mary, Michael and Lucifer: Folk Catholicism in Central Mexico*. Austin: University of Texas Press.

Islamoglu, H. and C. Keyder (1977) 'Agenda for Ottoman history', *Review* 1(1): 31–55.

James, Wendy (1973) 'The anthropologist as reluctant imperialist', in Talal Asad (ed.) *Anthropology and the Colonial Encounter*. London: Ithaca Press.

James, Winston (1993) 'Migration, racism and identity formation: the Caribbean experience in Britain', in Winston James and Clive Harris (eds) *Inside Babylon: The Caribbean Diaspora in Britain*. London: Verso.

Jayawardena, Chandra (1987) 'Analysis of a social situation in Acheh Besar: an exploration of micro-history', *Social Analysis*, Special Issue Series, no. 22: 30–46.

Jelin, Elizabeth, 1990, 'Introduction', in Elizabeth Jelin (ed.) *Women and Social Change in Latin America*. London: Zed Books.

Joseph, Gilbert M. and Daniel Nugent (eds) (1994) *Everyday Forms of State Formation: Revolution and the Negotiation of Rule in Modern Mexico*. Durham, NC and London: Duke University Press.

Kahn, Joel S. (1981) 'Mercantilism and the emergence of servile labour in colonial Indonesia', in J.S. Kahn and J.R. Llobera (eds) *The Anthropology of Pre-Capitalist Societies*. London: Macmillan.

Kapferer, Bruce (1988) *Legends of People, Myths of State: Violence, Intolerance and Political Culture in Sri Lanka and Australia*. Washington and London: Smithsonian Institution Press.

Kapferer, Bruce (1994) Ethnic Nationalism and the Discourses on Violence in Sri Lanka. Unpublished manuscript.

Kapferer, Bruce (1997) *The Feast of the Sorcerer: Practices of Consciousness and Power*. Chicago and London: University of Chicago Press.

Kaplan, Robert (1994) 'The coming anarchy: how scarcity, crime, overpopulation and disease are rapidly destroying the social fabric of our planet', *Atlantic Monthly* (February): 44–76.

Kay, Cristóbal (1989) *Latin American Theories of Development and Underdevelopment*. London: Routledge.

Kearney, Michael (1996) *Reconceptualizing the Peasantry: Anthropology in Global Perspective*. Boulder, CO and Oxford: Westview Press.

Keesing, Roger M. (1992) *Custom and Confrontation: The Kwaio Struggle for Cultural Autonomy*. Chicago: University of Chicago Press.

Knauft, Bruce M. (1997) 'Gender identity, political economy and modernity in Melanesia and Amazonia', *Journal of the Royal Anthropological Institute (N.S.)* 3(2): 233–59.

Knight, Alan (1986) *The Mexican Revolution*, vol. II: *Counter-revolution and Reconstruction*. Cambridge: Cambridge University Press.

Knight, Alan (1990) 'Historical continuities in social movements', in Joe Foweraker and Ann L. Craig (eds) *Popular Movements and Political Change in Mexico*. Boulder, CO: Lynne Reiner Publishers.

Knight, Alan (1992) 'The peculiarities of Mexican history: Mexico compared to Latin America, 1821–1992', *Journal of Latin American Studies* 24, Quincentenary Supplement: 99–144.

Krotz, Esteban (1997) 'Anthropologies of the South: their rise, their silencing, their characteristics', *Critique of Anthropology* 17(3): 237–51.

Kurtz, Donald V. (1996) 'Hegemony and anthropology: Gramsci, exegeses, reinterpretations', *Critique of Anthropology* 16(2): 103–35.

Laclau, Ernesto (1985) 'New social movements and the plurality of the social', in David Slater (ed.) *New Social Movements and the State in Latin America*. Dordrecht: CEDLA.

Laclau, Ernesto and Chantal Mouffe (1985) *Hegemony and Socialist Strategy: Towards a Radical Democratic Politics*. London: Verso.

Lancaster, Roger (1992) *Life is Hard: Machismo, Danger and the Intimacy of Power in Nicaragua*. Berkeley: University of California Press.

Larson, Brooke (1988) *Colonialism and Agrarian Transformation in Bolivia: Cochabamba, 1550–1900*. Princeton, NJ: Princeton University Press.

Lattimore, Owen (1962) *Studies in Frontier History: Collected Papers, 1928–58*. London: Oxford University Press.

Leach, Edmund (1954) *Political Systems of Highland Burma*. London: Athlone Press.

Leach, Belinda (1998) 'Citizenship and the politics of exclusion in a "post"-Fordist industrial city', *Critique of Anthropology* 18(2): 181–204.

Legassick, Martin (1977) 'Gold, agriculture and secondary industry in South Africa, 1885–1970: from periphery to sub-metropole as a forced labour system', in Robin Palmer and Neil Parsons (eds) *The Roots of Rural Poverty in Central and Southern Africa*. London: Heinemann Educational Books.

Lenin, V.I. (1967) 'What is to be done? Burning questions of our movement', in V.I. Lenin *Selected Works in Three Volumes*, vol. 1. Moscow: Progress Publishers.

León, Rosario (1990) 'Bartolina Sisa: the peasant women's organization in Bolivia', in Elizabeth Jelin (ed.) *Women and Social Change in Latin America*. London: Zed Books.

Lewellen, Ted C. (1992) *Political Anthropology: An Introduction*. 2nd edn. Westport, CT: Bergin and Garvey.

Leyva Solano, Xochitl (1995) 'Catequistas, misioneros y tradiciones en Las Cañadas', in Juan Pedro Viqueira and Mario Humberto Ruz (eds) *Chiapas: Los Rumbos de Otra Historia*. Mexico City: Universidad Nacional Autónoma de México.

Leyva Solano, Xochitl and Gabriel Ascencio Franco (1996) *Lacandonia al filo del agua*. Mexico City: Fondo de la Cultura Económica.

Lomnitz-Adler, Claudio (1992) *Exits from the Labyrinth: Culture and Ideology in the Mexican National Space*. Berkeley: University of California Press.

Macfarlane, Alan (1987) *The Culture of Capitalism*. Oxford: Basil Blackwell.

Macpherson, C.B. (1962) *The Political Theory of Possessive Individualism: Hobbes to Locke.* Oxford: Oxford University Press.

Mair, Lucy (1958) 'The millennium in Melanesia', *British Journal of Sociology* IX(2): 178–9.

Mair, Lucy (1962) *Primitive Government.* Harmondsworth: Penguin Books.

Mallon, Florencia E. (1992) 'Indian communities, political cultures and the state in Latin America', *Journal of Latin American Studies* 24, Quincentenary Supplement: 35–53.

Mallon, Florencia E. (1995) *Peasant and Nation: The Making of Postcolonial Mexico and Peru.* Berkeley, Los Angeles and London: University of California Press.

Mann, Michael (1986) *The Sources of Social Power: A History of Power from the Beginning to A.D. 1760.* Cambridge: Cambridge University Press.

Marcus, George and Michael Fisher (1986) *Anthropology as Cultural Critique.* Chicago: University of Chicago Press.

Mardin, Serif (1993) 'Religion and secularism in Turkey', in Albert Hourani, Philip S. Khoury and Mary C. Wilson (eds) *The Modern Middle East.* Berkeley and Los Angeles: I.B. Tauris.

Marty, Martin E. and Scott Appleby (1993) 'Conclusion: an interim report on a hypothetical family', in Martin E. Marty and Scott Appleby (eds) *Fundamentalism Observed.* Chicago: University of Chicago Press.

Marx, Karl (1968) 'The 18th Brumaire of Louis Bonaparte', in *Marx and Engels: Selected Works in One Volume.* London: Lawrence and Wishart.

Mattiace, Shannon I. (1997) '"¡Zapata vive!": the EZLN, indigenous politics, and the autonomy movement in Mexico', *Journal of Latin American Anthropology* 3(1): 32–71.

Mayer, P. (1961) *Townsmen and Tribesmen.* Cape Town: Oxford University Press.

McCallum, Cecilia (1994) 'Ritual and the origin of sexuality in the Alto Xingu', in Penelope Harvey and Peter Gow (eds) *Sex and Violence: Issues in Representation and Experience.* London and New York: Routledge.

McClintock, Cynthia (1989) 'Peru's Sendero Luminoso rebellion: origins and trajectory', in Susan Eckstein (ed.) *Power and Popular Protest.* Berkeley: University of California Press.

McDonald, James H. (1997) 'A fading Aztec sun: The Mexican opposition and the politics of everyday fear in 1994', *Critique of Anthropology* 17(3): 263–92.

Melucci, Alberto (1989) *Nomads of the Present: Social Movements and Individual Needs in Contemporary Society,* edited by John Keane and Paul Mier. London: Hutchinson Radius.

Meyer, Jean (1976) *The Cristero Rebellion: The Mexican People between Church and State, 1926–29.* Cambridge: Cambridge University Press.

Middleton, John and David Tait (eds) (1958) *Tribes without Rulers: Studies in African Segmentary Systems.* London: Routledge and Kegan Paul.

Mimica, Jadran (1988) *Intimations of Infinity: The Cultural Meanings of the Iqwaye Counting System and Number.* Oxford: Berg.

Mintz, Sidney W. (1985) *Sweetness and Power: The Place of Sugar in Modern History.* Harmondsworth: Penguin Books.

Mintz, Sidney W. (1998) 'The localization of anthropological practice: from area studies to transnationalism', *Critique of Anthropology* 18(2): 117–33.

Mitchell, Timothy (1991) *Colonising Egypt.* Berkeley: University of California Press.

Moguel, Julio (1994) 'The Mexican left and the social program of Salinismo', in Wayne A. Cornelius, Ann L. Craig and Jonathan Fox (eds) *Transforming State–Society Relations in Mexico: The National Solidarity Strategy.* La Jolla: Center for U.S.–Mexican Studies, UCSD.

Molyneux, Maxine (1977) 'Androcentrism in Marxist anthropology', *Critique of Anthropology* 9–10 (Women's Double Issue): 55–81.

Moore-Gilbert, Bart, Gareth Stanton and Willy Maley (eds) (1997) *Postcolonial Criticism.* London and New York: Longman.

Moreira Alves, María Helena (1993) 'Something old, something new: Brazil's Partido dos Trabalhadores', in Barry Carr and Steve Ellner (eds) *The Latin American Left: From the Fall of Allende to Perestroika.* Latin American Perspectives Series, no. 11. Boulder, CO and London: Westview Press and Latin American Bureau.

Morris, Barry (1989) *Domesticating Resistance: The Dhan-Gadi Aborigines and the Australian State.* Oxford: Berg.

Moulder, Frances V. (1977) *Japan, China and the Modern World Economy.* Cambridge: Cambridge University Press.

Murphy, Robert F. (1959) 'Social structure and sex antagonism', *Southwestern Journal of Anthropology* 15: 89–98.

Murray, M.J. (1984) 'The development of capitalism and the making of the working class in colonial Indochina', in B. Munslow and H. Finch (eds) *Proletarianization in the Third World.* London: Croom Helm.

Nairn, Tom (1988) *The Enchanted Glass: Britain and its Monarchy.* London: Radius Books.

Nash, June (1979) *We Eat the Mines and the Mines Eat Us: Dependency and Exploitation in Bolivian Tin Mines.* New York: Columbia University Press.

Nash, June (1994) 'Global integration and subsistence security', *American Anthropologist* 96(1): 7–30.

Nash, June (1997) 'When isms become wasms: structural functionalism, Marxism, feminism and postmodernism', *Critique of Anthropology* 17(1): 11–32.

Nederveen Pieterse, Jan (1998) 'My paradigm or yours? Alternative development, post-development, reflexive development', *Development and Change* 29: 343–73.

Nugent, Daniel (1993) *Spent Cartridges of Revolution: An Anthropological History of Namiquipa, Chihuahua.* Chicago and London: University of Chicago Press.

Nugent, David (1997) *Modernity at the Edge of Empire: State, Individual and Nation in the Northern Peruvian Andes, 1885–1935.* Stanford, CA: Stanford University Press.

Nugent, Stephen (1993) *Amazonian Caboclo Society: An Essay on Invisibility and Peasant Economy.* Oxford: Berg.

Nystrom, Derek and Kent Puckett (1998) *Against Bosses, Against Oligarchies: A Conversation with Richard Rorty.* Charlottesville, VA: Prickly Pear Press.

O'Donnell, Guillermo (1986) 'Introduction to Latin American Cases', in Guillermo O'Donnell, Philippe C. Schmitter and Lawrence Whitehead (eds) *Transitions from Authoritarian Rule: Latin America.* Baltimore, MD: Johns Hopkins University Press.

Ong, Aihwa (1996) 'Anthropology, China and modernities: the geopolitics of cultural knowledge', in Henrietta L. Moore (ed.) *The Future of Anthropological Knowledge.* London: Routledge.

Ong, Aihwa (1999) *Flexible Citizenship: The Cultural Logics of Transnationality.* Durham, NC and London: Duke University Press.

Onoge, O. (1977) 'Revolutionary imperatives in African sociology', in Peter C.W. Gutkind and Peter Waterman (eds) *African Social Studies: A Radical Reader.* London: Heinemann.

Ortner, Sherry (1995) 'Resistance and the problem of ethnographic refusal', *Comparative Studies in Society and History* 37(1): 173–93.

Palmer, David Scott (1986) 'Rebellion in rural Peru: the origins of *Sendero Luminoso*', *Comparative Politics* 18(2): 127–46.

Patterson, Thomas C. (1991) *The Inca Empire: The Formation and Disintegration of a Precapitalist State.* Oxford: Berg.

Patterson, Thomas C. (1993) *Archaeology: The Historical Development of Civilizations.* Englewood Cliffs, NJ: Prentice Hall.

Peña, Devon (1987) 'Tortuosidad: shop floor struggles of female maquiladora workers', in V. Ruiz and S. Tiano (eds) *Women on the U.S.–Mexico Border: Responses to Change.* Boston: Allen and Unwin.

Petras, James and Morris Morley (1990) *US Hegemony under Siege: Class, Politics and Development in Latin America.* London: Verso.

Petras, James and Morris Morley (1992) *Latin America in the Time of Cholera: Electoral Politics, Market Economics, and Permanent Crisis.* London and New York: Routledge.

Poole, Deborah and Gerardo Rénique (1991) 'The new chroniclers of Peru: US scholars and their "Shining Path" of peasant rebellion', *Bulletin of Latin American Research* 10 (2): 133–91.

Poole, Deborah and Gerardo Rénique (1992) *Peru: Time of Fear*. London: Latin American Bureau.

Portes, Alejandro and Robert L. Bach (1986) *Latin Journey: Cuban and Mexican Immigrants in the United States*. Berkeley: University of California Press.

Powell, Kathy (1996) 'Neoliberalism and nationalism', in Rob Aitken, Nikki Craske, Gareth A. Jones and David E. Stansfield (eds) *Dismantling the Mexican State?* Basingstoke: Macmillan Press.

Price, David H. (1998) 'Cold War anthropology: collaborators and victims of the national security state', *Identities* 4(3–4): 389–430.

Rabinow, Paul (1996) *Essays on the Anthropology of Reason*. Princeton, NJ: Princeton University Press.

Reno, William (1995) *Corruption and State Politics in Sierra Leone*. Cambridge: Cambridge University Press.

Rey, Pierre-Philipe (1975) 'The lineage mode of production', *Critique of Anthropology* 3: 27–79.

Reyna, Stephen P. (1998) 'Right and might: of approximate truths and moral judgement', *Identities* 4(3–4): 431–66.

Richards, Paul (1996) *Fighting for the Rain Forest: War, Youth and Resources in Sierra Leone*. International African Institute, in Association with James Currey (Oxford) and Heinemann (Portsmouth, New Hampshire).

Rimoldi, Max and Eleanor Rimoldi (1992) *Halalis and the Labour of Love: A Social Movement on Buka Island*. Oxford: Berg.

Roberts, Bryan (1978) *Cities of Peasants: The Political Economy of Urbanization in the Third World*. London: Edward Arnold.

Roediger, David R. (1994) *Towards the Abolition of Whiteness*. London and New York: Verso.

Roosevelt, Anna (1989) 'Chiefdoms in the Amazon and Orinoco', in R.D. Drennan and C.A. Uribe (eds) *Chiefdoms in the Americas*. Lanham, NY: University Press of America.

Rorty, Richard (1986) 'On ethnocentrism: a reply to Clifford Geertz', *Michigan Quarterly Review* 25(4): 525–34.

Rorty, Richard (1998) *Achieving our Country: Leftist Thought in Twentieth-Century America*. Cambridge, MA: Harvard University Press.

Roseberry, William (1989) *Anthropologies and Histories: Essays in Culture, History and Political Economy*. New Brunswick, NJ: Rutgers University Press.

Roseberry, William (1994) 'Hegemony and the language of contention', in Gilbert M. Joseph and Daniel Nugent (eds) *Everyday Forms of State Formation: Revolution and the Negotiation of Rule in Modern Mexico*. Durham, NC and London: Duke University Press.

Roseberry, William (1996) 'The unbearable lightness of anthropology', *Radical History Review* 65: 5–25.

Ross, Eric B. (1998) 'Cold warriors without weapons', *Identities* 4(3–4): 475–506.

Rowlands, Michael and Jean-Pierre Warnier (1988) 'Sorcery, power and the modern state in Cameroon', *Man* (N.S.) 23: 118–32.

Rubin, Jeffrey (1990) 'Popular mobilization and the myth of state corporatism', in Joe Foweraker and Ann L. Craig (eds) *Popular Movements and Political Change in Mexico*. Boulder, CO: Lynne Rienner Publications.

Rubin, Jeffrey W. (1996) 'Decentering the regime: culture and regional politics in Mexico', *Latin American Research Review* 31(3): 85–126.

Rus, Jan (1983) 'Whose caste war? Indians, Ladinos and the Chiapas "Caste War" of 1869', in Murdo J. MacLeod and Robert Wasserstrom (eds) *Spaniards and Indians in Southeastern Mesoamerica: Essays on the History of Ethnic Relations*. Lincoln: University of Nebraska Press.

Rus, Jan (1994) 'The "Comunidad Revolucionaria Institucional": the subversion of native government in highland Chiapas, 1936–1968', in Gilbert M. Joseph and Daniel Nugent (eds) *Everyday Forms of State Formation: Revolution and the Negotiation of Rule in Modern Mexico*. Durham, NC and London: Duke University Press.

Sahlins, Marshall (1974) *Stone-Age Economics*. London: Tavistock.

Sahlins, Marshall and Paul V. Kirch (1992) *Anahulu: The Anthropology of History in the Kingdom of Hawaii*. Chicago: University of Chicago Press.

Sahlins, Peter (1998) 'State formation and national identity in the Catalan borderlands during the eighteenth and nineteenth centuries', in Thomas M. Wilson and Hastings Donnan (eds) *Border Identities: Nation and State at International Frontiers*. Cambridge: Cambridge University Press.

Said, Edward W. (1978) *Orientalism*. New York: Pantheon Books.

Said, Edward W. (1993) *Culture and Imperialism*. London: Chatto and Windus.

Salzinger, Leslie (1991) 'A maid by any other name: the transformation of "dirty work" by Central American immigrants', in Michael Burawoy, Alice Burton, Ann Arnett Ferguson, Kathryn J. Fox, Joshua Gamson, Nadine Gartrell, Leslie Hurst, Charles Kurzman, Leslie Salzinger, Josepha Schiffman and Shiori Ui, *Ethnography Unbound: Power and Resistance in the Modern Metropolis*. Berkeley: University of California Press.

Sanderson, Steven E. (1981) *Agrarian Populism and the Mexican State*. Berkeley: University of California Press.

Salman, Ton (1994) 'The diffident movement: generation and gender in the vicissitudes of the Chilean shantytown organizations, 1973–1990', *Latin American Perspectives* 82, 21(3): 8–31.

Saragoza, Alex M. (1988) *The Monterrey Elite and the Mexican State, 1880–1940*. Austin: University of Texas Press.

Scheper-Hughes, Nancy (1992) *Death without Weeping: The Violence of Everyday Life in Brazil*. Berkeley: University of California Press.

Scheper-Hughes, Nancy (1995) 'The primacy of the ethical: propositions for a militant anthropology', *Current Anthropology* 36(3): 409–40.

Schneider, Harold K. (1974) *Economic Man: The Anthropology of Economics*. New York: Free Press.

Scott, David (1992) 'Criticism and culture: theory and post-colonial claims on anthropological disciplinarity', *Critique of Anthropology* 12 (4): 371–94.

Scott, James C. (1976) *The Moral Economy of the Peasant: rebellion and subsistence in Southeast Asia*. New Haven, CT: Yale University Press.

Scott, James C. (1985) *Weapons of the Weak: Everyday Forms of Peasant Resistance*. New Haven, CT: Yale University Press.

Scott, James C. (1990) *Domination and the Arts of Resistance: Hidden Transcripts*. New Haven, CT: Yale University Press.

Shore, Chris and Susan Wright (2000) 'Coercive accountability: the rise of audit culture in higher education', in Marilyn Strathern (ed.) *Accountability and Ethnography: Anthropological Studies in Audit, Ethics and the Academy*. London and New York: Routledge.

Silverblatt, Irene (1987) *Moon, Sun and Witches: Gender Ideologies and Class Formation in Inca and Colonial Peru*. Princeton, NJ: Princeton University Press.

Silverman, Sydel (1974) 'Bailey's politics', *Journal of Peasant Studies* 2: 111–20.

Skocpol, Theda (1979) *The State and Social Revolutions: A Comparative Analysis of France, Russia and China*. Cambridge: Cambridge University Press.

Smith, Carol A. (1984) 'Local history in global context: social and economic transitions in western Guatemala', *Comparative Studies in Society and History* 26: 193–228.

Smith, Carol (1990) 'The militarization of civil society in Guatemala: economic reorganization as a continuation of war', *Latin American Perspectives* 17(4): 8–41.

Smith, Robert (1997) 'Transnational localities: community, technology and the politics of membership within the context of Mexico–U.S. Migration', in Michael Peter Smith and Luis Guarnizo (eds) *Transnationalism from Below*. New Brunswick, NJ: Rutgers University Press.

Spalding, Karen (1984) *Huarochirí: An Andean Society under Inca and Spanish Rule*. Stanford, CA: Stanford University Press.

Spencer, Jonathan (1990) *A Sinhala Village in a Time of Trouble: Politics and Change in Rural Sri Lanka*. Delhi: Oxford University Press.

Spivak, Gayatri C. (1988) 'Can the subaltern speak?', in Cary Nelson and Lawrence Grossberg (eds) *Marxism and the Interpretation of Cultures*. Urbana: University of Illinois Press.

Spivak, Gayatri C. (1996) 'Subaltern studies: deconstructing historiography', in Donna Landry and Gerald MacLean (eds) *The Spivak Reader*. London and New York: Routledge.

Spivak, Gayatri C. (1999) *A Critique of Postcolonial Reason: Toward a History of the Vanishing Present*. Cambridge, MA: Harvard University Press.

Starn, Orin (1992) '"I dreamed of foxes and hawks": reflections on peasant protest, new social movements and the rondas campesinas of Northern Peru', in Arturo Escobar and Sonia E. Alvarez (eds) *The Making of Social Movements in Latin America: Identity, Strategy and Democracy*. Boulder, CO: Westview Press.

Stephen, Lynn (1993) 'Challenging gender inequality: grassroots organizing among women rural workers in Brazil and Chile', *Critique of Anthropology* 13(1): 33–55.

Stephen, Lynn (1997a) 'Redefined nationalism in building a movement for indigenous autonomy in Southern Mexico', *Journal of Latin American Anthropology* 3(1): 72–101.

Stephen, Lynn (1997b) 'Pro-Zapatista and pro-PRI: resolving the contradictions of Zapata in rural Oaxaca', *Latin American Research Review* 32(2): 41–70.

Stephen, Lynn (1997c) *Women and Social Movements in Latin America: Power from Below*. Austin: University of Texas Press.

Stoler, Ann (1995) *Race and the Education of Desire: Foucault's History of Sexuality and the Colonial Order of Things*. Durham, NC and London: Duke University Press.

Stoll, David (1999) *Rigoberta Menchú and the Story of All Poor Guatemalans*. Boulder, CO: Westview Press.

Strathern, Marilyn (1988) *The Gender of the Gift: Problems with Women and Problems with Society in Melanesia*. Berkeley: University of California Press.

Strathern, Marilyn (1997) '"Improving Ratings": audit in the British university system', *European Review* 5: 305–21.

Susser, Ida (1996) 'The construction of poverty and homelessness in US cities', *Annual Review of Anthropology* 25: 411–35.

Swartz, Marc, Victor Turner and Arthur Tuden (eds) (1966) *Political Anthropology*. Chicago: Aldine.

Szemiñski, Jan (1987) 'Why kill the Spaniard? New perspectives on Andean insurrectionary ideology in the 18th century', in Steve J. Stern (ed.) *Resistance, Rebellion and Consciousness in the Andean Peasant World, 18th to 20th Centuries*. Madison: University of Wisconsin Press.

Tambiah, Stanley J. (1976) *World Conqueror and World Renouncer: A Study of Buddhism and Polity in Thailand against a Historical Background*. Cambridge: Cambridge University Press.

Tambiah, Stanley J. (1985) 'The galactic polity in Southeast Asia', in *Culture, Thought and Social Action: An Anthropological Perspective*. Cambridge, MA: Harvard University Press.

Tambiah, Stanley J. (1986) *Sri Lanka: Ethnic Fratricide and the Dismantling of Democracy*. Chicago: University of Chicago Press.

Taussig, Michael (1980) *The Devil and Commodity Fetishism in Latin America*. Chapel Hill: University of North Carolina Press.

Taussig, Michael (1987) *Shamanism, Colonialism and the Wild Man: A Study in Terror and Healing*. Chicago: University of Chicago Press.

Therborn, Göran (1980) *The Ideology of Power and the Power of Ideology*. London: Verso.

Thompson, E.P. (1967) 'Time, work-discipline and industrial capitalism', *Past and Present* 38: 56–97.

Tonkinson (1991) '"Ideology and domination" in Aboriginal Australia: a Western Desert test case', in Tim Ingold, David Riches and James Woodburn (eds) *Hunters and Gatherers: Property Power and Ideology*. Oxford: Berg.

Toulabor, Comi (1994) 'Political satire past and present in Togo', *Critique of Anthropology* 14(1): 59–75.

Touraine, Alain (1977) *The Self-Production of Society*. Chicago: University of Chicago Press.

Touraine, Alain (1981) *The Voice and the Eye: An Analysis of Social Movements*. Cambridge: Cambridge University Press.

Touraine, Alain (1984) 'Social movements: special area or central problem in sociological analysis?', *Thesis Eleven* 9: 5–15.

Trejo Delarbre, Raúl (1986) 'The Mexican labour movement, 1917–1975', in Nora Hamilton and Timothy F. Harding (eds) *Modern Mexico: State, Economy and Social Conflict*. Newbury Park and London: Sage Publishers.

Turner, Bryan S. (1979) *Marx and the End of Orientalism*. London: Allen and Unwin.

Turner, Bryan S. (1994) *Orientalism, Postmodernism and Globalism*. London: Routledge.

Turner, Victor (1996) *Schism and Continuity in an African Society*. Reprinted with a new preface by Bruce Kapferer. Oxford: Berg. First published in 1957, Manchester: Manchester University Press.

Van de Port, Mattijs (1999) 'It takes a Serb to know a Serb', *Critique of Anthropology* 19(1): 7–30.

Varley, Ann (1993) 'Clientelism or technocracy? The politics of urban land regulation', in Neil Harvey (ed.) *Mexico: Dilemmas of Transition*. London: Institute of Latin American Studies and British Academic Press.

Vincent, Joan (1990) *Anthropology and Politics: Visions, Traditions and Trends*. Tucson: University of Arizona Press.

Viqueira, Juan Pedro (1999) 'Los peligros del Chiapas imaginario', *Letras Libres* 1: 20–8, 96–7.

Von Neumann, John and Oskar Morgenstern (1953) *Theory of Games and Economic Behaviour*. Princeton, NJ: Princeton University Press.

Wade, Peter (1995) 'The cultural politics of blackness in Colombia', *American Ethnologist* 22(2): 341–57.

Wade, Peter (1997) *Race and Ethnicity in Latin America*. London: Pluto Press.

Wallerstein, Immanuel (1974) *The Modern World System*, vol. 1: *Capitalist Agriculture and the Origins of the European World-Economy in the Sixteenth Century*. New York: Academic Press.

Wallerstein, Immanuel (1976) 'The three stages of African involvement in the world economy', in Immanuel Wallerstein and Peter C.W. Gutkind (eds) *The Political Economy of Contemporary Africa*. Beverley Hills and London: Sage Publications.

Wallerstein, Immanuel (1979) *The Capitalist World Economy*. Cambridge: Cambridge University Press.

Warman, Arturo (1988) 'The political project of Zapatismo', in Friedrich Katz (ed.) *Riot, Rebellion and Revolution: Rural Social Conflict in Mexico*. Princeton, NJ: Princeton University Press.

Warren, Kay B. (1998) *Indigenous Movements and Their Critics: Pan-Maya Activism in Guatemala*. Princeton, NJ: Princeton University Press.

Weber, Max (1951) *The Religion of China*. New York: Free Press.

Weber, Max (1978) *Economy and Society*, 2 vols, edited by Guenther Roth and Claus Wittich. Berkeley: University of California Press.

Werbner, Richard (1996) 'Introduction: multiple identities, plural arenas', in Richard Werbner and Terence Ranger (eds) *Postcolonial Identities in Africa*. London and New Jersey: Zed Books.

Whittaker, Elvi (1994) 'Public discourse on sacredness: the transfer of Ayers Rock to aboriginal ownership', *American Ethnologist* 21(2): 310–34.

Williams, Brackette (1991) *Stains on My Name, War in My Veins: Guyana and the Politics of Cultural Struggle*. Durham, NC: Duke University Press.

Wilson, Richard (1991) 'Machine guns and mountain spirits: the cultural effects of state repression among the Q'eqchi' of Guatemala', *Critique of Anthropology* 11(1): 33–61.

Wilson, Richard (1993a) 'Continued counterinsurgency: civilian rule in Guatemala', in Barry Gills, Joel Rocamora and Richard Wilson (eds) *Low Intensity Democracy: Political Power in the New World Order*. London: Pluto Press.

Wilson, Richard (1993b) 'Anchored communities: identity and history of the Maya-Q'eqchi'', *Man* 28(1): 121–38.

Wilson, Richard (1995) *Maya Resurgence in Guatemala: Q'eqchi' Experiences*. Norman: University of Oklahoma Press.

Wilson, Thomas M. and Hastings Donnan (1998) 'Nation, state and identity at international borders', in Thomas M. Wilson and Hastings Donnan (eds) *Border Identities: Nation and State at International Frontiers*. Cambridge: Cambridge University Press.

Wolf, Eric R. (1969) *Peasant Wars of the Twentieth Century*. New York: Harper and Row.

Wolf, Eric R. (1982) *Europe and the People without History*. Berkeley: University of California Press.

Wolf, Eric R. (1990) 'Distinguished Lecture: Facing power – old insights, new questions', *American Anthropologist* 92(3): 586–96.

Wolf, Eric R. (1999) *Envisioning Power: Ideologies of Dominance and Crisis*. Berkeley: University of California Press.

Wolf, Eric R. and Joseph G. Jorgensen (1970) 'Anthropologists on the warpath in Thailand', *New York Review of Books*, 19 November: 27.

Wolpe, Harold (1972) 'Capitalism and cheap labour-power in South Africa: from segregation to apartheid', *Economy and Society* 1: 425–56.

Wood, Ellen Meiksins (1986) *The Retreat from Class: A New 'True' Socialism*. London: Verso.

Wood, Ellen Meiksins (1991) *The Pristine Culture of Capitalism: A Historical Essay on Old Regimes and Modern States*. London: Verso.

Worsley, Peter (1970) *The Trumpet Shall Sound: A Study of 'Cargo Cults' in Melanesia*. 2nd edn. London: Paladin. (Hardback 1968 McGibbon and Kee.)

Worsley, Peter (1992) 'The practice of politics and the study of Australian kinship', in Christine Ward Gailey (ed.) *The Politics of Culture and Creativity: A Critique of Civilization*, vol. II of *Dialectical Anthropology: Essays in Honour of Stanley Diamond*. Gainsville: University Press of Florida.

Young, Michael (1983) '"Our name is woman: we are bought with limesticks and limepots": an analysis of the autobiographical narrative of a Kalauna woman', *Man* (N.S.) 18(3): 478–501.

Zuidema, R.T. (1964) *The Ceque System of Cuzco: The Social Organization of the Capital of the Inca*. International Archives of Ethnography. Leiden: E.J. Brill.

INDEX

social movements *cont.*
 of right and left as mirror images of
  each other, 184
 problems of eurocentrism in theories of,
  187–8, 193–4
 theories of, 185
 women's role in, 207–13
social revolution, 81
 in France, 50–1
 Skocpol's theory of, 48
social sciences, place of anthropology in,
  7–9
sorcery
 and terror in Sri Lanka, 180
 in African politics, 103
South Africa
 effects of deracination in, 160
 experience of Nancy Scheper-Hughes
  in, 227–8
 Gluckman's analysis of mechanisms of
  racist domination in, 70–1
 homelands policy in, 79–80
 political economy of, 72
Soviet Union
 as an empire, 154–5
 role of countries of former USSR in
  global arms trade, 161
 russification in, 154
 socialist political culture, 155
Spencer, J., 179
Spivak, G., 67–8, 90
SPLA (Sudanese People's Liberation
  Army), 42, 43
Sri Lanka
 alternative ontologies in, 148
 caste system in, 64–5, 182
 ethnic violence in, 177–83
 logic of myth in politics of, 147–8
 origins of Sinhala chauvinism in, 178
 paranoid state order in, 180
 role of youth in the JVP insurrection of
  1971 in, 178
state
 absolutist, 15, 48, 50–1, 54, 56
 administration of land by, in India, 65
 administrative-hegemonic, weaknesses
  of, 95–6
 and private property rights in Europe,
  55
 Australian, and aborigines, 149–50
 autonomy of, in Mexico, 111
 bourgeois, 49–50
 bureaucratic-authoritarian, 94

capitalist, in contemporary Asia,
  165–6
colonial, 72–3, 75–7, 87, 182
colonial, and anthropologists, 1–3, 42
colonial, impact on Nuer of, 42–3
colonial, role of surveillance in, 73
constitutionalist compared with
  absolutist, 54–5
corporate, 94, 111
custodial, in Indic civilization, 63
formation of as first rupture in human
  history, 12
hierarchic, in Sri Lanka, 148
Hindu-Buddhist, 62–6
incoherence of Islamic theories of the,
  60
inegalitarian logic of cosmic, in Sri
  Lanka, 183
mass-incorporating, 113
modern, contrasted with pre-modern
  states in Europe, 55
modern, European conceptions of, 10
modern, theories of distinctiveness of,
  15–18
official, 92, 104
organic, 55
origins of, 38
patrimonial, 99
post-colonial, 43, 101–2
post-colonial, and transnationalism,
  163
post-revolutionary, in Mexico, 111
pre-modern imperial, 12
shadow, 153
shadow, in Africa, 103–5
shadow, in Mexico, 116–7
strong versus weak tribute-based, 39
theatre state, in Bali, 63–4, 180
typologies of, in Africa, 94–100
state clientalism, 128
 in Brazilian politics, 107
 selective, in Mexico's neoliberal
  transition, 115
state terror, 156, 160, 171
 as possessing a dynamic of its own, 159
 in Guatemala, 122, 125
 in Peru, 172, 176–7
 in Sri Lanka, 179–80
 legitimated through label of terrorism,
  153
 routinization of, 159
 theatricalization of, in Sri Lanka, 179
stateless societies
 as a negative category, 13